POLITICAL ECOLOGY

This collection is drawn from a recent Global Political conference held to mark the centenary of the birth of Harold Innis, Canada's most important political economist. Throughout his life, Innis was concerned with topics which remain central to political ecology today, and these essays explore the main issues in the field under the following headings:

- the new global order and the environment
- economics, society and ecology
- planetary management
- environment, gender and development
- consumption
- ecology and politics.

Vital political and ethical questions, such as the nature of the new global order, the future of work and population growth are discussed throughout with a view to possible developments in the future. The contributors are an international group of scholars, a number of whom are recognized leaders in their respective fields.

Offering many fresh perspectives and a multidisciplinary approach, this volume will be of central interest to students interested in this increasingly significant area as well as to the more general reader.

Roger Keil, David V. J. Bell, Peter Penz and **Leesa Fawcett** are all based in the Faculty of Environmental Studies, York University, Ontario, Canada.

INNIS CENTENARY SERIES
Daniel Drache
Series Editor

Harold Innis, one of Canada's most distinguished economists, described the Canadian experience as no one else ever has. His visionary works in economic geography, political economy and communications theory have endured for over fifty years and have had tremendous influence on scholarship, the media and the business community.

The volumes in the Innis Centenary Series illustrate and expand Innis' legacy. Each volume is written and edited by distinguished members of the fields Innis touched. Each addressed provocative and challenging issues that have profound implications not only for Canada but for the 'new world order' including the impact of globalization on national decision-making; interactions among the state, social movements and the environment; the nature of the 'market' in the future; the effect of new communications technology on economic restructuring; and the role of the individual in effecting positive social change.

The complete series will provide a unique guide to many of the major challenges we face as we enter the twenty-first century.

The Innis Centenary Celebration was made possible by the generous support of Innis College, the University of Toronto, York University and through private donations.

POLITICAL ECOLOGY

Global and local

Edited by
Roger Keil, David V. J. Bell,
Peter Penz and Leesa Fawcett

London and New York

First published 1998
by Routledge
11 New Fetter Lane, London EC4P 4EE

Simultaneously published in the USA and Canada
by Routledge
29 West 35th Street, New York, NY 10001

© 1998 Roger Keil, David V.J. Bell,
Peter Penz and Leesa Fawcett

Typeset in Times by Routledge
Printed and bound in Great Britain by TJ International Ltd, Padstow, Cornwall

British Library Cataloguing in Publication Data
A catalogue record for this book is available from the British Library

Library of Congress Cataloging in Publication Data
A catalogue record for this book has been requested

ISBN 0–415–18380–4 (hbk)
ISBN 0–415–18381–2 (pbk)

CONTENTS

v

CONTENTS

CONTENTS

PART 4
Environment, gender and development

CONTENTS

CONTENTS

TABLES AND FIGURES

Tables

Figures

CONTRIBUTORS

Laurie E. Adkin is an Associate Professor in the Department of Political Science at the University of Alberta, where she teaches comparative politics and social theory. She also serves on the editorial board of the journal *Studies in Political Economy*. Her research interests include: contemporary social movements and theories of social change; the comparative analysis of political ecology, labour and women's movements; explanations for the emergence in the 1980s of nationalist-populist parties in the West. Her recent book, *The Politics of Sustainable Development: Citizens, Unions, and the Corporations* (1988), examines the roles of citizens' groups, environmental organizations, unions and corporations in shaping Canadian state regulation of industrial pollution, particularly in the petrochemical and automobile sectors, and in advancing or resisting alternatives to the dominant model of development. Her current research focuses on the French Green Party and its relations with other social and political actors, and comprises part of a comparative inquiry into the potential of political ecology as a discourse of radical democratization – one which seeks to articulate the interests and identities of diverse subjects in the 'postmodern' era.

Bina Agarwal is a Professor of Economics at the Institute of Economic Growth, Delhi. She has taught at Harvard University as visiting professor, and been a fellow of the Bunting Institute (Radcliffe College) and the Institute of Development Studies (University of Sussex). She has written extensively on poverty and inequality, rural development, environmental issues, technological change and property rights, especially from a political economy and gender perspective. Her authored books include: *Cold Hearths and Barren Slopes: The Woodfuel Crisis in the Third World* (1986), *Mechanization in Indian Agriculture* (1983) and *A Field of One's Own: Gender and Land Rights in South Asia* (1994). Her 'land rights' book has been awarded the Edgar Graham Book Prize 1996 (UK), the A.K. Coomaraswamy Book Prize 1996 (USA), and the K.H. Batheja Award 1995–6 (India).

Elmar Altvater is a Professor of Political Science at the Free University,

Berlin. His research interests include crisis theory, state theory, the ecological implications of global markets, economic growth and social development in West Germany, industrial relations and trade union strategies in Western Europe and the ecological impacts of development in the Amazon. Recent publications include 'The Future of the Market: an Essay on the Regulation of Money and Nature after the failure of "Real Socialism"' (1993) and 'The Price of Welfare or Environmental Pillage in the New World (Dis)order' (1994). He is also the co-editor of the social science quarterly *PROKLA*, a member of the scientific council of the Institute of Social–Ecological Research in Frankfurt and of the Institute for Ecological Research in Berlin.

Egon Becker is a physicist and Professor of Theory of Science and Sociology of Higher Education at the University of Frankfurt. He is a co-founder of the Institute of Social-Ecological Research (ISOE) in Frankfurt and a member of the scientific advisory council of the German Foundation for International Development. His fields of research are social ecology and history of science, as well as environmental development, on which he has published extensively. Recent publications include *Umwelt und Entwicklung* (1992) and *Risiko Wissenschaft* (1993) (with P. Wehling).

David V.J. Bell is Director of the York Centre for Applied Sustainability, Chair of the Ontario Learning for Sustainability Pertnership and the former Dean of the Faculty of Environmental Studies at York University. Dr Bell is also a former member of the Ontario Round Table on Environment and Economy. A political scientist by training, he received his PhD from Harvard University in 1969. His recent publications include: (with F. Fletcher *et al.*) *Reaching the Voter: Constituency Campaigning in Canada* (1993), *The Roots of Disunity: A Study of Canadian Political Culture* (1992); (with R. Logan) 'Communication and community: promoting world citizenship through electronic communications', in J. Rotblat (ed.) *World Citizenship: Allegiance to Humanity* (1997); 'Negotiation in workplaces: the view from a political linguist', in A. Firth (ed.), *The Discourse of Negotiation: Studies of Language in the Workplace* (1995); and has co-edited (with R. Keil and G.R. Wekerle) *Local Places in the Age of the Global City* (1996).

Robyn Eckersley is a Senior Lecturer in the Politics Department at Monash University in Australia. Her research interests include environmentalism, green politics and theory, modern social and political theory, environmental philosophy, environmental law and policy, and ecological economics. Eckersley has recently authored *Environmentalism and Political Theory: Toward an Ecocentric Approach* (1992) and edited *Markets, the State and the Environment: Towards Integration* (1995).

Leesa Fawcett is an Assistant Professor in the Faculty of Environmental

Studies at York University. She is currently completing a PhD in Biology/Ecology. Her areas of academic interest include human ecology, human/animal relationships, environmental thought, biological conservation and ecofeminism.

Harriet Friedmann is a Professor of Sociology at the University of Toronto. Her publications focus on power, poverty, and diets in the world food economy; international agrofood complexes; and the social and ecological effects of agricultural policies. Her recent research focuses on the cultural and material aspects of sustainable food economies; and on the place of food within the Cold War and post-Cold War shifts in international power and property relations. Friedmann has recently published chapters in *Food* (1994) edited by B. Harriss-White and R. Hoffenberg, and *Rethinking the Cold War* (1997) edited by A. Hunter.

Franz Hartmann is a PhD Candidate in the Department of Political Science at York University. His research focuses on ecological political economy within an urban context. He has been actively involved with a Toronto environmental group since 1990 and has worked on issues including waste management, sustainable community economic development and energy. He is also part of the Toronto editorial group of the journal *Capitalism, Nature, Socialism*.

Thomas Jahn is Director and founding member of the Institute for Social-Ecological Research (ISOE) in Frankfurt am Main, Germany and holds a PhD in Sociology. His areas of research are ecology and democracy, sustainability studies and urban ecology. He has worked as a scientific advisor for NGOs and local and federal government institutions. On behalf of the MOST-Programme of UNESCO he recently organized an international research project 'Sustainability as a Social Science Concept'. He is co-author of 'Sustainability: A cross-disciplinary concept for social transformation' (MOST-Policy Paper 6, 1997), and co-editor of a joint publication of the contributions to the sustainability project.

Roger Keil is an Associate Professor of Environmental Studies and Political Science at York University. His publications include the forthcoming *Los Angeles: City of the World. Globalization, Urbanization, and Social Struggles* (London: John Wiley and Sons) and *Local Places in the Age of the Global City* (Black Rose, 1996). He was co-editor of a special issue of Environment and Planning D: *Society and Space* on edge cities in 1994, and of a recent book on Zurich and Frankfurt, *Capitales Fatales*, published in Zurich in 1995. He has worked in planning projects and community groups in Frankfurt, Los Angeles and Toronto and is a member of the International Network for Urban Research and Action (INURA).

Bonnie Kettel is Associate Professor in the Faculty of Environmental Studies at York University. Her work includes five years as the Canadian co-ordinator for a large research initiative focused on women's local knowledge in eight African countries; policy contributions for CIDA, the Commonwealth Secretariat, the Women's Environment and Development Organization and the United Nations Commission on Science and Technology for Development; and environment advisor for the Fourth World Conference on Women. She is a manuscript referee for several journals including a *Canadian Woman Studies* special issue on women and environment. She wrote 'Gender and Environments: Lessons from WEDNET' in *Engendering Wealth and Well-being* edited by R. Blumberg *et al.*, 1994.

Nathan Keyfitz is a Professor of Population, Emeritus, at Harvard University. He is also involved with the Center on American Children. He has worked for extended periods in Indonesia, Sri Lanka, and India and is a member of the US National Academy of Sciences and the Royal Society of Canada. He has published on the mathematics of population and on the interconnections of population, development and environment. He is the author of *Introduction to the Mathematics of Population* (1968) and *Applied Mathematical Demography* (1977).

Mark W. Lutes is a PhD Candidate in the Faculty of Environmental Studies at York University. He was the Executive Director for the Conservation Council of New Brunswick and was a founding member of the Toronto Environmental Alliance's Climate and Energy Caucus. He is currently a member of the Toronto editorial collective of the journal *Capitalism, Nature, Socialism*.

Takeshi Murota is a Professor of Economics at Doshisha University in Kyoto, Japan. He was Senator of Hitotsubashi University from 1991–2 and was a member of the committee of Investigation of Global Warming Problems, Environment Agency of Japan. His fields of research are in ecological economics, entropy analysis of resources/energy questions, economics of uncertainty and information, economics of electric power industry, alternative schemes of waste management, and environmental-economic history. He has published several monographs as well as many articles in Japan and worldwide.

Robert Paehlke has researched and taught environmental politics and policy at Trent University since 1970. He was the founding editor of *Alternatives: Perspectives on Society, Technology, and Environment*, and has served as a consultant on environmental issues for several organizations. He is the author of *Environmentalism and the Future of Progressive Politics* (1989), is co-editor (with D. Torgerson) of *Managing Leviathan: Environmental Politics and the Administrative State* (1990), and is editor of *Conservation and Environmentalism: An Encyclopedia* (1995).

Rodney G. Peffer is a Professor of Philosophy at the University of San Diego. He specializes in social and political philosophy, ethics, theory of value and Marxism, and is also interested in environmental ethics. He has conducted presentations on issues of social justice, world justice, environment and population. He is the author of *Marxism, Morality, and Social Justice* (Princeton University Press, 1990) and, most recently, 'Towards a More Adequate Rawlsian Theory of Social Justice,' *Pacific Philosophical Quarterly* 75, 3–4, 1994.

Peter Penz is an Associate Professor in the Faculty of Environmental Studies at York University, Toronto. His books include *Consumer Sovereignty and Human Interests* (Cambridge University Press, 1986) and *Global Justice, Global Democracy* (Fernwood Press, 1997, co-edited). Recent writings have been on global justice and the environment, on development ethics, on development-induced population displacement, and on land-rights mobilization in Asia.

Patricia E. Perkins is an Assistant Professor in the Faculty of Environmental Studies at York University. She has worked as an Environment Policy Advisor and a Policy Coordinator for the Ontario government and has been a community representative for a local environmental liaison committee for several years. She is a vice president of the Canadian Society for Ecological Economics/Société Canadienne d'Economie Ecologique. Her areas of research include trade and environment, feminist ecological economics, international environmental agreements, and sustainable trade. She is working on a book (co-edited with Brian Milani) called *Green Toronto: Building a Sustainable Community Economy on the Shores of the Great Lakes in the Aftermath of Free Trade*.

Raymond A. Rogers has a PhD from the Faculty of Environmental Studies at York University, where he is now an Assistant Professor. Before returning to university, he spent twelve years as a commercial fisherman in Nova Scotia. His academic interests focus on the social relationship between humans and nature, as well as on the place of local community in an increasingly globalized world economy. Dr Rogers has recently published *Nature and the Crisis of Modernity: A Critique of Contemporary Discourse on Managing the Earth* (1994), *The Oceans are Emptying: Fish Wars and Sustainability* (1995), and *Solving History: The Challenge of Environmental Activism* (1997).

Catriona Sandilands is an Assistant Professor in the Faculty of Environmental Studies at York University. Her areas of interest include social and political theory, environmental thought, environmental politics and gender/feminist theory. Her new book, *The Good-Natured Feminist: Ecofeminism and the Quest for Democracy*, will be published by the University of Minnesota Press in 1998.

Peter Timmerman is a Research Associate of the Institute for Environmental Studies at the University of Toronto and a Research Fellow of the International Federation of Institutes for Advanced Study (IFIAS). He was the Co-convenor of the Canadian NGO Earth Charter Working Group for the 1992 'Rio' Earth Summit. His research interests include global environmental change such as hazardous waste management, environmental ethics and the impacts of global 'ecorestructuring'. He was a contributor to the original Sustainable Development of the Biosphere Project through the International Institute for Applied Systems Analysis, Austria and has recently contributed to *Buddhism and Ecology* (1992) published by the World Wildlife Fund.

Paul L. Wachtel is Distinguished Professor in the Doctoral Program in Clinical Psychology at the City University of New York. Among his books, the most relevant to the topic of the present volume is *The Poverty of Affluence: a Psychological Portrait of the American Way of Life* (1989). He has written widely on both the theory and practice of psychotherapy and on such issues of social concern as the relation between consumption and satisfaction and the dynamics of race relations. He is on the editorial boards of a wide variety of journals that reflect these diverse interests.

ACKNOWLEDGEMENTS

This book and the conference it sprung from would have not been possible without the assistance of many institutions and individuals. Most prominently, the editors wish to thank our friend and colleague Daniel Drache at York University, the spiritus rector and director of the Innis Centenary conferences of 1993 and 1994. He assembled scholars across Canada in a unique celebration of intellectual achievement from coast to coast. His encouragement helped make our conference a success.

Drache also has been the series editor of the resultant book publications. In our case, we would like to express our appreciation specifically for his inspiration and critical guidance in reviewing various drafts of this book. We would also like to thank the anonymous reviewers and Alison Kirk of Routledge for their comments and advice.

The conference and book projects also relied on generous contributions from the Social Sciences and Humanities Research Council, the President and Vice President (Academic) of York University and the Faculty of Environmental Studies.

Of the individuals who helped in various functions with the project, we would like to mention in particular Barb Brook, Constance Carr, Paule Cotter, Tanya Gerber, Stefan Kipfer, Oliver Krauss, Immie Manthei and Dianne Zecchino. Robert Milliken provided the splendid artwork for the conference poster and brochure. Special thanks go to Irit Kelmann, John Sandlos and Mark Wagner for their relentless pursuit of completion and style and to Carina Hernandez for seeing the project through all the way.

As the saying goes, the mistakes that remain are ours.

Toronto,
August 1997
The Editors.

EDITORS' INTRODUCTION

Perspectives on global political ecology

Roger Keil, David V.J. Bell, Peter Penz and Leesa Fawcett

This book emerged from the 'Global Political Ecology' conference organized by the Faculty of Environmental Studies, York University, Toronto. It was one of a series of events held across Canada during 1994 to honour the centenary of the birth of Harold Innis, arguably Canada's most important political economist. The great scholar, who had spent most of his career at the University of Toronto, was born in 1894 in Otterville, Ontario. When he died in 1953, Innis left Canadian scholarship a rich legacy of historical studies, a distinctive tradition of inquiry, and a number of interesting unresolved problematics that would be further explored by later generations of scholars inspired by his approach.

The conference was set up to pursue, from a contemporary perspective, topics Innis identified which now constitute problem areas at the core of today's political ecology. For the organizers this focus was 'natural', given our own academic home in Environmental Studies. In political economy we find many of the keys to building a political ecology for a sustainable globe, even though the issues in political economy are by no means resolved.

But what is political ecology?[1] For us it is simply a new approach rooted in political economy and cultural studies and critically branching out to understand relationships between society and the natural world. Political ecology is a relatively new area of critical exploration,[2] and at present it raises more questions than it answers. But these are timely, and in some cases unique questions. Attempts to come to grips with the environmental crisis have opened up previously unseen landscapes, and the theorizing has begun. Our conference attempted to expand the boundaries of theoretical frameworks and research paradigms in political ecology.

The legacy of Harold Innis

Long recognized as a seminal figure in the Canadian political economy tradition, Innis also provides important intellectual seeds for political ecology.

1

Innis devoted much of his intellectual life to understanding the link between culture and nature. Specifically, his work focused on the impact of the human presence on the natural environment. He emphasized particularly the role of the technology of resource extraction and transportation.

Innis taught us to appreciate the significance of space and time. His analysis of space took him to explore the impact (through markets and bureaucratic empire) of activities in one setting upon those in another. Here he provided insights into both politics and economics by explaining world empires and world markets. He put forward a compelling analysis of the material preconditions for the spread of authority across space; and from this derived his monumentally significant insights about the role of communications as the underpinning of political authority. At the same time, his staples theory of economic development was linked to a sophisticated analysis of world markets in the post-mercantile era and the interrelationship between economic and political control that characterized imperial domination in numerous settings and epochs (of course with special attention to the Canadian experience – see Drache 1995). In short, he was an early theorist of the prototype of what we now call globalization.

Similarly, Innis understood the significance of time in a way that few social scientists before him had even begun to grasp. It is interesting here to note the parallel between his insights and those of Marx and Engels. Engels believed that one of the most important contributions of their work was to inject into social scientific analysis an appreciation of change over time. We might characterize this as the developmental insight. In this respect, Engels said that he and Marx had done for the social sciences what Darwin had accomplished for the natural sciences by making clear the significance of historical change and historical analysis. The following comments by Engels (drawn from his critique of eighteenth century, non-dialectical materialism) show remarkable sophistication:

> The materialism of the last century was predominantly mechanical . . . . What the animal was to Descartes, man was to the materialists of the eighteenth century – a machine . . .
>
> [This materialism was unable] to comprehend the universe as a process, as matter undergoing uninterrupted historical development. This was in accordance with the level of the natural science of that time . . . . Nature – so much as was known – was in eternal motion. But according to the ideas of that time, this motion turned, also eternally, in a circle and therefore never moved from the spot; it produced the same results over and over again . . . . The history of the development of the earth, geology, was still totally unknown, and the conception that the animate natural beings of today are the result of a long sequence of development from the simple to the complex

2

could not at that time scientifically be put forward at all. The unhistorical view of nature was therefore inevitable.

(Engels in Feuer 1959: 211–12)[3]

Like Marx and Engels, Innis was acutely aware of the need to 'take time seriously' and study historical development as fundamental change over time. Accordingly, Innis extended his vision backwards through to the era of primitive civilization and derived seminal insights about the interrelationship between cultural transformation and the development of the means of communication and transportation.

Innis was also aware of the downside of development. For development uniquely entails changes that are irreversible. Whether they are also positive depends entirely on the value perspective from which they are assessed. This highlights another Innisian theme that ran through our conference and is reflected in many of these chapters. Innis was not the mere chronicler of change, nor was he an impartial theorist of space and time. On the contrary, he brought a passionate set of value commitments to his work. He insisted on passing judgements, making evaluations, and raising questions of ethics and justice which continue to challenge us today. In distinguishing between changes that were irreversible, partially reversible, or entirely reversible, Innis insisted that this sort of analysis entailed assessing outcomes in relation to value commitments. He saw all along that many of the irreversible changes that were occurring were of dubious value. He, almost uniquely among economic historians, distinguished growth from development and thereby provided an intellectual basis for a concept that has now come to be called sustainable development (which we increasingly realize may *not* involve growth).[4] He was especially sensitive to the damage (itself, of course, a value-laden term) to the natural environment wrought by resource exploitation. And he was aware of the injustices visited on colonies by empires. He sensed the unfairness of staple resource extraction, the distortions it engendered, and the resulting economic and political systems that grew up around staple extraction and export. He lamented the lack of autonomy of his own native land, which he said had gone from colony to nation to colony.

The brochure and poster for the 1994 conference symbolized the dimensions of this book in that it showed an image of Harold Innis in a canoe on an Ontario Lake which denoted the active scholar, the 'organic' intellectual whose situated knowledge (Haraway) is grounded in the experience of the natural world. The poster showed a human hand holding a fish head by a hook. The fishhead seems to grasp for oxygen and water even beyond death. The human hand seems firmly in control. A second glance reveals that the hook is a plastic tag on which the fish's commodifiable properties are imprinted. Beyond the symbolism of the interface between the non-human and the human, there is yet another discussion in which the poster expresses one of the core concerns of the book: with eyes squinted, human hand, hook, and fishhead blur into the continents of North and South America, an image of the dynamics regulating the relationships of the global North to the global South.

Political economy and the impact of environmentalism

In his famous 'Preface to "A Contribution to the Critique of Political Economy"', Karl Marx lists capital, landed property, wage labour, the state, foreign trade and the world market as the categories he deemed necessary to explore the field of political economy. This powerful brief piece also explains Marx's position on the base-superstructure problematic. To assess the impact of environmentalism on the field of political economy, it would be foolish to assume that we could just add 'the environment' to this list, simply expecting that it would (in neo-classical terms) fit in as another factor of production or (in Marxist terms) as another socially determined force in the process of material production. Matters are more complicated than that. The discourse about the environment and its relationship to the economy becomes a feature of the superstructure. In this sense, in much of mainstream discourse, discussion of environmental matters is co-opted into an ideology of development and growth.[5]

This is one side of the contemporary concern with the environment. The other side consists of the more radical voices within environmentalism. Both, however, are implicated in the process of economic and technological growth, either as an affirmative or a critical force. To use the more precise Gramscian terminology, 'competing discursive practices whose social bases are constantly forming and dissolving', articulate themselves as hegemonic or counter-hegemonic (Adkin 1992: 135).[6] And counter-hegemony, to some extent at least, has to respond within the framework established by the hegemonic ideology.

> But the environment is not just an ideological construct. It is also what has been called an 'articulating ideology' and a material praxis, an active part of the political economy. The way we conceptualize nature, ecology or environment is part of the material praxis of reorganizing the societal relationships with nature.
>
> (Keil 1994)

The fact that there is more involved than just adding the environment on to the economic equation has also started to dawn on the traditional practitioners of political economy in academia. In fact, some of them have reacted with force to reconceptualize a field which for several centuries now has been fairly stable, ideological differences notwithstanding. Several of the chapters of this book address this relationship directly: Elmar Altvater's lengthy treatment of the global order of the societal relationships with nature, Harriet

Friedmann's and Ellie Perkins' explorations into global economic regimes of food and trade, Nathan Keyfitz's elaboration on the relationships of population ecology and economics, Egon Becker and Thomas Jahn's revisiting of the 'limits to growth', Takeshi Murota's thermodynamical approach to political ecology as well as Ray Rogers' case study of the collapse of the cod fishery present different (and diverging) aspects of the economy-ecology relationship to whose reconceptualization the conference was intended to contribute.

From our perspective, there are two main currents in this effort of reconceptualization within political economy. First, there are critical 'ecological' economists like Herman Daly who have challenged the assumptions of neoclassical economics for failing to recognize the dependence of the economy on the natural environment (Daly and Cobb 1989; Georgescu-Roegen 1971). And second, there are economists in the Marxist tradition who attempt to redefine the revolutionary, anti-capitalist project in a way that includes ecological thought as a central feature.[7]

This book looks at some of the contradictions between economy and ecology and attempts to find new access points to each and syntheses between them.[8] In his contribution to this volume, Altvater provides an Innisian analysis of the relationship of fossil energies to capitalist production and accumulation, noting the potentially devastating consequences for the natural environment. The resulting global ecological impacts have brutally uneven effects in the South and the North, and pose a painful challenge for the future.

Cutting across the divides in political economy is the ethics of environment–society relations. It too has its divisions as laid out, for example, by Robyn Eckersley (1992: 33–47). She has distinguished between resource conservation, where the emphasis is on maintaining the resource base for continued economic development; human welfare ecology, where a broader notion of 'environmental quality' includes human health and environmental amenities; preservationism, which is based on human appreciation of wilderness; animal liberation, which extends the concern with human suffering and well-being to other sentient creatures; and ecocentrism, which values all forms of ecosystems regardless of their value to or appreciation by human beings. Most of the chapters in this volume fall into Eckersley's category of human welfare ecology, that is to say, they involve an enlightened anthropocentric approach to the environment. However, themes of preservationism and ecocentrism emerge as well. Eckersley herself closes the volume with an excellent assessment of 'rights discourse' as it applies to environmental issues, and provides a balanced critique of the views of 'rights skeptics'.

Innis' own methods as an economist and historian recognized the connection, today seen to be so important, between the physical and symbolic qualities of the natural world, and the social and economic aspects of human existence in the natural world. Innis' analysis of the history of the fur trade in Canada started with a description of the beaver; his tale of the fisheries in Atlantic Canada began with the image and physical properties of the codfish.

The objectification of nature, Innis seemed to recognize, started with the acknowledgement of some subjectivity of non-human existence: before the cod becomes a commodity, it is a fish; before it is exchange value and staple, it is a living being and part of the natural world, to which humans also belong.

Let us consider, for a moment, the time period just before and around Harold Innis' death in the early 1950s. In the aftermath of one of the most violent conflicts of its entire history, humankind had begun to face the possibility of extinction at its own hands. Years before Rachel Carson's *Silent Spring*, which exposed the creeping death caused by chemicals, the Nazi death machine and the nuclear threat had demonstrated the dialectics of the enlightenment with atrocious clarity. Yet, despite this horrible experience, modernization linked to unbridled industrialism and capitalist economies of scale had not run their course. On the contrary, a revived optimism or even euphoria linked to the victory of 'democracy' over totalitarianism seemed to sweep the lands under the *Pax Americana*: development became the mantra and doctrine of an economic-technological explosion under the neo-colonialist guidance of the American hegemon. Its successful application to all parts of the globe, particularly of course the 'undeveloped' countries of the Third World, promised economic and ideological salvation. Paul Wachtel (this volume) helps deflate this balloon of uncritical optimism, carefully explaining how, insofar as they treat nature as an 'externality', mainstream economic ideas actually contribute to environmental degradation.

As Nathan Keyfitz reminds us in his contribution to this volume, the new belief in development and human supremacy was so strong that after the 1930s and 1940s, land (= nature) drops out of the economic vision altogether 'with the realization that through technology unprecedented possibilities of substitution were emerging, and synthetics were everywhere'. By the time Innis died, economics seemed to have forgotten about that lone beaver and forlorn cod at the core of the Innisian economic world view, despite – and perhaps in reaction to – the warnings from political economists as diverse as Marx and Polanyi that exploiting nature was tampering with the very basis of our existence on the planet.

Almost half a century later, we have learned a few lessons – it seems. Those past five decades since the Second World War are congruent with a distinctive period of capitalist accumulation which has been termed Fordism by a group of French regulationist economists who followed the inspiration Antonio Gramsci had taken from his critical analysis of United States capitalism in the 1920s. The global social and ecological crisis (elaborated below) we see ourselves embroiled in today has many of its roots in the specific history of the Fordist period and its crisis since the 1970s.

Fordism is a model of societal-economic integration based on a social compromise in advanced capitalist countries between capital and labour. This social compromise was a national mode of regulation, which – as long as it lasted – allocated the product of social labour in such a way that the growth in

6

workers' wages corresponded to the growth rate of the national economy. The result was unprecedented economic growth, middle-class prosperity and mass consumerism in the western countries. Globally, the Fordist regime rested on American hegemony buttressed by the Bretton Woods institutions and the North Atlantic Treaty Organization. The USA controlled its own camp (through economic dominance and cultural imperialism), the Soviet camp (through the balance of terror) and the 'Third World' (through open warfare, colonial oppression, development policies and cultural dominance). While Fordism was not at home everywhere – not even in all of western Europe – its tentacles reached far and wide: from the 'core' areas of Detroit, Los Angeles, or the Ruhr to the 'peripheries' of the Amazon, the Sahel, or Indochina, as well as the oil fields of the Middle East.

The geo-political economy of Fordism was equally a geo-ecology of resourcism. As a result, any crisis of Fordism is a crisis of global ecological proportions. Those involved in the greening of political economy seem to agree that it is critical to understand the specific role of the Fordist accumulation regime and of its crisis in the definition of the current environmental crisis. 'Fossilist' Fordism (Altvater 1993) has been at the base of much of the large-scale ecological problems we are faced with today (accumulating waste, acid rain, the hole in the ozone layer and ozone pollution on the ground, global warming, issues of distributive justice concerning the use of the natural environment, etc.). One of the most important theoreticians who has linked the crisis of global Fordism to the crisis of the global environment is Alain Lipietz who writes that the liberal-productivism of the past decade has led to

> the most dramatic ecological crisis that humankind has ever faced. In the course of one century capitalism has multiplied world industrial output by a factor of fifty. However, four-fifths of this growth occurred in the Fordist period after the Second World War. As with Fordism, liberal-productivism fosters a use of the natural environment which makes no sense, as the ecological debt which past and present generations are handing on to future generations . . . will have to be paid for in the next forty years.
>
> (Lipietz 1992: 321)

As the Fordist crisis has left many industrial workers stranded and entire regions devastated by deindustrialization, it has also left us with an environmental legacy of unknown proportions.

Two of the chapters in this volume address one particular environmental legacy that is emerging as a result of such uncompromising productivism, namely the issue of global warming. They do so from the perspective of environmental justice and ethics. Rodney Peffer, a philosopher operating primarily within ideal theory, explores the implications of global justice for this issue. Drawing on a cosmopolitan approach to social-contract theory, he finds in this approach support for a global carbon-rights scheme. Under it, the poorer countries would have both an entitlement to redistribution from the affluent countries and incentives to skip over the 'dirty' phase of industrialization. In contrast to Peffer, Mark Lutes, who is equally concerned about global social justice, warns that a 'globalist' construction of the global-warming problem leads, in the framework of our global politico-economic system, to an inimical top-down approach. According to Lutes, not only is it hostile to local struggles to escape from structures of domination, but it will also be ineffective because of its coercive treatment of local communities and their conditions, institutions and interests.

Despite the obvious and lamentable damage resulting from Fordist productivism, this situation also offers the opportunity for social movements and political actors to change altogether the direction of industrial production and mass consumption (married under Fordism). It provides scope to raise questions concerning the purpose of all this production and the possibilities for environmentally friendly production and less alienated work conditions. We are certainly convinced that, as Alain Lipietz has stated, '[e]cologist economics is first and foremost a different way of working' (Lipietz 1995: 45). This book pursues this question of the relationship of the world of work (and its twin consumption) to the world of ecology in several of its chapters. Laurie Adkin, Robert Paehlke and Paul Wachtel examine different aspects of the debate around the future of work and consumption from a decidedly ecological point of view.

Political economy: modernization and progressive strategy

Marx's political economy and his historical materialism hinge on a modernizing strategy. Three main developments are being reflected in changes in political economic thought accordingly. They refer to the substance, the character and the scope of the current phase of restructuring in global capitalism. They address the problem of entropy and the need for production for use value; the changing accumulation regimes and their modes of production in various parts of the world; and the globalization of the economy.

While different societies articulate the relationship of the economy and ecology or the environment in unique ways, we can generalize that all modern capitalist societies share a set of common patterns that are linked to their reproduction: first, the growing importance of chemistry for production and consumption; second, the growing relevance of electronic information and steering systems for production and consumption; third, an energy system that treats energy simply as a commodity, the sale of which must be maximized; fourth, a transportation system whose components are characterized by ever greater individualization; and finally, a spatial distribution of economic activities that tends toward agglomeration (Beckenbach 1994).[9]

These characteristics seem to provide the background for a critical rethinking of the relationship of the economy and ecology in the current period. They lay down a framework which – negatively – defines the scope of reform of the productive relations inside capitalism. To ignore these concerns would be self-defeating for the environmental movement. Options for a fundamental turnaround in political economic dynamics require coming to grips with this complexity. The apparent dominance of the modern chemical and biochemical industries in production and consumption will continue to be a major impediment to cleaning up the environment, getting on top of the waste crisis, etc. until and unless the companies transform their operations and stop producing toxins and pollutants.[10] Changes in the labour process, and the growing importance of computer-aided production as well as other features of information technologies, mark both the terrain of struggles at the workplace and in the communities, and the vantage point for a fundamental critique of technology (Keil and Kipfer 1994). And finally, cities that expand into ever larger agglomerations are suffering from the growing collapse of the transportation system which rests on privatized automobilization and the growing reliance on single-occupancy vehicles (SOVs).[11] The nexus of urban process with the transportation mode is both central to the Fordist mode of regulation and a source of the environmental crisis of today.

Despite all of this, identifying the damaging traits of modern capitalism should not lead to a false dichotomy of society versus nature as often heard in popular discourse on 'nature'.

> It is fundamentally mistaken . . . to speak of the impact of society on the ecosystem as if these are two separate systems in interaction with each other. The typical manner of depicting the world in terms of a box called 'society' in interaction with a box 'labelled' environment not only makes little intuitive sense . . . but it also has just as little fundamental theoretical and historical justification.
>
> (Harvey 1993: 28)

Nature is not external to the economy, however much we characterize it in those terms. In reality, as Wally Seccombe has pointed out, 'industrial economies are immersed in nature; they operate, however, as if they had been built "on top" of a natural template that they could dig up, dump into, and trample upon with impunity' (Seccombe 1993: 103).

Economics and ecology, then, are connected, for better or for worse, in a modernization complex which opens a number of options for intervention and change. The contraposition of economy and ecology is misleading. Ecologies are always implicated in the economy-driven modernization process in and beyond capitalist societies. Rather than denying this implication by lapsing into a deceptive opposition of the two, it is their relationship which needs to be discussed as the foundation of a current critique of capitalist political economy. Precisely this concern lies at the heart of this book!

Yet, if we speak today of ecological modernization, we mean a specific discourse which has been hegemonic around the globe since the early 1980s. Rather than signifying merely an ideological trope, ecological modernization is a

> complex social project. At its centre stands the politico-administrative response to the latest manifestation of the ecological dilemma. Global ecological threats such as ozone layer depletion and global warming are met by a regulatory approach that starts from the assumption that economic growth and the resolution of ecological problems can, in principle, be reconciled . . . . [Ecological modernisation on the one hand] recognizes the structural character of the environmental problematic, while on the other ecological modernisation differs essentially from a radical green perspective.
>
> (Hajer 1996: 248–9)

The hegemony of ecological modernization translates into a dilemma for political ecology: While it cannot escape, it seems, from its cradle of liberal and Marxist traditions, having to deal with their ballast at every turn – making it part of the modernizing trajectory, it also has to position itself clearly and uncompromisingly outside of the modernization and development narrative in order to have any relevance beyond playing the global court jester.

The ecological crisis

Much of the current discourse on political ecology occurs under the influence of a sense of crisis. But the meaning of ecological crisis also needs a brief reconsideration. Our being in the world is inescapably linked to the ecological health of the planet. Yet, conversely, our concept of political ecology does not allow us to externalize the ecological crisis from our reach. The separation of nature and society had been a modernist legacy. It led to the attempt at domination of nature (both human and non-human) in modern societies and ultimately to an understanding of the ecological crisis linked to this domination. In contrast, some social ecologists have recently begun to formulate the ecological crisis as a 'crisis of the societal relationships with nature' (Jahn 1996: 58). This perspective integrates the understanding of the material human–nature relationships with the symbolic forms in which these material relationships are constructed. It means that all facets of the ecological crisis have social dimensions and all social critique needs to be mindful of the societal relationships with nature (Jahn 1996: 58).

The material-symbolic dialectics in the societal relationships with nature were reflected in the design of the conference and this volume: in both cases, we intended a dialogue between the critical traditions in political economy and cultural studies. We assumed that the strides that had recently been taken in greening political economy constituted great progress over the classical economy/ecology divide (see Keyfitz in this volume) but still left the discursive, political and cultural aspects of the ecological crisis underexplored. The combination of political economy and cultural studies also served as a reminder of the bridge that Innis himself had built between political economy and the study of communications as a field of culture studies. One of the implicit assumptions of the conference was, then, that the exploration and engagement of economy, ecology and culture would result in a better understanding of political ecology. Constraints, needs, and possibilities of human agency in the natural world would become visible through this combination.

In one sense, this assumption rested on the historical-empirical analysis of ecologism as the product of a certain 'stage' in the history of social movements under capitalism. According to Altvater (1993), the contradictions in the relationship of economy and ecology at the current stage produce a set of problems that open a window of opportunity for new forms of social activism. Increases in productivity happen due to an expansion of human (individual and social) appropriation of nature. This increase can be interpreted as an accelerated growth of entropy. Large-scale industrial production undermines the sources of its success: nature and labour. These contradictory societal relationships with nature, then, are increasingly being politicized, because the ecological-destructive process of increase in entropy means the withdrawal of current and future use values; as a consequence, the potential of social resistance is also growing. Historically, in capitalist societies, three types of social conflict can be identified: the defence of 'pre-modern' life-spaces; conflicts of distribution – the modern problematic; and post-modern, 'new' social conflicts and movements (Altvater 1993). The shift to the third type entails a fundamental reorientation of the productivist/consumptionist logic of earlier periods of struggle and conflict without ridding the new type of this logic altogether. As Altvater has argued, the principle of producing as little as possible entropy, and the mobilization of systemic intelligence (technology as well as new forms of production and reproduction) become the guiding ideas of social progress. Agents involved in environmental politics and policy formation, therefore, tend to differ from earlier social movements, decision-makers, etc. Monetary compensation is not the central goal of their efforts (Altvater 1993: 282f).

This brings us to the final pillar that is central to the book. We have emphasized so far political economy and ecology, with some reference to ethics as a third pillar. What is being introduced here is political discourse and political culture (Bell 1992). Discourse and culture frame the articulation and understanding of economics, ecology and ethics as well as the resulting forms of political ecology. It has now been widely accepted, as Maarten Hajer has recently pointed out, that 'the developments in environmental politics critically depend on the specific social construction of environmental problems' (Hajer 1995: 2). This discursive nature of the ecological crisis (which does not mean to deny the materiality of ecological problems) is not just about how we speak about pollution, degradation, etc. It is also about the culture and cultural politics of the environment.

Linked to the notion of crisis, in the recent literature on political ecology, 'risk' has become an important concept (Lash *et al*. 1996; Beck *et al*. 1994). It is seen as a determining factor of late modern or post-modern being in the world. The book explores several dimensions of this risk, most prominently the sharing of global environmental problems and the allocation of risk in the process. What the book avoids is taking either side of the polar extremism which separates widely the Pollyannaish position of mainstream economics from the apocalyptic notions of some ecologists (on this divide, see Keyfitz in this volume). The risk of the apocalypse (while not unlikely, specifically from a human point of view – see Athanasiou 1996), is a disenabling prospect. Again, throughout most of its chapters, the book takes a middle ground on which risk and improved regulation of the societal relationships with nature are brought together. Regulation in this sense is not the management of risk – a term fraught with the hubris of anthropocentrism. Rather, regulation is a contradictory process informed of the social and environmental conflicts and struggles that make up our existence:

> How is a 'contradiction' (as Marxists would say) – a relationship between each and everyone – to be regulated? In the same way as all social contradictions: by manners and customs (habits, values, or *habitus*, as the sociologist Pierre Bourdieu would say) and by institutions.
>
> (Lipietz 1995: 12–13)

We consider political ecology an important field in which the regulation of societal relationships with nature takes place. Yet, in contrast to Alain Lipietz, who sees political ecology as an ideology reaching beyond and replacing Marxist and liberal projects of social theory, we see political ecology as a complementary completion of these projects. We hope this volume can contribute to this goal.

What is needed (and has not yet emerged) is a new framework or paradigm,[12] that will allow humankind to lighten its 'ecological footprint'[13] while reforming the inequities within and between countries. Of course this is an enormous undertaking that will require rethinking our relationship not only with nature but also with each other. Feminist scholarship has stretched the boundaries between political discourse, ethics and cultural studies. Ecofeminism is a more far-reaching form of the anti-anthropocentric, non-dominance positions (Vance 1995), and has contributed significantly to opening up the horizon of questions that are considered legitimate. Attempts by ecofeminists to explore these concerns in a new discourse with a focus on gender, and to translate this project into programmes and action, are critically assessed by Bina Agarwal, Bonnie Kettel and Cate Sandilands in their contributions to this volume.

Often ignored in discussions of political ecology is politics itself. The challenge is to find new approaches to decision making that are democratic and yet sufficiently far reaching to take account of the needs and rights of future generations; that promote a global perspective without annihilating local autonomy; that ensure concern for the environment without destroying the economy – or vice versa; and that embody principles of justice and fairness appropriate to the global village of the twenty-first century. In short, we require a new politics of sustainability. The last section of the book addresses this challenge, with contributions from Peter Timmerman, Franz Hartmann, and Robyn Eckersley.

Notes

1 The term 'ecology' is complex and ideologically ambivalent; Neil Evernden reminds us that the popular understanding of 'ecology' in the sense that 'nature knows best and ecology knows nature' (Evernden 1992: 8), and the 'science of ecology' can be drastically different things. Ecology as a science has a pretty ahistorical, uncritical, economistic (theories of competition, exclusion, exploitation) base. Evernden's warning bears repeating:

> In choosing to ignore this somewhat dark side of ecology, even well-intentioned authors inadvertently create a new ecology to better serve their purposes – that is to better substantiate their arguments. . . . So far I have spoken of the use of ecology only by those in support of social reform. There is, however, a much heavier reliance on ecology by those who defend the status quo.
>
> (1992: 9)

2 Despite its newness, as might be expected political ecology is already the subject and title of a new academic journal (which is available in electronic format exclusively!). In the inaugural volume of *The Journal of Political Ecology*, the editors define it as 'a historical outgrowth of the central questions asked by the social sciences about the relations between human society, viewed in its bio-cultural-political complexity, and a significantly human nature'. They go on to identify the 'two major theoretical thrusts that have most influenced the formation of political ecology. These are political economy, with its insistence on the need to link the distribution of power with productive activity and ecological analysis, with its broader vision of bio-environmental relationships', James B. Greenberg and Thomas K. Park (1994) *The Journal of Political Ecology*, vol. 1, p. 1. Interestingly, a former colleague in the Faculty of Environmental Studies published one of the earliest essays on the subject nearly 20 years ago. See Grahame Beakhurst, 'Political Ecology', in William Leiss (ed.) *Ecology Versus Politics in Canada*, Toronto: University of Toronto Press, 1979.
3 Cf. also Engels, Speech at the Graveside of Karl Marx: 'Just as Darwin discovered the Law of Development of Organic Nature, so Marx discovered the Law of Development of Human History' (Tucker 1978: 681).

4 Herman Daly, one of the founders of 'ecological economics', has begun to write and lecture about 'uneconomic growth', a term that would be self-contradictory from the perspective of mainstream neo-classical economics. He explained what he means by this term in a lecture to the Faculty of Environmental Studies at York University (March 1997).

5 Sceptics noted that the term sustainable development reflected the relative power of the protagonists brought together under its umbrella: 'Environmentalists got the adjective; the business people got the noun'. To be sure, some have perverted the intention of the term, insisting that it refers to 'development that is sustained'. This perversion accounts for the increasing tendency to drop the term development all together, and substitute 'sustainability' for 'sustainable development'. Cf. Wackernagel and Rees (1996: 160): '[The] sustainability gap refers to the difference between ecological production and current human over-consumption. Developing sustainability (*a term I prefer to sustainable development*) means reducing the sustainability gap'. (Emphasis added.)

6 While any brand of environmentalism has some sort of implication for economic and accumulation logics, there are, of course, certain political rifts that help us differentiate their position in the public realm. Adkin likens the environmental movement to other new social movements and concludes: 'Insofar as there exists a consensus among left theorists about what a counter-hegemonic discourse is, it seems clear that such a discourse eludes many elements of these movements – those, for example, that reinforce the productivist, technocratic logic of growth, or post-Fordist strategies of capitalist accumulation – and rejects others that are conservative reactions to the crisis of modernity' (Adkin 1992: 135f).

7 Several Marxist economists (James O'Connor, Martinez-Alier, Altvater, Lipietz) have attempted to develop a theory of political economy that rejects the resourcist view of nature prevalent in older concepts. Within this perspective, a renewed debate on ecology and economy (Grundmann, Benton, Harvey) has occurred, much of it in the pages of the journal *Capitalism, Nature, Socialism* and *New Left Review*. O'Connor has emphasized the need to deal theoretically and practically with the 'second contradiction of capitalism', the relationship of capital and nature. Altvater, Déléage and Martinez-Alier have been influenced by the theory of thermodynamics and suggest that current capitalist production is geared towards a relentless increase in entropy and will first lead to an undermining of the conditions of production (as Marx said: land and labour) and finally to an end to human existence on earth as we know it.

8 Altvater (1993) sees five areas in which the economy and ecology are contradictory: (1) While the economy is caught up in cycles of quantitative change, natural processes are qualitative in nature; (2) In natural processes, real time and space (as material conditions) are central, whereas in economic thinking timelessness and spacelessness prevail; (3) Economic processes rest on the circularity and reversibility of their own dynamics, while the opposite is true in nature where change is irreversible; (4) Similarly, profit and interest appear as the ever renewable goals of economic activity while changes of entropy in natural processes are one-directional and final; (5) Finally, economic processes rely on some idea of rationality whereas natural processes are highly irrational.

9 All of these economies bear three kinds of social costs: economy-induced social costs; ecology-induced social costs; and labour-induced social costs (Beckenbach 1994).

10 Both chemical manufacturers and workers have initiated programs that attempt to reduce the harmful environmental effects of the industry. The Canadian Chemical Producers Association took the lead by introducing a 'Responsible Care'

programme in the early 1980s. Counterparts in dozens of countries around the globe have since adopted it.

11 See *A Strategy for Sustainable Transportation in Ontario*. Report of the Transportation Climate Change Collaborative, co-sponsored by the Ontario Round Table on Environment and Economy and National Round Table on the Environment and the Economy, November 1995.

12 Cf. Lipietz (1995): 'I am now convinced that political ecology can be this new paradigm, this framework of thinking to unite hopes . . . ' (xiii).

13 Wackernagel and Rees discuss the notion whereby 'modern cities and whole countries survive on ecological goods and services appropriated from natural flows or acquired through commercial trade from all over the world' and point to the 'Ecological Footprint' that represents the corresponding population's total 'appropriated carrying capacity' which includes the 'area of carbon sink land required to absorb the carbon dioxide released by per capita fossil fuel consumption (coal, oil and natural gas) assuming atmospheric stability as a goal' (Wackernagel and Rees 1996: 11).

References

Adkin, Laurie E. (1992) 'Counter-hegemony and environmental politics in Canada', in William K. Carroll (ed.) *Organizing Dissent: Contemporary Social Movements in Theory and Practice*, Toronto: Garamond Press.

Altvater, Elmar (1993) *The Future of the Market: An Essay on the Regulation of Money and Nature after the Collapse of 'Actually Existing Socialism'*, London: Verso.

Athanasiou, Tom (1996) *Divided Planet: The Ecology of Rich and Poor*, Boston: Little, Brown, and Company.

Beakhurst, Grahame (1979) 'Political ecology', in William Leiss (ed.) *Ecology Versus Politics in Canada*, Toronto: University of Toronto Press.

Beck, Ulrich, Giddens, Anthony and Lash, Scott (1994) *Reflexive Modernization: Politics, Tradition, and Aesthetics in the Modern Social Order*, Stanford: Stanford University Press.

Beckenbach, Frank (1994) 'Social costs in modern capitalism', in Martin O'Connor (ed.) *Is Capitalism Sustainable?: Political Economy and the Politics of Ecology*, New York: The Guilford Press.

Bell, David V.J. (1992) *The Roots of Disunity: A Study of Canadian Political Culture*, Toronto: Oxford University Press.

Carson, Rachel (1962) *Silent Spring*, Boston: Houghton Mifflin Company.

Daly, H. and Cobb, J. (1989) *For the Common Good: Redirecting the Economy Toward Community, the Environment, and a Sustainable Future*, New York: Beacon Press.

Drache, Daniel (ed.) (1995) *Staples, Markets and Cultural Change: The Selected Essays of Harold Innis*, Montreal: McGill-Queen's.

Eckersley, Robyn (1992) *Environmentalism and Political Theory*, Albany: State University of New York Press.

Evernden, Neil (1992) *The Social Creation of Nature*, Baltimore: Johns Hopkins University Press.

Feuer, Lewis C. (1959) *Basic Writings on Politics and Philosophy: Karl Marx and Friedrich Engels*, New York: Anchor Books.

Georgescu-Roegen, Nicholas (1971) *The Entropy Law and the Economic Process*, Cambridge, MA: Harvard University Press.

Hajer, Maarten A. (1995) *The Politics of Environmental Discourse: Ecological Modernization and the Policy Process*, Oxford: Clarendon Press.

—— (1996) 'Ecological modernisation as cultural politics', in S. Lash, B. Szerszyski and B. Wynne (eds) *Risk, Environment and Modernity: Towards a New Ecology*, London: Sage.

Harvey, David (1993) 'The nature of environment: dialectics of social and environmental change', in Ralph Miliband and Leo Panitch (eds) *Real Problems, False Solutions: The Socialist Register 1993*, London: Merlin Press.

Jahn, Thomas (1996) 'Urban ecology – perspectives of social-ecological urban research', *Capitalism, Nature, Socialism* 7, 2: 95–101.

Keil, Roger (1994) 'Green Work Alliances: the political economy of social ecology', *Studies in Political Economy* 44: 7–38.

Keil, Roger and Kipfer, Stefan (1994) 'Weltwirtschaft/wirtschaftswelten: globale transformationen im lokalen raum', in Peter Noller, Walter Prigge and Klaus Ronneberger (eds) *Stadt-Welt: Uber Die Globalisierung Stadtischer Milieus*, Frankfurt: Campus Verlag.

Lash, Scott, Szerszynski, Bronislaw and Wynne, Brian (1996) *Risk, Environment and Modernity: Towards a New Ecology*, London: Sage.

Lipietz, Alain (1992) *Towards a New Economic Order: PostFordism, Ecology And Democracy*, Oxford: Oxford University Press.

—— (1995) *Green Hopes: The Future of Political Ecology* (translated by Malcolm Slater), Oxford: Polity Press.

Marx, Karl (1955) 'Preface to "A contribution to the critique of political economy"', in *Karl Marx and Frederick Engels, Selected Works in Two Volumes*, Volume 1, Moscow: Foreign Languages Publishing House, pp. 361–5.

Seccombe, Wally (1993) 'Democracy and ecology: envisioning a transition to a green economy', in Greg Albo, David Langille and Leo Panitch (eds) *A Different Kind of State? Popular Power and Democratic Administration*, Toronto: Oxford University Press.

Transportation and Climate Change Collaborative (1995) *A Strategy for Sustainable Transportation in Ontario*. A report co-sponsored by the Ontario Round Table on Environment and Economy and National Round Table on the Environment and Economy.

Tucker, Robert C. (ed.) (1978) *The Marx-Engels Reader*, Second Edition, New York: W.W. Norton.

Vance, Linda (1995) 'Beyond Just-So Stories: Narrative, Animals, and Ethics', in Carol Adams and Josephine Donavan (eds) *Animals and Women: Feminist Theoretical Explorations*, Durham, NC: Duke University Press.

Wackernagel, Mathis and Rees, William (1996) *Our Ecological Footprint*, Gabriola Island, BC: New Society Publishers (New Catalyst Bioregional Series).

Part 1

THE NEW GLOBAL ORDER
AND THE ENVIRONMENT:
DEFINING THE ISSUES

1
GLOBAL ORDER AND NATURE

Elmar Altvater

Introduction

Only in the twentieth century is it possible, for the first time, to speak of 'world order'. Only during the Fordist phase of capitalist development did the great majority of humankind get integrated fully into global relations. As a result of the commodification of all spheres of life, or what Marx called the 'real subsumption of labour and nature under capital', nearly everywhere, all social relations are penetrated by the economic logic of capital valorization. Polanyi observed that 'the human economy is usually embedded in social relations. The transition from this social form to a society which, quite perversely, is embedded in the economic system was an entirely new development' (Polanyi 1957a: 135), which, we might add, reached maturity only during the Fordist mode of regulation.

The 'global orders' of the millennia and centuries preceding the advent of the capitalist mode of production in Europe had always only encompassed the 'world' which was known and accessible at the time.[1] To trace 'world-systems' to 'pre-history' (after the 'neolithic revolution') and interpret the rise and fall of world empires and world cultures as long economic, political and cultural cycles lasting several centuries only makes sense if one views the feeble long-distance trade relations and monetary flows (concentrated on a few cities) as the channels of communication of a system. Such a perspective privileges the formal over the real subsumption of social relations under the capitalist social form (Frank and Gills 1993). Before the advent of the modern age in Europe in the 'long' sixteenth century, only certain parts of commodity and monetary circulation spanned continents or the whole globe. Up until the nineteenth century, 90 per cent of the active population was working in agriculture and the overwhelming majority of economic activity took place on a local or at best regional level. Wallerstein may be right in concluding that a capitalist world system developed during the last five centuries (Wallerstein 1974; Modelski 1987). But images of the 'blue planet' and 'the unitary world' (*eine Welt*) were projected into popular imagery only after the launching of space-ship Apollo in the 1960s made it possible to take photos of our planet Earth.

19

As an economic system, political order, social unit and above all 'global ecosystem', the unitary world has been in existence only for a few decades and for this reason the discourse of 'world order' has only become more than metaphorical at the end of the twentieth century.

As long as 'the societal relationship with nature' was based on biotic energies, on the soil and the fruit it bore, on the speed and range of an ox or horse drawn cart, on the tonnage, manoeuvrability and speed of a sailing vessel and on the art of navigation, the material possibility of overcoming these limits of space and time was slight and the capacity of creating a world order remained restricted. In the twentieth century, however, the extraordinary density of economic and political ties among all regions of the world led to the emergence of world politics, the world economy and global ecological problems. In the *world economy*, corporations compete against each other at remote production sites and in highly integrated world markets, which only a few decades ago belonged to different worlds separated by geographical barriers. Japanese and German cars competing in Latin American markets – this would have been an absurd idea in the 1950s. The 'banana war' instigated by the European Union against cheap 'dollar bananas' from Central and South America would have been declared a bad joke twenty years ago. Corporations are not only multi- and transnationalized in core segments of the production process, they must also compare the profitability of invested capital with the interest rate formed in highly integrated international capital markets.

International competition forces corporations to adjust and thus leads to an equalization of production conditions, consumption norms and finally profit rates among previously distant regions of the world. As long as corporations do not produce for local markets only, their profitability must conform to a minimum level given by the interest rate formed in global capital markets. Keynes (1936) still assumed that the setting of interest rates was an indispensable element and a principal expression of national sovereignty. Today nation states have lost their sovereign power to determine interest rates (*Zinssouveränität*) (Scharpf 1987). The role of nation states changes once economic competition erodes the bases of political sovereignty, that is to say, when under a free trade regime territories can no longer be protected from competition from other regions in the world, when *citoyens* are no longer identical with *bourgeois*, and when the political power of states is undermined by market forces. In such a situation nation states and regions try to regain their sovereignty by compensating for what they have lost due to the interest rates, exchange rates and commodity prices with a political programme to boost the 'systemic competitiveness' of particular territories (Porter 1990). The reduction of labour costs (or less euphemistically: the reduction of wages and salaries), the creation of positive synergies in networks and technological impulses constitute the main pillars of micro- and macro-economic initiatives.[2] Costs must be reduced to stay competitive in given conditions determined by commodity prices, exchange rates and interest rates which are beyond the influence of individual states. In such a context the nation state is being transformed into a competitive state (*Wettbewerbsstaat*) (Hirsch 1997), which promotes 'its' production sites economically and defends them politically against 'foreign' producing regions. Such strategies are unproblematic as long as an expanding world market provides the conditions for a positive-sum-game. If however zero-sum games or even negative-sum games define the rules, competition policy becomes a ruinous race for rationalization (which displaces labour and increases unemployment) and a dangerous strategy of externalizing social and ecological costs.[3] In this situation one can observe tendencies towards 'macro-regionalism', that is to say the formation of regionally integrated economic spaces (EC, EFTA, CUSFTA and NAFTA), and 'micro-regionalism' below the level of nation states. As a result, nation states exhibit signs of disintegration (Cox 1993) and societies are exposed to the ideological stress of modern ethnic conflict.

The post-war order,[4] which provided the framework for *world politics*, lasted less than fifty years from 1945–89. In 1989, the fall of the Berlin wall symbolized the collapse of 'real existing socialism' and brought an end to bipolarity. Since that time some have begun to talk about a 'new world order' of 'unipolarity' (Krauthammer 1991). At the beginning of the twenty-first century – after the 'victory of the Cold War' and the 'end of history'[5] – there appears to be no alternative to the rationalism of world domination embodied in processes which are guided economically by markets and steered politically by formal democratic procedures. This apparent lack of alternatives expresses the fact that all dimensions of capitalist reproduction are subsumed not only formally but also substantially under the capitalist social formation.

Even if the process of 'determination' leaves plenty of room for individual action, *ecological* restrictions on the future of development have now become a reality. With the creation of an economic world system and a political world order, the 'metabolism' of humankind, society and nature has now reached a global scale. The societal relationship with nature is global and its regulation thus requires global rules. The common understanding necessary for the latter's creation and functioning is, if at all, just now beginning to emerge.

The pursuit of the rationalism of world domination has raised many questions to which new answers must be found within the 'new world order' because 'old' answers stemming from the period of bipolarity have proven to be inadequate if not counter-productive. Can modernization and industrialization modelled after the 'North' and the 'West' continue to constitute a realistic societal goal for all societies in all regions of the 'South' and the 'post-socialist' East? If yes, how should one deal with the failure of development efforts made during the last decades in the politically (not necessarily geographically) defined 'South'? What kind of regulatory frameworks will have to be agreed upon to 'order' the international financial and currency relations which are now out of control? And finally, how should one react to the fact that at the same time as the rationalism of world domination is being perfected, global ecosystems – water, air, land and ice caps – are threatened to be thrown out of balance? In the following pages, I will try to find answers to these pressing questions. For that purpose it makes sense to adopt a historical perspective in order to define the kinds of tasks the present must face in light of the aforementioned problems of world economy, world politics and global ecology.

The social form of surplus production and the energy system

The conquest of global space and the temporal acceleration of economic processes has a long history going back to the 'neolithic revolution' which lasted several hundred, if not a thousand years around 6000 BC.[6] Only from today's perspective do the developments in south-west Asia (mostly Mesopotamia), China or Mesoamerica appear as parallel evolutions, which was most certainly not the case (Ponting 1991: 37–67), notably because the contemporaries did not know of each other and thus invented gunpowder, the wheel, and the written word independently.

Still, it is possible with the advantage of historical hindsight to discern a logic in the history of human evolution (see Figure 1.1): initiated by what was probably a gender-specific specialization,[7] the transition to agriculture facilitated a more intensive utilization of natural resources. Increased labour productivity resulted in a surplus which allowed for social differentiation. With the deepening of the division of labour in society, classes and castes of warriors, priests, administrators, and rulers could form and assume the role of appropriating and distributing the surplus. At the same time, surplus production allowed for an expansion of trade within and, above all, among societies. The production of commodities for exchange and thus the principle of equivalence became a social norm. As monetary relationships spread and intensified, coins were introduced. Those able to exercise monopoly control over coinage were in the position to make a profit based on the difference between the nominal and the real value of currency (seigneurage).[8] The organization of production, distribution and storage of surplus became the source of power and privilege for the elites in the city. The accumulation of surplus constituted a project of domination which neither in Mesopotamia nor in Central America, Eastern Asia and Europe stopped short of the over-exploitation of human beings (super-exploitation) and nature (environmental degradation). Salinization (in Sumer), soil erosion (in China and Mesoamerica), deforestation (in Indus valley and the Mediterranean) destroyed world empires which we continue to admire because of their cultural achievements (scriptures, monuments, discoveries in astronomy). The disregard for ecological limits has a history which is much longer than that of industrial society. Nevertheless, the destruction of nature remained restricted to the local and regional level and never reached global proportions.

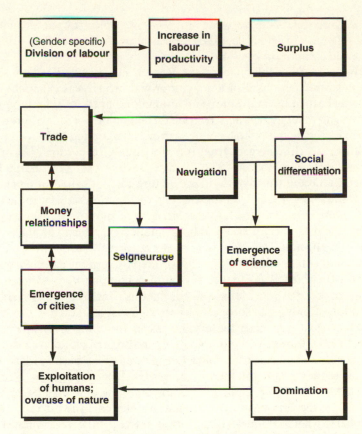

Figure 1.1 Elements of transition during the 'neolithic revolution'

The spatial dimensions of ecological problems are defined by the reach of energy systems. In modes of production based on biotic energy, labour productivity can grow only to a certain, limited level. The speed of a human being, a horse, or an ox can only be increased to the point of physical exhaustion. Yet the transition to fossil fuels and the concomitant technological systems of energy transformation (the industrial forces of production) and social formation (the capitalist mode of production) constituted a qualitative advance in human history which in this case is rightly called revolutionary. Since the late eighteenth century, the resort to fossil energy sources, 'exosomatic' forces (Lotka 1925; Smil 1993: 3), facilitated a quantum leap in the speed and reach of human activities. Enormous growth in labour productivity and social surplus production were made possible.[9] According to calculations by Angus Maddison, the average GDP per capita in international dollars (1980 prices) of OECD countries grew from $1,817 to $10,205 between 1900 and 1987, a six-fold increase, while in the USSR, which started off at a lower level of aggregate production, GDP increased by a factor of 7.45 during the same period (Maddison 1989: 19).

In this context Nicolas Georgescu-Roegen (1971, 1986) talked about a 'Promethean revolution' in productivity growth which was experienced first by European, then by 'neo-European' humankind in the re-orientation of its energy system to fossil fuels and the transformation of its mode of production and form of social and political organization. Humankind thus evolved from agriculture, which emerged from the 'neolithic revolution', to modern industry (Georgescu-Roegen 1971: 292). In 1870, 49 per cent of the labour force in OECD countries worked in agriculture compared to only 6 per cent in 1987 (Maddison 1989: 20). In his analysis of the 'process of production of capital', Marx demonstrated how the *ensemble* of motion, transmission, and machine tool machinery in heavy industry made it possible to produce relative surplus value by means of the real, not just the formal subsumption of labour under capital (Marx 1936: 342).[10] This principle expresses a type of productivity growth which is no longer slow and geographically restricted (as in agricultural societies) but global and continuously intensifying, driven by the competition of individual corporations on capitalist markets.[11]

The fact that ever since the discoveries in the 'long sixteenth century' (Braudel 1977), Europe could dominate the rest of the world even though in the thirteenth and fourteenth century Europe was still a 'backward' continent compared to the Chinese and Indian empires,[12] can be explained by the disintegrating tendencies within 'competing' empires (Frank and Gills 1993; Ponting 1991) and by the European expansion across the Atlantic into the Western Hemisphere, where conquest faced comparatively little resistance (Crosby 1986). Europe enriched itself during the centuries of ruthless exploitation following the discovery. Similar to Laurian silver in the case of Athens, Latin American silver became a significant factor in primitive capitalist accumulation in Western Europe. The importance of silver can be judged by the fact that in the nineteenth century the Ottoman empire, the Latin American states, the USA and tsarist Russia were all indebted (sometimes to the point of bankruptcy) to the European colonial powers (Kindleberger 1985: 213).

The colonies also benefited invaluably from the emigration of the surplus populations of Europe who could be induced to leave their countries for the Americas, Australia, New Zealand and, to a lesser extent, Africa. Between 1820 and 1930 Europe managed to 'rid itself' of about 50 million people. The costs of the accelerating process of accumulation were thus externalized. Indeed, these social costs were almost miraculously transformed into *social benefits*, for the colonies now had considerable purchasing power, developed new markets, delivered raw materials and absorbed capital. A virtuous cycle was thus set in motion. Capital accumulation fed colonial expansionism while the colonial expansion of Europe supported the internal accumulation of capital. In the sixteenth century, Europe became the hegemonic continent within the world system and retained its status up to the twentieth century. The functions of hegemony continued to be tied to nation states which got entangled in serious conflicts (as predicted by the theory of hegemonic cycles (Modelski 1987)), which finally culminated in two world wars and resulted in the weakening of not only the defeated but also the victorious European nations (Britain, France). Since the mid-twentieth century, the exercise of global hegemony has been in the hands of the United States.

Capital accumulation, global expansion, the subjection or extinction of other cultures and the exercise of political hegemony were thus mutually contingent processes. What distinguishes the new world system from older 'world empires' is the globality of order. The 'real subsumption of labour under capital' and the transformation of all conditions of life from material work to immaterial culture are based however on the availability of fossil fuels to feed the systems of energy and matter transformation in production, sustain daily households activities, and drive systems of transportation and communication. Social change becomes the norm of human and social existence (Cipolla 1985: 2) while continuity takes on the meaning of stagnation, even crisis. At the end of the 'great transformation' (Polanyi 1957b) to the market economy, which was connected to the 'Promethean revolution' and the emergence of industrial society (Georgescu-Roegen 1971) and supported by 'bourgeois revolutions' in England, France and the USA (including the subsequent breakthrough for human rights and democratic principles), the modern capitalist mode of production with its 'propagandistic tendency to create a world market' (*die propagandistische Tendenz, den Weltmarkt herzustellen* [see *Marx-Engels Collected Works* 1994]) had not only materialized but remained the victorious and – as many now think – only possible principle of organizing the metabolism between man and nature.

The expositions made so far can be summarized graphically (see Table 1.1). With the social organization of surplus production and productivity growth, human evolution has produced different energy systems and therefore also determined the distinct ways in which resources (elements and energy of dead and living nature) and sinks (in the global sphere) were utilized. The social form of production, utilization and distribution has been decisive for the social dynamics of social formations. The ecological effects on local, regional and global ecologies differ according to the economic and ecological scope of the activities in question. Each social formation ultimately reaches limits in its capacity to expand surplus production. The adoption of modes of regulation[13] within a social formation opens up a new range of options, which will shrink again at some point, however, unless energy systems and the social formation are transformed as well. These transformations in the neolithic, industrial and possibly the solar 'revolutions' (Altvater 1992) constitute the deep divides in human history even if we follow Ponting and Cameron's advice to apply the concept 'revolution' with caution.

Table 1.1 Brief characteristics of Promethean revolutions in the history of humankind

| Era | Resources | | Sinks | Productivity and surplus | Value/commodity/money | Societal reach | Social type of society |
	Energy	Matter					
Pre-neolithic	Solar	Renewable	No overload of carrying capacity of local ecosystems	No or small surplus	Rudimentary/reciprocity	Local	Hunters and gatherers
Neolithic	Solar	Renewable/non-renewable	Partial overload of regional ecosystems	Increase of productivity; surplus production in limits of agriculture	Partial monetization/reciprocity and equal exchange	Regional	Agriculture
Industrial society	Fossil	Renewable/non-renewable	Heavy overload of global ecosystems	Social rule of permanent increase of productivity; surplus in form of surplus value	Full monetization; reciprocity as a complementary rule	Global	Industry
Post-industrial – solar society	Solar	Renewable	Reduction of load in limits of carrying capacity of global ecosystems	Ecological productivity; surplus in socialized form	Partial monetization; rule of reciprocity	Global	Post-industrial society

The role of money in the 'fossil' mode of production

The contours of the industrial revolution's new historical dynamic become even starker if we consider the role of money in the process of capitalist industrialization. Given the limits of biotic energy, not only productivity growth and surplus production but also the potential increase in the sum of capital advanced are finite. Only as a result of overcoming these limits by means of fossil energy can positive interest rates become a social norm which stimulates economic activities without leading to the collapse of communal cohesion. The 'quantitativism (*Quantitativismus*) of money', which Aristotle (and later St Augustine or St Thomas Aquinas) still criticized because of its socially disintegrative effects,[14] can expand almost without limits once techno-energetic systems multiply, transform endosomatic forces of humans and animals into exosomatic energy and render the spatial and temporal limits of 'oikos' and 'polis' irrelevant for human activities. In modern monetary economies, fossil fuels propel the Promethean revolution, which makes the 'self-valorization of value' (see *Marx-Engels Collected Works* 1994) into a historical force and finally launches the latter into the nirvana of global financial speculation.

Within the Aristotelian tradition, St Thomas Aquinas taught that money is unproductive (Le Goff 1988: 27), a self-evident conclusion in a primarily agrarian society. Money can not reproduce (*nummus non parit nummos*), and usury is tantamount to death (Le Goff 1988: 31).[15] Money can be put to 'work' only once fossil energy sources make it possible for money to stimulate increases in real production and surplus creation. Of course money does not produce anything as the 'Fathers of the Church' maintained quite correctly. However, transformed into capital, money 'subsumes' labour and nature first formally and then substantially, reduces science and technology to a method of productivity growth and surplus extraction, and develops a type of labour organization which allows money to 'bear children' in the form of interest. The monetary value of interest demands an equivalent, materially produced surplus in the social form of profit. If profits are not sufficient to meet interest payments and the real surplus of material production is too small relative to monetary constraints, money is either devalued through inflation or the material basis of producers (debtors) is consumed. Without fossil energies neither the process of capitalist production and accumulation nor the modern monetary world market could exist. Fossil fuels have released the productive system from the shackles of biotic energy and allowed for the material growth which liberated monetary interest from the stigma of socially destructive and sinful usury, ennobled it to develop into a positive social rule (the monetary budget constraint), and even produced the contemporary institutions of the world economy with its 'flying circus' of bureaucrats and technocrats whose role is to enforce monetary restrictions. How could billions of dollars be transferred within seconds from Hong Kong to London or from Tokyo to London without electricity generated from fossil or atomic[16] energy? How could

World Bank officials apply their structural adjustment programmes in such different places as Brazil, Ghana and the Philippines without being able to fly from Brazil to Accra, and from there on to Washington and Manila? Only due to the annihilation of time and space by 'technological progress' (which makes it possible to talk coquettishly about the economy as a 'virtual' event), can real locations between the Rio Grande, Southern Ontario, Rhine, Po and Volga be forced to compete for liquid investment funds in the 'virtual' world monetary market by offering highly material factors of 'competitive advantage': wage costs, infrastructure, administrative efficiency, etc.[17]

Fossilism and the globalization of monetary relations (the global currency system and world financial markets) have by no means led to the harmonization and equalization of modern industrial development and to the integration of extraction with production systems everywhere in the world. Rather, the 'world order' of the second half of the twentieth century is characterized by the contradiction between systems of energy and matter transformation in the developed industrial societies of the 'North' on the one hand, and the less developed, resource-oriented extraction economies in the 'South' on the other hand. It is by no means certain that those countries and regions which are richly endowed with resource deposits ('syntropic islands') do have a better chance to accumulate wealth and affluence.[18] While in the nineteenth century resource endowment was an important factor of competitive advantage, the international division of labour in the twentieth century tends to favour those countries which do not depend on raw materials but have the skilled labour force as well as the organizational and technological potential to innovate and compete in world markets. With their raw material exports, resource-rich countries provide industrialized nations with the opportunity to maintain and increase their prosperity, while in their own territories only 'black holes' (Euclides da Cunha's description of the mines in Minas Gerais) remain after the completion of the extraction process.

The 'order' of the industrialized world is thus predicated on 'disorder' in extraction economies (Altvater 1992; 1993b) unless resource-exporting countries manage to direct factors of production (labour and capital) from the resource sector into a developing industrial sector by shaping relative factor prices through political means. Such a strategy is however conditional on the competitiveness of the countries' industrial products in the world market, a goal which is difficult enough to achieve. Fostering 'systemic competitiveness' implies that products (such as German cars, Brazilian iron ore, Canadian wine) will have to engage in intra-sectoral competition with comparable products manufactured in other countries (Japanese cars, Australian ore, French wine). This competition has two dimensions, however: intra-sectoral competition based on product price, cost, and quality (according to the classical rules of comparative advantage) and inter-sectoral competition based on profit rate differentials (for example between industrial and resource sectors). The difficulties of achieving a transfer of factors of production from the resource into the industrial sector are related to the obstacles less developed countries face under conditions of world market competition in generating industrial profit rates comparable to those in the resource sector. These problems were addressed in detail by Harold Innis in his analysis of staple products (cod, fur, lumber) in Canada (Innis 1965) and Steven Bunker (1985) in his attempt to explain the underdevelopment of the Amazon by means of thermodynamic categories (see also, Altvater 1987; 1993a). The same issues have also been discussed as effects of the 'Dutch disease' of inversely proportioned factor prices (Gregory 1976) and in terms of class-specific structures of interest.[19]

The reason why differences in developmental patterns between resource-extracting countries and resource-consuming industrial countries have been problematized is related to the globalization of standards and models of production and consumption, political forms of participation or cultural practices, all of which are mediated by the now comprehensive global systems of money and communication (Bell 1993: 159; Innis 1986; Godfrey 1986: IX). In globalized financial markets, where the minimum level of valorization is given by interest rates, this standardization is most evident. Measures and standards are not immutable, however. In what is another expression of the dynamics of the model, benchmarks are continuously raised by the most successful in the competitive race. The aforementioned quantitativism of money thus determines the rules and dynamics of international competition. Nothing remains in a position of stasis; all competitors are coerced into raising the standards of competition.

To the extent that the social norm of money (the monetary budget constraint), or, respectively, the principle of capital valorization in the production process and the energetic potentials of fossil energy sources (harnessed by modern industrial systems) are transforming the globe, ecological problems of global proportions have accumulated. Improved competitiveness results in growing production levels, surplus accumulation and increased growth.[20] Even under conditions of improved energy efficiency, mass production (and 'mass consumption') are only possible if the 'throughput' of matter and energy grows too (Daly 1991).[21] Global ecological problems have three main dimensions. First, finite, non-renewable resources are depleted and resources which are in principle renewable are harvested beyond their capacity to regenerate. This tendency is very old and has ruined many old cultures, as Ponting has demonstrated paradigmatically in the case of Easter Island (Ponting 1991: 1–7). Today, and in stark contrast to the latter example, the over-exploitation of renewable and non-renewable resources has reached global proportions and affects humanity as a whole. Second, as a result of the infinitely quantitative logic of the industrial capitalist mode of production, sinks are exploited to a point where their receptive and regenerative capacity is exceeded. This effect has predominated since the beginnings of industrialization and has reached global dimensions parallel to the material construction of a capitalist world system. Third, the over-utilization of resources and sinks threatens the habitats of those species which unlike humans have not developed 'exosomatic instruments' to construct a second nature adapted to changing environmental conditions. Species perish if environmental change is too rapid for their 'inner' nature to adjust. The catastrophe of modern ecological degradation consists in the fact that the principle of historic-geographical imperialism compresses time so much that the capacity to prepare for and quickly adjust to radically altered environments is drastically reduced. It has become increasingly evident that the contradiction between the monetary budget constraint, which has strongly stimulated capitalist market economies, and the 'ecological budget constraint' has deepened. So far this contradiction has, if at all, been described normatively (with reference to the 'sustainability' of production and consumption) but awaits rigid analytic treatment (O'Connor 1994).

We can now summarize the arguments presented up to this point. Monetary regulation forces economic activities and, consequently, the economic system to accelerate in time and expand in space. Monetary regulation can only grow into a historical force once fossil energy sources and the concomitant systems of energy and matter transformation allow for the real subsumption of labour and nature under the imperatives of capital. Previously the 'rules of money' had been tamed by the canonical or Islamic ban on interest rates or the social ostracism of usury. But in the wake of the industrial and fossil revolution both the ecological problems caused by the subsumption of nature and the social problems related to the subsumption of labour were globalized. The over-exploitation of global ecosystems and the economic inequalities in this world have thus become central issues to be addressed in the construction of a 'new world order'.

The politics of the ecological 'budget constraint': global apartheid or environmental regime?

Ecological limits manifest themselves as 'social limits of growth' (Hirsch 1977) on a global level. The pursuit of the 'rationalism of world domination' entails one 'tragic' result. The more this agenda is pushed ahead, the more it becomes impossible to truly dominate the world. For 'a society which does not take into account the repercussions of its transformation of nature can hardly be said to dominate nature at all' (Grundmann 1991: 109). The limits of exploiting natural resources, such as the emission of pollutants into the atmosphere, can not be defined in national, territorial terms and escape economic budget constraints. Attempts of this sort fail either because they can not be delimited territorially or because the pursuit of profitability puts a premium on the production of 'global costs of industrial society'. Instead, the definition of ecological limits requires an understanding of ecological 'budget' constraints which can be determined in two ways. They can be defined (first) 'passively', in terms of the carrying capacity of ecosystems relative to anthropocentric effects, and (second) 'actively', in terms of the burden imposed on the earth by human production and consumption. The boundary between ecological capacity and economic burden, between 'ecological scale' and 'economic scale' of production and accumulation has been called 'sustainability' in international debates following the publication of the Brundtland report in 1987 (Brundtland 1987). The concept carries normative undertones and lacks analytical rigour (O'Connor 1994). It makes more sense therefore to define 'sustainability' in thermodynamic terms (Daly 1991; Altvater 1992). The rate of entropy production[22] must equal zero on earth, that is to say that energy inputs (from the sun) must balance out the increase in entropy in the form of heat, sewage, waste, emissions, etc. (see the contribution by Murota in this volume). Ultimately this flow equilibrium can only be achieved by means of a 'solar strategy' (Altvater 1992; Scheer 1993).

The exploitation of ecosystems depends first of all on the amount of resources extracted from the environment and the amount of emissions sunk into ecosystems: the 'ecological scale of production and consumption'. This concept denotes the physical and energetic (use-value) side of production and consumption, the metabolism between nature and humankind. Second, the magnitude of resource extraction is determined by the level, the rate of growth and the distribution of income in world society, the 'economic scale of production and consumption'. In the latter case, we can talk about the monetary or value side of economic processes. The utilization of ecological resources and sinks (ecological scale) requires by necessity the setting of quantitative ceilings and qualitative standards in matters of, for example, CO_2 emissions, logging, water pollution and the production and treatment of waste, including recycling, etc. It seems obvious that the requirement of standard setting would provoke authoritarian solutions (for a critique, see Harvey 1993) which do not come close to meeting the regulatory challenge.

In principle one may stay within the limits of 'economic scale' by means of economic incentives which stimulate market participants to behave in ecologically sustainable ways: actors are induced to internalize the environmental costs they produce. For this purpose one might levy environmental charges, eliminate all environmentally destructive subsidies (in the transportation, agriculture and energy sectors), and institute adequate fee and fare systems in the public sector. At the same time, it is possible to influence pricing mechanisms in such a way as to calculate the 'costs' of exploiting the environment and include them in market prices. It is necessary however to question the feasibility of unburdening the environment by 'getting the prices right'. No method exists to attach market prices to the utilization of resources and sinks. Environmental economics tries to compensate for these difficulties by means of auxiliary devices (shadow prices), which even if they were 'rational' face a second fundamental difficulty: is it possible at all to dissect an interdependent ecosystem into individual pieces which then can be measured by prices? And even if that were possible, would a mechanism of rational price-formation not tear apart and destroy rather than protect nature?

A third, economic reason to doubt ecological strategies of internalization is related to the problem of market structure. Prices on world markets are not the result of free market forces but the outcome of the power of transnational corporations to administer prices micro-economically. At least 25 per cent of world trade must be considered intra-firm trade (OECD 1993). Most importantly, the price of money which is the source of the budget constraint in a capitalist money economy – the interest rate – is a highly volatile variable, particularly in times of economic instability. Contrary to the assumption of classical economists, the level of the interest rate does not reflect the real and 'natural' capacity of surplus production (indicated by the increase in production capacity) or investment demand and liquidity preference. Due to the global 'debt overhang', the internationality of credit in a world divided into national currency zones – a permanent incentive for speculation – the interest rate is a means to calculate risk. Financial instruments which serve the purpose of hedging risks, are fast becoming objects of speculation (financial derivatives), thus drastically diminishing the reliability of interest rates as the price of money. The productive surplus in the form of profit which can be produced with a given amount of capital is of little consequence for the calculation of return of innovative financial instruments in the monetary world market. The level of the interest rate has become detached from the real productive potential of debtors. In pre-capitalist and 'pre-fossil' times, such circumstances were the cause for the Aristotelian, canonical and Islamic prohibition of interest. While such a prohibition no longer exists, we are witnessing a growing global debt burden exemplified by the Third World debt crisis and its disastrous social and ecological effects in Latin America and Africa. Interest rate formation is certainly economically rational, for the price of money – a highly elastic market price – is 'theoretically exact'. If however the level of the interest rate becomes detached from the real conditions of surplus production and reflects the risk of debt more than anything else, the interest rate cannot be 'accurate' in ecological and social terms and fails to provide a basis for rational decision-making.

Economic mechanisms can solve ecological problems as little as they can mitigate developmental discrepancies between industrial and resource-oriented countries. What answers can be found then to the challenge posed by limited resources and sinks in a world of limitless industrial capitalist production and consumption? One answer can be described with the term 'containment' (Sachs 1992): confining the negative consequences of the over-exploitation of resources and sinks in the 'South' to perpetuate the accumulation model, mode of regulation and cherished life style of the privileged industrialized countries in the North. During the early *colonial* phase of capitalism the 'empty spots' on the globe were conquered, settled, oppressed, exploited and integrated in brutal, even genocidal ways into the sphere of influence of the capitalist metropolis. The *imperialist* states of the nineteenth and twentieth century did all they could to spatially re-organize an already sub-divided world, attempts which almost inevitably led to armed conflict and culminated in world wars. The strategy of *containment* is producing a fundamentally new spatial organization of the globe which builds on the structure of privilege emerging during the post-war period. Affluent societies try to secure their access to resources and sinks, but must ensure that others make the necessary sacrifices to stay within the recognized limits of global ecosystems. With the help of some sort of 'Maxwell's Demon', world society would be 'protected' from equality (in terms of income levels and access to natural resources) and the order of inequality would be perpetuated indefinitely (Martinez-Alier 1987).

The principle of equality of needs, wants and rights for all human beings in the world [23] is being replaced with another one: the principle of *rationing* limited resources of highly utilized and partly over-burdened ecosystems (resources and sinks). One part of humanity is assigned a large ration while another part gets only a small ration. In the 'new' world order, the rationing effects of the price mechanism (citizens of G7 countries with an annual income of $20,000 can claim larger shares than citizens of G77 countries with an annual per-capita income of $500) is being perfected by economic, political and military means.

An alternative to containment and global apartheid lies in the coordination of politics and cooperation among principally equal actors, that is to say in the formation of an international ecological regime based on common values, political norms, rules and above all capable institutions, within which actors could effectively communicate on an equal footing to discuss ecological questions. A series of observers have interpreted the UNCED Conference in Rio de Janeiro in June 1992 as a significant step towards regime formation (Buckmeier 1994; Simonis 1993; Oberthür 1993; Rowlands 1992), notably because the UNCED Conference was preceded by other conventions which dealt with the global regulation of the metabolism between nature and humankind.[24] Among the latter are the Washington Agreement on the protection of endangered species in 1973, the Montreal protocol on CFCs and ozone depletion (1987) and subsequent agreements, the Basel convention on transboundary movements of hazardous waste in 1989 which was strengthened in Geneva in March 1994, the Tropical Timber Trade Organization in Tokyo and Yokohama, and finally the now ratified CO_2 convention and the less binding agreements on the protection of forests and biological diversity all concluded in Rio de Janeiro. It would be an exaggeration to interpret these agreements as regimes with the above characteristics, which would circumscribe the framework and define the goals and strategies of environmental action taken by actors in the international arena. One thing all of the aforementioned regulations have in common is some form of conditionality which imposes (albeit very loose) restrictions on the imperatives of 'free trade' (the axiom of comparative advantage) and 'free enterprise' without embracing national protectionism, a principle with roots in the world order of the nineteenth century.

The principle of ecological conditionality (which cannot be ignored if the decisions reached at the UNCED in Rio are to be taken seriously) opens up alternative options: ecological norms are either controlled by nation states or anchored in international trade agreements and monitored by an international institution. In the first case 'eco-dumping' (the neglect of ecological costs in price formation) on the one hand and 'eco-protectionism' (tariffs or non-tariff barriers against products whose prices do not adequately reflect ecological costs) on the other are almost unavoidable and trade conflicts among states are easily predictable already. This prospect is by no means more disturbing than 'free trade' without environmental regulations. Indeed, the concept of 'comparative cost advantage' coined by classical economists is theoretically unfounded in times of extreme capital mobility and transnational labour migration (Daly and Cobb 1989). Ultimately the second option – an international institution (possibly within the framework of GATT) – would be preferable as a means to advance regime formation after UNCED (see Figure 1.2). Since financial contributions have to be made and environmental regimes would regulate rights of use of natural resources which are indispensable for the maintenance of income levels, regime formation is necessarily tied up with distributional conflicts among nation states.

Global civil society beyond nation states?

Yet on an international level, nation states are no longer the only, and in many respects possibly not even the decisive actors, even if the cultural, linguistic, political and historical legacies of redistributional policies implemented by nation states are more likely to have legitimizing effects than appeals to the abstract commonalities, rights and obligations of cosmopolites. Alongside groups of states such as the large and powerful European Union or the small and weak Alliance of Small Island States (AOSIS), beside loose alliances such as the Group of 77 and solidly institutionalized forums of coordination like the Group of 7, transnational banks and corporations act on the international scene with their economic muscle which translates into political power. International institutions like the World Bank or the International Monetary Fund (IMF), the GATT or the ILO often reinforce the economic and political might of industrialized countries while Non-Governmental Organizations (NGOs) participate in decision-making processes, notably in matters of environment and development.

All these actors pursue interests. The latter can be divided into the interests of polluters and the interests of sufferers, both of which cannot be neatly distinguished, however, due to the 'boomerang-effect' (Beck 1992): polluters are also sufferers. To those two types of interest, Prittwitz (1993) introduced a third category, the third-party interests of 'supporters' or 'assistants' (*Helferinteressen*). Such a matrix of actors and roles makes it possible to appreciate the complex and contradictory constellation of interests which

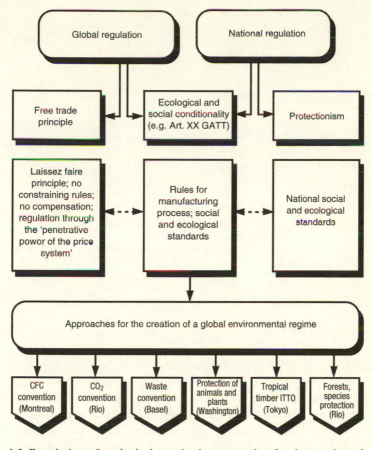

Figure 1.2 Regulation of ecological standards: approaches for the creation of an international regime

structure the negotiation of international regimes designed to regulate development and environment. Developed from Simonis (1993), Table 1.2 indicates these connections. As a result of global communications and global networks, nation states and the diplomats representing national governments are losing their monopoly in shaping international relations. 'Civil society' is in the process of becoming internationalized and transnationalized.[25] Even this tendency can be understood as an outcome of the globalization of fossil Fordism. The threat to the natural environment has led, on the one hand, to 'new concerns' (*neue Betroffenheiten*) and, on the other hand, to international networks[26] which are growing into organizational forms. In the meantime, NGOs have taken on important tasks in the negotiation of international agreements, particularly in the realm of environment and development. These trends raise questions relating to state theory.

Table 1.2 Actors and their interests in global environmental politics

International actors	Producers of emissions	Actors affected by emissions	Aid givers	Aid receivers
States and groups of states				
USA	strong	weak	strong	no problem
EU	strong	strong	strong	no problem
Eastern Europe	strong	strong	weak	strong
OPEC	strong	weak	weak	weak
Group of 77	weak	strong	weak	strong
AOSIS	less than weak	very strong	no problem	weak
Transnational corporations	strong	strong/weak	no problem	no problem
NGOs	no problem	strong	strong	strong
International institutions	no problem	no problem	strong	no problem

Sovereign states, which since the emergence of modernity have constituted the 'international order' and the point of departure for the 'realist school' of international relations, have been the actors endowed with the longest tradition, the most power, the least questioned legitimacy and the greatest expertise within the international system. The sovereignty of the nation state is defined and delimited in two ways. State power refers to a territory and thus has a territorial, spatial dimension. Also, state power is derived historically from the citizenry (*Staatsvolk*), which at least in democratic systems is the proper sovereign and bestows legitimacy and authority upon respective national governments. Both resources of power and sovereignty – territory and people – are finite. The boundaries of the nation state of the nineteenth and twentieth centuries are less and less compatible with the scope of economic processes and the spatial and temporal effects of matter and energy transformations. Due to the internationalization of the economy, the system of modern nation states has become 'fluid' (Ruggie 1993: 139).

It would be wrong however to infer from these tendencies that at the end of the twentieth century, the formerly decisive role of nation states is a thing of the past (see for example Panitch 1993; Cox 1993). Legitimacy for governmental action is still primarily derived from societies defined by nationality of the electorate. Yet the national citizenry is no longer a self-evident unit, if it ever was one. In European history, nation states had to invent their national peoples rather than receiving their integrity from pre-existing 'nations'.

Modern 'nomadism' is leading to a dissolution of non-territorial boundaries, such as those dividing rightful social insurance claimants. At the same time subnational, regionalist entities ('micro-regionalism' [Cox 1993]) are emerging and convey subnational identities which are no longer attached to the traditional nation state.

The territoriality of nation states is being 'unbundled', as Ruggie (1993) called the erosion of territorial nation states as functional entities and the undoing of national territories as symbols in the world of social imagery. As currency zones, nation states are paradoxically defined both in national and international terms. They are connected to each other by means of exchange rates, yet their economic relations with other nation states are calculated by means of national accounting measures and the balance of payments. The regulation of foreign exchange rates lies only to a limited degree within the realm of influence of nation states and international institutions. Exchange rates are the result of the interplay of unregulated monetary forces in currency markets, where today more than US$1000 billion are traded, of which only ten billion, or 1 per cent is required to transact world trade (which amounts to US$3500 billion annually). The remaining currency transactions are a result of speculation, which is necessary to defend the value of monetary assets against currency fluctuations in the context of national currency regulation and global capital movements but at the same time increases the volatility of currency fluctuations.

In light of the globality of economic and ecological problems and considering the limited sovereignty of nation states, one might argue that we are witnessing the formation of a global state in a unitary world (*eine Welt*) (Knieper 1991, 1993). To what extent a global state can be 'personified, symbolized, imagined' (Walzer 1967), and thus acquire legitimacy and elicit consensus as the state of a global society is a matter of debate. The nightmare of authoritarian ecologism looms large. These considerations immediately point to a political, economic and ecological paradox. Politics is about the regeneration of power, the setting of rules, the securing of legitimacy for political intervention, the generation and cultivation of consensus. Can these principles be globalized? Hardly, for the globalization of politics pre-supposes that the political principle of establishing boundaries be transformed into the boundlessness of a global system. Politics would have reached a turning point.

The temporal unevenness and the spatial and temporal incompatibility of economy, ecology and politics can be abolished neither by constructing a global state nor by invoking the tradition of nation statehood. Yet the question arises how this 'dys-functionality' of functional spaces on a unitary globe can become a productive force. If nation states are incapable of resolving global ecological and economic problems, and if a global state is an illusion, then intermediary institutions and organizations face a two-pronged complex of tasks in the process of building an international ecological regime. First, NGOs are becoming indispensable in mediating and strengthening consensus within national (or regional) societies so as to wrest from political institutions radical and at first unpopular measures to reduce air, soil and water pollution, manage resources sustainably and preserve spaces for species whose 'economic benefits' can not be calculated. Interests in the protection of the natural environment can not be ascribed to vertically divided class interests or horizontally juxtaposed interests of particular groups. They are present in every individual and concern all (vertical) classes and (horizontal) groups equally if one disregards for a minute class-specific avenues of escaping the effects of environmental degradation. In this sense Ulrich Beck is correct when he pointedly remarks that smog is 'democratic'. Rather than being reducible to specific class or group interests, NGOs play a general advocacy role.

Second, because they are situated beneath the realm of the state and escape the problems addressed within the realm of sovereignty and traditional diplomacy, NGOs uniquely can weave connecting links within international networks. Non-Governmental Organizations are thus constituents of an international civil society, as it were. 'Interests of humanity' (and, one must add, human rights and rights of nations) beyond national interests are better articulated by NGOs, which are not constrained by sovereignty and national territorial power, rather than by nation states, which enter into international negotiations but depend on intermediary procedures and regulations to have international agreements ratified. International networks of NGOs are the formal political expressions of the globality of ecological crisis. The experiences of Rio also indicate, however, that NGOs do not necessarily communicate on the same wave length simply because of their common political form and intermediary character. Rowlands detects 'an unprecedented level of cooperation among some members of the NGO community', but he also observes significant differences between NGOs from the North and those from the South in terms of the professionalism of their activities, the number of their connections to the grassroots, and their influence on representatives of large nation states or international institutions (Rowlands 1992: 215).

To conclude: as announced by the discourse of 'post-industrial society' (Bell 1976), the epoch of industrial capitalism is coming to an end in the same way as the pre-neolithic and neolithic eras faded during earlier historical times. Global ecological problems are as difficult to resolve as the market-induced inequality in the world, for in contrast to earlier historical epochs one single model of development not only determines the ideas and aspirations of humankind but also guides the politics of nation states and international institutions. The 'Maxwell's demon' of the 'new world order' is needed to sustain the order of global inequality and contain the ecological, political, social and ecological consequences of non-development: ecological destruction, conflict, war, poverty, misery. After the containment of the Cold War, a new form of containment emerges and is being replicated even by the new military strategies. Yet there are tendencies which may transgress this new world order. New actors have entered the stage, a solar energy model is no longer unrealistic. New social and political forms of regulation, however, remain to be found.

Chapter translated by Stefan Kipfer

Notes

1 Braudel (1977) explicitly distinguishes between '*économie-mondiale*' and '*économie-monde*'. '*Économie-monde*' denotes a 'world-for-itself' which does not necessarily encompass the whole globe ('économie-mondiale') as Braudel showed in his study of the Mediterranean of the sixteenth century.

2 The spread of 'systemic competitiveness' as a principle of policy making is a good indication of the fact that the capitalist mode of production has taken the form of a world system. In all parts of the world, the promotion of comparative advantage against competitors has become a paramount strategy (EU 1993; CEPAL 1990), a fact which explains the relevance of Friedrich List's argument that each nation should maximize its 'productive forces' before exposing itself to the 'cosmopolitanism' of world market competition (List 1841; Fallows 1993). Times have changed however since the first half of the nineteenth century. The prospects of protecting national economies behind 'educational' tariff walls are slim in light of globalized financial markets. Instead, all pertinent policy approaches developed by global actors such as the world bank, the IMF, or the new World Trade Organization demand further market liberalization.

3 In this context, Leo Panitch cites the story of the race between Alice and the Queen in 'Alice in Wonderland', where the runners do not advance despite their efforts to run as fast as possible. This analogy very clearly demonstrates the absurdity of the policy of competitiveness (Panitch 1993). Panitch's conclusion that the nation-state still constitutes the main space of capital accumulation may be realistic from a North American perspective but no longer applies to Western Europe.

4 The bipolar world order of the second half of the 'short' twentieth century, which lasted from 1917–89, was no longer primarily defined by the forces of repulsion and attraction of nation-states. Its main characteristic was the competition among two rival 'systems' and blocs of states, between Western capitalism and the real-socialist camp. Both systems claimed to offer alternative social orders to the world and wooed for influence in the non-aligned regions of the 'South'. In the West a differentiated, trans- and international web of rules and regulations emerged, which not only served the purpose of competing with the East Bloc but also provided a favourable framework for the temporal acceleration and spatial expansion of accumulation. It is not surprising that after the collapse of 'real existing socialism' and the end of bipolarity, nationalistic tendencies in East and West are intensifying and pose a growing danger to peaceful interdependence and cooperation.

5 For a review of the debate about 'posthistoire', which developed after the collapse of real existing socialism, see Niethammer (1992) and Anderson (1992).

6 Due to this long duration, Clive Ponting rejects the term 'revolution' to qualify the 'neolithic' transition from hunting and gathering societies (which themselves lasted several hundred thousand years) to agriculture and sedentary lifestyles (see also Cameron 1989: 24).

7 While men did the hunting, women began to breed plants and domesticate animals. This process of specialization lasted for centuries.

8 Cameron reports that the power of Athens was to a large extent dependent on seigneurage gains:

Silver from Laurium also helped finance Athens' persistently unfavourable balance of trade (shipping and financial services were also important sources of earnings), and thus indirectly aided in the construction of the great public buildings and monuments for which Athens became famous. The Athenian Golden Age, in fact, was made possible by the Laurian silver.

(Cameron 1989: 35)

9 The capitalist mode of production is so unique and coherent because it consistently combines psychological dispositions (the motivational principles of accumulation and performance), incentives for individual achievement (profit) and social rules (positive and negative sanctions in the competitive process) and fuels this regulatory *ensemble* with fossil energy. Referring to A.G. Frank, who in 1959 already demonstrated the existence of 'a perfect correlation between the given measures of growth of industrial capital stocks and the consumption of energy from fossil fuels both in the USA and in the UK', Martinez-Alier adds that 'neither Frank nor Wallerstein wrote the kind of ecological history which is now developing . . . '' (Martinez-Alier 1987: 15).

10 See Marx's elaborations in the Economic Manuscript of 1861–3:

the formal subsumption of labour under capital . . . is distinguished only *formally* from other modes of production . . . . As yet there is no difference in the *mode of production* itself. The labour process continues exactly as it did before – from the technological point of view – only as a labour process now *subordinated* to capital.

(Marx 1994: 95)

On real subsumption, Marx writes:

With the real subsumption of labour under capital, all the CHANGES we have discussed take place in the technological process, the labour process . . . in the relation of the worker to his own production and to capital – and finally, the development of the productive power of labour takes place, in that the productive forces of social labour are developed, and only at that point does the application of rational forces on a large scale, of science and machinery, to direct production become possible. Here, therefore, there is a change not only in the formal relation but in the labour process itself.

(Marx 1994: 106)

11 Industrial methods multiplied the productivity of agriculture as well and made it possible for the first time in human history to eradicate hunger, if only in the highly industrialized countries (Ponting 1991: 88).

12 The criterion of backwardness must be qualified. Precisely because at that time there was no developed world system comparable to that of the late twentieth century, no homogeneous model of development was in existence to justify the concept of backwardness.

13 This is the subject of regulation theory, which unfortunately cannot be discussed in more detail in this paper.

14 This doctrine was adhered to by Christianity (up to modern times) and by Islamic cultures (in some cases until today).

15 In medieval Europe every business transaction was called usury if it allowed someone to take more out of a transaction than she/he put in (*Usuram appellari et superabuntantiam quidquid illud est, si ab eo quod dederit plus acceperit*). In the Decretum Gartiani one can read: 'Everything which is demanded over and above capital is usury' (*Quicquid ultra sortem exigitur usura est*). According to this understanding, usury is more than a crime, it is a sin (Le Goff 1988: 24).

16 We cannot enter into a discussion of the differences between nuclear and fossil energy. Suffice it to say that the recourse to nuclear energy magnifies the problems of fossilism.

17 While in pre-modern times humans were limited in their capacity to transport energy sources (mainly wood) (Debeir 1991) and thus had to locate production in relative proximity to available energy sources, modern capitalist societies source energy and raw materials from all regions of the world and process them into use values in the centres of energy and matter transformation to fill the store windows of 'modern affluent societies' and display the 'wealth of nations'. All this presupposes elaborate storage capacities, extensive transportation systems and an easy transformability of primary and secondary energy sources into final energy products (coal into heat and motion, and, in turn, motion into heat and electricity). All these conditions are met by fossil fuels.

18 It is often argued that because of their endowment with natural resources, the countries of the former Soviet Union have good prospects of integrating successfully into world markets. It is more probable, however that these countries will have difficulties to develop modern industrial systems despite their natural wealth. The gap between the former Soviet republics and the industrialized countries will grow as raw materials are exported to fuel the industries in the modern, competitive industrialized countries.

19 It is not possible at this point to discuss these approaches in detail. We must also disregard the contribution made by Massarrat, who explains developmental blockages with the 'manipulations' of the 'North' within the 'dualism of the world economy' (*Dualsystem der Weltwirtschaft*) which have made it impossible that 'resource stocks in the developing countries of the South can take on the form of capital' (Massarrat 1993: 46).

20 This statement assumes that all other variables remain constant ('ceteris paribus').

21 OECD countries managed to reduce energy consumption per unit of gross national product after the oil shock of the 1970s. Nevertheless, energy production (and waste production) has increased because the gross national product grew more than energy efficiency (OECD 1991).

22 The use of this term in the social sciences has not remained unchallenged. It has strong anthropomorphic connotations because the concept of order as well as the concept of 'availability' of free energy in a closed system are defined according to human criteria (Georgescu-Roegen 1971; Martinez-Alier 1987; Altvater 1992).

23 Raising income levels in the 'Third World' to that of the 'First World' would require an increase in the product of (1) the ratio of the income level in industrial countries to that in developing countries, (2) population growth in developing countries, (3) a factor reflecting the assumed increase in the efficiency of production, and (4) a factor representing the population of the developing countries as a fraction of total world population. If one supposes that the share of developing countries of world population is 0.8, the increase in efficiency is 0.5, the population in developing countries doubles (factor 2) and the ratio of income between industrial and developing countries is 4, then incomes would have to increase by a factor of 3.2 ($0.8 \times 0.5 \times 2 \times 4 = 3.2$). Such an increase is largely unrealistic if one considers the weight of economic mechanisms (monetary constraints) and ecological limits (ecological constraints). A convergence in income levels can thus only be

achieved by means of global income re-distribution. The political will to achieve such a task can not be pre-supposed, however.

24 The OECD (1991) has compiled most international environmental agreements and conventions.

25 'Civil society' is not meant in a trite or idyllic way as in many recent analyses of the 'new world order' (Hein 1993). The internationalization of 'civil society' is nothing but the internationalization of the social relations of the capitalist social formation and thus all of the latter's contradictions and conflicts.

26 Thereby electronic data banks are becoming increasingly important for the international integration of NGOs (*Le Monde Diplomatique* July 1994).

References

Altvater, Elmar (1987) *Sachzwang Weltmarkt. Verschuldungskrise, blockierte Industrialisierung, ökologische Gefährdung-der Fall Brasilien*, Hamburg: VSA.

—— (1992) *Der Preis des Wohlstands. Umweltplünderung in der neuen Welt(un)ordnung*, Münster: Westfälisches Dampfboot.

—— (1993a) *The Future of the Market: An Essay on the Regulation of Money and Nature after the Collapse of 'Actually Existing Socialism'*, trans. Patrick Camiller, London: Verso.

—— (1993b) 'Die Ökologie der neuen Welt(un)ordnung', *Nord-Süd aktuell* 1: 72–84.

Anderson, Perry (1992) *A Zone of Engagement*, London and New York: Verso.

Beck, Ulrich (1992) *Risk Society: Towards a New Modernity*, London: Sage.

Bell, Daniel (1976) *The Coming of Post-Industrial Society: A Venture in Social Forecasting*, New York: Basic Books.

Bell, David V.J. (1993) 'Global communications, culture and values implications for global security', in David Dewitt, David Haglund, John Kirton (eds) *Building a New Global Order: Emerging Trends in International Security*, Oxford: Oxford University Press.

Braudel, Fernand (1977) *Afterthoughts on Material Culture and Capitalism*, trans. Patricia M. Ranum, Baltimore, MD: Johns Hopkins University Press.

Brundtland, Gro Harlem (1987) *Our Common Future: World Commission on Environment and Development*, Oxford and New York: Oxford University Press.

Buckmeier, Karl (1994) *Strategien globaler Umweltpolitik*, Münster: Westfälisches Dampfboot.

Bunker, Stephen (1985) *Underdeveloping the Amazon: Extraction, Unequal Exchange, and the Failure of the Modern State*, Chicago, IL: University of Illinois Press.

Cameron, Rondo (1989) *A Concise Economic History of the World: From Paleolithic Times to the Present*, New York and Oxford: Oxford University Press.

CEPAL (Comision Economica para America Latina y el Caribe) (1990) *Transformación Productiva con Equidad*, Santiago de Chile.

Cipolla, Carlo M. (1985) 'Die industrielle Revolution in der Weltgeschichte' in Cipolla and Borchardt (Hrsg) *Europäische Wirtschaftgeschichte*, Stuttgart and New York.

Cox, Robert (1993) 'Global perestroika', *Socialist Register* 30: 26–43.

Crosby, Alfred (1986) *Ecological Imperialism: The Biological Expansion of Europe, 900–1900*, Cambridge: Cambridge University Press (Deutsch: Die Früchte des weissen Mannes, Darmstadt).

Daly, Herman (1991) *Steady-State Economics*, Washington, DC: Island Press.

—— (1994) 'Die Gefahren des freien Handels', *Spektrum der Wissenschaft* (January): 40–6.

Daly, Herman E. and Cobb, John B. Jr. (1989) *For the Common Good*, Boston: Beacon Press.

Daly, Herman E. and Townsend, Kenneth N. (eds) (1993) *Valuing the Earth: Economics, Ecology, Ethics*, Cambridge: MIT Press.

Debeir, Jean-Claude, Deléage, Jean-Paul and Heméry, Daniel (1989) *Prometheus auf der Titanic: Geschichte der Energiesysteme*, Frankfurt: Campus.

EU (1993) Kommission der Europäischen Gemeinschaften: Wachstum, Wettbewerbs-fähigkeit, Beschäftigung. Herausforderungen der Gegenwart und Wege ins 21. Jahrhundert, Weißbuch, Bulletin der Europäischen Gemeinschaften, Beilage 6/93, Brüssel.

Fallows, James (1993) 'How the world works', *The Atlantic Monthly* 272 (December): 61–87.

Frank, André Gunder and Gills, Barry K. (1993) 'World system economic cycles and hegemonial shift to Europe 100 BC–AD 1500', *The Journal of European Economic History* 22, 1: 155–83.

Georgescu-Roegen, Nicholas (1971) 'The entropy law and the economic process in retrospect', *Eastern Economic Journal* 12, 1: 3–25.

Godfrey, David (1986) Foreword to *Innis, Harold A, Empire and Communications*, Toronto: Press Porcépic.

Gregory, R.G. (1971) *The Entropy Law and the Economic Process*, Cambridge, MA: Harvard University Press.

—— (1981) 'Some implications of the growth of the mineral sector', *The Australian Journal of Agricultural Economics* 20, 2: 71–91.

Grundmann, Reiner (1991) 'The ecological challenge to Marxism', *New Left Review* 187: 103–20.

Habermas, J. (1984, 1987) *Theory of Communicative Action*, Boston, MA: Beacon Press.

Hardin, Garrett (1968) 'The tragedy of the commons', *Science* 162: 1243–8.

Harvey, David (1993) 'The nature of environment: the dialectics of social and environ-mental change', *Socialist Register*, London: Merlin Press.

Hein, Wolfgang (1993) *Umweltorientierte Entwicklungspolitik*, Hamburg: Zweite erweiterte Auflage.

Hirsch, Fred (1977) *Social Limits to Growth*, London: Routledge and Kegan Paul.

Hirsch, Joachim (1997) 'Globalization of capital, nation-states and democracy', *Studies in Political Economy* 54, Fall: 39–58.

Innis, Harold A. (1956) *Essay in Canadian Economic History*, Toronto: University of Toronto Press.

—— (1986) *Empire and Communication*, ed. David Godfrey, Toronto: Press Porcépic.

Keynes, J.M. (1936) *The General Theory of Employment Interest and Money*, London: Macmillan.

Kindleberger, Charles (1985) *A Financial History of Western Europe*, London: Allen and Unwin.

Knieper, Rolf (1991) *Nationale Souveränität: Versuch über Ende und Anfang einer Weltordnung*, Frankfurt: Fischer.

—— (1993) 'Staat und Nationalstaat: Thesen gegen eine fragwürdige Identität', *PROKLA, Zeitschrift für kritische Sozialwissenschaft* 23: 65–71.

Krauthammer, Charles (1991) 'The Unipolar Moment', *Foreign Affairs* 70, 1: 23–33.

Le Goff, Jaques (1988) *Wucherzins und Höllenqualen. Ökonomie und Religion im Mittelalter*, Stuttgart: Klett-Kotta.

Lipietz, Alain (1993) *Berlin, Baghdad, Rio*, Münster: Westfälisches Dampfboot.

List, Friederich (1841) *Das nationale Systeme der politischen Ökonomie*, (repr. Berlin: Akademie Verlag, 1982).

Lotka, A.J. (1925) *Elements of Mathematical Biology*, Baltimore, MD: Williams and Wilkins.

Maddison, Angus (1989) *The World Economy in the Twentieth Century*, Paris: Development Centre of the Organization for Economic Co-operation and Development.

Martinez-Alier, Joan (1987) *Ecological Economics*, Oxford: Basil Blackwell.

Marx, Karl (1936) 'The production of relative surplus value', *Capital I: The Process of Capitalist Production*, New York: The Modern Library.

—— (1994) 'A contribution to the critique of political economy', (Economic Manuscript of 1861–1863) *Marx-Engels Collected Works* vol. 34. London: Lawrence and Wishart.

Massarrat, Mohssen (1993): *Endlichkeit der Natur und Überfluss in der Marktökonomie*, Marburg: Schritte zum Gleichgewicht.

Modelski, George (1987) *Long Cycles in World Politics*, London: Macmillan.

Niethammer, Lutz (1992) *Posthistoire: Has History Come to an End?*, New York: Verso.

O'Connor, Martin (ed.) (1994) *Is Sustainable Capitalism Possible?: Essays on Ecological Crisis in Market Society*, New York: Guilford.

Oberthür, Sebastian (1993) *Politik im Treibhaus: Die Entstehung des internationalen Klimaschutzregimes*, Berlin: Sigma.

OECD (1991) *OECD Environmental Data, Compendium 1991*, Paris.

—— (1993) *Intra-Firm Trade*, Paris.

Panitch, Leo (1993) *A Different Kind of State: Popular Power and Democratic Administration*, Toronto: Oxford University Press.

Polanyi, Karl (1957a) *Trade and Market in the Early Empires: Economies in History and Theory*, Glencoe, IL: Free Press.

—— (1957b) *The Great Transformation*, Boston, MA: Beacon Press.

Ponting, Clive (1991) *A Green History of the World: The Environment and the Collapse of Great Civilizations*, Harmondsworth: Penguin.

Porter, Michael E. (1990) *The Competitive Advantages of Nations*, London: Macmillan.

Prittwitz, Volker von (1990) *Das Katastrophenparadox: Elemente einer Theorie der Umweltpolitik*, Opladen: Leske und Budrich.

Rigaux, François (1991) 'Reflexionen über eine neue Weltordnung', *PROKLA* 84: 384–99.

Rowlands, Ian H. (1992) 'The international politics of evironment and development: the post-UNCED agenda', *Millennium: Journal of International Studies* 21, 2: 209–24.

Ruggie, John Gerard (1993) 'Territoriality and Beyond: Problematizing Modernity in International Relations', *International Organization* 47, 1: 139–74.

Sachs, Wolfgang (1992) 'Von der Vereitlung der Reichtümer zur Verteilung der Risiken', *Universitas* 9: 887–97.

Scharpf, Fritz W. (1987) *Sozialdemokratische Krisenpolitik in Europa*, Frankfurt and New York: Campus.

Scheer, Hermann (1993) *Sonnenstrategie: Politik ohne Alternative*, Zurich: Piper.

Simonis, Georg (1993) 'Der Erdgipfel von Rio–Versuch einer kritischen Verortung', *Peripherie* 51/52: 12–37.

Smil, Vaclav (1993) *Global Ecology: Environmental Change and Social Flexibility*, London: Routledge.

Wallerstein, Immanuel (1974) *The Modern World-System, Vol. 1*, New York: Academic Books.

Walzer, Michael (1967) 'On the Role of Symbolism in Political Thought', *Political Science Quarterly* (June).

2

SUSTAINABLE TRADE

Theoretical approaches[1]

Patricia E. Perkins

Introduction

In the global economy of the 1990s, attempts to define or implement policies for 'sustainability' at the local or national level are not sufficient. Transboundary pollution, global resource depletion, erosion of environmental standards and government capacity by trade agreements – all are signals that any meaningful concept of 'sustainability' must address and incorporate the issue of international trade: How much and/or what kind of trade can be considered 'sustainable'?

This question subsumes a range of others. For example: How does trade affect the 'sustainability' of the local or national economy? How can trade-related pressures to over-exploit resources and sacrifice environmental controls be successfully counterbalanced? In an era of fluid international capital, what remains of the concept of comparative advantage? How should local and far away 'claims' on scarce mineral or biological resources be mediated? How does trade contribute to the transformation of local environmental problems into international ones, and can this be overcome?

Alternative definitions of sustainable trade

The many different theoretical views of how trade affects sustainability can be arranged along a broad spectrum, from those which basically see any trade at all as damaging to the environment, community and sustainability, to those which see trade as good for sustainability. Much of the explanation for these widely diverging views lies in how each defines 'sustainable' – that is, a correlation is apparent between the way different authors define 'sustainability' and the way they view trade in relation to sustainability. In general, the more that ecological and social factors come into the definition of sustainability, the more negative are trade's perceived effects.

The following brief schematic categorization illustrates this tendency.

Deep ecology/bioregionalism/social ecology

For deep ecologists, the new paradigm which is necessary to bring about sustainable human habitation of the earth, in parallel or symbiosis with other species, involves rejecting many of the attributes of industrial society and allowing large tracts of wilderness to remain or re-establish themselves. Use of land and 'nature' in each ecological region should be limited by its carrying capacity for humans without undue harm to other species (Merchant 1992: 86–7).

From a bioregionalist point of view, trade's main effect is to contribute to the breakdown of community and to dependence on goods or services from outside the bioregion – thus, to a weakening of the region's sustainability as an internally independent whole. By definition, bioregionalism is:

> an effort to create economic and political systems within an area where it is possible for people to know, understand, and control the impact of their actions. This would stop the industrial world from using and wasting the resources of other areas of the world . . .
>
> As a community is seduced into wanting the products of another region they will become dependent on those products and give up, often unknowingly, the control over their community. The economic surplus created within a community is then sent out of the community to buy the wanted goods. If the surplus were spent in the community it would be much more prosperous.
>
> (Bioregionalism Congress 1991)

Another bioregional theorist explains that: 'The goal of an alternative bioregional economic development structure would be to make each individual bioregion as internally self-reliant across as broad a spectrum of production as possible' (Aberley).

A 'deep ecology' definition of a sustainable society terms it 'one that provides for successful human adaptation to a finite (and vulnerable) ecosystem on a long-term basis' (Catton 1980, quoted in Merchant 1992: 89). Trade in goods, from this perspective, would both stimulate over-use of the local ecosystem and interfere with the local development of new capabilities to meet local needs; on balance its effects would almost certainly be negative for the sustainability of local communities. Those human communities (for example, in desert areas) which depend on trade for their existence, bioregionalists would argue, are not sustainable, and humans should not try to live in such places (see Sale 1985: 75).

Jeremy Rifkin states:

> A global market affords the rich and well-to-do middle classes of the first world with an opulent consumer life-style. But it does so at the

expense of destroying the carrying capacity of the planet's ecosystems, undermining the health of the biosphere, and impoverishing the lives of millions of human beings in second and Third World nations. The bioregional market emphasizes necessities over luxuries and biospheric sustainability over geospheric expediency. Attention is placed on utilizing readily available resources in imaginative ways to provide food, clothing, shelter, transportation, and energy . . . . By establishing a sense of grounding in a local bioregion, people are making a political commitment to use only their fair share of the earth's resources.

(Rifkin 1991: 310; also see Sale 1985: 77)

Social ecologist Murray Bookchin argues that in order to avoid catastrophic ecological collapse, 'humans must recognize and live within the requirements of bioregions. The ecosystems within bioregions limit the range of human options to control nature. Technologies, agricultural practices, and community sizes appropriate to the specific conditions of the bioregion are needed' (Merchant 1992: 145). Leaving aside the question of what constitutes a bioregion (or assuming that, given any delimited bioregion, trade with the area outside the bioregion remains a possibility), such trade would interfere with sustainability by making it almost impossible for people to recognize when their consumption is exceeding the bounds which are ecologically sustainable.

While bioregionalists and deep ecologists seldom refer to the role of finance or capital movements, they decry the 'commoditization' of the natural environment. By implication, all forms of commerce beyond the bioregion – capital and services flows as well as trade in goods – are detrimental. The fact that financial transfers and trade in goods tend to be mutually reinforcing is further indication, from a bioregionalist viewpoint, that both should be avoided (Sale 1985: 46, 77).

A growing 'sustainable community development' movement identifies local communities as the place to start in countering trade's harmful social and ecological effects. Marcia Nozick's summary of this position is especially cogent:

To restore social and ecological balance to the world, we must shift our economic, cultural and political orientations away from global competition to a concern with local needs. The change makes sense both ecologically and economically. First, by concentrating on local production for local needs, we minimize the distances which products must travel for distribution, thus cutting down on transportation costs, wasteful energy use and pollution. Second, local demand for goods (community and surrounding region) can be met by smaller scale industries and technologies which can be more easily managed

48

by the community. Decentralized development – using a scaled down technology to produce smaller amounts for fewer people – disperses the impacts of development more evenly throughout the biosphere, giving nature more time to absorb and reprocess the waste. Third, by decentralizing industry and creating more small scale business to replace megaprojects, we can increase the numbers of jobs and people's access to them, thereby creating a more equitable distribution of wealth. Fourth, at smaller scale enterprises, workers can have greater say over their work environment and therefore find work more meaningful.

For all these reasons, community engendered and controlled development contributes toward a sustainable future for all.

(Nozick 1993: 14–15)[2]

Thus, the theoretical and philosophical underpinnings of much radical social and ecological thought are inherently antithetical to trade, for the following general reasons:

1   Trade damages community by making people dependent on goods and services from outside their bioregion, and by forcing them to produce for outside markets. It devalues what is local, and makes the local area vulnerable to externally generated instability.
2   Trade makes it difficult to see the limits of the local ecosystem and thus to know and feel when ecological boundaries are being trespassed. It complicates consensus on needed steps in the direction of sustainability.
3   Trade is an example of the way in which humans thoughtlessly assert their dominance over the non-human environment, in contravention of their position as one species in a complex global ecosystem – quite possibly with catastrophic results, as more and more local ecosystems are destroyed by trade induced pressures.
4   Trade can also exacerbate or perpetuate forms of social domination and injustice, serving as a force opposing the social transformation which is necessary to achieve community self-sufficiency.

From this perspective, then, sustainability implies humans learning to live without trade: If something can't be produced locally using local inputs, we can't sustainably consume it. Moreover, in a dynamic sense, trade acts as a drag on the processes of social change which are necessary to bring about a sustainable society.

Ecological economics

Emphasis on the benefits of protection and the drawbacks of 'free trade' is provided by Herman Daly and many other contributors to the rapidly

49

growing and loosely defined field of 'ecological economics'. These arguments begin by countering the basic economic trade theory of comparative advantage. The modern-day violation of the Ricardian assumption of capital immobility means that comparative advantage is without foundation as an applicable principle. In the words of Herman Daly and John Cobb, 'The free flow of capital and goods (instead of goods only) means that investment is governed by absolute profitability and not by comparative advantage' (Daly and Cobb 1989: 214).

From this viewpoint, unregulated international trade will not necessarily benefit all trade partners in a world where capital is free to roam the globe in search of the lowest costs of production. Instead, trade partners are forced to constantly compete for investment by lowering their environmental and labour standards.

While Daly and Cobb feel that trade is not justified by the theory of comparative advantage, and that the current 'volume and scope of free trade has passed the margin at which it does more harm than good to most of the nations that subject themselves to it', they also express the view that trade does have its merits (Daly and Cobb 1989: 363; see also Rees 1992). They advocate a sort of targeted protectionism to foster economic self-sufficiency, at least for the United States (Daly and Cobb 1989: 363–8).

Protection is justified in order to prevent the lowering of labour and environmental standards, the worsening of international income distribution, and the unsustainable growth of scale of the world economy.

Daly and other ecological economists have defined sustainability as 'a relationship between dynamic human economic systems and larger dynamic, but normally slower-changing ecological systems, in which (1) human life can continue indefinitely, (2) human individuals can flourish, and (3) human cultures can develop; but in which effects of human activities remain within bounds, so as not to destroy the diversity, complexity, and function of the ecological life support system' (Costanza *et al*. 1991: 8–9). The primacy of humans is clear in this definition, especially as compared to the bioregionalist definition of sustainability quoted above. Correspondingly, Daly's critique of trade – while scathing at times – is made from the viewpoint of an economist, not an ecologist.

According to Daly:

> Free trade sins against allocative efficiency by making it hard for nations to internalize external costs; it sins against distributive justice by widening the disparity between labour and capital in high wage countries; it sins against community by demanding more mobility and by further separating ownership and control; it sins against macroeconomic stability. Finally, it also sins against the criterion of sustainable scale.
>
> (Daly 1993: 129)

A related definition of sustainability is put forward by Donella H. Meadows, Dennis L. Meadows and Jorgen Randers. They define a sustainable society as 'one that can persist over generations, one that is far-seeing enough, flexible enough, and wise enough not to undermine either its physical or its social system of support' (Meadows *et al.* 1992: 209). From a systems viewpoint, they state, positive feedback loops causing exponential population and capital growth must be controlled; for social sustainability the material standard of living must be adequate and secure for everyone; and the society's throughput of materials and energy must not exceed regeneration rates (ibid. 209). They note the potential of trade to exacerbate and spread systemic collapse to other parts of the world, since different social, institutional or physical limits may be encountered first in different parts of the world: 'In an increasingly linked world economy, a society under stress anywhere sends out waves that are felt everywhere. Free trade enhances the likelihood that those parts of the world included in the free trade zone will reach limits simultaneously' (ibid. 179).

Daly concludes, 'The allocative, distributional, and scale problems stemming from free trade in today's world are sufficient to reverse the traditional default position in its favour. Measures to further globalize and integrate the world economy should now be treated as a bad idea unless proven otherwise in specific cases' (Daly 1993: 157).

This position represents a call to put the brakes on trade in today's world, because of trade's negative effects on movements toward economic sustainability (see also Daly and Goodland 1992). These effects can be summarized as follows:

1   Free trade hampers environmental quality by emphasizing the competitive advantage of those countries which do not internalize environmental costs, thus interfering with government policy measures aimed at making markets work more efficiently to force polluters to pay the clean up costs associated with their actions. Free trade therefore works against government efforts to foster environmentally benign economic development.
2   Free trade also contributes to uncertainty and to the uncontrolled growth in scale of the global economy, which must be limited as the most important step toward sustainability.
3   Free trade is bad for the cohesiveness of human communities and for society's ability to provide for its members. Social prerogatives justify some protectionism.

In comparison with the bioregionalist and deep ecology positions, the relationship between trade and sustainability here is seen as mediated by the economy of human societies; humans are not so much one species in a bioregion as controllers of what happens in the environment. The call is for responsibility in how we interact with and manage the global environment, instead of for humility and a smaller sense of our own importance, which is a thread running through bioregionalist writings.

Sustainable development

Many advocates of the nebulous term 'sustainable development' see trade as a necessary engine of economic growth which can make possible additional care for the environment, especially in poor countries. While negative environmental concomitants of trade are sometimes acknowledged, trade itself is not seen as the cause of environmental degradation. Rather, insufficient domestic environmental policy leads to environmental externalities in the domestic economy which create incorrect prices for goods. In turn, these incorrect prices can cause environmental degradation by influencing economic actors to over-exploit natural resources or over-produce pollution intensive products. International trade simply acts as a magnifier of externalities inherent in the domestic economy.

In *Trade and Sustainable Development*, Aaron Cosbey and David Runnalls note:

> For example, if a country is supporting unsustainable agricultural practices, then liberalizing trade may allow it to increase its agricultural exports, magnifying the problem. Or if the external pollution costs of producing a good are not internalized, then liberalizing trade may increase pollution problems by allowing more of the good to be produced for export. The implication is that sustainable development will not be achieved by trade liberalization policies alone; such policies must be accompanied by reform of other existing problems.
>
> (Cosbey and Runnalls 1992: 24)

Robert Repetto defines 'sustainable development' as

> a development strategy that manages all assets – natural and human resources, as well as financial and physical assets – for increasing wealth and well-being ... [It] rejects policies and practices that support current living standards by depleting the productive base, including natural resources, and that leave future generations with poorer prospects than our own.
>
> (Repetto 1993: 9–10)[3]

Repetto argues that trade liberalization and environmental regulation have similar goals, of increasing economic efficiency, and thus they reinforce each other (Repetto 1993: 1).

In this view, correcting domestic externalities will ensure that trade acts in support of sustainable development, rather than against it. This is the principle behind the Agenda 21 call for trade and environmental policies to be mutually supportive. Repetto points out that Third World countries need trade in order to take advantage of the 'labour services' of their large populations (Repetto 1993: 160–2).

The important role of private corporations in most countries means that these firms need to be involved in bringing about sustainable economies. Trade is a vital part of this process:

> Internationally competitive business believes that open markets are the most – and perhaps only – effective stimulus to the development of new products and technologies needed both to lower costs and to promote wider use of products and processes that will reduce environmentally destructive and wasteful practices. Open trade, buttressed by multilaterally agreed-upon rules that constrain arbitrary government actions, is the best way to assure that markets are in fact open to competition.
>
> (Morris 1993: 123)

If sustainability is a priority, however, it is up to governments to make corporations sit up and take notice. Frances Cairncross, environment editor of *The Economist*, argues that it can be cost-effective and conducive to competitiveness for corporations to adopt progressive environmental policies, but it is nearly always necessary for governments to play a role in forcing them to do so (Cairncross 1993: 299). From this viewpoint, government policy can encourage and induce private corporations to create sustainable economies – by allowing free trade, but setting and enforcing environmental priorities.[4]

This general perspective holds that national policies aimed at ensuring sustainability need not interfere with trade; in fact, trade as a contributor to economic growth is probably a positive factor helping to create the social conditions for sustainability. In summary, this is because:

1 Trade seems to bring economic benefits for all countries involved, and the resulting increase in standards of living has historically been associated with rising levels of environmental protection and conservation. Increasing exports of manufactured goods for example, may reduce pressures to export primary products (Repetto 1993: 160–2).

2 At present, sustainability seems only measurable and implementable at the national level, through policies of national governments. There is no *a priori* reason why national policies to bring about sustainable economies should be invalidated by trade (or the lack thereof), since traded goods follow the same rules as other goods.

Many advocates of sustainable development, in summary, tend to be supporters of the idea of trade, trusting to the policies of each trading nation to curb any excesses and bring about sustainability. Their definition of sustainability encompasses economic factors and management at the national level, thus representing a more limited perspective than either the bioregionalist or ecological economics views outlined above.

Property rights

For some analysts, the solution to most environmental problems, including how to achieve sustainability, lies with facilitating the workings of the free market. This implies that property rights to resources and other environmental amenities must be fully allocated; then their owners can negotiate through markets to bring about the socially optimal use or trade of those resources, engaging in the type of bargaining envisioned by the Coase theorem.[5] In the words of Terry Anderson and Donald Leal:

> Market processes with consumer and producer sovereignty have a demonstrated record for improving the quantity and quality of goods and services produced. Expanding these processes to include natural resources and environmental amenities offers the only possibility for improving environmental quality, raising living standards, and, perhaps most important, expanding individual liberty.
>
> (Anderson and Leal 1991: 147–8, 72)

While they do not set out their own definition of 'sustainability', these authors reject 'sustainable development' because it implicitly requires political controls and government regulation of the economy. Such management by government violates ecological principles, in their view, because 'it is impossible to concentrate knowledge about all the possible variations in an ecosystem, especially . . . the global environment' (Anderson and Leal 1991: 170). 'Free market environmentalism', in contrast, 'decentralizes power and harnesses self-interest through market incentives' (Anderson and Leal 1991: 172).

To bring about sustainable economies, governments' main responsibility is to create the conditions where the free market can operate without obstructions – that is, to allocate and enforce property rights.[6] Environmental policy *per se* would be unnecessary if property rights were unfettered. The same conditions hold internationally; trade is simply the inevitable and laudable working of the international market (see Yandle 1993: 9–10; Globerman 1993: 27–44).

From the property rights perspective, individual freedoms are seen as perhaps the most important aspect of sustainability. Gone are the emphases of bioregionalists on ecosystems, of ecological economists on economic scale, of sustainable development advocates on national policies. For property rights advocates, governments need only protect physical property, and let markets alone. In this perspective, trade is welcome because it facilitates Coase-type bargaining at the international level, making possible improvements in environmental quality based on property rights. Trade also provides a venue for the expression of producer and consumer sovereignty, a key element of social and economic sustainability.

This pro-trade stance corresponds to a vehemently libertarian definition of sustainability which includes little attention to non-human nature or even to community and diversity among humans.

Summary: trade and sustainability

The preceding categorization of perspectives on the relationship between trade and sustainability shows the link between how sustainability is defined and how trade is viewed. Let us now ask the question another way: if we embrace a strong definition of sustainability, one that bioregionalists would accept, does this necessarily imply no trade at all? Could a region which is entirely self-sufficient in basic necessities trade sustainably, in a limited way, with another self-sufficient region? Would this necessarily lead either region away from sustainability?

The deep ecologists' definition of a sustainable society cited above termed it as 'one that provides for successful human adaptation to a finite (and vulnerable) ecosystem on a long-term basis'. Implicit in this definition is the idea of balanced relationships not only between humans and nature, but also in interpersonal, political, and social human interactions. It is at least conceivable that trade in beads, artworks, baskets – anything 'nonessential' which is imported or exported in small quantities – could enrich the lives of people on each side of the trading arrangement without upsetting their own independent social, economic, and ecological equilibria.

Because of historical patterns of world trade, it is hard not to regard this possibility as naive. But what is it about trade that seems to lead to exploitation of the trading relationship, and thus to spiraling inequality? The growth of trade on a global scale has accompanied world social transformations, technological development, and the increasing commoditization of land, labour services, natural resources, and capital (Ponting 1991: 154–5). In calling for less trade as a means of de-commoditizing natural and human resources, perhaps critics are confusing the effect with the cause? As Ponting notes, in such matters it is difficult to disentangle cause and effect (Ponting 1991: 160).

One way to get around the 'commoditization' problem might be to trade via barter. Historical experience with large-scale barter, however, seems to indicate that this is a cumbersome and bureaucratic way of exchanging goods – and not necessarily a sustainable one, in the sense that it may engender external dependencies or deplete resources in the same ways as money-based trade.[7] There is perhaps a parallel, nonetheless, between barter and the sort of local exchange networks proposed by some bioregionalists and ecological economists, wherein goods and services are exchanged among community members on the basis of local supply and demand (see Linton and Greco 1990: 155). Again, however, the sustainability of such a trading system would seem to be linked to wholly voluntary participation, and to some limits on its size and on the volume of goods traded.

For our purposes it is sufficient to put forth the theoretical possibility that some limited trade could contribute to the dissemination of beauty, diversity and even world understanding without threatening sustainability.[8] In outline, such trade could only take place among sustainably self-sufficient trading partners, (i.e., it is almost inconceivable in today's world), it would involve no element of coercion, and it would be small in scale relative to the size of the trading economies. As a contribution to diversity, which is part of many definitions of sustainability, such limited trade could be a positive factor (see the sustainability principles outlined in Dale 1993: 2).

An extension of the above position would ask, if it is possible to trade beads for baskets without exploitation, why not rice for potatoes? In other words, once the door is opened to trade because diversity is pleasant and beneficial, where do we draw the line?

The crux of this perspective lies in setting out a rationale and mechanism for limiting the scale of trade, and ensuring that it is undertaken voluntarily by all parties involved. That is, not only 'sustainability', but also 'trade', must be carefully examined and defined. In effect, this approach requires the development of a set of criteria for measuring trade's beneficial and harmful effects with regard to the type of sustainability we seek.[9]

How 'sustainability' is defined clearly affects which indicators are useful. If natural capital and produced or financial capital are assumed to be infinitely substitutable, for example, trade (and indeed, global resource depletion) pose no significant problems. However, if we embrace a definition of sustainability which requires some level of natural resource conservation, then the effect of trade on resource depletion must be limited in some way for that trade to be considered 'sustainable'. Moreover, trade's effects on sustainability at the global or international level may be no less important than its effects within the trading nations or regions themselves.

The discussion which follows is based on a definition of sustainability that includes attention to:

1   protecting the long-term stability of global ecosystems;
2   preserving non-human nature and ecological diversity;
3   ensuring intergenerational equity for humans and other species;
4   maintaining stocks of renewable and non-renewable resources;
5   protecting the earth's waste assimilation capacities;
6   fostering human diversity and equity among individuals and among cultures, regions, countries, communities and social groups;

7   allowing for human mistakes in attempts to understand earth processes;
8   taking account of irreversibility, risks, and uncertainty.

The implications of this sort of sustainability for trade, and indicators of trade's effects on sustainability of this type, are the subject of the next section.

Indicators of sustainable trade

One way to approach the question of indicators, as noted above, is to set out criteria for sustainability within a country, and to say that once an individual country's economy meets these criteria, then trade of any surplus goods, services or capital would not violate sustainability. However, it is possible that the process of trade itself could be harmful in some way; the sustainability of local communities, and the entire global system, must also be considered.

To start off, we consider the work of Michael Jacobs, which addresses policies designed to bring about a 'green economy' – implicitly, at the national level. He sets out two definitions of sustainability, which he terms 'minimal' and 'maximal' sustainability. For 'minimal' sustainability, future generations are guaranteed the avoidance of environmental catastrophe; 'maximal' sustainability implies that future generations are left the opportunity to experience a level of environmental consumption at least equal to that of the present generation (Jacobs 1993: 72).

According to Jacobs, the goal of sustainability can be made operational by considering each of the economic functions of the environment in turn: its role in supplying renewable and non-renewable resources, in assimilating wastes, and in furnishing environmental services.

Renewable resources

For renewable resources, so long as the rate of harvest does not exceed the regeneration rate, the environmental capacity of the resource will be kept constant (and both minimal and maximal sustainability achieved) (Jacobs 1993: 89).[10] Technological change or yield increases would thus allow harvest rates to increase without violating sustainability.

Jacob notes that his discussion assumes that sustainability is defined in absolute, not per capita, terms; population growth rates would need to be factored in if per capita sustainability were desired, which would be an important component and indicator of the social sustainability of the system. It also deals only with flows, not stocks. If the current stock is deemed to be too small, then harvest rates would need to be below regeneration rates until the desired stock level was reattained (Jacobs 1993: 88). Jacobs states:

The important point about defining sustainability in this way is that each of these components of 'environmental capacity' – soil volume and productivity, the size of aquatic stocks and the quantity and quality of water supplies – is *measurable*. Moreover it is quite feasible, through proper management, to maintain them over time. This means that the principle of sustainability can be made operational. Rates of resource harvest and habitat quality can be identified which will maintain output (and therefore consumption) into the foreseeable future. If this is done, sustainability is turned from being a mere ideal into a practical guide to policy.

(Jacobs 1993: 89)

From a trade viewpoint, exports of renewable resources would be sustainable as long as they did not exceed the harvest rate criterion cited above. The caveats regarding per capita sustainability and stock size, however, could imply relatively large adjustments to the sustainability target if the global population were held to be the relevant one, i.e., if all humans were regarded as having an equal claim on the resource in question (see sections below). This, in turn, could mean substantial political difficulties for governments attempting to implement such sustainability-driven limits on consumption.[11]

Non-renewable resources

For non-renewable resources, according to Jacobs, the relevant concept for determining sustainable depletion rates is 'relative scarcity' or 'relative stock size': 'The depletion of a given resource may be said to satisfy the principle of intergenerational equity if it occurs at the same rate as demand for the resource declines. Although the absolute stock level of the resource is reduced, the stock level *relative to demand* is then kept constant. In this sense, sustainability requires policy to be directed at demand as well as supply' (Jacobs 1993: 90).

This definition of sustainability is different from that proposed by others, in which non-renewable resources should be depleted no faster than technological substitutes can be found for them (see Daly 1991a: 22; Peet 1992: 215; Rees 1991: 2).[12] In contrast, by Jacobs' definition, sustainable use rates for non-renewable resources are determined by three factors: the development of new economic reserves, reuse/recycling, and demand reduction (which includes substitution by other materials) (Jacobs 1993: 91).

As for renewable resources, this sustainability criterion would seem to imply quite different conclusions if trade is considered than if it is not. The inclusion of both demand and supply factors as determinants of sustainable use rates raises the question of *whose* demand is included. In a global economy with growing population, total world demand would appear to be the relevant measure. Again, the political implications for implementing such a policy are substantial.

Waste assimilation

Jacobs divides wastes into 'flow wastes', which can be assimilated by the natural environment through biological and geochemical processes, and 'stock wastes', such as nuclear residuals and heavy metals, which can only be stored. The sustainability criterion for 'flow wastes' is analogous to that for renewable resources: disposal of these wastes should not exceed the earth's assimilative capacity to neutralize them. For 'stock wastes', discharges should be permitted only as long as safe sites can be found for deposits. According to Jacobs:

> Sustainability requires that neither pollution, nor its damaging effects, increase over time. Since both ambient pollution levels (the purity of air, water, and soil) and the effects of such levels on health and ecosystems (diseases, tree loss, toxicity) are measurable, this is again an operational principle. Once 'acceptable' or 'optimal' pollution levels have been set, the waste emission rates which will maintain them can be identified, and policy then directed towards achieving such rates.
>
> (Jacobs 1993: 94)

The difficulty of controlling international trade in wastes has pointed up the global dimensions of this problem. Achieving international agreement on appropriate waste disposal rates and practices is likely to be very problematic.

Environmental services

The life support functions which humans consume can be measured by indicators such as average global temperatures and the incidence of ultraviolet radiation. The sustainability of environmental services can therefore be measured by the performance of these indicators (Jacobs 1993: 95). Policies to bring about sustainability must set targets for the determinants of those indicators – for example, controlling global warming involves targets for carbon dioxide emissions, vegetation cover available to absorb carbon dioxide, methane emissions, etc. (Jacobs 1993: 96). Achieving international consensus on such targets and especially their allocation is almost certain to be problematic, as attested by the slow progress in negotiating a global warming convention (Cairncross 1993: 160–75).

Transboundary pollution

Early efforts at pollution control often made international environmental problems out of local ones, by permitting the wider dispersal of emissions (sometimes into the stratosphere) rather than mandating their reduction.

With each new stage of environmental regulation, care must be taken that similar results do not arise. For example, limits on disposal of wastes of the type discussed above, imposed to achieve sustainability targets, could provide increased incentives for international diversion of wastes by raising local waste disposal costs. There is evidence that increasing trade has contributed to transboundary environmental conflicts (McRobert and Muldoon 1991: 190).

An important element of global sustainability, therefore, is the political and institutional context in which other policies for sustainability are adopted. Is there a forum for hearing international disputes on transboundary pollution and waste disposal? Are effective sanctions in place against dumping pollution on the weakest? Is the effort an international one, and how widespread is the global commitment to carry it out?

Human rights

The relationship between human rights and environmental protection – and thus, sustainability – has been outlined by many authors.[13] Clearly, a measure of the sustainability of any trade is the level of human rights enjoyed by people on each side of the trading relationship. This is because trade should be voluntary to be beneficial, according to most of the perspectives listed in the first section of this paper; moreover, as Jacobs notes:

> Environmental protection frequently requires challenging market-based ownership rights over natural resources such as fishing grounds, forests and agricultural land. Sustainable management of these resources has been shown in many cases to be best achieved by giving control over them to local, poor communities, whose livelihoods depend on them, and who therefore have a long-term interest in their conservation.
>
> (Jacobs 1993: 184)

The political sustainability of regimes which engage in trade based on social injustice is also questionable. Where low wage rates depend on political coercion and lack of democratic rights, child labour, and/or poor health care and social services, trade is exploitative. The process of including world populations in calculating sustainable resource use and waste assimilation according to the method cited above also implies justice in the eventual allocation of these resources.

Debt

Debt interferes with sustainability by injecting coercion into the trading relationship, in a way similar to human rights abuses. As long as countries are being pressured to pay international debts, they will find it difficult to implement and follow sustainable trade policies. For this reason, various authors have stated that sustainability implies a restructuring of international financial obligations and relationships (Jacobs 1993: 36–7, 184–8; Goodland and Daly 1993: 19–23; Cameron 1993: 7–63; Dawkins 1992: 7).

Community

Given the arguments, evidence and concerns advanced by many authors about the ways in which globalization breaks down local communities, and the importance of such communities for social, institutional and ecological sustainability, this factor merits specific attention. Criteria and methods are needed for gauging the effects of trade on local communities – and these may be as varied and as numerous as the communities themselves.

Communities also need more effective mechanisms for refusing to participate in wider trade relationships, and for public education on the issue of globalization. Alternatives to a trade-based local economy are also needed, and they are rapidly arising (see Nozick 1993; Lang and Hines 1993; Brandt 1995; Norgaard 1994).

A vital measure of the sustainability of trade is its effect on local communities.

Conclusion: comparative advantage revisited

From the perspective of sustainability which we have been developing, a measure of true 'comparative advantage' would include only those renewable and non-renewable resources, and waste assimilation and other environmental services, which are being used sustainably according to the above criteria – that is, following distribution of their benefits equitably among all people. Moreover, the desirability of trade at all should be subject to examination from the viewpoints of trans-boundary pollution, human rights, debt, and community sustainability. If, following the application of these criteria, one country has a surplus of a given good or environmental service which is available for export, then that country can be said to have a sustainable trading advantage in that good.[14]

Since global 'claims' on environmental resources and services would be factored into the sustainability criteria (ideally on a per capita basis), this trading advantage would depend almost entirely on each region or country's environmental/physical endowments of soils, climate, and mineral resources.[15] The inclusion of human rights and debt reduction/relief measures in the sustainability criteria would eliminate these from serving as components of any country's trading advantage. Without the inclusion of social and ecological sustainability criteria, any notion of comparative advantage obscures more than it illuminates.

Many of the indicators mentioned above imply government action, to set sustainability targets and to agree internationally on standards for global justice and transboundary environmental issues. How is this important role for governments, which may seem vital to operationalize sustainability, to be reconciled with the hands-off rationale behind trade? Jonathan Harris has stated the problem as follows:

> The goal of maximizing short-term welfare through free trade should be replaced with the goal of long-term sustainability. But sustainability requires a process of national, regional, and local resource and environmental planning, which is in direct conflict with the principle of free trade (and which) . . . inherently undermines community control of resources by eliminating export and import controls and replacing these with an impersonal control by international market allocation. This is not merely a side-effect associated with free trade – it is its very essence.
>
> (Harris 1993: 80)

In Harris' view, sustainability must be made a priority of trading governments and included as a goal in strategic trade planning, perhaps via sectoral trade agreements which incorporate sustainable development strategies (Harris 1993: 83).

The indicators listed above go beyond calling for governments to implement sustainability, however. For human rights and social equity, public participation in local communities is vital in setting and enforcing sustainability goals – just as it is for resource use, waste disposal, and other environmental services (Dawkins 1992: 16; Khor 1993: 97–107).

Moreover, there is growing evidence that government action is far from the only way in which economies move toward sustainability. The resurgence of locally based economic activity in many places, as an alternative or response to globalization, represents a new synthesis of decentralized community control with environmental sensitivity to the requirements and potentialities of particular bioregions.

The institutional changes which are needed at the local, national, regional and international level to bring sustainable trade closer to reality are the subject of a wide-ranging current discussion.[16] Much concern centres on the ways in which current initiatives toward liberalizing world trade, via agreements such as NAFTA and GATT, erode the long-term potential for making individual economies more sustainable (see papers in *The Case Against Free Trade*). Since this, as noted above, seems to be a prerequisite for sustainable trade, many of the dynamic processes now at work in the world economy do not evoke optimism. Finding the opportunities which are available, nonetheless, is the challenge the world faces.

Notes

An earlier version of this chapter entitled 'What is sustainable trade?' appeared in the volume *Globalization, Growth and Sustainability*, edited by Satya Dev Gupta with Nanda K. Choudhry, and published by Kluwer Academic Publishers in 1997.

1 The author gratefully acknowledges the research assistance for this paper provided by Cameron MacKay.
2 See also Rajan 1993; Norgaard 1994: 165–7; Brandt 1995: 147–55; Lang and Hines 1993: 125–31; Daly and Cobb 1989; Hug 1985.
3 For a similar definition, see Brown, Lester R., Flavin, C. and Postel, S. (1991) *Saving the Planet: How to Shape an Environmentally Sustainable Economy*, New York: Norton, page 30.
4 GATT economists Kym Anderson and Richard Blackhurst recognize the possibility that, for countries without 'appropriate environmental policies in place, conventional estimates of the gains from trade may overstate the net gain to society. It is even possible in such a situation that trade or trade liberalization could reduce a country's overall welfare. For this to happen, two conditions must hold: first, that the increased trade adds to environmental degradation; and second, that the conventional gains from increased international specialization are not sufficient to outweigh the negative effect of the reduction in environmental quality'. See Anderson and Blackhurst (1992) *Greening of World Trade Issue*, New York: Harvester, Wheatsheaf, page 19.
5 A hallmark of standard environmental economics, the Coase theorem argues that polluters can compensate pollution sufferers, or vice versa, to attain an economically efficient level of pollution control.
6 On property rights and intergenerational equity, see Borcherding 1990: 95–116. On trade bans to protect endangered species, Block 1990: 281–331.
7 On US barter trade, see US Congress 1956: 224–9. On East Bloc barter trade, see Lindert 1986: 189–90.
8 It is perhaps instructive to recall J.M. Keynes' views on the subject:

> I sympathize, therefore, with those who would minimize, rather than those who would maximize, economic entanglement between nations. Ideas, knowledge, art, hospitality, travel – these are the things which should of their nature be international. But let goods be homespun whenever it is reasonably and conveniently possible; and above all, let finance be primarily national.
>
> (Keynes vol. 21 1982: 236)

9 James Robertson mentions a similar 'international regulatory framework for trade as a means of encouraging greater self-reliance and a more conserving use of resources' (Robertson 1990: 75). Tim Lang and Colin Hines also speak of the need for new trade rules that 'ensure that economic activity provides maximum protection for the environment and for people' (Lang and Hines 1993: 130). Many other authors echo these views (see also Brown *et al.* 1992: 309–28; Van den Bergh and Van der Straaten 1994: 245).
10 This criterion is also set out in Daly 1991b: 45.
11 Stating that all people's claims on resources found in a given area should be considered in determining the sustainability of that area's ability to trade away such resources, is in theory directly contrary to the bioregional position that people in each local place should live within the parameters of the natural environment which exists there. But since bioregionalists oppose trade in any case, and the effect

of estimating global per capita resource claims incorporating population growth rates is to reduce desirable resource use to extremely small levels, in fact the position put forward here is largely consistent with a more purely bioregional strategy. When coupled with consideration of community effects as discussed below, which also allow for local discretion regarding participation in global markets, this principle of first assessing an area's resource position *vis-à-vis* the rest of humanity may provide some interesting and useful information.

12 The view that natural and human-made capital are substitutes (as in H. Daly's 'weak sustainability') is not pursued in this paper (see also Victor 1991).

13 See, for example: Cuauhtemoc, Cardenas (1992) 'Free Trade, the Environment, and the Need for a Social Charter', *Loyola of Los Angeles International and Comparative Law Journal* 15, 1 (December): 71–8; Goodland, Robert and Daly, Herman (1993) *Poverty Alleviation is Essential for Environmental Sustainability*, World Bank Environment Department Divisional Working Paper: 42, Washington, DC: World Bank; Brown, George E. Jr, Gould, William and Cavanagh, John (1992) 'Making Trade Fair', *World Policy Journal* Spring: 309–27; Harris, Jonathan M. (1993) '"Free" Trade and Environmental Sustainability: An Ecological Economics Perspective', *Praxis* 10, 2 (Summer): 77–84; and papers presented at the conference on 'Human Rights Approaches to Environmental Protection in the Commonwealth and Beyond', 27–8 May 1993, Commonwealth Institute, London. The approach of Richard Norgaard in 'treating sustainability as an equity objective rather than as a technical constraint' is also relevant in this context; see Norgaard, Richard (1992) 'Sustainability as Intergenerational Equity: Economic Theory and Environmental Planning', *Environmental Impact Assessment Review* 12: 85–124.

14 Note that this procedure for determining sustainable trading advantage follows the three steps laid out by Herman Daly for ordering allocation, efficiency and scale: it requires that optimal scale (ecological sustainability) be set out at the beginning, distributes rights corresponding to the chosen scale, and then allows reallocation among individuals through markets in the interests of efficiency (see Daly 1992: 188).

15 As noted above, however, desirable use rates of such resources, especially nonrenewable ones, might appear vanishingly small.

16 See, for example: Friends of the Earth International Trade and Environment Project (1993) 'International Trade, Sustainable Development and Environmental Protection: What Role Should the Multilateral Trade Organization Play?' Friends of the Earth, England, Wales and Northern Ireland; Kox, Henk L.M. (1992) 'Towards International Instruments for Sustainable Development', Amsterdam: Environment and Development Resource Centre; Dale and Kimball (1992) 'Forging International Agreement: Strengthening Intergovernmental Institutions for Environment and Development', United Nations Environment Programme/World Resources Institute; Opschoor, H. and Van der Straaten, J. (1993) 'Sustainable Development: An Institutional Approach', *Ecological Economics* 7, 3: 203–22.

References

Aberley, Douglas, 'A bioregional approach to community economic development', a working paper presented at the Fourth North American Bioregional Congress.

Anderson, Terry L. and Leal, Donald R. (1991) *Free Market Environmentalism*, Boulder, CO: Westview Press.

'Introduction to Bioregionalism' (1991) A working paper presented at the Fourth North American Bioregional Congress, Turtle Island Office.

Block, Walter E. (1990) 'Environmental problems, private property rights solutions', in Walter E. Block (ed.) *Economics and the Environment: A Reconciliation*, Vancouver: The Fraser Institute.

Borcherding, Thomas E. (1990) 'Natural resources and transgenerational equity', in Walter E. Block (ed.) *Economics and the Environment: A Reconciliation*, Vancouver: The Fraser Institute.

Brandt, Barbara (1995) *Whole Life Economics*, Philadelphia, PA and Gabriola Island, BC: New Society Publishers.

Brown, George E., Jr, Gould, J.W. and Cavanagh, J. (1992) 'Making trade fair', *World Policy Journal* 9, 2: 309–28.

Cairncross, Frances (1993) *Costing the Earth*, Boston, MA: Harvard Business School Press.

Cameron, Bruce (1993) 'Globalization, trade agreements and sustainability', in *The Environmental Implications of Trade Agreements*, Canadian Environmental Law Association. Toronto: Ontario Ministry of Environment and Energy.

Catton, William R., Jr and Dunlap, Riley E. (1980) 'A new ecological paradigm for post-exuberant sociology', in *American Behavioral Scientist* 20, 1: 36.

Cosbey, Aaron, and Runnalls, David (1992) *Trade and Sustainable Development: A Survey of the Issues and A New Research Agenda*, Winnipeg: International Institute for Sustainable Development.

Costanza, Robert, Daly, Herman E. and Bartholomew, Joy A. (1991) 'Goals, agenda, and policy recommendations for ecological economics', in *Ecological Economics: The Science and Management of Sustainability*, New York: Columbia University Press.

Dale, Ann (1993) 'A charter for the environment', *Sustainable Development Research Institute Newsletter*, University of British Columbia, Summer/Fall: 2.

Daly, Herman (1991a) 'Elements of environmental macroeconomics', in Robert Costanza (ed.) *Ecological Economics*, New York: Columbia University Press.

—— (1991b) *Steady State Economics*, Washington, DC: Island Press.

—— (1992) 'Allocation, distribution, and scale: towards an economics that is efficient, just, and sustainable', *Ecological Economics* 6, 3: 188.

—— (1993a) 'Problems with free trade: neoclassical and steady-state perspectives', in Durwood Zaelhke *et al.* (eds) *Trade and the Environment*, Washington, DC: Island Press.

—— (1993b) 'From adjustment to sustainable development: the obstacle of free trade', in *The Case Against Free Trade: GATT, NAFTA, and the Globalization of Corporate Power*, San Francisco: Earth Island Books.

Daly, Herman and Cobb, John, Jr (1989) *For the Common Good: Redirecting the Economy Toward Community, the Environment, and a Sustainable Future*, New York: Beacon Press.

Daly, Herman and Goodland, Robert (1992) 'An ecological–economic assessment of deregulation of international commerce under GATT', Environment Department, The World Bank, Washington DC: World Bank.

Dawkins, Kristins (1992) 'Balancing: policies for just and sustainable trade', Minneapolis, MN: Institute for Agriculture and Trade Policy.

Globerman, Steven (1993) 'The environmental impacts of trade liberalization', in Terry L. Anderson (ed.) *NAFTA and the Environment*, San Francisco: Pacific Research Institute for Public Policy.

Goodland, Robert and Daly, Herman (1993) *Poverty Alleviation is Essential for Environmental Sustainability*, World Bank Environment Department Divisional Working Paper: 19–23, Washington DC: World Bank.

Harris, Jonathan M. (1993) '"Free" trade and environmental sustainability: an ecological economics perspective', *Praxis* 10, 2 (Summer): 77–84.

Hug, A.M. (1985) 'The doctrine of international trade: a Gandhian perspective', in Romesh Diwan and Mark Lutz (eds) *Essays in Gandhian Economics*, New Delhi: Gandhi Peace Foundation.

Jacobs, Michael (1993) *The Green Economy*, Vancouver: UBC Press.

Keynes, J.M. (1982) 'National self-sufficiency', in D.M. Moggridge (ed.) *The Collected Writings of John Maynard Keynes*, vol. 21. London: Macmillan.

Khor, Martin (1993) 'Free trade and the third world', in *The Case Against Free Trade*, San Francisco: Earth Island Books.

Lang, Tim and Hines, Colin (1993) *The New Protectionism*, New York: The New Press.

Lindert, Peter (1986) *International Economics*, Homewood, IL: Irwin.

Linton, Michael and Greco, Thomas (1990) 'LETS: the local exchange trading system', in Van Andruss *et al.* (eds) *Home!: A Bioregional Reader*, New Society Publishers.

McRobert, David and Muldoon, Paul (1991) 'Toward a bioregional perspective on international resource-use conflicts: lessons for the future', in *Proceedings of the Fifth Canadian Institute of Resources Law Conference*.

Meadows, D.H., Meadows, D.L. and Randers, J. (1992) *Beyond the Limits: Confronting Global Collapse*, Post Mills, VT: Chelsea Green Publishing Co.

Merchant, Carolyn (1992) *Radical Ecology*, New York: Routledge.

Morris, Robert J. (1993) 'A business perspective on trade and the environment', in Durwood Zaelhke *et al.* (eds) *Trade and the Environment*, Washington, DC: Island Press.

Norgaard, Richard B. (1994) *Development Betrayed*, London and New York: Routledge.

Nozick, Marsha (1993) *No Place Like Home*, Ottawa: Canadian Council for Social Development.

Peet, John (1992) *Energy and the Ecological Economics of Sustainability*, Washington, DC: Island Press.

Ponting, Clive (1991) *A Green History of the World*, New York: Penguin.

Rajan, Vithal (ed.) (1993) *Rebuilding Communities: Experiences and Experiments in Europe*, Foxhold, Darlington: Green Books.

Rees, William E. (1991) 'The ecology of world trade: implications for sustainable development', (manuscript) University of British Columbia, School of Community and Regional Planning.

—— (1992) 'Natural capital in relation to regional/global concepts of carrying capacity', in *Ecological Economics: Emergence of a New Development Paradigm*, Workshop Proceedings, Institute for Research on Environment and Economy, University of Ottawa, 7–10 November 1992.

Repetto, Robert (1993) 'Trade and environment policies: achieving complementarities and avoiding conflicts', World Resources Institute.

Rifkin, Jeremy (1991) *Biosphere Politics*, New York: Harper Collins.

Robertson, James (1990) *Future Wealth*, New York: Bootstrap Press.

Sale, Kirkpatrick (1985) *Dwellers in the Land*, San Francisco: Sierra Club Books.

US Congress, Senate, Committee on Interior and Insular Affairs, Subcommittee on Minerals, Materials, and Fuels (1956) *Hearings: Extension of Purchase Programs of Strategic and Critical Minerals*, 84th Congress, 2nd Session, April 19, 20, 21, 25, May 16, 24, and 25, 1956.

Van den Bergh, J. and Van der Straaten, J. (eds) (1994) *Toward Sustainable Development*, Washington, DC: Island Press.

Victor, Peter (1991) 'Indicators of sustainable development: some lessons from capital theory', in *Economic, Ecological, and Decision Theories*, Ottawa: Canadian Environmental Advisory Council.

Yandle, Bruce (1993) 'Is free trade an enemy of environmental quality?' in Terry L. Anderson (ed.) *NAFTA and the Environment*, San Francisco: Pacific Research Institute for Public Policy.

3

GROWTH OR DEVELOPMENT?[1]

Egon Becker and Thomas Jahn

> The wealth of societies in which capitalist modes of production
> prevail appears as an enormous accumulation of commodities.
>
> Karl Marx (1867)

Historical reminiscences

When Karl Marx investigated how social wealth was produced and
distributed in his time, he discovered a strange entity that keeps itself alive
only by continuous growth and by progressively transforming the entire world
to fulfil its life requirements, namely capital. Marx was convinced that, as this
entity grows, it 'saps the original sources of all wealth: the soil and the
labourer'.[2] The production and distribution of social wealth under capitalist
conditions was for him technicalized and scientific production. He noted that
it destroyed all forms of a purely natural 'metabolism' between human beings
and nature, while at the same time science and technology endowed this
exchange process with a 'form adequate for full human development', operating as a 'systematic law of regulating social production'. Although,
according to Marx, this transforms the instrument of labour into a 'means of
enslaving, exploiting, and impoverishing the labourer', and transforms 'the
social combination and organization of labour processes' into 'an organized
mode of crushing out the workman's individual vitality, freedom, and independence', Marx nevertheless shared the faith of the rising bourgeoisie of his
time in science and progress, and was firmly convinced that the expansion of
the capitalist mode of production would be accompanied by the development
of world society towards ever higher forms. For him, capital was not only an
exploitive but also a civilizing force. His revolutionary optimism was rooted in
the firm conviction that capitalist modernization would reimburse humanity a
thousandfold in multiplied and enriched form for that which had been stolen
from labourers and nature. Behind capital, the revolutionary thinker discovered something much more powerful and valuable: human productivity and
creativity. Marx hoped that the dynamics of capitalist expansion would open

68

the pathway to the realm of liberty, to the socialist society of the free and the equal. Today such tidings echo like dreams from a lost world.

In that lost world of philosophical critique, economic analysis and political hope, many a nightmare also lurked. The economists of the nineteenth century were convinced not only that capital grew but also that the number of people producing under its direction increased constantly. As early as 1789, Robert Malthus in his 'Essay on the Principle of Population' put forward the thesis that the population of a country grew more rapidly than did food production, thereby permanently undermining any economic progress attained. Two hundred years later, the Malthus doctrine has come back into fashion, albeit in a radically changed world and in a completely new theoretical context.

The state of this world was described in drastic terms in 1972 by the Club of Rome – an international association of scientists, politicians and industrialists (Meadows *et al.* 1972). Here we find once again the problem of capitalist expansion addressed by Marx a century earlier, but brushed with neo-Malthusian scepticism. The differences are considerable. Marx described the unlimited expansion of capitalist accumulation. By contrast, the Club of Rome wrote about economic growth as a 'world *problematique*' spanning societies from the First to the Third World, both capitalist and state socialist countries. Marx hoped that a constantly growing, productive humankind would give birth to a revolutionary working class bent on winning the battle for socialism. The Club of Rome, by contrast, saw population growth meshed in a calamitous dynamic with economic growth, destroying the still open path to a society of the free and equal, and driving us to disaster if not halted. To prevent this outcome, the Club of Rome – together with numerous global thinkers of the present – has for two decades been seeking a growth-limiting world *resolutique* adapted to the world *problematique*.

We are thus faced by two theoretical worlds that seem to share no common ground. On the basis of Hegel's dialectical logic, Marx analysed the accumulation of capital as continuous change in the economic forms of wealth involving the transition from commodity to money and from money to capital, the 'self-expansion of value'. The Club of Rome, by contrast, regards economic growth as a physical process, as the continuous accumulation of quantities, of products and production plants, driven by the steady flow of materials and of energy. The process of growth is enmeshed with other processes dependent on its dynamics, especially resource consumption and environmental pollution, but also population growth and food production. With the tools of modern systems analysis, the dynamically interlocking processes can be represented and simulated on the computer. Another difference is also apparent. The Marxian world is one of revolutionary change. That of the Club of Rome is one of disturbed equilibrium, in which the linkage between economic and demographic reproduction determines the long-term stability of the world system.

A new order in the discourse on development[3]

The discourse on development we wish to address in this context moves between the lost world of socialist hopes on the one hand and the modern world with its models of economic growth, its international organizations, networked information flows and disaster scenarios on the other. In both worlds there is a development problem. In the former the question is whether capitalism can spread world-wide without collapsing under its own contradictions. In the latter the issue is whether modern industrialized civilization can eliminate poverty, hunger and illiteracy without destroying nature.

Is it important to consider the meaning of development? After all, the meaning of words become apparent only when the historical experience they encompass is decoded. They do not lend themselves to succinct definition, since they semiotically summarize a whole process. In this sense the word development carries historical connotations that cannot simply be defined away. It is the focal point of a semantic field, surrounded by mutually supportive concepts such as progress, modernization, growth, evolution, or maturity. This field both structures scientific and political attention and imposes specific restrictions on thought, speech and action. Development means more than mere alteration or historical change. The process indicated is a directional one. A societal state to be attained is given a normative designation, developed society. But what does the term refer to? To a still distant and unattained utopia, a society in which human potential can attain optimum expression, perhaps even in harmony with nature? Marx thought so. Or does it refer to existing societies, such as the wealthy industrialized countries of the West and the North? This is the position taken by the international development discourse. Here societies are considered developed if they manifest certain indicators. Until very recently development was largely equated with industrialization, and mean per capita income was regarded as the most important indicator of the degree of development attained by a national economy. This dogma was appropriate both in the Marxian world and in that of modern development theories.[4]

It is not the fading of the revolutionary Marxian message but the manifest ecological crisis that dissolves and invalidates the development dogma. Its decline leaves a theoretical gap that has lately been filled by versatile magic formulas. A particularly influential one was coined in 1987 by the Brundtland Commission of the United Nations, 'sustainable development'. The report declares that sustainable development has become 'a goal not just for the developing nations, but for industrial ones as well' (World Commission on Environment and Development (WCED) 1987: 4). 'Those who are more affluent' are required to 'adopt life-styles within the planet's ecological means – in their use of energy, for example' (WCED 1987: 9). The Commission warns poor developing countries that 'rapidly growing populations can increase the pressure on resources and slow any rise in living standards; thus sustainable development can only be pursued if population size and growth are in harmony with the changing productive potential of the ecosystem' (WCED 1987: 9). Global ecological equilibrium is at risk from two sides simultaneously, from environmental destruction related to industrialization and that related to poverty. Sustainable development thus requires both the elimination of poverty in the developing countries and the limitation of wealth and affluence in the developed countries. For the future it must be recognized that consumption habits and lifestyles in the Western industrialized countries cannot be transferred to the entire present and future world population. The empirical evidence for the validity of this thesis is overwhelming. In the Marxian world it could lend support to a reformulated theory of crisis and collapse. In the development discourse it imposes a new order. For, from a global ecological point of view, there exists now one development problem for the poor countries of the South, and another for the wealthy countries of the North. The common point of reference is the global ecological equilibrium – a highly problematic abstract benchmark that is difficult to operationalize, and which can hardly be reconciled with the immediate interests of the people. Whose individual behaviour is guided by the global ecological equilibrium? Or to put it in more concrete terms, what couple thinks about the size of the world population when planning a family? When in 1972 the Club of Rome earned such vehement public reaction to its attempt at describing the state of the world, such doubts still played no part. The abstract benchmark was on the contrary redefined as a global limit to growth: non-renewable raw materials and the limited arable land available for food production were declared to be imperilled in the long-term if destructive growth processes could not be limited. The problems of developing countries were related first to the endangered global ecological equilibrium and second to rapid demographic growth.

In 1972, the 'development of underdeveloped nations' and the 'conservation of the environment' appeared to the Club of Rome to be the two most vital world problems. They wrote at the time:

> We recognize that world equilibrium can become a reality only if the lot of the so-called developing countries is substantially improved, both in absolute terms and relative to the economically developed nations . . . . We unequivocally support the contention that a brake imposed on world demographic and economic growth spirals must not lead to a freezing of the status quo of economic development of the world's nations.

> (WCED 1987: 194)

This muted plea for 'catching-up development' met with scepticism. Since the early seventies there has been discussion on whether the global policy of international resource management and of limiting economic and demographic growth proposed by the Club of Rome is not pernicious to

71

development; whether, despite numerous assurances to the contrary, it does not in effect deprive the underdeveloped countries of their opportunity to develop. It is precisely the representatives of these countries who stress repeatedly that they consider development through economic growth to be indispensable. They claim that, instead of calculating limits to growth with problematic world models, and introducing an abstract global ecological equilibrium as a political norm, it would be more useful to deploy technology and science to displace the limits to growth. Growth should not be limited: the limits should grow. This alone would at the same time trigger development processes in the Third World that would lead to a more just distribution of social wealth throughout the world. Limited supplies of raw materials and energy, limited arable land in agriculture, or limited biosphere capacities for pollutants were seen as limits to growth only if the present methods of production, property rights, and distribution of goods were not changed regionally and globally. The problem was not material limits to growth, but socio-economic barriers to development.

With its frequently vague statements, the Club of Rome has provided sufficient leeway for this sort of criticism. This criticism has been taken into account and the latest report states that, in the two decades since 1972, the underlying causes of the contemporary *problematique* remained the same, but that it differed in its 'mix of issues and its points of emphasis' (King and Schneider 1991). In 1992 the most dangerous elements were the 'population explosion in the South' and the 'global greenhouse effect'. Like the Brundtland Commission, a differentiated and sustainable development strategy is called for: economic growth in the poor countries of the South and East should be combined with limited growth in the rich industrialized countries of the North and West.

This sounds reasonable, but its political implementation remains unclear. At the mammoth conference held in June 1992 in Rio de Janeiro, it became clear that the thematic and tactical linking of environment and development does not necessarily produce a new conception of development, and that, on the contrary, it creates a new dimension in the North–South distribution conflict. The initially separate fields of international environmental policy and development policy were discursively linked and placed in symbolic relation to political power. What had been seen by the Club of Rome as a 'world *resolutique*' transformed itself at the conference into purely tactical politicking, with lobbying, coalescing and fractionating, with new conferences and organizations, trade-offs between economic and political interests, and participation strategies. In the course of the conference, attention was occupied almost exclusively by deadlines, costs, obligations, controls and sanctions – and only peripherally by divergent political objectives.[5] The physical link between problems played only a subordinate part, although it sometimes showed through, for example with regard to limit values for CO_2 emissions for individual countries and regions.

This reduction of ecology to politics was made possible by changes in the ecological discourse itself. Usually ecology is defined as a science of the inter-active relationship between living things and their animate and inanimate environment. Its subject matter is thus primarily spatially defined aspects of nature, individual biotopes or entire landscapes. Whoever turns an ecologi-cally trained eye on natural living conditions of human beings will discover highly variant spatial distributions of population and social wealth. Moreover, differently defined economic, political, or cultural 'functional spaces' overlap in these milieux. The traditional ecological discourse regional-izes and differentiates problem perception, and in the transition to a social ecology this possibility should be used. But ecology has meanwhile developed from a biological and geographical sub-discipline into an interdisciplinary concept in which anthropogenic disturbances to natural life contexts are represented in model form. In modern systems ecology – as applied in the Club of Rome studies – the 'interactive relationships' between human beings and their environment are construed as flows of materials and energy, and the inhabitants as increasing or decreasing populations. Ecological problems then appear as disturbances to the metabolism or energy exchange of ecosystems. Most models attempt to represent ecosystems' undisturbed state in terms of feedback loops and self-stabilizing equilibrium. The conditions for stability and limits to the burdening of ecosystems disturbed and polluted by human beings can thus be determined, and strategies for problem management elabo-rated. But regional socio-economic development can hardly be analysed in this manner, for social, cultural, or economic activities appear in most of the ecosystemic models merely as unexplained exogenous factors, and not in their social context. Despite such theoretical weaknesses, the importance of systems ecology should not be underestimated. It was only the detour via models of global ecological problems that permitted 'environment' and 'society' to be related within an ecological conceptual framework. In such models, socially provoked disturbances no longer affect single local or regional ecosystems, but the biosphere as a whole.

Since the 1980s, a still more marked globalization of ecological problems has been effected by the startling model calculations of climatologists. The prognosticated greenhouse effect and the ozone hole, discovered by means of complicated measurements and calculations, provide new points of reference for both ecological discourse and development discourse. Social factors such as demographic growth, energy consumption, and food requirements appear to be indissolubly coupled with the predicted climatic changes. Global envi-ronmental problems thus define the hard core of the 'world *problematique*', and consequently also the central development problem of world society. It was the transition from a regionalizing ecology to a globalizing one that re-ordered the discourse on environment and development. In the model world of global ecology, the differences between developed and underdeveloped societies appear as differing contributions to global ecological problems. In the process, environmental policy and development policy mesh internationally, appearing as attempts to solve distribution and redistribution problems on a global scale. In the reality of international politics, the area for new global distribution contests is thus staked out. Then, for example, the effects of rapid demographic growth in the southern hemisphere can be politically balanced with the excessive consumption of fossil fuels and the related CO_2 emissions in the northern industrialized countries.[6]

Nevertheless a new common ground between developed and underdeveloped countries becomes apparent in the ecological dimension, which is repeatedly and prematurely interpreted as a species interest of mankind in joint survival. In the formula for sustainable development, this interest has been given a convenient handle. But appearances are deceptive. The devastation of an arable area is of a different order of significance in a rich industrialized country than in a poor agricultural one. Rich countries can withstand a decline in crops harvest without the population's food supply deteriorating drastically. More would simply be imported. In the poor countries there is no option of renunciation. Environmental destruction almost automatically implies hunger and misery. Moreover, the rich industrialized countries have significantly more resources available for preventive and curative environmental protection. They can deploy a specific environmental protection technique innovatively, and thus obtain competitive advantages for themselves in the world market as far as ecology and environment are concerned. New forms of international social inequality are emerging, to which the affected groups also react. Thus the interplay between poverty and environmental destruction, for example, intensifies the tendency for large numbers of people to migrate from poverty stricken areas to rich industrialized countries. This, too, provokes reactions. Development policy and environmental policy become more and more closely intertwined in an internationally coordinated population policy, which attempts to contain both the 'population explosion' and the 'streams of refugees'.

The concept of sustainable development, which depends on the idea of a global problem community, assumes a different importance against the background of new social inequalities. Since the Rio Conference it has become clear that the concept has little correspondence with practical measures. This experience must receive serious theoretical attention. We doubt whether, independently of the industrialized countries, something is possible in the 'developing nations' which we waive for economic reasons; namely that politics, economics, law, or science will trim their sails consistently to overcoming the ecological crisis. The far more difficult and more dangerous development problem is probably not located in the poor South but in the rich capitalist industrialized countries of the North. Not only forms of consumption and lifestyles must be fundamentally changed, but also an entire mode of production. Capital, according to Marx, can sustain itself only if it constantly expands. And he was convinced that, although the capitalist mode of production civilized the world, it would nevertheless perish of its internal contradictions. In a world in which there appear to be no attractive alternatives to capitalism left, we have to put another question: will the social wealth produced under capitalist conditions perhaps bring final destruction to the natural basis for the life of humanity – or is there a realistic possibility of civilizing capital both socially and ecologically? The answer to this question will decide whether sustainable development is merely an ideological slogan or a signpost pointing the way to a new concrete utopia.

There can no longer be much empirical doubt that the consumption habits and lifestyle of Western capitalist industrialized countries now serve as the explicit or implicit model for most countries in the world. Clearly, however, this model of civilization cannot be transferred to the entire present and future world population. This contradiction permits strongly diverging conclusions. We shall indicate only several of them:

- The old economic model of 'catching-up' development, which would finally lead to a global monoculture, can no longer be seriously entertained. It is replaced by conceptions of culturally and economically differentiated regional development.
- The differences between the poor and the rich nations are reinforced economically, politically, and militarily. The 'Fortress Europe' appears as one of the possible forms of reaction, which can be ideologically supported by radical cultural relativism, and be developed right up to the horror scenario of a racist policy with 'ethnic cleansing'.
- The development problem of world society can be split up. The excessive energy and resource consumption by the rich industrialized countries can be counteracted by scientific–technical innovation and an efficiency revolution, which would at the same time create international competitive advantages for these countries. The surpluses obtained can then be transferred to the poor agricultural countries of the South and used in the fight against poverty and to support a modern population policy.
- A new model of welfare which can be universally applied in both the North and the South could be developed, based either on regionalization with modernized forms of subsistence economy, or on a world-wide efficiency revolution.

A different scenario for future developments corresponds to each programme, and each scenario can be inserted in a model of sustainable development.

Growth and development

Whichever programme achieves final historical realization, there is already a discernible hegemony discourse in which global ecological problems determine thinking and political action. It is making its mark both through international organizations and through national interest politics. But there are signs of countervailing movements, one of which comes out of the model world of global ecology itself.

Twenty years after the *Limits to Growth*, the Meadows have repeated their simulations of global development trends with an updated data base and the World3 computer model used for the first study. They now introduce a distinction, which, while indicating the limits to their model world, can nevertheless show the way out of it: '"To grow" means to increase in size by the assimilation or accretion of materials. "To develop" means to expand or realize the potentialities of; to bring to a fuller, greater, or better state. When something grows it gets quantitatively bigger; when it develops it gets qualitatively better, or at least different. Quantitative growth and qualitative improvement follow different laws. Our planet develops over time without growing. Our economy, a subsystem of the finite and non-growing earth, must eventually adapt to a similar pattern of development' (Meadows *et al.* 1992: xix). The authors come to the conclusion that, 'although there are limits to growth, there need be no limits to development' (Meadows *et al.* 1992: xix).

We should consider this line of reasoning carefully, for it could indicate an avenue out of the chaos prevailing in the development theory discussion. First an analytical comment: in the way that Meadows draws a distinction between quantitative growth and qualitative development, two dimensions are condensed in one, namely that of material/non-material and that of quantitative/qualitative. This is doubly problematic. On the one hand the material world also organizes itself and develops, for there are qualitatively quite distinct, historically changeable relationships between its various elements; and on the other hand there are in the non-material world quantifiable elements and even pure quantities (such as numbers) cohabiting with purely qualitative elements (such as the meanings of linguistic utterances for instance). Since the simulation studies condense the two dimensions into one, only quantitative changes in material factors can be recorded.[7]

What does this mean? The simulation model defines single state properties of the 'world system': population size, industrial and food production, raw materials and energy consumption, environmental pollution. They result either from the summation of similar individuals to a statistical totality (such as 'population'), or by summation of physical measurement properties (e.g., mass or energy) to aggregate values (such as 'raw materials consumption'). Growth is then defined as the quantitative increase in these state properties. From the 'sources' of natural resources, materials and energy flow into an open system, are used up by humanity, and are then delivered back to the 'sinks' in the environment in the form of wastes and pollutants. Limits to growth are defined by the output capacity of the sources and the absorbing capacity of the sinks. The dynamics of the world system arise from positive or negative feedback loops, which in their turn are closely networked. The systems dynamics and the restraints placed on growth processes by the available sources and sinks finally give rise to a world *problematique*, which is now beginning to exert ever greater influence on the new ordering of the development discourse.

With the concentration on quantitative changes in material properties, material motives for growth processes must also be identified:

> Because of their potential for self-reproduction, population and industrial capital are the driving forces behind exponential growth in the world system. Because of their potential for production, societies encourage their growth. We assume in World3 that population and capital have the structural potential for both reproduction and production. We also assume that those potentials cannot be realized without continuous outputs of pollution and wastes. People need food, water, air, and nutrients to grow, to maintain their bodies, and to produce new people. Machines need energy, water, and air plus an enormous variety of minerals, chemicals, and biological materials to produce goods and services, to maintain themselves, and to make more machines. According to the most fundamental laws of the planet, the materials and energy used by the population and the capital plant do not disappear. Materials are either recycled or they become wastes or pollutants. Energy is dissipated into unusable heat.
>
> (Meadows *et al*. 1992: 44)

In the model, there are thus two powerful forces driving this entropic process, in which constantly highly organized structures are elaborated and demolished: human beings and industrial capital. Both are claimed to possess the capacity to reproduce themselves. The other sectors with growth tendencies – food production, natural resources consumption, and environmental pollution – are structurally incapable of reproducing themselves. They are, by contrast, 'driven' to growth [8] by increases in population and industrial capital. Living things multiply by self-reproduction. The more individuals there are in a species, the more offspring they can produce. It therefore seems obvious to construe the dynamics of self-reproduction of the population – as in biology – in terms of population ecology. Strangely enough, however, World3 construes the self-reproduction of industrial capital with the same mathematical model of population growth, thus excising all theoretical problems of classical capital and growth theory at one fell blow.

In the Meadows' model world, capital is represented only by material means of production. Industrial capital refers not to money values but to physical plant: the hardware, machines, factories, and equipment that produce manufactured products – including new production plants. The more there are, the more production facilities can be constructed. Production occurs 'with the help, of course, of labour, energy, raw materials, land, water, technology, finance, management, and the services of the natural ecosystems of the planet' (Meadows *et al.* 1992: 33). Capital without money necessarily corresponds to an economy without money and without financial capital, but with networked flows of raw material, energy, products and rubbish. For the Meadows, money has the sole function of supplying information on the relative costs and the value of industrial capital. Money flows 'mediate and motivate the flows of physical capital and products' (Meadows *et al.* 1992: 33–4). But money flows are not subject to the material constraints of the planet, and are thus of little interest to the model builders. This model world knows only the material–energetic aspect of the economy, not movements of value, money and information flows. We find ourselves in a conceptual world governed by a naturalistic concept of capital.

In this world, however, there is also no place for all those processes that, under the heading of development, were previously distinguished from material growth. The term development was taken to mean qualitative change in the organization of material processes, such as changes in form, which can in their turn affect various growth processes – either retarding or accelerating them. Consequently, although there are material limits to growth, there need be no limits to development. Human knowledge, social behaviour, love and kindness, lifestyles and artistic forms of expression are in this sense of the term capable of unlimited development. But precisely these factors are almost completely excluded from the neo-Malthusian model world. It can register only the effects of qualitative change on quantitative growth or shrinkage process. The cultural aspect of society, located in conceptless limbo, is beyond the bounds of the model world.

But the close linkage to population dynamics also gives a distorted model of the natural aspect of society. Nature could after all provide growth models quite different from that of population ecology. With grasses and trees, animals and human beings, growth in size is always coupled with the development of forms and shapes (Thompson 1966). In biological growth processes, there is something in the way of 'biomechanical shape optimization' (Mattheck 1992), which under specific marginal conditions leads to a minimizing of material and energy consumption. If one were to derive growth models from this, scientific attention would be diverted from statistical totalities towards detail, towards the variegated wealth of form and shape in nature. The paradigmatic linkage of the world model to population growth not only transports a powerful Malthusian prejudice, but also a conceptual blindness to the form aspect of change.[9]

Socio-ecological transformations

Following the collapse of the industrialist development dogma, many scholars and practitioners of development policy had hoped that the 'ideal of ecology' could on the one hand permit a new political orientation, and on the other conceptually restructure the increasingly diffuse development debate. This hope has proved deceptive. Ecology provides no firm basis for dealing theoretically with social problems and processes. There is at present similar semantic chaos in the development discourse. It can be eliminated neither by adopting ecological concepts, nor by simple theoretical operations, nor by means of global world models. The development concept cannot be easily removed from its well-established semantic field, nor can ecology be easily inserted into this semantic field. This appears at first glance to be a merely academic problem. But how this dense, unordered mix of interlinked, interactive difficulties and problems, of which the Club of Rome speaks, is to be handled conceptually is a very real practical and political problem. If the disorderly problem mix can give rise to a world *problematique*, there must be strict order in the model world. Theoretically it is defined by neo-Malthusian *problematique* at the level of global ecology, which at the same time directs political attention repeatedly to population growth.

We would like to indicate at least one alternative. In this context the 'founding distinction' developed/underdeveloped is abolished and the development concept replaced by a concept with ecological meaning. New light is then thrown on the usual empirical distinctions – such as those between modern and traditional, between urban and rural culture, between industrial and agricultural production (Becker 1992). Wherever thinking is strictly 'ecological', there is a danger that social problems and processes are treated as if they were natural occurrences. On the other hand, strictly sociological thinking runs the risk of neglecting the natural preconditions for human life in society, reducing society to communication.[10]

However, in considering the ecological crisis, it is precisely the multifarious relationships between human beings, nature and society that are profoundly disturbed. Even those who are convinced that society can no longer be understood without nature, nor nature without society, must nevertheless draw a distinction between society and nature in order to avoid the naturalistic trap. Without symbolic activities, society is non-existent. This is obvious with regard to language, art, religion, myth, or science; with respect to the economy it suffices perhaps to mention money. But society is not a purely symbolic context. Societal processes always have a material side, too.[11] Only a distorted comprehension of the disturbed relationships between human beings, society, and nature is possible in a pure ecological conceptualization. A careful distinction must therefore be drawn between material and symbolic occurrences. In the global ecological model world, this difference is smoothed over, and society represented as a purely natural context.

If one re-introduces this distinction, then, following Meadows, growth can usefully refer only to changes in material properties. However, different notions of growth are conceivable. The Meadows' growth model is quite clearly based on population ecology, and in this model world only quantitative growth can therefore find a place. If natural or social changes owing to

79

changes in form are to be recorded, one cannot avoid the vague notion of qualitative growth. Now in nature and society there are probably hardly any changes in which only form, shape or structure alters – and in which material factors such as quantity of material, energy, or entropy do not also increase or diminish. In reality, such processes almost always occur in both a quantitative and a qualitative dimension. Development processes thus mesh with growth processes – and, conversely, changes in form also constitute aspects of physical growth processes. Social development, however described, never relates to a purely material context. There is always a symbolic side to it. It is a matter of manifold material–symbolic change that cannot be adequately comprehended by either an industrialistic growth concept or by a culturalistic development concept.

Distinguishing quantitative from qualitative dimensions as well as material from symbolic dimensions gives rise to a more complex and sophisticated analysis of change (see Table 3.1).

We suggest renouncing the concept of development and substituting the rather inelegant constructed concept of 'socio-ecological transformation'. It is free of the connotations of the development paradigm, emphasizes form change, but also includes material growth processes. At the level of concrete human activities, where, for example, basic needs crucial to survival are satisfied, it still has a defined meaning: in every society there are specific relationships with the natural co-world, with other people, and with a given culture which change in the event of socio-ecological transformations. Here we are referring to 'societal relationships with nature' that have to be subject to permanent regulation if human life is to be possible and if the social life process is to be propagated from generation to generation. Its material regulation is effected in a cultural nexus impossible without labour and production. Production not only of food, tools, clothing and shelter, or means of transport, but also of symbolic forms, taken together constitute a culture (Cassirer 1944). And, finally, what is to be regarded as sufficient, clean, healthy, safe, satisfying, enjoyable and beautiful is also predetermined by cultural stan-

Table 3.1 Distinguishing dimensions in the analysis of change

	Quantitative	*Qualitative*
Material	Quantitative growth of material factors (e.g. populations)	Qualitative growth through changes of form (e.g. metamorphosis)
Symbolic	Quantitative increase of symbolic entities (e.g. knowledge)	Qualitative development of symbolic orders (e.g. marriage rules)

dards. If for no other reason, the different societal relationship with nature must not only be materially regulated, but always culturally symbolized as well. The cultural regulation of sexuality and reproduction takes a privileged position, which, beside labour and production, constitute a second pole where the regulation of all other natural relationships condense symbolically in differences of sex and gender. Labour and production, eating and drinking, locomotion and reproduction are basic relationships on which others (such as clothing, shelter and protection against danger) depend. The various material forms of regulation have corresponding elements in a symbolic order – mediated via language, rite, myth, religion, art and science. And they determine the forms of individual participation in social life.

What is at the present time being discussed as the ecological crisis is in essence a crisis in societal relationships with nature and problem solution means intervention in their dynamics – with often unpredictable and unwanted, dangerous side-effects. Against this background, let us once again take a brief look at the indicators representing quantitative growth occurrences in global ecological world models. Despite all abstraction and aggregation on a high data level, they always relate back to the totality of different natural relationships in society, whence they draw their meaning and significance.

We have referred to changes to this ensemble by the decidedly complicated term 'socio-ecological transformation'. The consumption of material resources and production of environmental pollution are on the one hand the precondition and on the other the consequence of the regulation of a central societal relationship with nature, namely human production. Destructive growth processes indicate that material forms of regulation are disturbed, from which it follows that symbolic order shatters throughout the world. Labour and production now proceed almost completely under the direction of capital. A fundamental societal relationship with nature in society has thereby been largely de-linked from the satisfaction of basic human needs, and has become an element in the 'self-expansion of value' (Marx) or the 'self-reproduction of industrial capital' (Meadows *et al.* 1992). In this process, the traditional forms regulating reproduction and sexuality, the second pole in every symbolic order, diverge from production relations and forfeit their cultural significance. The regulation of demographic growth in accordance with economic or ecological requirements is doomed in practical terms alone by the fact that sexual reproduction and capital reproduction cannot be synchronized. But this not only changes the traditional patterns of symbolic orders, but also plunges the entirety of societal relationship with nature into crisis. The global ecological crisis as depicted in world models is merely the quantitative expression of this crisis. If one makes a serious attempt to deal with it, the links between economic and demographic growth are indeed decisive. It is not only a matter of limits to growth, but of more profound changes in production relations on the one hand and the relations between the sexes and generations on the other. Marx saw only one of these aspects clearly, and was partly blinded by revolutionary optimism. He thus suppressed his own insight that capitalist expansion undermines the 'sources of all wealth', namely 'the earth and the labourer'. And he overlooked the possibility that the crisis of the capitalist mode of production could result in ecological disaster. Today, a nineteenth-century revolutionary thinker can easily be forgiven his economic one-sidedness and historical optimism. For those born later there can be no excuse.

Notes

1 Paper presented at the conference 'The First Global Revolution. Two Decades of the Club of Rome' organized by the Protestant Academy Arnoldshain and the Institute for Social–Ecological Research in Frankfurt, February 1993.

2 All quotations from: Karl Marx, Gesamtausgabe: (MEGA), (eds) Inst. für Geschichte der Arbeiterbewegung, Berlin and Inst. für Marxismus–Leninismus beim Zk. d. KPDSU–Berlin: Abt. 2. 'Das Kapital' und Vorarbeiten, Bd. 9. Capital, a critical analysis of capitalist production. London 1887, text 1990, part 4, chs 13 and 14.

3 See also Egon Becker, Ökologische Modernisierung der Entwicklungspolitik?, in Prokla. Zeitschrift für kritische Sozialwissenschaft, 22. Jg., Nr. 86, March 1992, pp. 47–60.

4 Cf., in lieu of many others: Gustavo Esteva's Essay 'Development', in Wolfgang Sachs (ed.) The Development Dictionary. A Guide to Knowledge as Power, London, 1992.

5 Cf., Lothar Brock, Nord–Süd-Kontroversen in der internationalen Umweltpolitik: Von der taktischen Verknüpfung zur Integration von Umwelt und Entwicklung (HFSK – Report 7/1992), Frankfurt am Main 1992.

6 In complete contrast to the liberal economic doctrine, there is economization of scarce environmental goods and the formation of regulatory mechanisms and markets, but a politicization of international distribution conflicts. It is a mystery how the much vaunted ecological market economy is supposed to function. (See the critical comment by Elmar Altvater, Der Preis des Wohlstands – oder Umweltplünderung und neue Welt(un)ordnung. Münster 1992).

7 This applies with regard both to the 1972 study and to the reiteration twenty years later. It is no counter-argument that the text nevertheless contains numerous qualitative statements. Such 'qualitative' provisions are naturally incorporated in the model construct if only because there are interrelationships between the different variables, because definitions are given, models of structural propositions built, etc.

8 'Exponential growth happens for one to two reasons: because a growing entity reproduces itself, or because a growing entity is driven by something that reproduces itself out of itself' (Meadows et al. 1992: 20).

9 This is, for example, evident in a naturalistic concept of capital incapable of dealing with form changes. Whereas, in complete contrast, Marx's Critique of Political Economy and the capital concept developed there aims to decipher economic social forms.

10 Our two major competing grand theories in Germany find common ground in this reduction – Luhmann's theory of social systems on the one hand and Habermas' theory of communicative action on the other.

11 The late Talcott Parsons was quite clearly aware of this relationship. See his Action Theory and the Human Condition, New York and London, 1978.

References

Becker, Egon (ed.) (1992) *Umwelt und Entwicklung* (Jahrbuch 1989/90 Pädagogik: Dritte Welt), Frankfurt am Main.

Cassirer, Ernst (1944) *An Essay on Man: An Introduction to a Philosophy of Human Culture*, New Haven, CT: Yale University Press.

King, Alexander and Schneider, Bertrand (1991) *The First Global Revolution: A Report by the Council of the Club of Rome*, New York: Pantheon Books.

Marx, Karl (1971) *A Contribution to the Critique of Political Economy*, London: Lawrence and Wishart.

Mattheck, Claus (1992) *Design in der Natur, Der Baum als Lehrmeister*, Berlin: Springer-Verlag.

Meadows, Donella H., Meadows, Dennis L., Randers, Jorgen and Behrens, III, William W. (1972) *The Limits of Growth. A Report for the Club of Rome's Project on the Predicament of Mankind*, New York: Universe Books.

Meadows, Donella H., Meadows, Dennis L. and Randers, Jorgen (1992) *Beyond the Limits: Confronting Global Collapse, Envisioning a Sustainable Future*, Vermont: Post Mills.

Thompson, D'Arcy Wentworth (1966) *On Growth and Form (abridged edition)*, Cambridge: Cambridge University Press.

World Commission on Environment and Development (WCED) (1987) *Our Common Future*, Oxford: Oxford University Press.

Part 2

ECONOMICS, SOCIETY AND ECOLOGY

4

A SUSTAINABLE WORLD
FOOD ECONOMY

Harriet Friedmann

Introduction

Food offers a useful insight into the world economy and politics, because it is central both to accumulation of capital, and to livelihood and community. Plants and animals are at once nourishment for human beings, and edible commodities. Land is at once a natural habitat of human communities and a resource for production. Diets are at once cuisines expressing cultural relations to nature, to families and communities, and to the body – and bundles of substitutable, variously priced nutrients offered to consumers.

This chapter outlines how the world food economy worked in the 'golden age' of the 1950s and 1960s, and how alternatives have been taking shape during the prolonged restructuring of the 1970s, 1980s and 1990s. It begins with a brief account of the choices made after the Second World War, which rejected international coordination of agricultural trade in favour of systems that were highly regulated by national states, including trade restrictions and subsidies. Next it traces the main changes in production and diet that occurred in the 1950s and 1960s, which created a 'Fordist' international food regime, based on standard agricultural products, such as wheat and milk. The chapter concludes by describing the competing models for a new food regime: the liberal–productivist model and alternative development models.

Background to the Fordist food regime

In 1947, the Food and Agriculture Organization met to decide on the proposal for a World Food Board, an idea which had originated during the Second World War at a famous meeting in Hot Springs, Arkansas, in 1943. The proposal for a World Food Board had wide support among the victorious Allies, as an expression of the larger purposes of the fight to defeat fascism. The institutions to manage international stocks were already in place. During the Second World War governments on both sides undertook massive, coordinated efforts to direct the production and distribution of food. The Allies continued to control food after the war for relief and rehabilitation of war-torn areas.

The world in 1947 was open to alternative ways of organizing food and agriculture, but they did not include unregulated markets. These had collapsed during the 1930s Depression leaving unsaleable surpluses of grain and widespread hunger, both within countries and internationally. For the major grain import countries, especially Great Britain, the Depression had seen the first systematic studies linking poverty and nutrition. During the Second World War, advocacy for public intervention to ensure minimal diets led to maternal and infant food programmes, and canteens for workers as part of the war effort. In the United States, organized farm lobbies – a key to the New Deal alliance of the governing Democratic Party – gained support for farmers in the form of government purchases to support prices. The result was the creation of publicly held surpluses and distribution of surplus foods to the poor via food stamps.

The problems of hunger and farm surpluses, both linked to violent market fluctuations, precluded a return to free markets. In Great Britain, the home of Free Trade, bread rationing was introduced a year after the war ended, to prevent a return of the hunger and social unrest of the Depression years. The countries of the continental Europe, both victors and vanquished, required assistance until they could reconstruct farming and food distribution. Farmers in the major grain export countries were concerned that the end of government purchases would revive Depression conditions of lack of demand due to unemployment, and collapse of international trade (conditions compounded in the United States by the ecological crisis of the dust bowl). The Roosevelt administration solved the farm crisis and the hunger crisis by government purchase and distribution of agricultural commodities. In doing this, it institutionalized government-held agricultural surpluses.

The World Food Board proposal built on the international institutions inherited from the Depression and the Second World War. The first was an International Commodity Agreement for wheat (as for sugar, metals and other raw materials in international trade). This was a forum for import and export governments to negotiate minimum and maximum quantities to buy or sell, respectively, designed to manage the volatility of international markets (Rowe 1965). Second, the Food and Agriculture Organization, part of the League of Nations, was to be the institution managing the World Food Board along the lines of the international commodity agreements. It would have been a key component of a strong United Nations had that project not been overtaken by power struggles related to the Cold War and decolonization. Third, the Allied war effort and subsequent relief agencies had established massive public distribution of food throughout war-torn Europe. The institutions were in place to consolidate cooperative planning of food supplies and allocations.

Yet the proposal was caught in contradictions of its time. First, it did not find a way to address the conflicting interests of farmers (and export countries) and consumers (and import countries). The main opponents in the end were the two most powerful allies, the United States and Great Britain. British opposition came from a concern by the Labour government that farm export interests, which wanted high prices, would eventually prevail over consumer (and import country) interests in low prices, and saw the alternative in reviving purchasing power (Peterson 1979:181). The American story is more paradoxical. Managed trade, particularly the import controls necessary to the United States farm program, would be inconsistent with larger free trade goals pursued in its initiative for an International Trade Organization. In the end, however, the ITO, approved at an international conference in Havana, died at American hands; it was brought to Congress but was withdrawn before it could be ratified because of opposition from those who wanted trade protection for farm programmes. These protective measures were achieved via exceptions made for agriculture, at the United States' insistence, in the less formal General Agreement on Tariffs and Trade (GATT).

Second, although it might have accommodated independence of European colonies, the proposal for a World Food Board presumed 'national planning' that included the empires of France and Britain. More centrally for the food story, it addressed the problems of an era when food and agriculture were pretty transparent. The food people bought was related to plants and animals: potatoes, bread, meats, dairy products, fruits and vegetables. Agriculture was closely tied to climate and other natural features: the main commodities in international trade were wheat from the temperate zones and sugar, coffee, cocoa, palm and coconut oils from the tropics.

The proposed World Food Board was a multilateral, negotiated alternative to ad hoc practices which reflected national economic power. In practice, multilateral planning would have avoided the central dilemma of overcoming dollar shortages to allow US food surpluses to be traded. The proposal was defeated. In its absence, a nationally regulated, surplus-driven food regime emerged by default.

The food regime

The regime that arose by default was the most intensely state regulated of all the sectors of 'Fordist' economies (Lipietz 1992). It began with American ambivalence about free trade in agricultural commodities. The US agricultural depression had preceded its general depression, and because its European customers had turned elsewhere for imports (particularly Great Britain to the Sterling bloc), the United States had the greatest agricultural collapse of any of the export countries. Its farm programmes had led the New Deal interventionist programme, and had reinforced the agricultural lobby which was crucial to the Democratic majority and prevented reversals of policy. Consequently, the United States clung to its right to restrict agricultural trade, and amended the GATT (the now famous Article XI) to exclude agricultural products.

United States farm programmes required that it control imports. The American government was offering above market prices to its farmers. Without import controls, all the world's grain, sugar and other supported crops would have flowed to US Commodity Credit Corporation. The United States disposed of surpluses through food aid, an extension abroad of the distribution outside market channels to domestic food stamp recipients. International food aid went first to Europe and Japan, then to the Third World, where it played its part in reconstructing international trade (towards American exports) and agricultural production (in specialized, chemical and mechanical intensive forms of the 'American model'). Finally, decades later, in a desperate attempt to shore up the centrality of American exports in face of changed world conditions, aid went to the Soviet Union/Russia. For two key decades, from the mid-1950s to the mid-1970s, the United States managed world trade and set the standard for production by means of powerful controls over agriculture.

The response of other states was to regulate agriculture just as intensely as the United States. Both Europe and Japan adapted American policies to a context of import substitution, which required stricter import controls and higher price supports. In Europe, the Common Agricultural Policy was the second basis of the Economic Community, after Coal and Steel. Similarly, Japan's Marshall Aid helped to reconstruct agriculture, and Japan's import and domestic farm policies aimed to ensure national self-sufficiency in the basic food grain (rice). Eventually the European Community created publicly held surpluses, and competed with the United States to subsidize exports to the Third World and later the socialist countries.

Third World countries extended controls inherited from the colonial period and adopted new ones to complement the food regime dominated by surplus disposal through subsidized exports. None of the advanced capitalist import countries, with their own regulated agriculture, was in a position to object to marketing boards and even producer agreements to negotiate exports of tropical products. The new state intervention was part of larger modernization and state building projects: food subsidies to urban workers, the latter often managed through food aid. New states (and also in Latin America, long-standing states) accepted aid at the expense of their own agricultural sectors, in order to speed the availability of urban wage labourers for industrial employment (Friedmann 1981, 1992). Beginning somewhat later, a counteracting trend was to accept Green Revolution techniques based on the hybrid seeds and chemical inputs modelled on those which had transformed American corn production in the interwar period (Kloppenberg 1984, 1988).

This regime was the object of prolonged and acrimonious negotiations at the Uruguay Round of the GATT, and finally last December was undone at the insistence of the United States, which had originated it.

Changes in the Fordist food regime

What changed between the 1960s, with food aid and rising standards of diet, and the 1980s and after, with trade wars and growing hunger throughout the world? As Lipietz puts it, 'a development model holds good only as long as its promises coincide with a certain possible conception of happiness' (Lipietz 1992: 3), a conception which collapses 'either when the model can no longer guarantee it, or when the disadvantages of the model are more and more glaring'. The Fordist model was based on intensely national, state regulated agriculture and food distribution, organized by implicitly managed trade of surpluses generated by this regulation. Several aspects of this model changed in tandem with development of the international food regime.

From the point of view of *consumption*, two major shifts occurred in the advanced capitalist countries. First, a dietary model called 'American', very heavy in beef, came to be part of the mode of consumption. This rested on higher incomes and a European cultural heritage. It created an incentive for industrial livestock production and crops to feed the animals.

Second, as much as Kraft, Unilever, Nestlé and the other giant processing companies could make it, food became a durable consumer good (Friedmann 1991, 1995). New foods were invented, such as Cheez Wiz and Miracle Whip. Frozen foods required the miniaturization and proliferation of appliances such as fridges and freezers in households and shops. Meals such as TV dinners were industrially produced. This promoted the concentration of wholesaling and retailing, eventually leading to the dominance of retail chains within (at least) North American agrofood complexes. Other European dietary favourites, sweeteners and fats, were incorporated in increasing, and difficult to monitor quantities, into complex edible commodities invented with ever-increasing rapidity by the industrial kitchens of the food manufacturers.

From the point of view of *production*, agriculture changed in two important ways. First, the mixed grain-livestock model of the earlier regime became specialized into grains and intensive livestock operations, with grave ecological consequences. Despite soil conservation and other programmes to deal with the effects of monoculture on prairie soils, the pressure, felt also in Canada, Europe, and elsewhere, to monoculture was stronger. As the grains shifted from human to animal feed, maize production increased and soy was introduced into the rotation. Capital intensive feed manufacturers, transnational from the start, became the link between the two monocultures, and between both and intensive poultry, pig and cattle operations (Berlan 1991).

Second, many farms became suppliers of raw materials for industrial food manufacturing. Not only feed grain and livestock producers, but also market gardening became subordinated to industrial capitals. Tomatoes for ketchup, vegetables for freezing, and a wide variety of substitutable ingredients for the increasingly complex edibles concocted in the kitchens of food manufacturers, such as thickeners, sweeteners and oils, replaced crops brought to markets by farmers. Farm products were increasingly combined with chemicals such as emulsifiers, preservatives, and the like. Farmers adopted specialized, high chemical and mechanical input farming, often with hybrid seeds that came in packages of complementary chemicals with specific instructions that replaced traditional knowledge (Goodman *et al.* 1989).

From the point of *international trade*, tropical exports were often disadvantaged due to substitution by First World crops and synthetic substitutes. Many Third World countries had declining terms of trade, particularly for tropical oils, substituted by temperate ones, particularly soya oil. The latter was an important subsidized export through American food aid in the 1950s and 1960s, and continued to be available at favourable market prices because it is jointly produced with soya-based animal feed. Tropical cane sugar lost much of its historic demand in industrial countries, where it had always faced competition from domestic beets, because of sweeteners made from subsidized temperate crops, such as maize, and from chemicals, such as aspartame. For bananas and other crops not easily substituted, transnational corporations in conjunction with land reform initiatives, encouraged plantations to give way to smaller farms dependent on sales to export companies, often through production contracts (Friedmann 1992).

As a *sector*, Fordist agriculture generally tended to the model of small units (the 'family farm') compared to the capitalist farms of the eighteenth-century agricultural revolution in England and the colonial plantations established for export crops in Latin America, Asia, and parts of Africa. In the United States and Europe, agricultural programmes supported smaller farms that would have succumbed to consolidation through unregulated competition. At the same time, however, they encouraged growth through ever-greater use of chemical and mechanical inputs, which implied scale economies, high land values, and continuing use of credit. Farmers became organized into commodity specific lobbies, locked into state commodity programmes, monocultures, the technical treadmill and loan repayments.

Politically, farmers' numbers declined faster than their political weight, and their autonomy gave way to subordination within an agrofood complex dominated by industrial and financial capital. Agrofood corporations had outgrown the nationally regulated regimes which spawned them, and consumers gained equal weight with farmers in agrofood politics.

The GATT agreement thus sealed a fate written in the changes of the Fordist food regime. Still, it took two chaotic decades to agree to abolish the founding rules of the regime. The specific changes to implement those agreements are now beginning to unfold. They will take shape through the practical efforts and conflicts of farmers, consumers, political activists and corporations with divergent projects involving different roles for the state in technical assistance, research and trade.

Alternatives

For the agrofood sector, the 1980s accelerated international restructuring of the food regime, mainly along lines described by Lipietz as the liberal productivist model. Meanwhile, the alternatives pointing towards socially and ecologically sustainable models began to bubble up more quietly here and there. Most examples have elements of both possibilities at once. A few examples may illustrate the real choices that will eventually be made, by intention or by default.

Post-Fordist *consumption* led to a conspicuous triumph of capitalism in the 1980s: the revival and renewal of handcrafted or specialty foods. The speculative booms of the decade fostered a large category of newly rich professionals, bankers, consultants, and others, whose consumption animated demand for old craft foods, such as wines, cheeses and regional dishes, and new syncretic cuisines and ingredients. Niche markets emerged which had quite distinct effects on production of commodities at the top and at the bottom of the new 'hourglass' distribution of incomes. Paradoxically, the regional aspect of niche products accompanied globalization of markets, along with standardization of expensive as well as mass consumption.

For example, boxed beef was a new product of the livestock industry. Standard, highly mechanized slaughtering and packaging fostered the global centralization of the livestock complex, and the relocation and restructuring of labour processes. Thus, meat packing was shifted to new places and labour forces within the United States (Stanley 1994). It was also reorganized around new axes of trade, especially in the Pacific Rim (McMichael and Kim 1994; Lawrence and Vanclay 1994). These changes created in various locales what Stephen Sanderson (1986) has called (in parallel to the 'world car') the 'world steer'. In Mexico, he argues, the introduction of world standard beef slaughter and packaging cut deeply into the mix of subsistence activities in the countryside. By displacing local markets, central production undermined sideline production of cows for milk, meat, leather and tallow, for many self-provisioning communities, and even led to their import for the commercial part of the economy.

Another example of privileged consumption leading to global markets is exotic fruits and vegetables. Starfruit and kiwi in Northern markets (like pears and apples in Southern markets), and nonedible crops such as ornamental plants, became the basis for new export sectors in Third World countries. Under pressure of debt payments and often directly imposed austerity measures by the International Monetary Fund, land and labour are shifted from food and traditional exports to supply fluid foreign markets. These changes are often highly destabilizing, undercutting subsistence within the context of volatile markets. The flexibility of production is at the expense of the stability of farmers and farmworkers (Raynolds 1994).

At the bottom of the hourglass, proliferation of new edible commodities intensified the corporate search for substitutable ingredients on land and sea. For example, the quest for palatable textures led to the systematic harvest of a new natural ingredient, carrageenan, which is derived from sea plants in Southeast Asia (Blanchetti-Revelli 1995). Like harvesting of shellfish, this is a new enclosure of the commons, driving out traditional fishers and pricing out traditional eaters (Skladany and Harris 1995).

For *production*, as the liberal–productivist model undercuts the Fordist one, social and ecological problems multiply. Biotechnology, which holds promise in principle for enhancing social and ecological sustainability, threatens in practice to compound the negative effects of the old chemical and mechanical technologies. Corporate domination of the farm sector, and often of agricultural lobbies, accelerates technical change which promotes consolidation of farms. Most recently, bovine somatotropin (BST) has become the topic of intense political conflict. At present, proponents seem to have the upper hand in the United States, opponents in the European Community; in Canada the balance is yet to be determined during the one year moratorium which ends in the summer of 1995. With pressures from the United States and transnational corporations to deregulate agriculture, concentration of dairy farms, and relocation, seems likely.

International restructuring, in agriculture as in industry, involves a shift from stable, national subsectors to flexible, international subcontracting arrangements. The new focus on profits and competition encourages ever-shorter time horizons and ever-diminishing accountability for social and ecological consequences of reorganizing and abandoning production in any locale. Flexible production systems often mean fly-by-night entrepreneurs who set up production speculatively, leaving the workers or peasants to fend for themselves if the markets turn out wrong (Raynolds 1994). There is a shift towards private power at the expense of public responsibility – for managing surpluses, stabilizing farm sectors, promoting parallel models in the Third World.

The transition from mass to batch production means a shift in labour forces, away from male farmers and industrial workers, towards women and minorities. Like Benetton capitalism for clothing, flexibility for entrepreneurs is inflicted mainly on women, often at the expense of employment for men. At the top of the hourglass, crafted foods and personal food services are usually provided by women who must adjust to changing volume and design requirements. At the bottom of the hourglass, in North America there is a concerted attack on unionized labour in meat packing, food processing, and distribution, with pressure to accept 'on-call' conditions of employment as well as lower wages and benefits. In the Third World, government officials and entrepreneurs sometimes encourage rural women to add to their other work, the planting of the newest fashion fruit or vegetable for Europe. At harvest the trucks may or may not come by.

Alternatives to the liberal–productivist model may come from sustainable trade, in support of (and built upon) diverse, locally organized production systems. Sustainable trade depends on sustainable development strategies (Perkins, this volume). Consumers may choose to support Canadian, Ontarian, or Great Lakes Bioregion food production, as individuals and as citizens demanding local buying policies by public and quasipublic institutions. We may go further to support communities to renew employment in more labour intensive, environmentally sensitive agriculture and in the manufacture and sale of culturally appropriate, seasonal foods. As citizens we may promote policies to support a transition to sustainable agriculture, with respect to inputs, credit, and markets. By trading with parallel groups in other countries, bypassing corporate channels, we may promote a similar transition to sustainable trade in the Third World.

While debt is the major stick coercing Third World exports at the expense of local livelihoods, demand is the part of the equation under potential control of ordinary people in the North. If the North reduces demand by refocusing on its own regional food economies, the South will have the option to (re)construct regional food economies as well. This is better than moralism or philanthropy to correct for the destabilizing and impoverishing effects of present patterns of demand.

This is also crucial to the deepening threat to genetic diversity of food crops brought by the liberal–productivist model. As Lipietz argues, 'biodiversity depends on ethnodiversity'. In the Third World where genetic diversity flourishes, it is especially urgent to support embeddedness of communities in specific bioregional settings. Ethnodiversity is as important in the North, and can be grounded in reconstructing agriculture to supply a mix of cultural diets. Consumers who buy locally and farmers who sell locally share concerns to use the land in complex, sustainable ways, and to create the foods that support individuals and communities.

What are the elements of a sustainable food regime? First is to begin with the demographic shift to urban populations and the post-Fordist economic shift to niche consumer markets. Facing unemployment and problems of access to food, combined with concerns about the dubious health effects of much industrially produced food, urban populations may choose between charities institutionalized alongside (and in symbiosis with) the giant private enterprises of the liberal–productivist model; or self-help organizations which combine *negotiated involvement* with community work schemes. Lipietz describes these as self-managed, contractually bound to end-users, and part of a logic of local development founded on partnership (Lipietz 1992: 145). Many of the main actors in both liberal productivist and alternative models are women. As consumers, paid workers and community volunteers, women can be important strategically.

From their side, farmers may choose to continue the battle to protect Fordist regulation, or actively to engage with the choice between models (in the short-term these may be complementary). On one side are the corporate links offered by the liberal–productivist model. I recently saw how quickly this has proceeded in Alberta, where the public has withdrawn or, in the case of the Wheat Board, moved to restructure along private lines. The language to describe this shift is adopted from industry, but has the extraordinary effect of reversing the meaning in agriculture. Leaders of farm organizations, public officials, and staff members of agricultural organizations share a view of what I am calling the transition from Fordist to liberal–productivist agriculture. They speak of adapting to 'the market'. The examples make clear that in practice this means discovering what Cargill or Mitsubishi wants them to grow, seeking contracts for the season, and hoping that the corporation remains interested in Alberta crops and farmers. Despite their own experience of public marketing, which is responsive to price and sells to the world of bidders, they paradoxically see the search for serial monopoly buyers as a shift to 'competition'. On the other hand, farmers who want to sustain cooperation and avoid complete dependence on corporate buyers, may seek an alternative based on negotiated involvement with consumers, retailers, input suppliers and governments.

Local economy and politics

Governments at various levels have untried potential to support diverse, environmentally sound farming practices and local, culturally diverse cuisines. These employ the skills and time of members of the community in personally enriching and financially stable ways. Starting from local (municipal) government, food policy councils are being formed in North America, which may turn out to be counterparts to some of the more successful regions of Europe (Fanfani 1994). The Toronto Food Policy Council (TFPC) is one of these.

Some of the activities of the TFPC and related groups in the local food economy suggest the alternative vision of food as part of the health and livelihood of individuals and communities. First among these activities is advocacy to establish the right to food, tied to a project to reconstruct a local food economy grounded in socially determined land use. In the Toronto context, this has evolved through health care policy, and now joins with anti-poverty and employment agendas. One idea is to issue universal vouchers to redeem for local farm produce in neighbourhood shops, as part of the publicly funded health care system. The argument is that public funds for staple foods are an aspect of preventative or public health (the branch of government that houses the TFPC).

Toronto Board of Health calculations suggest that public provision of the total dietary costs of at-risk pregnant women would cost about one-tenth the health care costs of low birth weight babies in their first two years alone. Similar calculations for known diet related diseases show that costs of public provision of healthy foods would be repaid within only a few years. Many believe that the health savings from improved diets are potentially much greater than those measured for specific cancers, heart conditions, and the like. The same argument applies to environmental savings from low-chemical input agriculture, and social savings from reducing dependence on debilitating forms of social assistance and charity.

Second, within the framework of social justice to include all citizens is the relinking of local agrofood chains. Liberal trade agreements present great challenges, and the TFPC has opposed them. Yet they also open new possibilities by forcing changes to agricultural regulation (Skogstad 1994). The restructuring of Fordist agrofood economy leads to both wider markets – the liberal–productivist model – and the breakup into niche markets. The latter include the revival of culinary interest among privileged consumers, and the revival of barter and other arrangements to cope with the shrinking incomes from Fordist employment and transfer payments. At the upper end of the income scale, prominent chefs have formed links with organic farmers (some have changed roles) and created an organization called 'Knives and Forks' which sponsors a farmers' market in central Toronto (in addition to the larger non-organic one) and educates a monied clientele about local, seasonal food and its social and ecological requirements.

At the other end, a quasipublic organization called FoodShare organizes direct buying through trips to farms by residents of social housing, and organizes direct deliveries of farm produce to social housing on a regular schedule. The Good Food Box, adapted from the American programmes, is the most ambitious of the 'Field-to-Table' projects. It uses social marketing techniques to attract consumers to group buying of boxes of fresh fruits and vegetables, ordered and delivered once a month, and providing good value through joint buying. It is a different way to shop and eat, reviving the seasonal and the fresh, and reconstructing choice, community, and the social relation to food.

Of course the most direct connections are smaller, but can have a large combined effect. The TFPC supports Community Share Agriculture, in which farmers and farm communities sell shares in the harvest in advance of planting and deliver produce as it matures. Another project is urban gardening in allotments on rooftops, privately, in schools, senior citizens' homes, and other common spaces.

Third, again parallel to dynamic European regions, government relations to markets and social provision are more complex than is captured by the state–market divide. Public purchases offer great possibilities for shifting economies of scale for local organic produce relative to continental commercial networks. Larger turnover, allowing lower prices and greater freshness, could shift markets for private consumers. This involves lobbying not only municipal government, of which it is a part, but also Provincial and even federal governments. At present, this is administratively difficult, and its consistency with trade agreements is dubious. However, use of intrinsically desirable health and environmental criteria, requiring low chemical inputs and additives and high standards of freshness could have the desired effects without directly discriminating in favour of local caterers, manufacturers and farmers. These are easily justified for hospitals, schools, and seniors, where health standards should be high.

School programmes are a way to combine culturally appropriate meals, local employment, and direct purchases of local fresh and prepared foods. The cultural diversity of Toronto provides opportunities for public purchases to specify cultural criteria favourable to local cultural groups. Contracts can be let in public buildings to feature a variety of local cuisines and local products. Flexible public programmes at the local level, a feature of the pilot school nutrition programme sponsored by the TFPC (and recently extended to Ontario) allow school committees to integrate food delivery with education on nutrition, gardening, and food economies. Inspired in part by the experience of the London (UK) Food Commission about a decade ago (Haringey Women's Employment Project n.d.), the intention is to combine health, education, revaluation of women's work and cultural diversity, through creative public food programmes.

Finally, local food distribution and provisioning provide opportunities for empowerment of individuals and communities in relation to livelihood and provisions. Food-related employment is not declining in the liberal–productivist model, but shifting to lower-paid, part-time and less secure jobs, in manufacturing, retailing and services. Import replacement can at least partly reverse the Fordist trend to national/continental sourcing and marketing, and the post-Fordist, liberal–productivist trend to global sourcing and marketing. The TFPC promoted a 'food fair' on the site of the recently closed stockyards, to include a farmers' market, shared facilities for refrigeration, composting, and related needs, and approved equipment to be rented for batch processing by small or new entrepreneurs (many of whom would likely be women with family recipes). Local community members, both in business and residents, were involved. This idea has now become part of the City's plan for revitalization of the district. The idea is spreading to other sites.

These types of local initiatives require support at higher levels of government. In the United States, the vision is usually limited to the (very large) national government. In Canada, the need for international agreements is just as plain, and one of the main requirements from the national government is to protect local initiatives against international rules prohibiting local preferences.

At the level of government which regulates agriculture (provincial in Canada), it is important to change policies from those promoting Fordist agriculture via credit, marketing, health regulations, and the like. Agricultural extension services which mimic corporate technological packages and accompanying advice, are not appropriate either to liberal productivism or to alternate strategies centred on community, social justice and environmental sensitivity. Rather than reduce or privatize, it might be well to change them to foster conversion from chemical–mechanical intensive farming to low-input, diverse agriculture. Research and development in government funded institutions could also promote new technologies for farmers who are as needy of appropriate technologies as those in the Third World. Pluriactivity and rural enterprises, as well as hobby farmers who might become serious, are a new base to complement converting farmers.

At national and international levels, it is important to seek multilateral alternatives to monetary rules constraining domestic policies in favour of debt payments and open trade. Green policies to promote new types of employment; shorter work hours to realize the benefits of increased productivity; and economic–social recognition for presently unpaid social labour in support of families and communities, are all aspects of support for local communities. At the same time, support for social/ecological alternatives in the North creates space for Third World survival and development. Moreover, recognition of the importance of indigenous knowledge finally privileges parts of the Third World where it still lives, and particularly women's knowledge (Kloppenburg 1991). The craft knowledge of agriculture in much of North America has almost been destroyed in my own generation (Berry 1978). New types of science that build on site-specific knowledge and experience, as well as education, credit, and technical support, are alternative directions to promote to achieve stability and sustainability.

Conclusion

In the future, is it conceivable that there will be self-governing communities federated into nested bioregions? The international commodity agreements, which in the inter-war years tried to solve problems arising from volatile agricultural markets, led to the rejected World Food Board proposal. The actual framework of surplus disposal through food aid and other subsidies then caused transnational corporations to vie with sovereign states in regulating agricultural markets and the farmers who supplied raw materials. Now, by cultivating tastes for industrial food among urban consumers and organizing raw materials and markets on an ever-larger scale, the liberal–productivist model pushes the shift of power away from national states.

Meanwhile, the national state is all that stands between consumers, farmers, and communities on one side, and transnational corporations on the other. Within that frame, if Polanyi is correct, the time is right for self-protective movements to protect communities and their habitats from the harm caused by ever-faster moving markets. Perhaps with the possibilities opened by the breakup of markets, and commitment to creating regional food economies, the alternative could promote negotiated food systems supportive of livelihood, health, and sustainability.

References

Blanchetti-Revelli, Lafranco (1995) 'Canadian misfortunes and Filipino fortunes: the invention of seaweed mariculture and the geographical reorganization of seaweed production', in Philip McMichael (ed.) *Food and Agrarian Orders in the World Economy*, Westport, CT: Praeger.

Berlan, Jean-Pierre (1991) 'The historical roots of the present agricultural crisis', in William H. Friedland, Lawrence Busch, Frederick H. Buttel and Alan P. Rudy (eds) *Towards a New Political Economy of Agriculture*, Boulder, CO: Westview.

Berry, Wendell (1978) *The Unsettling of America: Culture and Agriculture*, New York: Avon.

Fanfani, Roberto (1994) 'Agrofood district: a new dimension for policy making and the role of institutions', in Conference Papers *Restructuring the Agro-Food System: Global Processes and National Responses*, Trondheim, Norway, 2–4 May.

Friedmann, Harriet (1982) 'The political economy of food: the rise and fall of the postwar international food order', *American Journal of Sociology* 88 (supplement): 248–86.

—— (1991) 'Agro-food industries and export agriculture: changing international division of labour', in William H. Friedland *et al.* (eds) *Towards a New Political Economy of Agriculture*, Boulder, CO: Westview.

—— (1992) 'Distance and durability: shaky foundations of the world food economy', *Third World Quarterly* 13, 2: 371–83.

—— (1995) 'Food politics: new dangers, new possibilities', in Philip McMichael (ed.) *Food and Agrarian Orders in the World Economy*, Westport, CT: Praeger.

Goodman, David, Sorj, B. and Wilkinson, J. (1987) *From Farming to Biotechnology: A Theory of Agro-Industrial Development*, Oxford: Basil Blackwell.

Haringey Women's Employment Project (n.d.) 'Women and privatization: school meals in Haringey, a campaign strategy for school meals and women's jobs based around a radical food policy', London: London Food Commission.

Kloppenberg, Jack, Jr (1984) 'The social impacts of biogenetic technology in agriculture: past and future', in Gigi M. Berardi and Charles C. Geisler (eds) *The Social Consequences and Challenges of New Agricultural Technologies*, Boulder, CO: Westview.

—— (1988) *First the Seed: The Political Economy of Plant Biotechnology, 1492–2000*, Cambridge: Cambridge University Press.

—— (1991) 'Social theory and the de/reconstruction of agricultural science: local knowledge for an alternative agriculture', *Rural Sociology* 56, 4: 519–48.

Lawrence, Geoffry and Vanclay, Frank (1994) 'Agricultural change in the semiperiphery: the Murray-Darling Basin, Australia', in Philip McMichael (ed.) *The Global Restructuring of Agro-Food Systems*, Ithaca, NY: Cornell University Press.

Lipietz, Alain (1992) *Towards a New Economic Order: Postfordism, Ecology, and Democracy*, New York: Oxford.

McMichael, Philip and Kim, Chul-Kyoo (1994) 'Japanese and Korean agricultural restructuring in comparative and global perspectives', in Philip McMichael (ed.) *The Global Restructuring of Agro-Food Systems*, Ithaca, NY: Cornell University Press.

Peterson, Martin (1979) *Interest Organizations and the Transmutation of Postwar Society*, Stockholm: Almquist and Wicksell.

Raynolds, Laura (1994) 'The restructuring of Third World agro-exports: changing production relations in the Dominican Republic', in Philip McMichael (ed.) *The Global Restructuring of Agro-Food Systems*, Ithaca, NY: Cornell University Press.

Rowe, D.W.F. (1965) *Primary Commodities in International Trade*, Cambridge: Cambridge University Press.

Skladany, Mike and Harris, Craig K. (1995) 'On global pond: international development and commodity chains in the shrimp industry', in Philip McMichael (ed.) *Food and Agrarian Orders in the World Economy*, Westport, CT: Praeger.

Skogstad, Grace (1994) 'Policy under siege: supply management in agricultural marketing', *Canadian Public Administration* 36, 1: 1–23.

Sanderson, Stephen (1986) *The Transformation of Mexican Agriculture: International Structure and the Politics of Rural Change*, Princeton, NJ: Princeton University Press.

Stanley, Kathleen (1994) 'Industrial and labour market transformation in the US meatpacking industry', in Philip McMichael (ed.) *The Global Restructuring of Agro-Food Systems*, Ithaca, NY: Cornell University Press.

Toronto Food Policy Council (TFPC) (1994) 'If the Health Care System Believed You Are What You Eat: Strategies to Integrate Our Food and Health Systems', Discussion Paper No. 3.

5

THE ATLANTIC FISHERY

Raymond A. Rogers

The cod appears to be one of the most prolifick kind of fish. Of
this there need be no other proof than the great number of ships
which anually load with it . . .
Antonio de Ulloa 1758 (in Innis 1954: 2)

No other industry has engaged the activities of any people in
North America over such a long period of time and in such a
restricted area.
Harold Innis (1954: 2)

Arising out of this plenitude of fish and human activity, Innis' monumental
work *The Cod Fishery: The History of an International Economy* (1954)
provides an interesting commentary on an industry that is now – on the east
Coast of Canada in the 1990s – in a state of almost complete ecological and
economic collapse. Innis' emphasis on the cod as a staple in the colonial
period can inform an environmental perspective on the political economy of
depletion and dependence. Central to the correlations between Innis' work
and those based on depletion and dependence are the relationships of international political economy which promote overexploitation in particular
geographic realities and natural processes, and at the same time, foster frameworks of dependence which leave local communities in exceedingly vulnerable
positions as they attempt to cope with the aftermath of ecological and
economic collapse. It is this condition of depletion and dependence which
links the plight of Atlantic Canadian coastal communities with that of local
cultures in the South as they struggle for survival in the context of resource
overexploitation and international trade and debt arrangements.

For Innis, both political economy and natural community required a
comprehensive analysis for there to be an understanding of the relationships
that existed in the fishery. Innis summarizes the Canadian interrelationship
between natural systems and economic history in this way:

The economic history of the regions adjacent to the submerged areas extending to the northeast of America's north Atlantic seaboard is in striking contrast to that of the continental regions. In the continent's northern area the St Lawrence facilitated expansion westward and a concentration on fur, lumber, and wheat; in the submerged areas innumerable small, drowned river valleys in the form of bays and harbours facilitated expansion eastward and a concentration on fish. Drainage basins bring about centralization, submerged drainage basins decentralization . . . . Unity of structure in the economic organization of the St Lawrence was in sharp contrast with the lack of unity in the fishing regions . . . . In the interior, economic history was marked by changes to new staple industries; on the Atlantic, changes were centred in a single industry.

(Innis 1954: 484)

In the view of later economists who had become enamoured by the adaptability of capital and expanded forces of production, this recognition of the importance of natural and geographic realities could appear to be an almost physiocratic linking of nature and economy. But from the perspective of the current collapse of marine communities in Atlantic Canada, Innis' attention to natural processes is noteworthy, and is in sharp contrast to the corresponding invisibility of ecological realities in later economists and managers – like the ones who were part of the Kirby Task Force's study on the fishery *Navigating Troubled Water* (Kirby 1983) – whose economic priorities took little account of the limits of the workings of natural communities, and were more concerned with creating large vertically integrated fish companies as a solution to the problems in the fishery. As Barbara Neis states with regard to Fordist economies-of-scale generally:

The Fordist relationship between capitalism and nature was based on seeking out, at a global level, large, dependable supplies of relatively homogeneous raw materials such as oil and wheat. In other words, Fordism relied heavily on direct and indirect control of such natural resources by large multinational corporations and relatively little knowledge about nature and on the efforts to transform nature.

(Neis 1993: 90)

Neis also points out that a great many theorists who attempt to analyse the transformation from Fordist to post-Fordist approaches to production 'neglect the barriers to capital accumulation which nature imposes' (Neis 1993: 88).

The political economy of depletion and dependence returns analysis necessarily to the staple of the process without which nothing else can happen. It also counters the homelessness of capital in affirming the located sense of the relationship between human community and natural community – not only as operands of the production process – but in terms of their interrelated and situated contexts.

Because it promotes dependence in coastal communities through its centralized regulatory infrastructure and accepts the economic realities which have caused the depletion of biotic communities in Canada's East Coast fishery, the resource management perspective of the Canadian Government remains as an impediment to significant analysis of the aftermath of collapse. By contrast, Harold Innis' study of the cod fishery can provide a starting point for analysis which would move away from the attribution of blame among the various actors, and toward a problematic examination of the assumptions which inform the relationship between modern society and the natural world.

Innis and marine life

Innis begins his study of the economic history of Northeastern North America with an in-depth discussion of the biological characteristics of the cod fish and the marine area it inhabited: 'An interpretation of [the cod's] significance in the economic history of the area depends on an understanding of its geographical background and habits' (Innis 1954: 1). A submerged analysis of underwater realities leads Innis to give details on water temperature, egg laying, available food for cod at different times of year, behaviour of small fry, and the effects of ocean current and wind direction on food availability and school migration. This recognition of the importance of natural realities locates economic activity in a particular context:

> The great wealth and complex interdependence of animal life along the seaboard of the Maritimes have as yet baffled the scientist, and only small areas which have yielded to economic exploitation have come under the range of intensive investigation. The Banks are subjected primarily to ocean phenomena, and are not influenced by rivers from Newfoundland or by fresh water from the Gulf of St Lawrence. The Gulf Stream and the Labrador Current, a variety of conditions of temperature and climate, and a food supply varying from plankton to the larger fish in the vicinity of the Grand Banks are responsible for the abundance and diversity of the animal life which supports the extensive but fluctuating cod fishery
>
> (Innis 1954: 2)

As well as pointing out the many natural characteristics which are of great significance to economic activity in the fishery, Innis alludes to the fact that 'only small areas which have yielded to economic exploitation have come under the range of intensive investigation'. The importance of the linking of scientific study and economic activity in the fishery cannot be overestimated in an examination of ecological collapse. What Innis' statement points to is that science operates in the service of economics rather than in the service of biological conservation. This has certainly been the case in the history of the fishery. The resource management myth that for each economic imperative there is an equal and opposite regulatory response in the name of conservation bears no relation to the events.

In his discussion of nature's economy, Innis discusses the specific habits of the cod fish:

> The cod prefers a salinity of 34 per thousand and a temperature of 40 to 50 degrees, but its range is far beyond these limits. It frequents chiefly rocky, pebbly, sandy, or gravely grounds in general from 20 to 70 fathoms in depth, although it has been taken at 250 fathoms and thrives in temperatures as low as 34 degrees. The cod usually spawns in water less than 30 fathoms deep and apparently in fairly restricted areas. A female 40 inches long will produce 3,000,000 eggs, and it has been estimated that a 52-inch fish weighing 51 pounds would produce nearly 9,000,000. The eggs float in the upper layers of water, where they are fertilized and hatched . . . . Experiments have shown that a temperature of 47 degrees will lead to hatching in 10 or 11 days, of 43 degrees in 14 or 15 days, of 38 or 39 degrees in 20 to 23 days, and of 32 degrees in 40 days or more.
>
> (Innis 1954: 3)

This is followed by a detailed anatomical description of the cod fish, and a discussion of the seasonal role of herring, capelin, squid and crustaceans in the diet of the cod. This analysis of the habits and characteristics of cod concludes by pointing out the way these realities affected both the fishing activity of those engaged in the industry, as well as the curing and preserving methods which made the cod a tradable commodity which became important to the economic history of northeastern North America.

The attempt to include natural processes in economic analysis is currently considered to be of major importance in analysing environmental problems and developing a perspective which would promote sustainable use of living natural resources. This is in contrast to the expansionary approaches associated with Fordist capitalism which took little or no account of the relationships in natural communities. Alternatively, Innis' work links human economy and nature's economy despite the fact that there were few problems related to overexploitation when he was doing his research. The very real likelihood that the cod fishery will disappear in economic terms in Atlantic Canada, necessarily creates a new context in which to examine Innis' study of the centrality of the cod fishery to the economic history of the region and to the recognition of the centrality of natural communities to the well-being of human communities.

Innis and international political economy

Most of *The Cod Fishery: The History of an International Economy* is devoted to an analysis of the colonial relationships competing for dominance in north-eastern North America and the affect these struggles – and the accompanying trade and commerce arrangements which informed the colonial powers' exploitation of the cod – had on local political and economic realities, such as the development of responsible government. This desire of colonial powers such as the French, British and Spaniards to use the cod in their three-way trade with colonies in the Caribbean had the indirect result of limiting the development of the colonies directly adjacent to the fish. As Innis states:

> The activity of commercialism based in the fishing industry and the relative articles of shipbuilding and trade fostered by the navigation system had significant implications for constitutional develop-ment .... While such legislation coincided with the demands of West Country [of Great Britain] commercial interests, it clashed with the interests of the colonies under the Crown .... The problem of empires was one of constitutional as well as economic organization.
>
> (Innis 1954: 506)

This led to conflicts where:

> The West Country opposed the formation of settlements in Newfoundland to the point of hastening the rise of the fishing industry in New England. Nova Scotia, in turn, resisted the control of New England and accentuated the isolation of Newfoundland .... Exports of sugar from the British West Indies led to the emergence of vested interests which fostered legislation opposed to the trade of New England and the colonies .... Direct trading between the West Indies and England flourished at the expense of the auxiliary trading between the colonies and the West Indies.
>
> (Innis 1954: 500–1)

Although 'an expanding commercial system broke the bonds of a rigid political structure defended by vested interest' (Innis 1954: 502), it was followed by a more directly capitalist arrangement after 1783 whereby 'the new empire was more firmly based on direct exports to Great Britain in return for finished products, and the monopolies of the old empire became impossible because of the importance of trade with the United States' (Innis 1954: 502). These colonial arrangements weakened during the nineteenth century, but this centre–periphery reality still exists today in the relationship between Atlantic Provinces and the Canadian government, and undermines conservation measures because of the demand for economic growth in a perceived 'have-not' region which still does not control economic and trade arrangements.

The context of international exploitation of the cod has continued to be important throughout the last fifty years and has played a central role in the collapse of marine communities. The centrality of these international forces has had both direct and indirect results. In direct terms, the unregulated international distant water fleet – which included up to twenty industrialized nations – expanded dramatically after the Second World War and exploited the cod to the point of collapse in the early 1970s. Indirectly, the massive catching capacity of international factory freezer trawlers led to a lack of development of the Canadian fleet, which remained in large part artisanal. There was also a lack of development in accompanying regulatory frameworks in Canada while the industry remained international, and – after the declaration of the 200-mile limit in 1977 and the Canadianization of the industry – this 'underdevelopment' resulted in a confusion of expansion and restriction in an attempt to both regulate and increase the exploitation of a newly nationalized resource.

Innis' emphasis on the economic ramifications of the shift from a salt fishery to a fresh frozen industry and Atlantic Canadian underdevelopment is of special significance. By focusing on underdevelopment in the region and the increased pressure on marine communities brought on by changes in international economic relations, Innis' work in the 1930s describes the relationships which promoted the severe ecological problems which occurred for the first time in the late 1960s.

Innis gives this description of the shift from salt-fish to fresh-fish and the complex arrangements which were central to this shift:

> The spread of industrialism evident in urbanization, improved transport, and refrigeration had profound effects on an industry that had its life in a commodity which depended on salt as a preservative if its product was to be sold in distant and tropical countries . . . . The overhead costs of large-scale equipment in the fresh-fish industry tended to force dried cod into the position of a by-product.
>
> (Innis 1954: 418–19)

Other changes in technology and communications accelerated this process of transformation which made fresh and frozen fish more readily available:

> the broadening of the market in the United States, together with refrigeration and improved communications by telephone, telegraph, and radio, brought about improved facilities for handling fresh fish . . . . The introduction of the filleting process in 1921 and the marketing of packaged fillets reduced the weight of fish and expanded the market . . . . A rapid increase in trawlers accompanied

an expanding market . . . . With the decline of the fishery on Georges
Bank in 1931 [due to overfishing], there was a sharp increase on the
other banks, which became more accessible due to more rapid steam
and motor ships.

(Innis 1954: 423)

The shift from the low investment levels needed for salt-preserving and
longline technology used on salt-bankers such as the *Bluenose* to the high-
investment trawlers – or draggers as they are now called – and the consequent
demand for a regular supply of fish which accompanied this increased investment is described by Innis:

Trawlers, while not needing bait, require an abundance of coal and
ice. They can support with greater dependability, and under a variety
of weather conditions, a market demanding larger quantities of fish
on certain days of the week and during certain seasons of the
year . . . the large-scale capital investment now essential to the fresh-
fish industry – that is, an investment in cold-storage equipment,
packing equipment, and by-products plant, extending in some cases
to the ownership of mills for the production of lumber – demands a
continuous supply of raw material.

(Innis 1954: 435)

This shift from salt-fish to fresh-fish intensified the pressure of capital
because it converted the fish off Canada's East Coast from what had been a
slave's food in tropical countries as part of the triangular colonial trade in the
Atlantic, to a commodity available to prosperous countries.

The shift from salt to fresh was also a shift from low standard of living
countries to high standard of living countries. This increased the importance
of capitalist modes of production and consumption (Innis 1954: 443).

Innis' analysis of the colonial relationships which competed for the fish off
the Northeast Coast of North America provide an important background for
understanding the relationships which were involved in the events leading to
the ecological collapse of the cod. The postcolonial intensification of
exploitation by the international fleet ended with the collapse of a range of
Atlantic species in the early 1970s. The access the international fleet had to the
fish also led to the limited development of the Canadian fleet and Canadian
regulatory infrastructure. When the coastal zone was nationalized in 1977,
this sole access and regulatory mandate proclaimed by the government of
Canada led to a collision of the perspectives of expansion and regulation.
This resulted in a situation where there was the expansion of Fordist industrial arrangements in the national context, and the internalization and
re-entrenchment within Canada of centre–periphery 'colonial' relationships
as represented by Ottawa, on the one hand, and Atlantic coastal communities

on the other. It is this history of depletion and dependence which now characterizes the current crisis in Canada's East Coast fishery.

Ecological brinkmanship

the Canadian Government considers customary international law inadequate to protect Canada's interest in the protection of the marine environment and its renewable resources.

Law of the Sea Conference (1974: 3)

The catching-capacity of the international distant water fleet increased dramatically after the Second World War as war ships were converted to draggers and technologies developed during the war such as powerful engines, hydraulic winches, radar, and sonar were put to use in the fishery. As the stocks became depleted off the coasts of Europe, this fleet of Russians, Poles, Spaniards, French, Portuguese and German boats moved into the Northwest Atlantic off Canada's East Coast. A volunteer umbrella organization called the International Commission for the Northwest Atlantic Fishery (ICNAF) was set up in 1949 to gather information on fishing activity in the area.

During this period of industrial expansion, the number of draggers fishing in the region went from 620 in 1954, to 1537 in 1974. The gross tonnage of boats increased 500 per cent, while the index of fishing effort (a combination of days fished and gross tonnage) increased from 13,280 to 241,453. In an attempt to keep pace with this expansion, the Canadian fleet over 50 tons increased its catching capacity by 320 per cent during the 1960s. A stark indication of impending doom is reflected in the fact that while the catching capacity of the Canadian fleet increased by 320 per cent, its actual catch only increased by 18 per cent. In Fordist terms, the international factory freezer trawlers

were characterized by a highly destructive and wasteful relationship between production and nature . . . .The profitable operation of FFTs absolutely required access to fish stocks that were dense and relatively homogeneous and thus suited to automated harvesting and processing.

(Neis 1993: 93)

In the aftermath of the collapse of marine communities which resulted from international exploitation, ICNAF attempted to impose gear restrictions and country by country quotas in the mid-1970s. Because of the international context and the resulting lack of enforcement capability, ICNAF – as a volunteer, umbrella organization – failed to limit fishing effort and this led coastal states to nationalize unilaterally the 200-mile Exclusive

Economic Zones in 1977 as a first step toward replacing 'customary international law' and putting in place the regulatory framework needed to overcome the destructive exploitation patterns of the past.

Nationalization of marine life and the emergence of resource management

the Progressives assumed that lawmaking was somehow divorced from competition in the market place and not . . . in many respects a struggle for resources carried on by other means.

Arthur McEvoy (1987: 295)

The implementation of a resource management institutional capability formed the basis of the Canadian government's and other coastal states' claims to the high seas 200 miles from their coasts. Within this national regulatory framework, resource management perspectives now became the context in which discussions of fisheries issues occurred. This represents a significant transformation in analysis from the political economy approaches of theorists such as Innis. Unlike political economy critiques of capital and markets which struggle 'to find a frame of reference to which the market itself is referable', to quote Polanyi (1968: 174), the critical ability of resource management perspectives is limited by its implicit acceptance of the workings of modern economy. Resource management is an approach which strategizes with – but does not question – the demands that appear on the market. As McEvoy states with regard to the limited mandate of resource management in the California fishery:

external to the theory [of resource management] were the forces that drove the harvest: demand, technology, and other variables were factors that fishery managers had to cope with, but were not variables to be controlled.

(McEvoy 1987: 295)

It is precisely these forces of demand and technology which political economists such as Innis identified as being central to understanding the relationship between economic processes and natural processes.

In one of its few proactive policy initiatives in the fishery, the Canadian Government set out its first comprehensive approach to the fishery on the eve of the declaration of the 200-mile limit in 1977. With the aim of overcoming the chronic economic and ecological instability which had plagued the fishery in the international context, the *Policy for Canada's Commercial Fisheries* announced the following management goals:

- Obtain national control of the exploitation of fishery resources throughout a zone extending at least 200 nautical miles from Canada's coasts.
- Institute a co-ordinated research and administrative capability to control fishery resource use on an ecological basis and in accordance with the best interests (economic and social) of Canadian society.
- Develop a fully effective capability for the monitoring of information on resource and oceanic conditions, for the surveillance of fleet activity and for the enforcement of management regulations.

(Fisheries and Marine Service 1976: 63–4)

It is worthwhile to compare a well-known normative model of the way resource management should take place with the above mission statement of the Canadian government. Bruce Mitchell outlines an ideal resource management process whereby a 'natural resource becomes a commodity or service as it is shaped by human attitudes, technology, financial and economic arrangements, and political realities' (Mitchell 1979: 1–5). For Mitchell, this process should occur in three stages:

1 Resource analysis – determines the quality, quantity, and availability, as well as demand for product.
2 Resource planning – the actual decisions which allocate and set the conditions of resource development.
3 Resource development – the process whereby the resource becomes a commodity or service.

In these terms, first there is an analysis of the size and quality of the resource, then, once it is decided that the resource provides a viable basis for exploitation, a management framework is put in place to ensure economic and ecological stability. After these first two stages are complete, then resource development begins and the resource is converted to a commodity or service available to society.

As well as presenting an 'ideal' of the resource management process, Mitchell's model also provides an analytical tool for managers to assess the possible reasons for success or failure of particular instances of resource development. The management goals set forth in *Policy for Canada's Commercial Fishery* corresponded to Mitchell's model of how resource management should take place. Did the failure in the fishery result from the poor or untimely implementation of these management goals? Or was there something seriously wrong with the resource management model? I contend that the most important reality in the failure of the fishery – which can be identified through the use of Mitchell's model – is that the marine biotic community was 'developed' to the point of collapse before there was any consideration that there should be resource analysis or resource planning.

Although not directly concerned with depletion of natural communities, Innis' analysis of the cod fishery points to two reasons this ecological failure was the direct and indirect result of the colonial period: (1) the expansion of commodity relations in the context of an increasingly industrialized fishery put intense pressure on marine communities; and (2) the history of international relations left Atlantic Canada in a state of dependence both economically and politically and this caused the fishery to be seen as an engine of development and therefore weakened the mandate for conservation of marine communities. It was these earlier realities which – during the resource management mandate in the period from 1977–94 – undermined the conservation goals set out in the *Policy for Canada's Commercial Fisheries* on the eve of the declaration of the 200-mile limit.

Since the collapse of the stocks in the early 1970s and the various regulatory responses to that collapse (including nationalizing the stocks), resource managers have been attempting to control exploitation, and at the same time trying to understand the workings of marine biotic communities that have been destabilized by overexploitation. What this has amounted to, finally, is resource management as crisis management. Almost all fishery policy that now exists has come about from inquiries into breakdowns in the industry. Thus these policies reflect not the fulfilling of the twin mandates of conservation and economic stability, but rather the sacrificing of conservation policy to assuage the cries for more fish. This crises management is understandable within the context of the historic dependence of Atlantic Canada which was identified by Innis as the legacy of colonialism. In the period immediately following the nationalization of the stocks, the fishing industry was seen as an engine of jobs and economic activity when, in fact, it had been made very vulnerable by the overexploitation of the international fleet.

This national policy of using the fishery as the engine of development to overcome regional disparity within Canada appeared most intensely in the expansion of the processing and catching capacity of the larger fish companies, subsidized by agencies such as the Federal Department of Regional Economic Expansion. Barrett sums up the history of the relationship between government and large fish companies such as National Sea Products in this way:

> The history of National Sea Products is one of growth and expansion under the protective wing of a developmentist state, especially in the 1970s. In payment for this public tutelage, the company took advantage of every opportunity to exploit underutilized species or new species of fish, and to expand efforts into more traditional fisheries. Centralism, concentration, and technological modernization became its hallmarks. In spite of this seeming orderly expansion, however,

anarchy and frenzied overexploitation prevailed. When fish stocks were threatened, the company could only respond by increasing efforts in other areas or by diverting capital out of the fishery or out of the country altogether. To such an organization, conservation and rational management were an anathema.

(Barrett 1984: 96)

When the recession of the early 1980s set in, this expansion caused a debt and liquidity crisis in the recently expanded fish companies which had huge stock piles of inventory which they couldn't sell. This crisis led the federal government to set up the *Kirby Task Force* to inquire into the problems in the fishery and the task force report identified the Canadian government's conflictual response to fishery issues after the declaration of the 200-mile limit in 1977:

Provinces with no trawler fleets wanted them; provinces with trawlers wanted to add more and bigger vessels. Companies poised themselves for the growth in resources. Processing plants expanded; new ones were built . . . . While the Department of Fisheries and Oceans was slowly tightening up the licensing regime with one hand (and preaching constraint), it was passing out subsidies for fishing vessel construction with the other, as were provincial loan boards.

(Kirby 1983: 20)

This drive for economic development led to a situation where, by 1981, the domestic Canadian fleet surpassed the catching capacity of the international fleet which had decimated marine communities in the 1970s. Despite its massive expenditure on regulatory infrastructure, the Canadian government ended up doing little more than internalizing the very processes of industrial expansion which had destroyed the marine communities in the international context.

Because of the expansion of the Canadian fleet, catch levels increased throughout the early 1980s and levelled off in the mid-1980s before beginning to drop dramatically. Prices paid for fish were at an all-time high in the mid-1980s, so despite falling catches the increased value promoted exploitation of marine communities which were on the brink of collapse. What became clear in the aftermath of collapse is that the fish were always in a vulnerable state, and it was only the increased efficiency and catching capacity of the Canadian fleet which generated increased catches, and not the recovery of the health of marine communities.

In 1989, the *Scotia-Fundy Groundfish Task Force Report* – an inquiry into overcapacity in the groundfish fleet – stated that there was five times the catching capacity in the fleet needed to harvest the annual quota. Along with the recognition of overcapacity in the fleet, the report reflects a fundamental change in the federal government's approach to the fishery. In contrast to *Policy for Canada's Commercial Fisheries* (1976) which saw its mandate in terms of putting in place a centralized and publicly funded regulatory infrastructure to manage the fishery, the 1989 report was more interested in moving toward the wider government initiative linked to privatization and deregulation of economic activity:

> Fisheries management employs public resources to generate private gain. The process should be made as efficient as possible to minimize the cost to Canadian taxpayers. Management has evolved toward a system demanding a high degree of administrative, scientific, and enforcement support while manpower and financial resources have been declining. In this light more efficient management measures must be sought.
>
> (Hache 1989: 10)

A central aspect of this increased efficiency was the expansion of the Enterprise Allocation programme which turned the fish in the ocean into transferable private property – in the form of ownership of a share of the annual Total Allowable Catch – which was granted to the larger participants in the industry. This approach assumed that private property promoted more rational use of the resource, as opposed to the 'rush to fish' impetus which was inherent to the quota system.

With this shift in the Canadian government's overall approach to the public–private relationship, and as it became clear in the late 1980s that the regulatory mandate as set out in *Policy for Canada's Commercial Fisheries* had failed in specific terms, the Federal Department of Fisheries and Oceans set about abandoning the mandate of a comprehensive regulatory infrastructure funded by Canadian taxpayers. By beginning a programme to privatize and deregulate the fishery, the Canadian government acknowledged that it had manifestly failed to fulfil the goals of promoting ecologic and economic stability in Atlantic Canada which had formed the basis of their declaration of the 200-mile limit. By doing so, it was promoting the global processes which had depleted biotic communities, and at the same time, increasing the vulnerability of coastal communities which had come to depend on that more fickle source of life, the federal government.

Conclusion: the political economy of depletion and dependence

A long list of stocks endangers in 1970 would be longer still in 1980, the only removals being those stocks that have collapsed. Despite the wealth of helpful theory, there have been very few success stories of fisheries management in practice.

Pitcher and Hart (1982: 344)

In the Spring of 1989, the 'Independent Review of the State of the Northern Cod', chaired by Leslie Harris submitted its interim report which confirmed that the northern cod were on the verge of ecological collapse. The report stated that 'there has been a serious underestimate of fishing mortality rates in the years between 1977 and 1989' (Harris 1989: ii). This time period corresponds to the entire mandate of the Canadian government's management of the East Coast fishery. Despite the 'wealth of helpful theory' referred to above by Pitcher and Hart, the resource management perspectives under which the Federal Department of Fisheries and Oceans operated led to the depletion of marine communities and dependence in Atlantic human communities. As Neis states, the failure to take natural barriers into account 'contributed to the crisis in Fordism in the fishery and these have continued to hamper efforts to establish a new effective regime of accumulation, not only in the North Atlantic, but globally as well' (Neis 1993: 102).

Although forever mired in an ongoing economic and ecological crisis, fishery managers nonetheless could not or would not acknowledge the 'financial vortex [of] . . . massive high-tech fishing for profit' (Mowat 1990: 10) which undermined any conservation initiatives. Instead, managers saw the problems in the fishery in terms of its 'poor fit' into modern economic categories. It is possible to convey this failure of analysis in the fishery by examining the way the 'common-property problem' has been understood in the fishery.

In fisheries literature, an open-access situation has been repeatedly mistaken for a common property problem. The reason this misreading occurs is that – as with the most well-known example of this in Garret Hardin's 'Tragedy of the Commons' metaphor – the imperatives of modern economic processes and competitive and atomistic capitalist behaviour are universalized so that the only aspect of the situation that does not fit this modern paradigm is the lack of property rights. The lack of property rights is then seen as the source of overexploitation. The conclusion is that what is required to promote increased efficiency of resource use is the granting of property rights. This assumption is not borne out in reality as there is no indication that property rights limit the drive to overexploit. The *Report of the Workshop on Scotia-Fundy Groundfish Management from 1977 to 1993* published by the Department of Fisheries and Oceans states:

all of the analyses [of fish catches] inferred dumping, discarding, and highgrading (by both mobile gear and fixed gear) due to trip limits, EAs, ITGs, and imbalances between quota and abundance for the CHP species mix in a given area. The observer evidence infers that these practices have increased rather than decreased within introduction of property at the level of an enterprise. The port technician anecdotal information and the interviews infers that property at the individual level (IQs) is providing more incentives for illegal fishing practices at sea, but the levels of such practices cannot be quantified.

(Angel *et al.* 1994: 115)

What this statement makes clear is that exploitation patterns are not mitigated by the granting of property rights, and conversely, that the common property problem of the 'race to fish' may not be what causes depletion.

From the perspective of the political economy of depletion and dependence, then, common property – defined as the recognition of specific members of a group having access to a resource under culturally and socially defined limits – is not the source of the problem of overexploitation. Rather, this kind of stable social arrangement – as it has existed in other cultures at other times – is undermined by the predatory incursions of open-access capitalism which has no recognition of the limits of natural processes or of community-imposed limits to exploitation. The assumptions that regulatory frameworks on a national scale – which was the initial basis of Canada's claim to the fish – or the granting of individual or corporate property rights – which evolved later – could provide this same stability in the modern context have been proven wrong.

Although referred to in comments within the workshop report is the statement quoted above that property rights are 'providing more incentive for illegal fishing practices at sea' which are driven by the expansionary requirements of capital, the introduction to the report sets out the standard view that the 'race to fish' inherent to common property has caused many of the problems in the fishery, as well as causing undue strife between regulators and exploiters, and therefore the Department of Fisheries and Oceans embarked on a programme of privatizing fish stocks as a way of integrating conservation into development:

These programmes aimed to change the fundamental motivations in common property systems by issuing quotas to companies or individual fishers. Enhanced ownership is expected to mitigate the 'race for quota' and allow individual fishers to tailor capacity and ultimately to target fishing effort to the quotas they control. Fishers would then be able to maximize profits without having to maximize the volume for competitive quotas. EA programmes were introduced to offshore fleets in 1982, vessels 65–100 ft. in 1988, and to the inshore mobile gear fleet in 1991.

(Angel *et al.* 1994: 2)

This summary statement is not qualified in any way with reference to the failures of these programmes in reality. It is this kind of analytical failure which continues to plague any worthwhile discussion of the problems in the fishery.

What the 'race for quota' is really referring to is not the common property problem, but the location of conservation – as it operates in a quota system – within modern political economy. Conservation is not an on/off switch for destructive behaviour imposed by an external authority at some upper level of exploitation at the last minute. In other words, to allow the modern economy to operate solely in response to technology and economic pressure, and then expect all this to grind to a halt when catch levels are reached, is the analytical equivalent of solving waste management problems by standing at the gate of the landfill site with a whistle.

This resistance to useful analysis is reflected again in the *Report of the Workshop on Scotia-Fundy Groundfish Management from 1977 to 1993*. Presented in the report is a table which conveys over 300 instances where discarding, dumping, misreporting, and highgrading of catches – activities which are promoted by the 'last minute' location of the quota system as exploiters attempt to both meet quota requirements and maximize economic return – were seen as the central problem in gathering reliable data for the purposes of developing a groundfish management plan. The report then goes on to state that:

> It has been interpreted that changes in environmental conditions [read: colder water] have been a major contributor to the declines in northern cod off Newfoundland and Labrador. By inference, it has been concluded by some that environmental conditions have increased natural mortality in other areas where stocks have also declined steadily since the late 1980s. The continuous growth of the gray seal populations since the extension of jurisdiction has also been considered to be important.
>
> (Angel *et al*. 1994: 115)

Once again, although the information on dumping and misreporting is included within the text of the workshop report, along with the discussion of seals and cold water, the abstract of the report makes no mention of misreporting and dumping, but states that 'Two papers . . . evaluated the degree to which changes in natural mortality (by, respectively, environmental trends and seal predation) over time have compromised our ability to attain management objectives' (Angel *et al*. 1994: 1).

Although never directly concerned with the ecological collapse of natural communities, Harold Innis' political economy analysis of the cod fishery in the 1930s is far more able to make a contribution to the political economy of depletion and dependence in the 1990s than is resource management fisheries literature, or global sustainability literature, which shares many of the same assumptions as fisheries literature. The goals and strategies of the resource management approach in the fishery are all but identical with the goals and strategies of sustainability based on the integration of conservation and development, and both fail to make the processes of development sufficiently problematic.

By recognizing the significance of the relationship between natural processes and the exploitive pressures of commodity production and the relationships which accompany this form of production, Innis engaged in an analysis which makes a contribution to understanding the problems in the fishery. Of the dislocation of Atlantic Canadian communities, Innis expressed this concern in the midst of economic changes in the 1930s:

> Nova Scotia turned to the interior in Canada and the United States, and retreated from world markets where she found herself in competition with the capacity of large-scale fish production in other important countries. The results of the retreat were evident in the revolution from an economy facing the sea with a large number of ports to an economy dependent on a central port [Halifax] and railways to the interior . . . . The disappearance of an active commercial region as a result of the impact of machine industry has been a major calamity to the fishing regions of France, New England, Nova Scotia, and Newfoundland . . . . The transition from dependence on a maritime economy to dependence on a commercial economy has been slow, painful, and disastrous.
>
> (Innis 1954: 507–8)

In comparison to the slow, painful, and disastrous transition of the 1930s, it is hard to imagine the words required to describe the transition in the 1990s for these same communities.

If it is accepted that a definition of conservation related to the quota system has not provided a viable basis for conserving natural communities, and that we need something more than an on/off switch for destructive behaviour, it then becomes possible to see common property not as the source of the problems in the fishery – as it has been described in the resource management literature – but rather as a possible solution to both depletion and dependence in the fishery. In this context, conservation can mean the implicit acceptance of one's place in human community and natural community. In large part, then, conservation is a social and cultural issue, not a regulatory problem. Like aboriginal people in Canada – who in full recognition of their cultural difference have set about reclaiming their sense of community from the Department of Indian Affairs; or like local communities in the Southern hemisphere who struggle against the edicts of international financial institutions; Atlantic coastal communities can set about initiating a 'sea claim' to reclaim control of nearby natural communities on which they depend. In contrast to the regulatory basis of Canada's declaration of the 200-mile limit coastal communities require a social and cultural basis for conservation of community which can begin to challenge the forces of depletion and dependence.

References

Angel, J.R., Burke, D.L., O'Boyle, R.N., Peacock, F.G., Sinclair, M. and Zwanenburg, K.C.T. (1994) *Report of the Workshop of Scotia-Fundy Groundfish Management from 1977 to 1993*, Can. Tech. Rep. Fish. Aquat. Sci. 1979.

Barrett, L.G. (1984) 'Capital and the state in Atlantic Canada: the structural context of fisheries policy between 1939 and 1977', in C. Lamson and A. Hanson (eds) *Atlantic Fisheries and Coastal Communities: Fisheries Decision-Making Case Studies*, Halifax: Dalhousie Ocean Studies Programme.

Clark, Colin (1990) *Mathematical Bioeconomics*, New York: Wiley.

Fisheries and Marine Service (1976) *Policy for Canada's Commercial Fisheries*, Ottawa: Department of the Environment.

Gordon, H.S. (1954) 'The economic theory of the common property resource: the fishery', *Journal of Political Economy* 62: 124–42.

Hache, J.E. (1989) *Scotia-Fundy Groundfish Task Force Report*, Ottawa: Minister of Supply and Services.

Hardin, G. and Baden, J. (1977) *Managing the Commons*, San Fransisco: Freeman.

Harris, Leslie (1989) *Independent Review of the State of the Northern Cod Stock*, Prepared for the Department of Fisheries and Oceans, May 15.

Innis, Harold (1954) *The Cod Fishery: The History of an International Economy*, Toronto: University of Toronto Press.

Kirby, Michael (1983) *Navigating Troubled Waters: Report for the Task Force on the Atlantic Fisheries*, Ottawa: Minister of Supply and Services.

Law of the Sea Discussion Paper, (1974) Ottawa: Department of External Affairs.

McCay, B. and Acheson, J. (1987) *The Question of the Commons*, Tuscon: University of Arizona Press.

McEvoy, Arthur (1987) 'Toward an interactive theory of nature and culture: ecology, production, and cognition in the California fishing industry', *Environmental Review* 11, 4: 289–305.

Mitchell, Bruce (1979) *Geography and Resource Analysis*, New York: Longman.

Mowat, Farley (1990) Quoted in G. Wheeler, 'Hibernia blues', *Now Magazine* 10, 4.

Neis, Barbara (1993) 'Flexible specialization: what's that got to do with the price of fish?', in Jane Jenson, Rianne Mahon, and Manfred Bienefeld (eds) *Production, Space, Identity: Political Economy Faces the 21st Century*, Toronto: Canadian Scholars Press Inc., pp. 83–110.

Pitcher, T.J. and Hart, P. (1982) *Fisheries Ecology*, London: Croom Helm.

Polanyi, Karl (1982) *Primitive, Archaic, and Modern Economies*, ed. George Dalton, New York: Doubleday Anchor.

Taussig, Michael (1980) *The Devil and Commodity Fetishism in South America*, Chapel Hill, NC: University of North Carolina Press.

World Commission on Environment and Development (1987) *Our Common Future*, New York: Oxford University Press.

World Conservation Union, United Nations Environment Programme, and World Wide Fund for Nature (1991) *Caring for the Earth: A Strategy for Sustainable Living*, Gland, Switzerland.

6

MATERIAL CYCLE AND SUSTAINABLE ECONOMY

Takeshi Murota

Introduction

Sustainable development has been frequently discussed in recent years in the context of global environmental problems. However, substantive conditions for sustainability have not been analysed in a precise manner. While it is easy to construct a formal, imaginary model[1] of a sustainable economy, one might also be able to present a counterargument that sustainability is impossible given the universal tendency of matter/energy degradation according to the entropy law.

Posed this way, the question of sustainability resembles the one of the recycling of diffused materials or of dissipated matter, which was a focal point of controversy between Kenneth Boulding and Nicholas Georgescu-Roegen. In his widely known article, 'The Economics of the Coming Spaceship Earth', Boulding (1968:279) asserted that 'there is, fortunately, no law of increasing material entropy, as there is in the corresponding case of energy, as it is quite possible to concentrate diffused materials if energy inputs are allowed'. Georgescu-Roegen (1976, 1980) severely criticized this position on the ground that, like energy, matter is subject to the entropy law and moves in a one-way direction of dissipation. He contends that, if the once-dissipated matter ever reassembles itself into its original form such a process will take an infinite amount of time so that its recycling is practically impossible, however abundant the supply of available energy.

In response to such criticisms, Boulding was obliged to make a concession. In his later work (Boulding 1981:164–5), he writes, 'Concentrating the diffuse, however, takes energy, and it may take a great deal of energy. We cannot assume too easily that there is an ultimate solution in recycling, except perhaps at a lower level of input than we have now'. As yet, the fact remains that certain substances are showing long-lasting, cyclic behaviours in renewable fashions. The water cycle and the convection of air in the atmosphere are the typical examples.

At this point, it is worthwhile to recollect that Quesnay (1764), one of the founders of modern economics, recognized that an economy could make sense as such if and only if human economic activities repeated themselves as circulations (or cycles), but not as finite processes. Most economic models since Quesnay have explicitly or implicitly retained a cyclic nature. For example, money circulates among economic sectors and the manner of its circulation affects the direction the economy takes. In addition, Quesnay was quite aware that each economic sector, especially the agrarian sector, was embedded in the environment from which resources were taken.

However, neither he nor his successors were sufficiently aware that production as well as consumption are waste generating processes. We must therefore find routes through which wastes can go directly back to a production sector to become its new, raw materials; or if this is impossible or insignificant for some reason, indirectly back to the environment at large without causing its destruction. A sustainable economy can not be realized only by human endeavours of direct recycling and of resource/energy conservation. Instead the issue will have to be settled on the whole ground of the material cycle.

Water cycle which makes the earth 'alive'

The earth, as a system, is open in terms of energy, but practically closed in terms of matter. Countless organic and inorganic activities that have been repeatedly taking place in this system, have recently been threatened by global environmental problems. Given that all activities are entropy-increasing processes,[2] there must be some mechanism of surplus entropy disposal. Generally speaking, a disequilibrated but steady system is characterized by the entropy balance:

$$S_{in} + S_{gen} = S_{out} \qquad (1)$$

where S_{in} is the incoming entropy to the system, S_{gen} is the entropy generated inside, and S_{out} is outgoing entropy, all in a given period of time. As long as the earth maintains its open nature, this basic equation (1) must be satisfied.

Typically, however, we have been offered a different, mysterious interpretation of the earth. It is often said that the negative entropy of solar energy cancels out the surplus entropy. But the solar energy once trapped in the earth's atmosphere gets thermalized and its entropy level increases. At this point, we need to recognize the significance of the water cycle, which – together with the convection of air – is the fundamental component of the material cycle of the earth.

The earth's surface receives the energy from the sun at relatively high temperatures averaging 15°C (288 K, where K stands for Kelvin), causing the air to become warmer and water to evaporate from the earth's surface and to transpire from plants' leaves. Water vapour and warmed air, which are lighter than the surrounding air, obtain buoyancy and ascend to the sky. At higher altitudes, the pressure decreases. Then, the formation of clouds and cold air result from adiabatic expansion and the cooling of the water vapour and warm air. At this instant, the heat carried by vapour and air radiates towards outer space with relatively low temperatures averaging -18° C (255 K). Given the solar constant; 257 kcal/cm^2/yr, it is known that some 30 per cent of it, approximately 77 kcal/cm^2/yr, is taken up by the water cycle and the convection of air.[3] This means that the earth sends 308 cal/K of entropy for each cm^2 towards outer space per annum while it receives 267 cal/K of entropy from outside.

The above consideration can be restated in the following way. Let S_{in} and S_{out} denote the incoming and outgoing entropies for each cm^2 per annum. Then, we have

$$S_{in} = 267 \quad (cal/K) \quad and \quad S_{out} = 308 \quad (cal/K) \qquad (2)$$

$$S_{in} + S_{gen} = S_{out} \qquad (3)$$

where the equation (3) is nothing but the restatement of (1) above. From these equations, we obtain $S_{gen} = 41$ (cal/K) per cm^2 of the earth surface per annum. This amount of S_{gen} accounts for the entropy generated in the earth system through various organic and inorganic activities.

In other words, the radiation of heat at low temperatures to the outer space allows the surplus entropy given as S_{gen} to leave the system together with that heat. The room stemming from the difference $(S_{out}-S_{in})$ between the incoming and outgoing entropies, has been the source of maintaining the earth as a living system by itself (i.e. 'living', in a broad sense.)

From the sky, water (rain) and cold air, which are relatively heavier than the surrounding air, come back down to the earth's surface, thus ending one cycle of water and air. It can be shown that the water cycle contributes to about 80 per cent of S_{out} and the convection of air accounts for the remaining 20 per cent (see Figure 6.1).[4]

Coming back to the thesis of Georgescu-Roegen, matter certainly dissipates, and water, which is also matter, does so to a gaseous form. But it returns to its original liquid form after disposing of surplus entropy. The water cycle occurs not only due to the law of increasing entropy but due also to the law of universal gravity coupled with the phase change of water. As we will see later, other kinds of matter also show cyclic behaviours without contradicting the law of entropy. In theorizing about a sustainable economy, total negation of the importance of natural cycles is conceptually dangerous while total reliance on the recycling of wastes can be practically unhelpful in some cases. This is particularly true for mechanistic types of recycling which is done without the long-term help of natural forces, e.g. the recycling of plastic bottles.

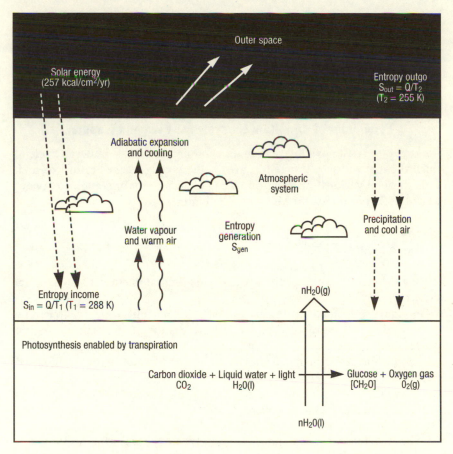

Figure 6.1 Entropy disposal of the earth system and the role of transpiration of water in photosynthesis

Note: Q = 77kcal/cm^2/yr. Condition for a steady system: $S_{in} + S_{gen} = S_{out}$; [CH$_2$O] = (1/6)C$_6H_{12}O_6$; n = 23 for the monochromatic light of wave length = 0.65 micron (Net entropy increase = 784 cal/K/molCO$_2$; n = 521 for the sunlight (net entropy increase = 16,565 cal/K/molCO$_2$. [(l) and (g) refer to liquid and gas respectively.]

I will now discuss the tendency of available matter to be lost from lands down to the oceans as a result of the law of gravity. Since this could potentially result in the degradation and impoverishment of the environment, we face a question as to how the environment itself is countering this tendency and how human beings can contribute to this process. No object on earth, whether it is organic or inorganic, can escape from the traction force proportional to its mass due to the universal law of gravity. This seems to imply that all kinds of nutrients eventually descend from high lands to the bottoms of the ocean. If, however, this process was uni-directional, lands would lose all their nutrients to become completely barren and the oceans would receive them to become overly eutrophicated. In such a world, human economy could not exist, nor could other living activities continue on the lands. Since this is obviously not the case, there must be some mechanism by which the movement of nutrients occurs in the opposite direction.

Economics of upwelling ecosystems: Peru and Canada

The key to the sustainability of human economy lies in the material cycle in which the matters once trapped in low lands or deep oceans return to high lands through various routes. From the ecological–economic point of view, the material cycle (hereafter MC) is divided into:

(1) non-human MC;
(2) economy-driven MC.

Leaving the consideration of the MC(2) aside for a moment, let us first characterize the MC(1).

One may be tempted to regard the MC(1) as a phenomenon that only occurs over a long lapse of time, i.e., of thousands of thousand years. Of course, such a long-term cycle is important. But the main concerns in this chapter are the cycles of much shorter time, i.e., the ones within a hundred years or so. Let us first consider the phosphorus cycle. Phosphorus is one of the essential elements for all living organisms. Charton (1988: 217) tells us about its circulation in the biosphere:

> Through the erosion of phosphate rocks, or the use of phosphate fertilizer, phosphorus enters the soil and is taken up by plants, which are eaten by animals. The dead animals or plants are then decomposed by bacteria, and the released phosphorus salts, re-enters the soil or is carried into the sea by runoff water. New phosphate rock is eventually formed from marine sediments.

According to such an explanation, land plants receive phosphorus mostly from phosphate fertilizers and dead land animals/plants in the short-run while, in the long run, it is mainly supplied through the weathering of the rocks made of marine sediments. It seems that something is missing here in an intermediate perspective of a few decades or so.

Charton (1988: 292), however, seems to hint at an answer when she explains the phenomenon of upwelling which is 'the rise of subsurface cold, dense water'. She continues:

> The deep water coming up does so to replace wind-displaced surface water . . . . If the deep water is nutrient-rich, the result is a bloom of

plankton at the surface. This in turn feeds a large fish and bird population, as evidenced on Antarctica and along the Chile–Peru coast of South America.

Martinez-Alier (1987, 1991) mentions the political economy of guano, the dung of seabirds, in Peru. He describes the colonial policy of European countries which massively shipped guano to be used as fertilizer from Peru to their lands without much return to the Peruvians. We attempt to go a bit further into its ecological economy from the viewpoint of the MC.

The driving force towards the formation of Peruvian guano is the upwelling[5] occurring in the Peru coastal current. The following causal chain is found:

upwelling → nutrients from the deep part of the ocean rising → phytoplankton (and then zooplankton) growth → fish propagation → birds propagation → massive excreta drops on coastal areas and on islands → accumulation of bird droppings under the dry weather.

This shows the large potential of non-human MC. (For an illustration of this point, see Figure 6.2.) However, the guano did not contribute to the enrichment of the economic cycle of Peru. Instead, European countries, especially England, imported a great amount of guano from Peru mostly in 1840–80.

Marx (1867) thought the reason for such import was that English fields had been exhausted of fertility.[6] But Duncan (1989: 95–6) negates this view. He writes that; 'the farmers added guano enthusiastically in order to INCREASE the absolute quantity of nutrients in their soil, not to compensate for a supposed deprivation'. Regardless of the reason, the massive application of guano was the beginning of modern agriculture's dependency on external fertilizers.

With the exhaustion of high-quality guano[7] in Peru, it was discovered that there were phosphate rocks on Nauru and Ocean Islands in the Pacific Oceans as well as on Christmas Island in the Indian Ocean. As Williams and Macdonald (1985) describe in detail, Britain then started to establish rights of extraction of the rocks and imported them en mass as raw material for phosphate fertilizer in the early twentieth century. In Peru, the government realized, by then, that the domestic agriculture badly needed the guano, and set up the Guano Administration Company in 1909. With demands for guano increasing, the guano administration decided to end its exports in 1928, and adopted a policy of seabirds conservation. Prior to this, layers of accumulated guano had been extracted for exports as if being mined (like coal or iron ore). As the new policy was implemented, however, the guano became a subject of harvest as a crop. Each guano-bearing island along the Peruvian coast has then turned out to be a place 'visited in rotation every few years after the birds have laid down a new guano layer several inches thick' (Levin 1960: 112).

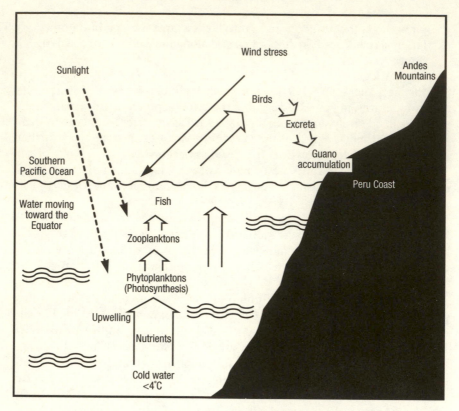

Figure 6.2 Upwelling of Peru coastal current and the formation of guano

It is worthwhile noting that an upwelling can also occur fairly deeply inside a continent. As a special example of upwelling ecosystems, let us consider the St Lawrence River, which originates in the Great Lakes in the US–Canadian border area and empties its water into the Gulf of St Lawrence. Jacques Cartier (1491–1557), the Breton explorer, made three voyages to North America under the commission of Francis I. During his second voyage 1535–6, he stayed on the south shore of the St Lawrence, opposite the mouth of the Saguenay River and waited for a favorable tide condition before continuing upstream. On 3 September 1535, he observed:

> we made sail and got under way in order to push forward, and discovered a species of fish, which none of us had ever seen or heard of. This fish is as large as a porpoise but has no fin. It is very similar to a greyhound about the body and head and is as white as snow, without a spot upon it. Of these there are a very large number in this river,

between the salt and fresh water. The people of the country call them *Adhothuys* and told us that they are very good to eat.

(Cartier 1545: 117)

This was one of the places the Basque whalers frequented in the sixteenth century as is shown in Proulx (1993). As Innis (1940) investigated in detail, the cod fishery attracted many fishermen of Europe to the eastern coasts of Canada. Similarly, whaling formed another international economy there. The whale mentioned above is beluga. The town developed along this part of the St Lawrence River is Tadoussac.

Near this town, the riverbed suddenly drops from a depth of 25 to 300 meters. It is a meeting place of cold sea water coming up from the Gulf of St Lawrence at the time of high tide, relatively warm fresh water coming down from the Great Lakes, and cold fresh water of the Saguenay River coming down from the wooded areas of Northern Quebec. As a result of both this topography and these thermal difference in waters, strong upwelling has been occurring in this hydrosphere to push nutrients from the riverbed upward (Luoma 1989). This provides feed for numerous fish, and they in turn feed many whales, not only beluga but much bigger whales such as the blue whale. (For an illustration of this point, see Figure 6.3.) An upwelling hydrosphere is the space of affluence. Unfortunately, many belugas have been dying recently. It is suspected that toxic chemicals discharged into the Great Lakes may be one of its causes as is reported by Bull (1993). From a viewpoint of political ecology, it has to be understood that the upwelling areas are of prime importance to sustain the material cycle.[8] Oceanographers classify the upwelling into three categories (1) coastal upwelling, (2) equatorial upwelling, and (3) esturial upwelling, the sum of whose areas consists of only 0.1 per cent of the total ocean surface of the earth. Yet, such a small sum of upwelling areas is estimated to contribute to nearly 50 per cent of the total fish production in the world's oceans! Dividing the oceans into (a) oceanic, (b) coastal (but not upwelling area), and (c) upwelling, the oceanic occupies 90 per cent, and the coastal 9.9 per cent of their total surface areas. In contrast to such shares, the fish production in (a), (b), and (c) are estimated to be 0.2, 12, and 12 (10^6 tonnes carbon per year), respectively (see Lalli and Parsons 1993, p. 120, table 5.1).

These comparative figures illuminate the enormously high productivity of the upwelling ecosystems. The sea along the Peru coast is the world's strongest example of coastal upwelling. The mouth of the St Lawrence river is one of the esturial upwelling areas. Some of the many small islands along the equator are endowed with guano of various degrees of quality as a fertilizer thanks to the equatorial (open ocean) upwellings surrounding them. Skaggs (1994) vividly describes the guano-seeking history of the territorial expansion of the United States, which was a late comer in the world scene of the guano trade in the early nineteenth and twentieth centuries.

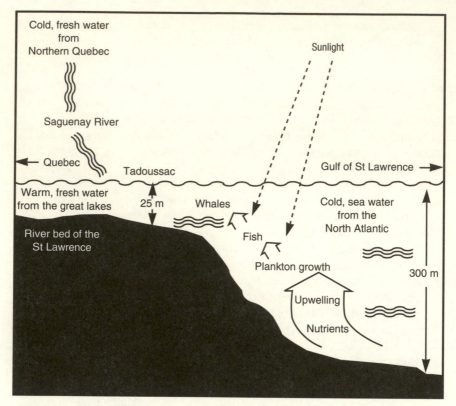

Figure 6.3 Upwelling and whales in the St Lawrence River

The Edo (early Tokyo) model of economy-driven material cycle

The economy-driven MC is a new concept and needs to be clarified with empirical support. For this, one can trace out a model of human-driven MC from the history of Japan.[9] Edo (present-day Tokyo) had been chosen as the capital city of Japan by the Tokugawa shogunate family in 1603. Its population was some twenty thousands in the first several decades, but increased to as many as one million by the middle of the Edo era (1603–1867). The then world's largest city was quite prosperous both economically and culturally, despite the complete lack of modern technology. The key to understanding the miraculous achievements lies in the fact that the economic activities were performed in such a cyclic way as to prompt the MC among sea, city, and suburbs.

Within 100–200 km to the north and to the west of Edo there were heavily wooded mountains and there was a bay on its south-eastern front. Its north-eastern lands were mostly marshes, while its western lands were *daichi* (terraced land) and hills, scarce in water. The bay, then sometimes called *kantokai* (present-day Tokyo Bay), was only narrowly connected with the Pacific Ocean. Into this half-closed sea, nutrient-rich rivers flowed down from the mountains, as did exhaust waters from the active city. It was then so productive that it raised a large population of sea plants and animals including shellfish and seaweed.

If the bay had remained untouched, then it would have become overly eutrophicated. Nonetheless, the historical facts show the coexistence of clean sea water and biologically high productivity. The reason of this coexistence lay in the fishery. The people of Edo developed the habit of eating various kinds of fresh fish as well as shellfish and seaweeds harvested in the bay. To meet their demands, fishermen were busy bringing sea-based food to land against the law of gravity.

In addition, there was another important activity which also worked against gravity. The farmers of suburban villages regularly collected the excreta of the city populace as precious fertilizer for their agricultural lands. Though the usefulness of human excreta as fertilizer had been occasionally recognized among some farmers in Japan during the Middle Ages, full systematic utilization of it started in the Edo era. Each of the warlord families and citizens of Edo made annual or longer contracts with suburban farmers to take the accumulations out of each toilet on a regular basis and to bring them uphill to the farmland. In return, they received a certain combination of fresh vegetables in many cases, or a grain or cash in other cases. This barter exchange performed the key role both of hygienically cleaning the world's largest city without a sewage system and nourishing the suburban soils, which had not been fertile enough before the Edo era. (Figure 6.4 gives an illustration of the Edo model described here.)

It is worthwhile noting that the German chemist Liebig (1885) stated:

> The urine contains the soluble, the solid excreta the insoluble, constituents of the soil derived from the crops used as food, and reaped from the soil. It is clear that by adding manure, or liquid and solid excreta, to the soil, that soil recovers those constituents which have been removed from it in the crops.
>
> (cited from Pomeroy 1974: 15)

For a long time before this statement, however, the farmers in Japan had been practising the return of human excreta to the soil not in an accidental but in a systematic, economic way.

Of course, the lives of the Edo people were not supported solely by the bay's sea organisms and suburban vegetables, wheat and barley. Large quantities of rice came in from the Kanto Plain and far more northern areas. In return, Edo sent a variety of commercially manufactured goods to those areas. With regard to suburban agriculture, the role of dried fish, in particular,

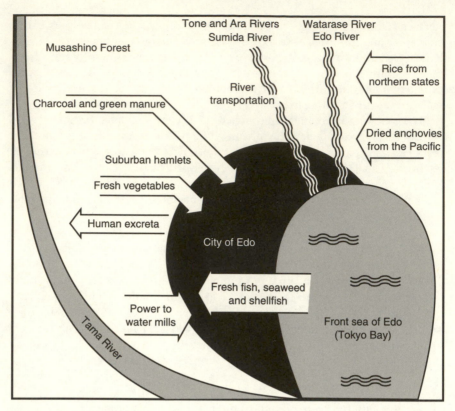

Figure 6.4 Edo model of economy-driven material cycle

of dried anchovy was also important. A great catch of anchovy was made mostly outside of the bay, east off the Boso Peninsula. Some of the catch was eaten by people, but an even larger amount went through a process of drying and heating for fats to be extracted, which became fertilizers in uphill areas.[10]

Forest attracts fish or fish nourishes forest?

In the Edo era, some people in Japan started to notice that forests along seashores or rivers attracted fish. It was considered that a forest could benefit fish by providing shadow as shelter, nutrients, and so on. This consideration remained in the minds of people living near waterfronts or forests after the Meiji Restoration (1868). When the first forest act was passed at the beginning of the twentieth century, it contained the article ordering the conservation of *uo-tsuki-rin*, which literally meant 'fish attaching forest'. This article is still valid in the present-day forest act of Japan.

With regard to this *uo-tsuki-rin*, Shibatani (1992), the Japanese biologist,

130

raises an interesting question. He thinks that it may be the fish that helps forests to grow rather than forests providing fish with comfortable spaces. This hypothesis comes from his research on the forests in Maritime Territories of Eastern Siberia, specifically along the Ussuri River, a tributary of the Amur River. This area is subject to cold temperatures and receives very little sunshine, but there has been forest growth for a long period of time. Nutrients must have been carried from somewhere. But as there are no significant mountains in the upstream areas, the nutrients must have come from downstream, or more exactly, from the Northern Pacific, and the salmon as well as some other kinds of fish are likely to play a significant role as their carriers (see Figure 6.5).

His hypothesis on the area along the Ussuri River may be generalized to many areas along the Amur River. This river is 4,440 km in length (including the Argun River) and abounds in fish. With monsoonal rains in summer and only a little snow in winter, its water level shows large, seasonal fluctuations. The highest and lowest levels differ as much as 10–15 m in its upper and

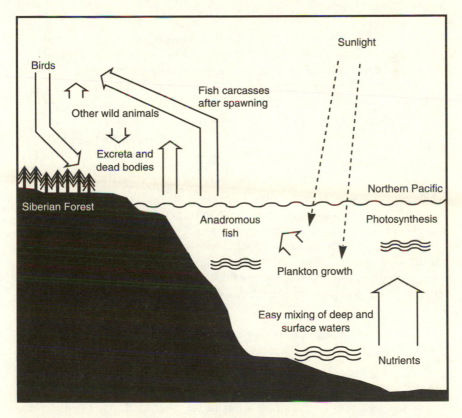

Figure 6.5 Anadromous fish and the Siberian Forest

middle courses and by 6–7 m in its lower one.[11] About one hundred species of fish live in the lower course and sixty in the upper course. According to *Britannica Macropaedis* (1992, vol 1: 211), this river is very peculiar in that 'the large number of fish species' develop 'in the sea and river' to escape 'exposure to the sharp changes in water level that occur in the river during the summer'. Along the river, there are many crows, bears and other wildlife. Bigger animals first catch and eat salmon while left-overs are then taken care of by smaller animals. The excreta deposited on the soil becomes nutrients for forest growth. An American study of a similar nature is found in Cederholm *et al.* (1989).

In the case of Peruvian guano, it had only kept accumulating on the coastal rocks without nourishing forests inside the South American Continent. This shows the rich potential of an upwelling ecosystem, but no more than that. In contrast to this, the salmon growing up in the Northern Pacific go deep inside the continent of north-east Asia and enrich forest soils there.

In relation to this, we find another of Jaques Cartier's observations very interesting. During the already mentioned second voyage to the present-day Canada, he was near the mouth of Saguenay River on 1 September 1535, and saw the following scenery:

> This river issues from between lofty mountains of bare rock with but little soil upon them. Notwithstanding this, a large number of various kinds of trees grow upon this naked rock as in good soil, in such sort that we saw there a tree tall enough to make a mast for a ship of thirty tons, which was as green as possible, and grew out of the rock without any trace of earth about it.
>
> (Cartier 1545: 114)

This could only be explained by the propagation of birds in the area which fed on a great number of fish in the upwelling water of the St Lawrence. Cartier did not write about the kinds of birds in that particular area, but listed their names which he saw in his upstream trip from the 19 to the 28 September. Namely, he saw cranes, swans, bustards, geese, ducks, larks, pheasants, partridges, blackbirds, thrushes, turtledoves, goldfinches, canaries, linnets, nightingales, sparrows and other birds 'in great numbers'. It is a possibility that the droppings of a vast number of different kinds of birds had provided nutrients to soil-less rocks to nourish trees in the area of Tadoussac.

Tasks of political ecology to activate material cycle

From what we have discussed thus far on several kinds of material cycles, what are the implications for policies of sustainability? To consider this problem of political ecology, let us first go back to the issue of human excreta. If we take the present situation of Japan as an example, the development of sewers coupled with wide use of flush toilets takes excreta of urban dwellers into wastewater treatment systems, many of which allow storm water to flow in together. Most of the wastewater treatment plants there adopt the activated sludge process, where the activated sludge is a partially decomposed brown mass with earthy smell taken out of the liquid flow of sewage. The activated sludge process is one of the sewage treatment processes that has been widely adopted in the contemporary cities of the world. The process involves putting the activated sludge in sewage water aeration tanks, where organic matter quickly undergoes aerobic decomposition by micro-organisms. The remaining waste sludge and liquid are then separated in a settling tank. The liquid, after treatment by chlorination or oxidation, is led to a natural aquifer (usually a river) next to the sewage treatment plant. But there remain at least two problems. First, nitrogen and phosphorus cannot be completely removed from the processed water so that the discharged water from the plants often causes over-eutrophication of rivers and seas. Second, a voluminous amount of dead sludge accumulates in the plants and its treatment becomes difficult, requiring the massive input of energy. Then, one cannot say that this method is the best. The use of oxidation ponds is known to be a good alternative, but it requires a vast area which is not affordable under extremely high land prices in urban and suburban areas in contemporary Japan.

The modern history of western countries shows that sewers were first introduced to the city of London as a device of quickly collecting storm water on the streets and discharging it into nearby waterways. This kind of sewer then spread to Paris, New York, Boston, and so on. A notorious problem, however, occurred in London when its citizens were obliged to discharge their night soils into such sewers due to the prohibition of the uses of cesspits in the late 1840s. Many of those sewers emptied their sewage into the Thames so that the river itself became an open sewer, or more bluntly, an open cesspool. The Thames, where even the salmon had come up until 1800, started to smell badly. In the summer of 1858, it reached such a stage that:

> the climax arrived in what came to be called the GREAT STINK when the windows of the House of Parliament had to be draped with curtains soaked in chloride of lime to mitigate the disgusting smell. Tons of chalk lime, chloride of lime and carbonic acid were tipped into the river with little effect. . . .
>
> (Weinreb and Hibbert 1984: 237)

Similar problems, though less in extent, were experienced in other cities in Europe and the United States. In response, not only were sewers extended to suburban areas but wastewater treatment technologies were also developed. The trickling filter and the activated sludge process, among others, were developed and came to be commonly used in big cities in the world. Modern sewers in Tokyo and other major cities in Japan had also been started as public works for storm water disposal. But they too allowed the intake of human excretion after a while. Though the activated sludge process is widely adopted, the two problems mentioned above remain unsolved.

One positive alternative to the already existing technologies is the soil purification method developed in Japan. This method relies on the soil microbes, earth worms, and many other small living creatures actively living in shallow parts of topsoil, less than one metre deep. Wastewater is led, first into a settlement tank covered by a layer of topsoil, and then into loosely connected ceramic pipes which are horizontally set under the ground, 50 or 60 cm below the surface. Wastewater slowly flows out from the open connection parts of the pipes and leaks into the topsoil full of the above mentioned creatures and the roots of plants. Since water has the property of capillary siphoning movement, which forces it to spread out horizontally in soil with numerous, small open spaces, it will not easily sink down to the ground water level. It is advised, however, that a waterproof sheet is placed at the depth of about one metre below the pipes in order to prevent its occasional, direct sinking. As a means of wastewater disposal, land application is currently very popular in the United States because of the Clean Water Act. While the method of soil purification appears to be similar, it is quite different from the traditional land application in that it fully takes advantage of soil plants and animals living in shallow parts of topsoil.[12] Since this method had faced opposition from government officials and civil engineers, the speed of its propagation has been slow. But more people are now paying attention to it. In Japan, the number of municipalities which adopt this method is increasing.

Coming back to the question of the fish–forest relationship, the tradition of *uo-tsuki-rin* conservation is now reviving in Hokkaido, the large, northern island of Japan. The women's section of the Hokkaido Association of Fishery Cooperatives recently launched a campaign called 'Plant Trees to Increase Fish'. A fishery cooperative is a fishermen's hamlet-based legal organization authorised to exercise an exclusive right to fish in a specified sea area, with the implicit obligation to protect marine lives in a sustainable fashion. Behind the rise of this movement, there is a fact that people have recently faced the decline of catches in the coastal lines in Hokkaido. The reason for this decline cannot be attributed to a single cause. One can list many possibilities. But one thing which is certain is that the forest conditions in both inland and coastal areas have deteriorated through erosion and other factors due to over logging in the past few decades. To counter this situation, women members of fishery cooperatives have decided to manually plant trees on coasts, sometimes with help from the forestry cooperatives. Inspired by these efforts in Hokkaido, the process of reevaluating the implications of *uo-tsuki-rin* is also under way in other parts of Japan.

Thus far, we have listed several measures of active response to environmental problems. This does not mean that passive responses are not important. The reduction in the production of polluting materials would be such a passive response. The production of toxic chemicals and the handling of radioactive substances should be minimized in order for them not to enter the material cycle in general and the food chain in particular. Institutional banning of them may be mandatory in some cases and the levying of heavy taxes on them may be appropriate in other cases. Dam construction must be stopped or truly effective fish paths must be devised and implemented. More thoughtful construction of fish paths not only for river fishery but for forest ecosystems is required.

Conclusion

Economic cycles in the contemporary age have largely functioned to destroy the material cycle. What is needed now is to embed the economic cycles inside the material cycle. This is different from the internalization of external diseconomy. Such an internalization is only an attempt to minimize the level of environmental disruption. Beyond this level, political ecology has to go further to let the economic cycles prompt and enrich the material cycle by being its active partner.

With regard to the question of wastes, the total negation of the possibility of recycling is an exaggeration of the truth of material diffusion. At the same time, excessive emphasis on the human endeavour of recycling may end up with the self-deception of anthropocentrism. Urgent tasks are to reduce or to stop production of chemical and radioactive toxins to prevent them from entering the material cycles. Recycling becomes meaningful if it is understood to include help from birds, fish and so on.

These are the conditions for sustainability. Policies for sustainable development have only been mentioned in the context of Japan in this paper. Much more remains to be formulated in the light of the variety of creative experiences in many regions and nations in the world.

Notes

1 The concepts of 'substantive' and 'formal' here are intended to correspond to the notions of Karl Polanyi (1977) who differentiated these two meanings of 'economic'.

2 The entropy S associated with the amount of heat Q(calorie) under the absolute temperature T (Kelvin) is defined by $S = Q/T$, where T is approximately equal to the Celsius temperature degree plus 273. The Second Law of Thermodynamics states that the transfer of heat occurs only from a hot body to a cold body, not the other way around unless there is an outside intervention. Suppose that a system isolated from the outer environment is divided into two subsystems, one with high temperature T_1 and another with low temperature T_2. Consider, then, the case where a small amount of heat s moves between these two subsystems, small to the extent that it does not noticeably change their temperatures. According to the Second Law, such a heat transfer occurs from the subsystem with T_1 to the one with T_2 to result in the situation that the former loses heat s which the latter gains. The former thus loses the entropy s/T_1 and the latter gains the entropy s/T_2, so that

the system as a whole incurs the entropy change of $-(s/T_1) + (s/T_2)$, which is positive since $T_1 > T_2 > 0$ and $s > 0$ in this context. In other words, the entropy in an isolated system increases if some thermal change occurs in it (or it stays constant if nothing changes). Hence, the Second Law is alternatively called the law of increasing entropy.

3 1 kcal = 1,000 cal. In natural sciences, it is now common to use the joule as a unit of measurement of energy. The conversion ratio of calories into joules is: 1 cal = 4.1814 joule.

4 Of course the Gaia Hypothesis presented by James Lovelock (1979) also recognizes the earth as a living system by itself. But it lacks an entropy-theoretic reasoning and misses the vital role of the water cycle which is essentially of a non-biological nature. Katsuki (1985) and Tsuchida and Murota (1987) show by quantitatively computed results that the photosynthesis of plants is also an entropy increasing process and that the surplus entropy generated within the plants' bodies is carried away from them mostly by the transpiration of water. Figure 6.1 gives an illustration of this point. Due to the traditional view that sunshine is the supplier of low entropy to plants, the highest propagation of plants would occur in tropical deserts with plenty of sunshine, which utterly contradicts reality and ignores the role of water in the plant cycle.

5 Its detailed observation was first made in 1976–7 and its result is shown in Brink et al. (1978).

6 Marx (1967 English edition: 239) stated the following,

> Apart from the working class movement that daily grew more threatening, the limiting of factory labour was dictated by the same necessity which spread guano over the English fields. The same blind eagerness for plunder that in one case exhausted the soil, had, in the other, torn up by the roots of living force of the nation.

7 In this case, 'high quality' means rich in nitrogen and phosphorus contents.

8 The density of pure water is greatest at $4°C$ while that of sea water is greatest at slightly lower temperatures. This means that the cold water between $4°C$ and nearly $0°C$ tends to be at the bottom of an ocean while ice and warmer water with lighter densities locate themselves nearer the surface. It is a general tendency in a tropical ocean that, surface water receiving a great amount of sunshine remains very warm while deep water remains cold so that their vertical mixture is unlikely to occur frequently, unless powerful winds are applied to the surface water for it to be moved away. In contrast, in an ocean of high latitudes surface water is also cold, thus there is not much difference in density between surface and deep waters. In such a hydrosphere, their vertical mix easily occurs and the nutrients once trapped in the bottom water have greater chances to come up toward the surface. This is the main reason why world-wide large scale catches of fish have been observed in dark, cold seas, but not in shiny, tropical oceans.

9 While its rough characterization was given in Tananoi et al. (1984), I shall go a bit further than that here.

10 In passing, it may be worthwhile to note that bats, as avian mammals, are performing a behaviour on inland terrains that is similar to the one of sea birds along coastal lines in terms of their excreta. As far as the experience in Japan is concerned, their excreta accumulated in some of limestone caves and nearby farmers used to scratch those out to utilize them as a fertilizer in their cultivated lands (Iwasaki 1992). Thomson (1964: 348) refers to the same tradition in the

south-east Asian countries such as Burma (present-day Myammer), Thailand, Malaysia and Indonesia.

11 Such differences in water levels are shown in the *Great Soviet Encyclopedia* (1973, vol.1: 364).

12 For the details of the soil purification method of wastewater treatment, see, for example, Yahata (1981).

References

Boulding, Kenneth (1968) *Beyond Economics: Essays on Society, Religion, and Ethics*, Ann Arbor, MI: The University of Michigan Press.

Boulding, Kenneth (1981) *Evolutionary Economics*, Beverly Hills: Sage Publications.

Brink, Kenneth H., Allen, J.S. and Smith, Robert L. (1978) 'A study of low frequency fluctuations near the Peru coast', *Journal of Physical Oceanography* 8: 1025–41.

Britannica Macropaedia (1992) 1, 14. Chicago: Encyclopaedia Britannica.

Bull, Rob (1993) 'Belugas in peril', *The Toronto Sun*, Monday 18 October: News 35.

Cartier, Jacques (1924) 'The second voyage 1535–1536', *The Voyages of Jacques Cartier*, 1545; trans. H.P. Biggar, Ottawa: F.A. Acland.

Cederholm, C.J. *et al.* (1989) 'Fate of Coho salmon carcasses in spawning streams', *Canadian Journal of Fisheries and Aquatic Sciences* 46: 1347–55.

Charton, Barbara (ed.) (1988) *The Facts on File Dictionary of Marine Science*, New York: Facts on File Publications.

Devai, I., Felfoldy, L., Witter, I. and Plosz, S. (1988) 'Detection of phosphine: new aspects of the phosphorus cycle in the hydrosphere', *Nature* 333, 6171: 343–5.

Duncan, Colin (1989) 'The centrality of agriculture: between humankind and the rest of nature', unpublished Ph.D. Thesis, York University.

Georgescu-Roegen, N. (1976) *Energy and Economic Myths: Institutional and Analytical Economic Essays*, New York: Pergamon Press.

—— (1980) 'Matter: a resource ignored by thermodynamics', in *Entropy and the Economic Process: A Seminar*, Ottawa: Science Council of Canada.

Great Soviet Encyclopaedia: Volume 1 (1973) London: Macmillan.

Innis, Harold A. (1940) *The Cod Fisheries: The History of an International Economy*, Toronto: University of Toronto Press.

Iwasaki, Hiromichi (1992) private communication with the author, Tokyo.

Katsuki, A. (1985) 'Entoropi teki na Shiten kara mita Seibutsu to Chikyu' (Living organisms and the earth: an entropic view), in S. Ono *et al.* (eds) *Entropy*, Tokyo: Asakura Shoten. In Japanese.

Liebig, J. (1974) 'Principles of agricultural chemistry with special reference to the late researches made in England, 1885', in Lawrence R. Pomeroy (ed.) *Cycles of Essential Elements*, Stroudsburg, PA: Dowden, Hutchinson and Ross.

Lalli, Carol M. and Parsons, Timothy R. (1993) Biological Oceanography: An Introduction, Oxford: Pergamon Press.

Lovelock, James (1979) *Gaia: A New Look at Life on Earth*, Oxford: Oxford University Press.

Luoma, Jon R. (1989) 'Doomed canaries of Tadoussac', *Audubon* 91, 2: 92–97.

Martinez-Alier, J. (1987) *Ecological Economics – Energy, Environment and Society*, Oxford: Basil Blackwell.

—— (1991) 'The ecological interpretation of socio-economic history: Andean examples', *Capitalism, Nature, Socialism* 7: 101–119.

Marx, Karl (1967) *Capital; Volume I*, New York: International Publishers, 1st German edn, 1867.

Polanyi, Karl (1977) *The Livelihood of Man*, New York: Academic Press.

Proulx, Jean-Pierre (1993) *Basque Whaling in Labrador in the Sixteenth Century*, Ottawa: Environment Canada.

Quesnay, François (1764) *Quesnay's Tableau Economique*, (3rd edn, 1972 trans. M. Kuczynski and R.L. Meak) London: Macmillan.

Sage, Bryan (1986) *The Arctic and Its Wildlife*, New York: Facts on File Publications.

Siegfried, W.R., Condy, P.R. and Laws, R.M. (eds) (1985) *Antarctic Nutrient Cycles and Food Webs*, Berlin: Springer-Verlag.

Skaggs, Jimmy M. (1994) The Great Guano Rush: Entrepreneurs and American Overseas Expansion, New York: St Martin's Press.

Summerhayes, C.P., Prell, W.L. and Emeis, K.C. (eds) (1992) *Upwelling Systems: Evolution since the Early Miocene*, London: The Geological Society.

Shibatani, A. (1992) 'Sake wa Naze Kawa wo Sojyo Suruno ka (Why do salmon go up rivers)', in *Chuo Koron*. In Japanese.

Tamanoi, Y., Tsuchida, A. and Murota, T. (1984) 'Towards an entropic theory of economy and ecology', *Economie appliquee*, 37, 2: 279–94.

Thomson, A.L. (ed.) (1964) *A New Dictionary of Birds*, London: Thomas Nelson and Sons.

Tsuchida, A. and Murota, T. (1985) 'Fundamentals in the entropy theory of watercycle, ecocycle and human economy', in Tsuchida *et al.*, *Entropy Studies on Ecology and Economy*. A booklet for limited circulation. Tokyo.

Watanabe, Z. (1983a) *Toshi to Noson no Aida: Toshi Kinko Nogyoshi Ron* (Between Cities and Agricultural Villages: A Histriography of Suburban Agriculture), Tokyo: Ronso Sha. In Japanese.

—— (1983b) *Kyodai Toshi Edo ga Washoku wo Tsukutta* (Japanese Cuisines Which the Giant City Edo Invented), Tokyo: Nobunkyo 1989. In Japanese.

Weinreb, B. and Hibbert, C. (eds) (1984) 'Drains and sewers', *The London Encyclopaedia*, London: Macmillan.

Williams, Maslyn and Macdonald, Barrie (1985) *The Phosphateers: A History of the British Phosphate Commissioners and the Christmas Island Phophate Commission*, Carlton, Victoria: Melbourne University Press.

Yahata, T. (1981) 'Wastewater treatment through surface soil', *Do Joker System 58*, Special English Issue: 2–7.

Part 3

PLANETARY MANAGEMENT: TOMORROW'S WORLD

7

WORLD JUSTICE, CARBON CREDIT SCHEMES AND PLANETARY MANAGEMENT AUTHORITIES

Rodney G. Peffer

The present situation and catastrophic climate change

We – the residents of earth at this particular point in history – are facing an interrelated set of global problems that relate not only to the issue of world justice but also to the prospect of maintaining the minimum social and material conditions within which principles of justice can sensibly be said to apply. This is not the prediction of a fringe-dwelling doomsayer but, rather, merely a statement of what has come to be accepted as mainstream thought. For while there has always been human poverty and misery in the world, disease and natural catastrophes, our species has never before been in a position of imminently despoiling the entire planet's natural environment (for both ourselves and almost all other species). And while the danger of nuclear holocaust seems to be at least temporarily off the agenda, there is still the danger in the foreseeable future of the world's civilization buckling beneath the combined pressures of poverty, population growth, environmental degradation, the depletion of natural resources, and (quite possibly) catastrophic climate changes.

For example, besides the direct health problems that hydrocarbons and other air pollutants pose for people, animals and plants a potentially even more important consequence of contemporary air pollution is an intensification of the greenhouse effect. It is the commonly accepted view among scientists who have studied the problem that the increasing carbon emissions (and the emission of other so-called 'greenhouse gases') together with the destruction of the world's tropical rain forests and the possible extinction of the phytoplankton in the world's oceans (which are the two main sources of removing carbon from the atmosphere and recycling oxygen back into it) will result in a run-away greenhouse effect which will lead to a significant increase

141

in the world's average temperature. This, in turn, will transform much presently arable land into desert as well as melt a portion of the polar icecaps, flooding many coastal areas.

Although some scientists point out the possibility that increased particulate emission (which reflects sunlight) may at least temporarily offset global warming, few of them are betting against global warming in the long run, given current trends. In fact, some scientists – like James Burke[1] – assert that it is too late to prevent significant global warming and suggest that our goal should be to *contain* the global rise in temperature to no more than 6 to 8 degrees centigrade at the equator and, thus, to no more than 20 degrees centigrade at the poles. But even this will cause a minimum three-foot rise in the oceans which will mean that many low-lying coastal areas will be under water. In addition to many inhabited islands these areas include approximately one-third of Bangladesh, the southern half of Florida, New Orleans and the bottom part of the Mississippi Delta, the delta area of the Nile (including Cairo), and many manufacturing centres along the coasts of Great Britain, Northern Europe, and China. And even if it should turn out that the effects are only half this bad we would still have a serious problem on our hands.[2]

But the truth about this problem – as with many of the other contemporary environmental problems – is, first, that it can't be solved by the piecemeal policy decisions of individual nations; second, that its solution is intimately tied up with considerations of social justice and, indeed, social justice on a planetary scale; and, third, we need some 'intermediate' institutions as viable mechanisms to achieve these goals. As Bernard Rollin puts it:

> even a cursory examination of some major environmental issues affecting the non-sentient environment indicates that those problems are insoluble outside of the context of international justice. The question then becomes: What, if any, philosophical basis exists for a system of international justice in this area?
>
> (Rollin 1988: 136)

the relevance of a viable mechanism of international justice to environmental ethical concerns is manifest. Indeed, many if not most environmental issues, and certainly the most vexing and important ones, entail major global consequences and thus cannot be restricted to local issues of sovereignty. An environmental ethics is inseparable from a system of international justice, not only in terms of policing global dangers and verifying and monitoring compliance with international agreements, but also in terms of implementing the distributive justice necessary to prevent poor countries from looking only at short-term gains. The rain forests are not only a problem for the countries in which they are found; if other developed nations are to benefit from the continued existence of the rain forests, we must be prepared to pay for that benefit. No country should be expected to bear the full brunt of environmental concerns. Classical economics does not work for ecological and environmental concerns; each unit pursuing its own interest will not enrich the biosphere, but deplete and devastate it.

(Rollin 1988: 138–9)

It seems obvious that social justice requires that the North transfer to the South emergency and developmental aid (funnelled through the governments of the developing countries and/or various non-government organizations such as UNICEF or the Red Cross) and, in addition, that there should also be transfers in terms of cancellation or rescheduling of debts, more equitable trade relations, monetary reforms, and other measures proposed by the New International Economic Order movement in the United Nations in the 1970s.[3] In addition, the strategy of 'autarchy' or autonomous development – of which the policy of national food self-reliance is a part – also seems an important part of the solution. But all of this would mean not merely a transfer of wealth from North to South but a transfer of decision-making power as well.

Even though the transfer of developmental aid from North to South to eliminate absolute poverty in the Third World would be considerable, the aid necessary also to save and regenerate the natural environment in the Third World may be much more substantial. This fact, together with the fact that affluent Northerners must reduce their consumption of resources *regardless* of what they do *vis-à-vis* the Third World if the environment is not to be substantially damaged, would seem to indicate that the standard of living of such affluent Northerners must, indeed, be substantially reduced. While greater efficiency can go some way toward the goals of saving the environment and slowing resource depletion, an absolute reduction in the North's consumption also seems necessary. (To be sure not all Northerners are affluent but all but the genuinely poor in the North will be required to consume less resources. Clearly, though, morality and justice may require the poor in the North to receive more resources just as they may also require affluent persons in the South to accept a reduced standard of living.)

In addition to improved efficiency, how much of a reduction in the standard of living is required will, of course, also depend on the rate at which the economies of the North and the South are growing as well as on how much internal, intranational redistribution is taking place. As to the latter point, an adequate theory of justice will put at least as much emphasis on *intra*national redistribution as on *inter*national redistribution. In any case, when it comes to deriving practical policies from such a theory of justice in the nonideal world in which we live, it seems fairly obvious that working-class and middle-class persons in the more affluent North are probably not going to be willing to accept reduced consumption unless the truly wealthy sectors of the population in *both* the North and the South are also willing to make proportionate sacrifices.[4]

Principles of justice for international redistributions

What, specifically, are the theoretical normative grounds for undertaking such measures – particularly, the massive transfer of income and wealth (and power) from the North to the South? One proposed ground, of course, is that of prudence. All of the UN-sponsored reports go out of their way to argue that a redistribution of wealth from North to South is in the long-term best interests of all of the countries involved. They assert that the trade and monetary reforms, tariff reductions, and greater concessional and non-concessional economic aid to the Third World will ultimately make for a healthier world economy and a more stable world political order. But while the empirical claims here are perhaps true, this 'prudential' justification must be taken with a grain of salt when it is offered as providing reasons for individuals or social classes to accept these policies, programmes, and institutions.

Although it may be true that in some sense it is in the public's interest or a nation's interest or even the world's interest that these measures be implemented, it is clearly false that it is literally in every individual's interest to have them implemented. Even if the meaning of one's 'self-interest' is broadened to include the interest one has in seeing one's family and friends do well – which is, of course, part of what Rawls' does in specifying what it is for people to be 'mutually disinterested' within the original position – it still does not follow that such programmes are in everyone's prudential interests. In fact, most relatively affluent Northerners whose disposable incomes will be significantly reduced will clearly not benefit by such programmes. And even if one's grandchildren and great-grandchildren are brought into the equation (so-to-speak) and we concentrate on the health effects that the degradation of the natural environment will have on future generations it is still not clear that everyone evaluating the alternatives from a purely self-interested point of view must rationally opt for the measures in question even if they believe that this is the only way to prevent environmental degradation. Very wealthy people, for example, may calculate that their greater ability to protect themselves from the effects of a noxious environment through better housing and medical care, less necessity to be exposed to its effects, etc. would more than compensate them for such environmental degradation and would be far superior to submitting to an egalitarian redistribution of their income and/or wealth.

This is why such appeals to purely prudential reasons or Hobbesian modes of reasoning – e.g., Bernard Rollin's Hobbesian argument for international cooperation to control pollution (Rollin 1988: 137–9) – do not work when taken literally and applied to all individuals. This is not to say that this general kind of argument is worthless or completely off the mark. In a sufficiently broad sense, it is true that it is in the public interest to implement these measures; but the argument in this broad sense seems to be at least as much a moral argument as a purely prudential one.

Although these quasi-prudential public-interest arguments are valuable motivational tools, the correct normative theoretical justification must be based on an adequate theory of social justice which is broad enough to include the Duty to Aid and/or its correlative Basic Rights Principle. A modification of John Rawls' social contract theory of social justice provides a sound basis for this. This modified theory is composed of the following four principles in order of priority:

1   Everyone's basic security and subsistence rights are to be met: that is, everyone's physical integrity is to be respected and everyone is to be guaranteed a minimum level of material well-being including basic needs, i.e., those needs that must be met in order to remain a normally functioning human being.
2   There is to be a maximum system of equal basic liberties, including freedom of speech and assembly, liberty of conscience and freedom of thought, freedom of the person along with the right to hold (personal) property, and freedom from arbitrary arrest and seizure as defined by the concept of the rule of law.
3   There is to be (a) equal opportunity to attain social positions and offices, and (b) an equal right to participate in all social decision-making processes within institutions of which one is a part.
4   Social and economic inequalities are justified if and only if they benefit the least advantaged, consistent with a just savings principle, but are not to exceed levels that will seriously undermine equal worth of liberty or the good of self-respect (Peffer 1990: 14).[5]

These principles can be labelled (1) the Basic Rights Principle, (2) the Maximum Equal Basic Liberties Principle, (3) The Equal Opportunity and Democracy Principle and (4) the Modified Difference Principle. These principles are priorized 'lexically', i.e. they are to be fulfilled one after the other, in order of priority.[6]

Although it is impossible in the absence of a world government and a common political constitution and legal system to implement all of these principles internationally, we can – and should – seek to apply the economic components of this theory globally at the present time. That is, we ought first and foremost to ensure that people's security and subsistence rights are met and then – all things being equal – we ought to adopt programmes and policies which at least approach the implementation of the Difference Principle. In addition, there are two other principles that at least prima facie ought to apply to the international economy. One is the Equality of Resources Principle, i.e., an equal per capita distribution of the benefits from the planet's natural resources, argued for by Charles Beitz (Beitz 1979). The other is simply the standard principles of compensatory justice as applied to the international economy, i.e., that restitution must be paid for past international injustices.

From the perspective of ideal theory all four of these principles provide a basis for a radical redistribution of material wealth from the First World to the Third (at least if one assumes the truth of a number of plausible empirical theses). These principles can be listed in the following order in terms of their strength of justification (at least in the sense of how many people will find them acceptable upon reflection):

1   a Basic Rights Principle (which is a corollary of the Duty of Mutual Aid or, more simply, the Duty to Aid);
2   the Principle of Equality of Resources applied between nations;
3   the Difference Principle; and
4   the Principles of Compensatory Justice.

As we pass from the first principle to the fourth it seems clear that the amount of the redistribution demanded increases while the strength of argument for redistribution – at least in most people's view – decreases. But of these four principles the Basic Rights Principle and its correlative Duty of Mutual Aid (as Rawls defines it) and the Equality of Resources Principle do not require there to have been any exchanges between the people of developed nations and people of developing nations in order to take effect. On the other hand, the Principle of Compensatory Justice requires there to have been harmful interactions between some of these parties; and Rawls' Difference Principle (which states that inequalities must be limited to those which, because of their incentive effects, benefit the most disadvantaged) requires the parties at least to belong to common institutions (which are defined as 'cooperative ventures for mutual advantage'). But the Basic Rights Principle/Duty of Mutual Aid holds between individuals regardless of whether they are part of the same institutions. Since this duty requires us 'to help another when he is in jeopardy, provided that one can do so without excessive risk or loss to oneself' (Rawls 1971: 114), and since Rawls, like J.S. Mill and many others, draws no strong line between acts of omission and acts of commission, it would seem that this principle issues in the demand that we each do (at least) our fair share to make sure that people's basic needs are met wherever they happen to live. (Since this task is probably much more effectively carried out by governments than by individuals or private charitable organizations at least part of this duty will presumably be to do our fair share in convincing our respective governments to take effective action along these lines.) And here it should be kept in mind that this duty enjoins the provision not only of emergency relief aid but also of long-term developmental aid of the sort that genuinely helps to improve the condition of the vast majority of people in Third World countries who are impoverished, without destroying the natural environment.

The Equality of Resources Principle is related to Charles Beitz's use of Rawls' social contract theory. The latter consists of a thought experiment involving a hypothetical choice situation in which rational, mutually disinterested, and non-envious persons have all the general knowledge they need to formulate acceptable principles of social justice but have no specific knowledge of themselves (including what their natural abilities and disabilities are, what their social and economic position in the real world is, etc.) According to Beitz, ignorance about themselves must also include the period in history and the part of the world in which they live. They consequently would choose to make sure that they are not arbitrarily disadvantaged by being born in a country or area of the world that happens to be extremely poor in natural resources. Thus, they would choose – if possible – to implement policies and institutions that would more fairly distribute resources either directly or through compensatory payments between countries regardless of whether they were part of a 'cooperative scheme for mutual advantage'. Presumably, this would generally require greater transfers between the North and South than merely meeting people's subsistence needs internationally.

But as much as it may cost the advanced industrialized nations – through monetary reforms, cancellation or rescheduling of debts, and more equitable trade relations as well as direct economic aid – to meet their citizens' duties correlative to the Basic Rights Principle and the Equality of Resources Principle, it would presumably cost much more to implement at the international level Rawls' Difference Principle which limits inequalities to those that benefit the worst-off. To answer the common objection that this constitutes a *reductio ad absurdum* of this demand, unless the sacrifices on the part of people in advanced societies (and/or local elites) are so great that they would go beyond what Rawls calls the 'strains of commitment' as judged from the 'original position' of the social contract, not from the perspective of one's position in the actual world, this is no objection (within ideal theory) to the demand that the Difference Principle be so applied. After all, there are people in real life who cannot even bring themselves to accept the Difference Principle as applied to their own society and some who can not bring themselves to accept any moral principles at all, yet this does not count against the correctness of these principles.

This brings out an important distinction that can and should be made between what is morally required of us as free and equal moral beings and what policies and programmes a particular population will find acceptable at any particular time. Although the international application of Rawls' Difference Principle may require large transfers of wealth from the First (and Second?) to the Third World, it is a practical political question as to how rapidly or to what degree such a programme could be implemented, given a particular population in a particular developed society at a particular time. Although Rawls does not delve into this issue, since he does not spend much time on 'partial compliance theory', as a practical political matter it may be necessary to implement such policies and programmes more or less gradually and to do so in conjunction with extensive educational campaigns.

To anticipate another objection, although Rawls stipulates that the Difference Principle is to be applied only within 'cooperative schemes for mutual advantage', the way that he defines these schemes makes it clear that they include any system of economic transactions. Since there now exists what is essentially a world economy, it seems obvious that in Rawls' theory the parties in the original position would choose to have the Difference Principle apply internationally. So, unless there is some other very strong moral reason for not applying it, it must be so applied. But Rawls has so far refused to commit himself to this view.[7] Now perhaps part of Rawls' reticence to allow the international application of the Difference Principle is that the demand for its application is usually not explicitly accompanied by a *ceteris paribus* ('all things being equal') proviso. But Rawls' own theory already makes clear that this principle *cannot* be applied to the detriment of either the Maximum Equal Basic Liberties Principle or his Fair Equality of Opportunity Principle. Thus, there is certainly no case for transfers of this sort from wealthier to poorer countries in cases in which doing so would support or strengthen autocratic or totalitarian regimes that are, for example, violating people's security or subsistence rights.[8] Finally, it should also be noted that this argument provides a somewhat weaker justification for massive transfers from the developed to the developing nations at least in the sense that (presumably) fewer persons will find Rawls' Difference Principle acceptable than will find the Duty of Mutual Aid (or a Basic Rights Principle) acceptable or even the Equality of Resources Principle.

The fourth basis for such transfers is that of compensatory justice. To quote Manuel Velasquez:

> Compensatory justice concerns the justice of restoring to a person what the person lost when he or she was wronged by someone else. We generally hold that when one person wrongfully harms the interests of another person, the wrongdoer has a moral duty to provide some form of restitution to the person he or she wronged. If, for example, I destroy someone's property or injure him bodily, I will be held morally responsible for paying him damages.
>
> (Velasquez 1982: 89)

> Traditional moralists have argued that a person has a moral obligation to compensate an injured party only if three conditions are present: (1) The action that inflicted the injury was wrong or negligent . . . . (2) The person's action was the real cause of the injury . . . . (3) The person inflicted the injury voluntarily.
>
> (Velasquez 1982: 90)

The principle of compensatory justice would presumably also hold in cases of coercive or unfair economic practices. Then, *if* it could be shown that the economic practices of various transnational (or at least international) corporations and the governments that supported them were coercive and/or unfair to various developing nations (and/or some or most of their inhabitants) and that their economic (or other) interests were damaged by these practices, there would exist a strong prima facie case that the developed world (or some individuals or groups within it) owed the developing world (or some individuals or groups within it) massive reparations. And this, of course, is precisely what many economists and others – both Marxist and non-Marxist – hold to be true. Some of the larger difficulties that such an attempt would run into, however, are: (1) delimiting the individuals or groups (e.g. corporations) responsible for the purported wrongdoing, (2) delimiting the individuals or groups (in the developing societies) that have been harmed by this wrongdoing, (3) deciding whether reparations for the wealth which was (presumably) unfairly extracted from developing societies (or from individuals or groups within those societies) in the past is now owed to the present government or to the descendants of those who were harmed in the past or to some other party, and (4) determining the amount of the damages involved.[9]

Although on rather plausible empirical assumptions truly incredible transfers of wealth from the developed to the developing nations might be justified, it must be admitted that this may be the weakest of the four arguments for such transfers since the correct principles of compensatory justice are perhaps more problematic than the other principles of justice discussed and since there would probably be considerable dispute over whether or not the present case fell under these principles: for example, whether or not the economic transactions involved were truly coercive or in some other way unfair and whether they constituted an actual injury to the interests of the developing societies. (Some might argue, for example, that the people in the developing societies would have been worse off without these economic transactions and, thus, that they have not been harmed or injured by them.[10]) Moreover, there are bound to be vehement disputes over the truth of the other empirical claims at issue as well.

But perhaps, in the final analysis, it is not very important whether this argument works. The fact is that at the practical level – at the level of what Rawls calls nonideal and, more specifically, partial compliance theory – it will be difficult enough to convince the people that will be disadvantaged by transfers of wealth from the developed to the developing world to accept even the amount of transfers advocated by the Basic Rights Principle, the Equality of Resources Principle, and/or the international application of the Difference Principle. It is arguable, however, that in terms of a well-functioning global economy, as well as political stability, even the generalized self-interest of the governments and peoples of the developed nations dictates that substantial transfers take place. But regardless of this fact, if we are to conform to the dictates of morality and justice, relatively massive transfers are necessary.

Carbon-credit schemes and planetary management authorities

A properly formulated 'carbon rights' or 'carbon credit' scheme can function both as a scheme to save the environment and a way to achieve world justice. Moreover, it provides a strong theoretical and pedagogical basis for arguing for a new global order in which both wealth and power are transferred from North to South and in which extreme poverty is eliminated everywhere in the world. According to the scenario outlined by James Burke in his video *After the Warming, Episode Two* – which serves as a working hypothesis – the goal now is to keep the earth from warming more than eight degrees Celsius at the equator and stabilize it at that temperature by the year 2050. To accomplish this goal the world-wide emission of greenhouse gases for the next 100 years must be cut in half (from 6 billion tons per year to 3 billion tons per year). According to Burke's fascinating, yet not fantastical, hypothetical history covering 1990 to 2050, to accomplish *this* goal the world's nations band together in 1997 to form the PMA (planetary management authority) head-quartered in Japan and then – in the year 2000 – adopt a carbon-credit plan. This plan specifies that one-half of the total three hundred billion-ton carbon budget for the next century be allocated to the industrialized countries (including the former Eastern-bloc) and the other half to the developing countries. Then each country in the North and South respectively receives a specific share proportional to their populations at the time the plan goes into effect. For example, since the industrialized nations (including the 'Four Tigers' in Asia) have approximately 1.5 billion people, an allocation of 1.5 billion tons of greenhouse gases per year means that each country gets allocated one ton per person (of their present populations) for the century. Thus, with approximately 250 million people, the US would receive an allocation of 250 million tons for the century, while Japan (with a population of approximately 125 million) would receive 125 million tons of carbon rights for the century.

At first glance this distribution may seem terribly unfair to the developing countries since they receive only 1.5 billion tons of carbon credits for their present population of 3.5 to 4 billion, while the industrialized countries receive the same amount of carbon credits for their present population of approximately 1.5 billion. (In addition, of course, the former's population is growing at a much faster rate than the latter's.) But, on the other hand, given current rates of greenhouse gas emissions, the industrialized nations of the North will use up all of their carbon credits well before the end of the twenty-first century. The most energy-efficient countries of the North (e.g., Japan) may have up to 80 years of greenhouse emissions available at current rates of use, whereas the least energy efficient (e.g., Luxembourg or Canada or the United States) may have only 10 or 15 years before they run out. At their current rates of emission, of course, the developing countries will not use their allocations up for, say, 200 to 300 years. From this perspective it may well be people in the North who are tempted to label the scheme unjust. But, of course, the whole point of this sort of carbon credit scheme is that, as a matter of justice, the North must bear the brunt of the environmental clean-up since it has disproportionately fouled (and continues to foul) the natural environment. And I take it that Burke's suggested allocation of carbon credits is arrived at by a rough estimate of what the populations of both the North and South can be expected willingly to accede to under real world circumstances.

Justice comes into play in this scheme because of the fact that the industrialized nations must 'buy' – actually barter for – carbon credits from the developing nations by transferring to them massive developmental aid for infrastructural improvements, clean energy technology, reforestation and agroforestry, telecommunication systems, educational resources, etc. Thus, for holding back on immediate industrial development by means of the less expensive 'dirty' industrial technology (now much used in the North) and for conserving their internationally important natural resources (e.g., their rain forests) the developing countries receive a much larger share of the world's income, wealth, and decision-making power than they enjoy under current arrangements.

Another essential component of this general approach is that it allows the South to leapfrog over the dirty industrial technology period that the North went through to an era of 'clean' energy technology and genuinely sustainable ecodevelopment. In the meantime, the North is provided incentives to convert to clean and efficient energy technology through a combination of: (1) considerations of competition and efficiency, (2) government tax incentives, and (3) a 6 per cent surtax on all fossil fuel consumption in the North (which provides the bulk of the money to run the Planetary Management Authority which administers the carbon credit programme and related international programmes and policies).

On the basis of this programme Burke projected that we would be able to save the earth's essential natural resources (including the remaining rain forests) and halt the earth's warming by 2050. In addition, family planning programmes promoted and funded by the PMA accelerates the demographic transition so that the earth's population stabilizes at 9 billion at mid-century and begins slowly to decline thereafter. Finally, Burke avers that decentralized, micro-scale energy systems – particularly, solar energy panels and small hydroelectric dams – together with the universal provision of computers and telecommunications technology (and, thus, educational opportunities) encourages people to remain in their traditional villages or areas in the developing countries and, in fact, encourages people all over the world to move out of the overcrowded cities to live in smaller communities. In this way some of the major problems of the overburdened urban areas can also be alleviated.

Now for an assessment of Burke's carbon credit scheme and similar proposals. First, it is important to note that not all such carbon credit or carbon rights schemes have equity considerations built into them. There are examples of both national and international carbon credit schemes that, as their critics contend, are little more than ideological justifications for unabated atmospheric pollution which unfairly benefits the corporations, governments, and nations of the industrialized North. This is precisely why we should promote carbon credit schemes that will, in fact, strive toward an equalization of material wealth and decision-making power between the North and South (as well as between classes within societies in both the North and South).[11]

It is also important to note that Burke's carbon credit proposal (which he says is based on a 1989 Dutch government report) is only the bare bones of a scheme for which many important details need to be discussed and worked out. For example, there is a debate over whether such a scheme should be based on a schedule of carbon emission rights or on taxes on carbon emissions (or a combination of the two). And if a tax is accepted, there is the further issue over whether this tax should be only on fossil fuel consumption or on all forms of energy consumption and, further, whether this should occur only in the North or in both the North and South. (Burke's proposal is that the 6 per cent energy tax apply only to fossil fuel energy consumption and only in the North.)

Moreover, while Burke proposes a barter system between North and South wherein the latter can only barter for clean (i.e. environmentally sound) technology, telecommunication equipment, educational resources, etc., most other proposals are based on the sale of carbon credits by the South to the North in which no provisions are made as to what the developing nations can buy with the proceeds. Another complication concerns the issue of whether there should be any time constraints on the developing nations' sale of carbon credits. One of the main worries here is that contemporary elites in the Third World may – at the encouragement of the multinationals – sell the farm (so to speak) for sake of their own aggrandizement, even though the credits may be much more valuable later on. Although Burke is not clear about this, one interpretation of his presentation is that nations could only sell off – or barter away – their 'excess' carbon credits for the present year (and accumulated credits, if any, that weren't sold off or bartered away in previous years). Economists such as Elmar Altvater and Alain Lipietz also feel strongly that the developing countries should not be allowed to sell off all or most of their carbon emission rights at the beginning of the period covered since such a shortsighted policy may have dire economic and ecological consequences over the long run.[12]

Moreover, despite my agreement with most of Burke's analysis and suggestions, I do have a few criticisms. First, he seems to think that such industrialized countries as the US can more or less maintain their present standard of living into the future and do so simply by becoming more efficient, whereas I think that a genuine reduction in consumption will be necessary as well. Second, Burke ignores class-based inequalities within societies, whereas I think we can expect the poorest segments in industrialized countries to accede to massive transfers of wealth from North to South *only if* they are assured a minimally decent standard of living and can see that the wealthiest segments of society (both in the North and the South) are willing to sacrifice proportionately in order to create a just society on both a national and international level. (Whether this is possible within present-day institutions is, of course, another question – albeit one of the most important ones. I do not believe that this is possible within a world capitalist system.)

Nevertheless, I have found Burke's carbon credit scheme an invaluable tool in raising people's global social and environmental consciousness. Its appeal to both long-term, enlightened self-interest and (implicitly) to considerations of social justice makes it a powerful pedagogical device. Burke's carbon credit or carbon rights scheme is an excellent example of an 'intermediate' institution or policy of this sort that we need to explore seriously. (By 'intermediate' here I mean intermediate between the current system which is largely based on the particular decisions of particular countries – and their good will in signing and abiding by essentially unenforceable international treaties and agreements – and a world government which, by definition, would be able to enforce its policies world-wide.) Burke's scheme is, in reality, both a programme for saving the environment and a scheme of international economic justice in that it would effectively redistribute wealth on an international scale in accordance with the ideal of reciprocity or a fair sharing of burdens. For these reasons I think that such schemes can and should become a focal point for debates over saving the environment and achieving sustainable development. I also believe that it is one of the most promising tools for motivating people toward favouring such policies even though their adoption would probably mean a somewhat lower standard of living for most people in the industrialized countries. This last point is one that Burke goes out of his way *not* to stress (presumably because he doesn't want to alienate his target audience in the industrialized countries before they hear him out and reflect on his proposals), but the massive emergency and development aid to the Third World, the steep taxes on fossil fuels in the North, and the necessary retooling of industry in the industrialized countries make this all but inevitable.

Another strong point of Burke's analysis is that his vision of the possibilities of international cooperation toward these ends avoids the false dichotomy between the so-called political 'realists' who see the international arena as a Hobbesian war of all against all with no possibility of significant cooperation between nations and the so-called 'idealists' who see world government as a panacea which is just around the corner. For the near and medium future Burke's hypothetical Planetary Management Authority – which has greater powers than the present United Nations but much less than even a federative world government would have – seems within the realm of plausibility, whereas an actual world government does not. It seems to me that as scholars and teachers we need to think seriously about such 'intermediate' international institutions and encourage others to start thinking about them as well.

Notes

1 James Burke, *After the Warming: Episode Two* (Ambrose Video Publishing, Inc., 1290 Avenue of the Americas, Suite 2245, New York 10104). 'Episode One' of Burke's video concerns the long-term history of the earth's climate, but the second episode can profitably be viewed by itself. The second episode also explains a Dutch government proposal for a Carbon-Rights Scheme and an associated Planetary Management Authority aimed at achieving economic justice between North and South as well as saving the world's natural environment.

2 Some scientists project considerably lower figures. Nevertheless, significant endangerment and displacement of populations due to major disruptions in the geographic pattern of agricultural productivity and to a rise in sea-level resulting from a partial melting of the polar icecaps remain part of the scenario.

For other estimates of the extent of global warming and its probable consequences, however, see: Harold Coward and Thomas Hurka (eds) (1993) *Ethics and Climate Change: The Greenhouse Effect*, Waterloo, Ontario: Wilfrid Laurier University Press; Lydia Dotto (1993) *Ethical Choices and Global Greenhouse Warming*, Waterloo, Ontario: Wilfrid Laurier University Press; and Wilfred Beckerman (1992) 'Global Warming and International Action: An Economic Perspective', in Andrew Hurrell and Benedict Kingsbury (eds) *The International Politics of the Environment: Actors, Interests, and Institutions*, Oxford: Clarendon Press, pp. 253–89.

The Editors: A more recent consensus in the scientific community is to anticipate a range of increases of 1.5 to 4.5 degrees centigrade.

3 See 'Declaration on the Establishment of a New International Economic Order', Resolution 3, 201 (S-VI), 1 May 1974, in *Official Records: Sixth Special Session*, Supp. No. 1 (A/9, 559), New York, p. 3. See also Paul B. Thompson (1992) *The Ethics of Aid and Trade: US Food Policy, Foreign Competition, and the Social Contract*, New York: Cambridge University Press.

4 But even if it is true that economic growth is necessary for a 'healthy investment climate' and if it is also true – as it seems to be – that owners of large amounts of capital will generally not invest in the absence of such a 'healthy' climate, there may still be a cogent argument for having public control over capital investments, if not outright ownership of capital and large-scale productive property. Obviously, however, this depends upon a great many other factors which we cannot consider here. But this does seem to be a point at which the socialist and environmentalist movements tend to converge. I have, in fact, defended the view that only a worldwide federation of democratic, self-managing socialist societies (with market socialist economies) can solve the world's major problems and achieve global justice. One of the most important focal points for this ongoing debate is the journal *Capitalism, Nature, Socialism* which regularly has articles on the so-called Second Contradiction of Capitalism (i.e., the contradiction between capitalism and the environment), the discussion of which began with Editor-in-Chief James O'Connor's seminal article by that title, now available in *Conference Papers*, Santa Cruz, CA: CES/CNS Pamphlet 1.

However, since not all people of good will agree on the empirical views underlying this assessment, I think it is important to leave this general institutional question initially open when discussing global justice and saving the environment. Once the general policies and measures needed are specified then, as a second matter, one can argue over whether a reformed capitalism or a democratic form of socialism can best meet these demands.

5 See also pp. 418–33 for a comparison of my theory of social justice to those of John Rawls and Kai Nielsen. I also compare and contrast my theory and Rawls'

theory in (1990) 'Marxism, Moral Theory, and Moral Truisms: Response to Kei Nielsen', *Radical Philosophy*, no. 60, Great Britain. For John Rawls' assessment of my modification of his theory see his (1993) *Political Liberalism*, Columbia University Press, p. 7, where he endorses all of my principles with the exception of 3(b). An updated version of my theory can be found in 'Towards a More Adequate Rawlsian Theory of Social Justice', *Pacific Philosophical Quarterly*, Special Double Issue: John Rawls' *Political Liberalism*, 75 (3&4) Sept/Dec 1994, pp. 251–71.

6 For present purposes I shall ignore the differences between my modified version of Rawls' theory and his original version. Thus, when I speak of the Difference Principle, for example, I will not distinguish Rawls' original formulation of it (which lacks the last clause concerning equal worth of liberty and the good of self-respect) and my version of it since at the (literally) global level we are concerned with in the present essay these differences probably do not add up to much; i.e. both versions of the Difference Principle are extremely egalitarian.

7 For arguments that the Difference Principle should be applied internationally see: Beitz, op. cit., pp. 125–76; Brian Barry, *The Liberal Theory of Justice*, Oxford: Clarendon Press, pp. 129–33; Thomas W. Pogge (1989) *Realizing Rawls*, Ithaca, New York: Cornell University Press, pp. 196–280; and my *MMSJ*, pp. 404–12. Rawls' arguments for his position that the Difference Principle should *not* be applied internationally – which I have not yet had time to absorb and evaluate – are contained in his 'Law of the Peoples' in *On Human Rights*, Stephen Shute and Susan Hurley (eds) New York: Basic Books, 1993. See also Darrel Moellendorf (1996) 'Constructing the law of peoples', *Pacific Philosophical Quarterly*, 77, and 'Liberal values and socialist models', *Theoria*, June 1997.

8 This, of course, is precisely the justification that the US has traditionally given for economically boycotting Cuba, Nicaragua under the Sandinista government, and, previously, China. But since the US at the same time has not only failed to boycott but has economically supported many governments of capitalist Third World countries which have far worse records on security rights violations, this justification can only be judged a cynical ruse.

9 According to Edward S. Greenberg:

> the well-being of the United States is dependent upon the extraction of wealth from less-developed areas. In modern capitalism, this extraction is accomplished through a complex international economic network of trade, finance, and direct investment under the direction of American multinational corporations . . .
>
> The elaborate structure of the world capitalist system which ties together core and periphery nations in relations of superordination and subordination is reflected in regularized and predictable social and economic distortions in the latter . . . the overall relationship between core and periphery is defined by the significant net transfer of value from the latter to the former . . . . While estimates of the dimensions of this transfer are a matter of some dispute, there is no gainsaying its impressive scale. Estimates range from ratios of two to one all the way to four to one. That is to say, the total of expatriated profits, trade imbalances, licensing fees, royalty payments, and the like, have been, on average, from two to four times greater than the total of invested capital, foreign aid, and public and private loans from the United States.

Taken from 'In Order to Save It, We Had to Destroy It: Reflections on the

United States and International Human Rights', in Patricia H. Werhane *et al*. (eds) (1986) *Philosophical Issues in Human Rights*, New York: Random House.

See also Noam Chomsky (1985) *Turning the Tide: US Intervention in Central America and the Struggle for Peace*, Boston, MA: South End Press, and the volumes in *The Political Economy of Human Rights* series by Noam Chomsky and Edward Herman including (1979) *The Washington Connection and Third World Fascism*, Boston, MA: South End Press, and (1979) *After the Cataclysm: Post War Indochina and the Reconstruction of Imperial Ideology*, Boston, MA: South End Press.

10 Conservatives often cite P.T. Bauer's (1981) *Equality, the Third World, and Economic Delusion*, Harvard University Press, as evidence to the contrary. While Bauer never goes so far as to deny that the developed capitalist nations take more value out of the developing world than they put into it, he does make the incredible claim that the poverty and underdevelopment of the Third World is not (even partially) caused by these economic relations and, thus, that the West bears no moral responsibility in this regard.

11 Here the New International Economic Order promoted in the United Nations in the 1970s is a good starting point, as are such major international reports as the Brandt Report, the Brundtland Report, and the Rio Earth Summit proclamations. The Brandt Report is formally known as the Report of the Independent Commission on International Development Issues (1980) *North-South: A Programme for Survival*, Cambridge, MA: MIT Press. (See also Teresa Hayter (1981) *The Creation of World Poverty: An Alternative View to the Brandt Report*, London: Pluto Press.) The Brundtland Report is actually the World Commission on Environment and Development's (1987) *Our Common Future*, New York: Oxford University Press. For the Rio proclamations see Daniel Sitarz (ed.) (1993) *Agenda 21: The Earth Summit Strategy to Save Our Planet*, Boulder, CO: Earthpress. On the reduction of inequalities within developing societies, see Paul Streeten *et al*. (1981) *First Things First: Meeting Basic Human Needs in Developing Countries*, New York: Oxford University Press, and Denis Goulet (1989) *Incentives for Development: The Key to Equity*, New York: New Horizons Press.

12 See Altvater's contribution to the present volume as well as Lipietz's 'Enclosing the Global Commons', in V. Bhaskar and A. Glyn (eds) (1995) *The North, the South and the Environment: Ecological Constraints and the Global Economy*, New York: St Martin's Press.

References

Beitz, Charles R. (1979) *Political Theory and International Relations*, Princeton, NJ: Princeton University Press.

Burke, James (1991) *After the Warming: Episode Two*, Ambrose Video Publishing, Inc.

Peffer, Rodney G. (1990) *Marxism, Morality, and Social Justice*, Princeton, NJ: Princeton University Press.

Rawls, John (1971) *A Theory of Justice*, Cambridge, MA: Belkap Press of Harvard University Press.

Rollin, Bernard E. (1988) 'Environmental Ethics and International Justice', in Steven Luper-Foy (ed.) *Problems of International Justice*, Boulder, CO: Westview Press.

Velasquez, Manuel G. (1982) *Business Ethics*, Englewood Cliffs, NJ: Prentice-Hall.

8

GLOBAL CLIMATIC CHANGE

Mark W. Lutes

Of all the stories told these days of impending environmental destruction, few have aroused such grand rhetoric and powerful images as global warming.[1] For *New Yorker* writer Bill McKibbon (1989), global warming means that 'we are at the end of nature'. Respectable scientific conferences report that the 'ultimate consequences could be second only to a global nuclear war'.[2] The popular literature on global warming is rife with fictionalized futures of drought, famines, floods, wars, locusts and the general collapse of civilization. Such rhetorical flourishes can be easily justified in the interests of motivating a jaded public and recalcitrant political apparatus to action. Such overtly literary and exhortatory techniques might also, it would seem, be easily distinguished from the hard scientific, economic and policy analyses and theories from which they derived their 'factual' basis. However, the distinction between fact and fiction, between scientific theories and journalistic stories, is not so sharply drawn, and whatever the nature of their difference, there is much traffic between them. This chapter examines some more pedestrian stories, or constructions, of the global warming issue in 'serious' scientific, economic and policy circles. It explores the influence of scientific, economic and policy discourses on the construction of the issue of global warming, and problematizes aspects of the currently dominant construction.

Since the issue of global climate change was propelled to the top of policy agendas in the late 1980s, powerful forces have been struggling to control the dominant definition of the issue, and construct it in ways that protect and promote their own interests. In the complex political and ethical dynamics surrounding global warming, there is a considerable danger of exacerbating social inequalities, advancing dangerous technologies and promoting a 'green globalism' reinforcing the hegemony of neo-liberal ideology and the intrusion of market mechanisms into more and more areas of social life (Lohmann 1993). Underlying particular policy choices (e.g., nuclear versus renewable options), or allocations of national reduction targets, are fundamental assumptions and concepts that structure our understanding of the issue. The key concepts on which the global warming debate now turns – uncertainty, competitiveness, efficiency, and the 'global' nature of the issue – should not be uncritically accepted as inherent elements of the policy issue. Rather, they are best seen as social constructs[3] created in particular contexts for particular purposes.

In particular, the 'global' construction of the issue requires careful scrutiny, not least because it privileges certain potential policy responses for controlling greenhouse gas emissions. These responses include some form of global planetary management through international agreements or by a supra-national organization; and further extension of market mechanisms and property rights to control emissions. Many current proposals, including various of emissions-trading schemes, involve some combination of these two. Because they concentrate power and authority in institutions ever further from the reach of people and communities, these trends have potentially negative implications for social justice and the prospects for democratizing the institutions that govern our lives. Perhaps an examination of the interests and processes involved in the 'global' constructions of the climate issue will reveal that such trends are not as inevitable or rational as they would at first appear.

The issue of global warming or climate change has become a lightning rod for a wide range of fundamental controversies. Debates around humans' place in nature, obligations to future generations, overconsumption versus overpopulation, environmental protection versus poverty alleviation, North versus South, free markets versus state and international regulation, science versus values and local versus global responses have all found prominent places in discussions of global warming issues. Since 1988, many environmental activists have used the issue of global warming to highlight fundamental contradictions within modern industrial society, and to reinforce other elements of the environmental agenda. The issue was often presented as showing most clearly the existence of ecological limits on continued economic growth and revealing the urgent need for economic, political and lifestyle transformations. As Ross (1990: 219) states

> Whether the hypothesis of global warming is proven or not, the recent spotlight on the climate debates has provided the single best opportunity for ecological condemnations of capitalist growth and development to win a hearing in the most powerful circles of decision-making.

Global warming was also initially conceived by many environmentalists to be the result of primarily Northern industrialization and fossil-fuel consumption. The first chapter of Oppenheimer and Boyle's *Dead Heat: The Race Against the Greenhouse Effect* (1990) was entitled 'Cause and Effect: The Wages of Industrialism', and focused on the American consumption of fossil fuels. Even the World Resources Institute, which would later be strongly criticized for bias against Southern countries, emphasized industrialized country emissions in their book *The Greenhouse Trap* (1990), aimed at the US mass market:

158

Currently, the world's industrialized countries contribute over 80 per cent of the emissions that commit the planet to future global warming. During the next decades, greenhouse gas emissions from developing countries are sure to increase. With the responsibility thus divided, the first item of business must be to reduce emissions in industrialized countries substantially. The equally important longer-term challenge is to help developing countries obtain the highly energy-efficient technologies that don't emit more pollution than Earth and its inhabitants can handle.

(1990: 103)

More recently, however, the current shape of political and scientific discourse around climate change have attracted accusations that these constructions of the issue support a Northern agenda at the expense of the South (Agarwal and Narain 1991; Shiva 1993), and that it advances the concentration of power in corporate, state, and international institutions (e.g., Sachs 1993; Ross 1991; Boehmer-Christiansen 1994). At the same time, the global warming issue has a much diminished status on the public policy agenda throughout the industrialized world. When the issue rose to prominence in the late 1980s there was a high public concern for environmental issues generally. Robust economies, hot dry summers in the US and Canada, and high average global temperatures helped publicize global warming which was a relatively novel issue supported by a well-placed and aggressive international scientific community. Since 1992, except for the recent publicity surrounding the Kyoto Conference, the mass media and politicians are now largely ignoring the issue. The vast majority of industrialized countries have admitted that they will not manage to stabilize their emissions of greenhouse gas emissions at 1990 levels by the year 2000, as called for in the Framework Convention on Climate Change. Lacking any strong impetus for action, governments have allowed the three factors that Brunner (1991) identified as problematic aspects of the dominant construction of the issue – questions about scientific uncertainties, the anticipated costs relative to benefits of action, and the lack of a widespread international commitment to reductions – to stand as obstacles to any concerted action. These aspects of the currently dominant construction are not natural or inevitable outcomes; they are the result of the efforts of particular sets of actors working within specific institutionalized discourses and contexts. We will now examine some of the processes involved in these constructions.

Climate science and the construction of uncertainty

Our awareness of the climate change issue is influenced by information from two rather disparate sources. At one extreme, most humans directly experience climate every day – it is nothing but the spatial and temporal extension of that most common-place of human experience, the weather. At the other, climate change researchers use the world's most advanced computers in modelling the dynamics of the global atmosphere and its interactions with land, oceans, outer space and solar radiation. Somewhere in this seamless local/global continuum, changes are occurring as a result of human actions that could significantly alter the conditions of life for a large proportion of the human and non-human inhabitants of the planet. But despite the various scales involved in weather/climate changes, the fundamental unit of analysis in the dominant construction of the climate change issue is the entire planet as an interconnected system. In some respects, this global construction of the issue is unavoidable and useful, but when it becomes the only way of perceiving the problem, it privileges one pole of the local/global dichotomy over the other, and becomes a powerful rhetorical device for privileging particular scientific, economic and managerial discourses over others in the framing of the problem. Also, when the globalist construction in scientific discourse is carried over into the economic and policy discussions, as we will see later, it can lead to an exclusive adoption of a global lens in these areas also.

The role of science in issues of public policy has been the subject of a large and growing literature. A recurring theme has been a challenge to the view that science can provide objective and value-free assessment of the risks or dangers posed to society by environmental hazards. Recent attempts in the US to institutionalize the separation of a supposedly objective and value-free risk assessment and the value-laden and political risk management have been widely criticized. Yet in the issue of climate change, this separation is largely taken for granted, even by the so-called 'skeptics' who argue against the scientific consensus that humans are changing the climate. Thus, while the particular findings of scientific bodies have been thoroughly debated, the role of climate science as providing the proper factual basis for policy decisions has been virtually unchallenged. The stated need to achieve greater scientific certainty is a key rhetorical strategy for opponents of action to mitigate climate change.

This uncritical acceptance of the autonomous and primary role of science as an input to policy decisions has been seen as problematic for a number of reasons. First, it creates a hierarchy between the scientific experts and the non-scientific public, limiting the role for the non-scientists as the passive recipient of 'facts' produced by natural scientists. Second, it ignores the interests of the scientific community itself in legitimating itself and securing resources (see Ingram *et al.* 1992). Third, it obscures the role that access to scientific knowledge plays in legitimating decision-making processes and particular decisions made by state and international bodies.

Several writers have recently proposed approaches to environment issues that take into account the socially constructed and culturally influenced nature of scientific knowledge in the area of environmental issues. Bradbury (1989) has identified two distinct concepts of risk:

One concept reflects a view of scientific knowledge as composed of objective facts: these facts provide the basis for decisions. A second concept reflects the view that facts cannot be separated from values in policy-related science contexts.

(Bradbury 1989: 381)

In the latter view, risk is conceived 'as a socially constructed attribute, rather than as a physical entity that exists independently of the humans who assess and experience its effects' (Bradbury 1989: 381). This view does not deny a role for scientific knowledge, but argues for an explicit recognition of the role of values, interests and social, cultural and discursive practices in the formulation of risk issues. Since values are implicit in 'scientific' accounts of complex societal issues, there is an argument for greater public participation in the construction of knowledge about risks, rather than leaving it to scientists alone.

The most concerted and thoroughgoing effort to analyse the production of scientific knowledge as a social construction has been in the area broadly defined as the social studies of science (eg., Latour and Woolgar 1986; Latour 1987; Jasanoff *et al.* 1995; Star and Greisemer 1989; Shackley and Wynne 1995). In a recent assessment of the limitations of environmental sociology, Buttel and Taylor (1992: 213) have argued that 'given the many intersections of science, social change and ecopolitics in global environmental issues . . . environmental sociology will need to elaborate an explicit sociology of environmental science'.

The climate change issue owes much to the scientific community for its rise to prominence. The scientific community played a key role in getting the issue of climate change onto the policy agendas of national governments and international institutions (Ingram et al. 1992; Schneider 1990). In fact, without the active and well-organized advocacy of the climate science community, the issue would probably not even have made it onto official policy agendas (Boehmer-Christiansen 1993, 1994). However, it is possible to make visible the cultural, institutional, political and discursive sources and implications of science. By doing this, we can bring into question the popular view of science as a socially neutral source of facts and information, and see how, as a powerful societal institution with its own unique culture and rules, it can constrain and restrict as well as inform discussions of important social and environmental issues.

One tendency of scientific discourse is to construct the world in the model of the laboratory where the experimental subject can be controlled and manipulated. The widely quoted opening statement from the Toronto Conference in the changing atmosphere claimed that 'humanity is conducting an unintended, uncontrolled, globally pervasive experiment whose ultimate consequences could be second only to a global nuclear war'. While the attitude of scientists appears to have changed from the time a few decades earlier, when 'the scientific literature . . . had seemed to welcome the inadvertent experiment of global climate change – provided that the experiment was well documented and that scientists could learn from it' (Hart and Victor 1993: 662), the language of experimentation and the image of the planet as a laboratory has remained. For Andrew Ross, this view of global warming as an experiment

> undercuts our best hopes for reclaiming the environmental sciences as an ecological ally . . . . The experimental attitude, especially when it takes the whole planet for its laboratory, becomes a form of constructive power that reshapes the world in a different image, detaching it from meaning and value and delivering it up to the rationality of technical description and control.
>
> (Ross 1991: 212)

The notion of global warming as experiment also reinforces the idea that scientists should play the lead role in structuring the debates around what appears as their natural territory.

One of the hazards of an uncritical reliance on scientific claims by environmentalists is that science is almost invariably open to many different interpretations, not all of which support environmentalist goals. Even with global warming, where the vast majority of climate scientists agree with the general global warming thesis, scientific research is often translated into policy discourse in such a way as to undermine action to prevent global warming. A key science-generated concept used almost universally in global warming policy debates is that of 'uncertainty'. Scientists are generally in agreement about the basic physics of the greenhouse effect, that greenhouse gases are accumulating in the atmosphere as a result of human activities, and that this is likely to lead to global warming and long-term changes in existing weather systems. The uncertainty surrounds questions of the timing and extent of the warming, the impacts on climatic systems, and the regional impacts on temperature and precipitation.

It is significant here that the areas of uncertainty in climate change are those that can only be resolved by computer modelling, involving extremely complex programming and the most advanced computers available. Scientists do not attach a great deal of certainty to the projected regional effects generated by these models, and there are quite wide variations in the predicted rate and extent of changes. Nor do most climate scientists expect significant advances in certainty within the next decade. This indeed appears to be a case where 'increases in knowledge may well have the effect of increasing uncertainty and complexity' (Holtzner 1972: 167). In contrast to the relative certainty of the greenhouse effect and the measurable accumulation of greenhouse gases in the atmosphere, the modelling technology generates uncertainty which it cannot realistically resolve. It does this by creating the discursive context for consideration of regional and local impacts and detailed projections of atmospheric dynamics, while there is little confidence and wide margins of error in the actual projections. The discursive ground is thus shifted to the greatest areas of uncertainty.

This uncertainty is a great resource for those industries and governments who oppose any action to reduce emissions. In scientific discourse, uncertainty is common-place, and a ubiquitous element of scientific work. Indeed, it is a precondition for on-going scientific research. However, while scientists often readily acknowledge some degree of uncertainty in certain areas of their work, this can be construed quite differently in policy discussions. When the term is appropriated into the policy discourse around a high-stakes and hotly contested policy issue, it serves to undermine the basis for action. In the case of global warming, the issue of uncertainty can become the best argument for inaction available. The existence of such uncertainties have enabled a minority of climate scientists known as 'greenhouse skeptics', who are often linked with right-wing organizations such as the Marshall Institute (1989) and the Cato Institute (Michaels 1993), to challenge the broad scientific consensus around the global warming hypothesis generated by the Intergovernmental Panel on Climate Change, and other scientific and political fora.

Rather than reducing emissions based on the relatively certain knowledge that significant and potentially catastrophic climatic changes will result from current practices, the potential for exact prediction based on climate modelling, however unrealizable this is in practice, promises the basis for a more rigorous assessment of the costs and benefits of climatic changes. This privileges arguments to wait until the uncertainties are resolved before actions are taken, lest 'sub-optimal' allocations of resources are made. If scientific certainty is in principal possible, its absence becomes an especially powerful argument for inaction in the context of neo-classical economics, where efficiency of market allocations is a primary virtue.

Economics and the discourse of efficiency

Part of the appeal of the global warming issue for many environmental activists was its apparent promise to, once and for all, reveal the essential contradictions and unsustainability of market capitalism. However, as it turned out, the global warming issue has proven fertile ground for advocates of market-based measures to address global warming. These measures, far from challenging global capitalism, will further institutionalize it and extend market mechanisms and the commodity form into new areas, including the planetary sinks, the capacity of the planet to absorb pollutants. As the earth's limited capacity as a sink for wastes is recognized and measured, this absorptive capacity becomes a scarce resource which, given an appropriate institutional framework, can be allocated, rationed, or sold and traded on newly created markets.

163

Much of the discussion about global warming policy is now focusing on the role of 'economic instruments', measures which promise to harness the power of the market in achieving environmental goals. The term economic instruments includes a wide variety of measures, such as waste disposal fees, pollution taxes, and tradable emission permits. For greenhouse gas emission reductions, considerable discussion has revolved around carbon taxes, 'joint implementation' and tradable permit systems. Carbon taxes are most likely to be applied within national boundaries, but both joint implementation and tradable permits are being considered as international mechanisms for transferring credit for emission reductions from one country to another (see Peffer, this volume). Joint implementation allows corporations or nations to meet their reduction targets by bringing about emission reductions in other countries, where they may be cheaper. These mechanisms have been criticized for a number of reasons, but primarily because they would allow industrialized countries to keep their current levels of emissions, while paying the South to keep theirs down. Most environmental groups and developing countries themselves have been highly critical of such measures.

> [D]eveloping countries suspected that it would become a new way of entrenching an 'eco-colonial' division of the world's resources, with high consumption in the North compensated by investments in the South in forests, energy efficiency projects, and so on.
>
> (Paterson 1996: 66)

Of all such 'market-based measures', joint implementation has received the most support from governments and industry, and even some NGOs, such as Canada's free-market oriented Energy Probe.

In 1992, the Economic Instruments Collaborative, a consensus building exercise in Canada which involved industry and environmental NGO representatives (with government 'observers'), was formed as an exercise to see if there was any room for consensus among the groups represented regarding the application of economic instruments to address atmospheric issues (acid rain, urban smog and global warming).[4] There was substantial agreement among the industry and environmental representatives on the potential for economic instruments. Much of the input from industry members stressed their need to remain competitive, the need to recognize the uncertainties in the science and therefore not act quickly or strongly, the importance of efficient and cost-effective actions, and the need to avoid 'command-and-control'[5] regulations. Most ENGO representatives present were reluctant to dispute these arguments strongly, largely because they felt that this was a promising venue to achieve some action on global warming, faced with a business-oriented Conservative government which appeared to be dropping global warming from its policy agenda.

The Collaborative eventually agreed on a proposal for a combination of a

164

carbon charge with offsets for large stationary sources. This would allow corporations with large emissions to offset their carbon charge by investing in carbon sinks such as tree plantations, or by investing in energy efficiency technologies in places (usually overseas) where, for instance, coal plants were much less efficient than in Canada. However, the group did not reach unanimity on the issue of whether charge offsets for overseas reductions should count towards Canada's goal which at that time was stabilization of carbon dioxide emissions at 1990 levels by the year 2000. The industry representatives argued strongly that overseas reductions should count towards this goal, but most environmentalists present disagreed.

Much of the discussion in the Collaborative adopted the language of neo-classical economics. This discursive context privileges efficiency and cost-effectiveness as the dominant virtue, and renders irrelevant or downplays such things as levels of consumption and which economic actors are responsible for the most historical or current emissions. Within this discourse, it is more difficult to avoid treating emissions everywhere as the same, and because carbon dioxide emissions are only harmful inasmuch as they contribute to global atmospheric levels, it makes no difference where emissions are reduced, as long as it is done at the least cost. The ideal is to reduce emissions where it is the cheapest to do so.

The value of economic instruments is held to be their promotion of efficiency – they reward individuals and companies who find cost-effective ways to reduce their emissions. The environmental argument for their use is that they promote the largest reduction of emissions possible for a given amount of investment. They also, it is claimed, will result in a transfer of funds from North to South to be used to clean up serious environmental problems there. Within the logic of economics these arguments are very persuasive and, with the public discussions of climate change increasingly oriented along neo-classical and free-market lines, they are finding support among many environmental advocates.

A 'global' issue – WRI/CSE debate

Global warming, or global climate change, usually comes at or near the top of most people's list of 'global' issues, along with other problems such as ozone depletion, overpopulation and loss of biodiversity. The 'global' credentials of this issue are, on the surface, irrefutable. The world's climate is understood as an interdependent global system, where any serious climatic disruptions will potentially affect the entire surface of the planet. Also, greenhouse gases, and especially carbon dioxide, are emitted by most life forms, and by a wide range of human activities throughout the world.

But when the term 'global' is applied to the human causes and consequences of climatic change, it is much more problematic. Efforts to define the human component of climate change as global has led to some very heated

165

North–South disputes. In 1990, the World Resources Institute (WRI) released a report with a chapter titled 'Climate Change: A Global Concern'. In this now infamous report, the WRI went to great pains to argue that climate change was a global issue – not just in terms of atmospheric dynamics, but also in terms of cause and effect. The report contained WRI's Global Warming Index, which attempted to reduce each country's total contribution to global warming to a single figure representing the equivalent in carbon dioxide warming potential. It then used this ranking to argue that the blame for climate change is widely shared, and as the chapter title indicates, global. In the words of the report:

> Sources of greenhouse gases are distributed widely around the world, with both developed and developing countries sharing major responsibility for emissions . . .
> The key greenhouse gases responsible for most of the projected warming emanate from a wide variety of human activities, ranging from fossil fuel combustion to wet rice cultivation.
>
> (WRI 1990: 13)

> What is evident is that responsibility for greenhouse emissions is spread widely around the world . . . . Such widespread responsibility for significant greenhouse gas emissions means that any effective agreement to stabilize or reduce these emissions will have to be equally widely based. Global warming is truly a global phenomenon, in both cause and potential effect.
>
> (WRI 1990: 15–17)

> To one degree or another, virtually all elements of human societies are involved in creating the problem. All must play a role in bringing it under control.
>
> (WRI 1990: 30)

This report was almost immediately challenged by the Centre for Science and Environment (CSE) in India, in a report titled *Global Warming in an Unequal World: A Case of Environmental Colonialism* (Agarwal and Narain 1991). The three main arguments used by the CSE to challenge WRI's global construction of climate change were that:

- WRI erred in science by overestimating Brazil and India's emissions from deforestation;
- WRI unjustly treated 'survival emissions' required by people in the South to meet basic needs, as equivalent to 'luxury emissions' which result from overconsumption in the North;
- WRI subtracted the planet's capacity to absorb greenhouse gases

(e.g., oceans) proportionately from all emissions to get the net warming potential, thus proportionately distributing entitlement to the planet's absorption capacity between countries according to their emission levels, while CSE argued for distribution on a per capita basis.

The ensuing debate around the reports highlighted the political nature of economic and scientific knowledge when used as a basis for policy decisions. The CSE did not, however, challenge the globalist scientific and economic constructions of the climate change issue. Instead, they attempted to incorporate equity concerns within this global construction. They went on to propose a global emissions trading mechanism based on the per capita allocation of emission rights, with emissions kept to a level at which no further emissions would accumulate in the atmosphere. Under this system, according to the CSE's calculations, most industrialized countries would have emissions far exceeding their cap, and would have to purchase emissions credits from the populous Southern countries who would be under-emitting. The result would be large transfers of funds from North to South, in exchange for emissions permits.

While the CSE succeeded in raising issues of equity within the dominant discourse of science and economics, the chances of their system being implemented seem slim, at best. According to Sheila Jasanoff,

> Few would argue that a regime of emission rights based on a per capita approach is a realistic goal. Such a formula not only risks rejection by the North but impairs the possibility of productive cooperation with smaller developing countries at a time when India is acutely conscious of the need for regional coalition building.
>
> (1993: 35)

In this case, their more enduring legacy may be in reinforcing the globalist construction of the issue, with its attendant need for appropriate global agreements or institutions, and legitimating the notion of emissions trading systems, no matter how inequitable the system might be which is finally implemented.

This global construction of the issue can have other perverse consequences, not the least of which is that it provides a ready excuse for any government to resist limiting its own emissions until a global agreement is in place. In Canada, the House of Commons Standing Committee on Energy, Mines and Resources released a report which claimed that

> unlike the acid rain problem or ground-level ozone, global climate change, as the name suggests, is a truly global problem whose solution, as many countries, including Canada, have come to realize,

requires a substantial degree of international cooperation and coordination.

(1993: 153)

This argument of the global nature of the problem also informed the Committee's preliminary report, timed for release just before the June 1992 Rio Earth Summit, which recommended

> that, at UNCED, the federal government reconfirm its stated commitment to stabilize greenhouse-gas emissions . . . at 1990 levels by the year 2000, and that it also seek a global commitment to a reduction of total global, anthropogenic greenhouse-gas emissions by 20 per cent from 1990 levels by the year 2005, to be achieved by coordinated global efforts.

(1992: 8)

The committee also stated its reservations about even the stabilization target, and their view that it was announced without due consultation with the industry sectors represented. But the report was voicing the clear concerns of the Canadian fossil fuel and mining industry that they would oppose any commitments to further reductions, on the grounds that reductions by Canada would be meaningless in the absence of some global agreement. The reluctance of Northern based industry and governments to make commitments that would mean significant changes to their domestic economies is, as the recommendation of the Economic Instruments Collaborative for 'international offsets' exemplifies, leading to pressure to allow Northern countries to export their reductions outside their borders. While the CSE proposal would allow this to some extent, at a significant cost to the purchaser of permits, other mechanisms are being proposed that do not have similar equity considerations built in.

The global per capita allocation of emission credits proposed by the CSE is only one possible (and probably the least likely) basis for emissions trading systems now being discussed. Rather than a per capita basis for emission allocations, an alternative is to take as the baseline current national emission levels, a practice which is known as 'grand-fathering' and which was employed by the WRI Study. This has the effect of rewarding the countries with current high emissions, and does not confer any rewards on countries with low emissions. This approach was strongly opposed by southern NGOs, as a basis for an international climate change regime, and in 1994 a broad coalition of them proposed a per capita allocation of emission entitlements as the basis for a North–South transfer of resources (ECO 1994). A report from the South Asian NGO Summit found that the most serious flaw in the Climate Convention is the idea of 'responsibility by capability'. The only morally acceptable and authentic position can be that of 'responsibility by liability' . . . [The Climate] Convention, in its preamble, accepts the responsibility of the rich in creating this global crisis, but the text ignores the requisite 'liability' that goes with this 'responsibility'.

(South Asian NGO Summit 1994)

However, an international process based on the principles of economic efficiency and based on a monolithically global definition of the problem, and where the most powerful members are also the largest polluters, is unlikely to make ideas of responsibility and equity a fundamental part of its agenda.

In the negotiations leading up to the First Conference of the Parties (COP 1) in 1995, a group of countries called JUSCANZ, which includes Japan, the US, Canada, Australia, New Zealand, and Norway, applied strong pressure to formalize a system of Joint Implementation where the sponsoring countries could get reduction credits for emissions reduced in another country. Because of strong resistance from the EU countries and the G77, a full JI programme was not approved. Rather, the proponents had to settle for a pilot phase, which would last until the year 2000, during which no transfer of credits could take place. In spite of the lack of credits, many industrialized countries have established registries for 'voluntary actions' to reduce emissions, and this includes international reductions, which could be recognized under some future agreement on Joint Implementation.

The most important outcome of COP 1 was the Berlin Mandate, an agreement to establish negotiations on new and binding reductions commitments, to be presented as a formal protocol in time for the Third Conference of the Parties in late 1997. As a result of pressure from the EU and G77, and again in the face of resistance from most countries of the JUSCANZ group, part of the Berlin Mandate an agreement that there would be no new commitments for developing countries. However, some industrialized countries, particularly the US and Australia, as well as fossil fuel and industry lobbies in many industrialized countries, have repeatedly invoked the lack of developing country commitments as a reason to refuse further commitments (or in many cases, achieving their current ones) to reduce emissions.

At the Third Conference of the Parties (CoP 3) in Kyoto in December 1997, a protocol to the Climate Convention was negotiated with binding targets for the Annex 1 industrialized countries. But at the insistence of the United States, the protocol allows countries considerable flexibility in meeting their targets, including joint implementation and emissions trading between Annex 1 countries, which will allow high-emission countries like the US to purchase emission credits from Russia, whose emissions are substantially below 1990 levels because of the collapse of the economy. Although 'joint implementation' is restricted to industrialized countries, the protocol does provide for a 'Clean Development Mechanism' to fund emission reduction projects in non-industrialized countries. Originally proposed by Brazil as a fund supported by penalties on industrialized countries which exceed their emission targets, it was changed, largely because of the influence of the US, to a voluntary fund. Countries contributing to this fund will be able to claim the credits for emissions reductions enabled by their contributions, thus making the fund, in effect, a joint implementation mechanism.

Thus, even though the fact that any binding emissions reduction agreement was achieved at Kyoto was considered by many to be a breakthrough, it is far from a satisfactory outcome. The rhetoric of the negotiations and lobbying for the Kyoto protocol shows how the issue is still heavily influenced by a framing of the issues which reifies contingent features as universal and absolute. The most vociferous opponents of the protocol, the largely US based fossil fuel industry, made strategic use of the 'global' nature of the issue in its demands that the US refuse any agreement that does not include the major southern countries. This attempt to undermine the consensus reached in the Berlin Mandate, that commitments would only apply to industrialized countries, was widely understood as a cynical strategy to disrupt the negotiations, but demands for southern country commitments actually became the official US negotiating position for a time, and is still alive and well as an argument against congressional ratification of the Protocol. Also, the goal of efficiency is a key rationale for the various forms of 'flexibility' built into the protocol, which will enable industrialized countries to continue to delay and avoid the actions necessary to reduce greenhouse gas emissions, and to continue business as usual while claiming to be making progress on the issue.

Conclusion

The point of this chapter is not that, if the issue were framed differently, the very complex and difficult ethical and social justice issues involved in dealing with global warming would disappear. However, the framing of the debate has a profound impact on how ethical issues get interpreted, what mechanisms are proposed for resolving them, and which interests are privileged. In this case, the 'globalist' construction of the scientific, economic and policy issues involved in climate change privilege top-down economic and political measures that in many ways are in direct conflict with the struggles of people and communities to escape from existing or emerging structures of domination. Not only are such measures potentially dangerous, they may not even be effective in achieving their goals. As Brunner (1991: 300) argues, 'policies that make sense only from the top down are difficult to enact and prohibitively expensive to enforce on national or global scales'.

The global warming issue appears to be losing its potential for progressive change. The agenda is being appropriated by state and corporate institutions more interested in maintaining profits and keeping the world safe for corporate capitalism, than in creating a world in which society and nature can reconcile their differences in a mutually supportive manner. To counter this tendency, we must pay close attention to the nature of particular constructions of the global warming issue, and directly or indirectly challenge those constructions. We must also promote alternative constructions and strategies for addressing the issue which can lead to progressive change.

But is it possible, or even advisable, to think about human influences on the climate in terms other than the dominant globalist view emerging from science, economics and policy discourses? Donna Haraway, in her paper 'Situated Knowledges: the Science Question in Feminism and the Privilege of Partial Perspective', provides some direction:

> So, I think 'my' problem and 'our' problem is how to have simultaneously an account of radical historical contingency of all knowledge claims and knowing subjects, a critical practice for recognizing our own 'semiotic technologies' for making meanings, and a no-nonsense commitment to faithful accounts of a 'real' world, one that can be partially shared and friendly to earth-wide projects of finite freedom, adequate material abundance, modest meaning in suffering, and limited happiness . . . . We also don't want to theorize the world, much less act within it, in terms of Global Systems, but we do need an earth-wide network of connections, including the ability partially to translate knowledges among very different – and power-differentiated – communities.
>
> (Haraway 1991: 187)

Haraway's insistence on 'situated knowledges', while not necessarily invalidating scientific knowledge claims, suggests approaching the issue of climate change in a way that validates local and situated constructions of reality; thus reconceptualizing the 'global' without romanticizing and reifying the 'local'.

Attention to the political strategies and the discursive techniques behind particular articulations of 'global' environmental issues can allow a broader response to these issues, both in terms of the nature of political critique with which they can be allied, and concrete strategies to respond effectively to these real and pressing issues. It can create a more potent discursive and political space to contest the meanings that get attached to 'global' issues, and to resist being drawn into the inexorable logic of the pro-capitalist, technocratic and northern construction of the issue.

I would like to thank Peter Penz, Ray Rogers, and the members of the Toronto editorial group of *Capitalism, Nature, Socialism* for helpful comments and stimulating discussions.

Notes

1   In this paper, the terms climate and global warming are used interchangeably, to refer to the warming of the lower atmosphere and associated climatic disturbances as a result of anthropogenic emissions of radiatively active gases. In other contexts, however, different meanings have been attributed to the terms. Friends of the Earth Canada had a policy in the early 1990s of using the term climate change rather than global warming, since it referred to climatic impacts beyond just an increase in temperature, which with Canada's cold winters could be seen positively. Paterson notes that: 'The US administration felt "global warming" to be too alarming a term, and insisted on it being called "climate change" which, to them, sounded more innocuous. However, this backfired to an extent since, at least in the UK, "climate change" was felt to be more sinister, implying general uncertainty, while "global warming" simply meant to many people hotter summers, which they were not particularly concerned about' (1996: 154).

2   This reference appeared in the statement of the Toronto Conference on the Changing Atmosphere in 1988. In the post-Cold War euphoric amnesia about the nuclear stockpiles that are still largely intact, this could qualify global warming as second to none, as environmental problems go.

3   Donna Haraway writes provocatively of our ideas of nature as artefacts or constructions. In elaborating on her notion of Nature as 'figure, construction, artefact, movement, displacement (which) . . . cannot pre-exist its construction', Haraway says that we should see this construction as a process in which the non-human world actively participates. 'In its scientific embodiments as well as in other forms, nature is made, but not entirely by humans; it is a co-construction among humans and non-humans' (1992: 296–7).

4   I represented Friends of the Earth Canada on the Climate Change Group of the EIC in the latter part of their deliberations, from September 1992 to November 1993.

5   One of our small victories at my first meeting was to get the industry representatives not to use the term 'command and control', since it was a pejorative, not a descriptive term. Alternatives to this term were 'traditional regulation' or 'rule-based regulation'. I initially proposed that 'suggest and negotiate' might be a more appropriate name for them.

References

Agarwal, Anil and Narain, Sunita (1991) *Global Warming in an Unequal World: A Case of Environmental Colonialism*, New Delhi: Center for Science and Environment.

Athanasiou, Tom (1991) 'Greenhouse blues', *Socialist Review* 21, 2: 85–109.

Boehmer-Christiansen, Sonja (1993) 'Science policy, the IPCC and the Climate Convention: the codification of a global research agenda', *Energy and Environment* 4, 4: 362–407.

——— (1994) 'Scientific uncertainty and power politics: the framework convention on climate change and the role of scientific advice', in *Negotiating International Regimes: Lessons Learned from the United Nations Conference on Environment and Development*, Great Britain: Graham and Trotman.

Bradbury, Judith A. (1989) 'The policy implications of differing concepts of risk', *Science, Technology, & Human Values* 14, 4: 380–99.

Brunner, Ronald D. (1991) 'Global climate change: defining the policy problem', *Policy Sciences* 24: 291–311.

Buttel, Frederick H. and Taylor, Peter J. (1992) 'Environmental sociology and global environmental change: a critical assessment', *Society and Natural Resources* 5: 211–30.

Canada, House of Commons Standing Committee on Energy, Mines and Resources (1992) *Sustainable Energy and the Response to the Environmental Challenge: An Interim Report on the Issue of Global Climate Change*, Ottawa.

Conference Proceedings (1988) *The Changing Atmosphere: Implications for Global Security*, Toronto: WMO, Geneva.

Coon, David (1992) *Climate Upheaval: Whose Problem? (Third Draft)*, Fredericton: Conservation Council of New Brunswick.

Corbett, Julia (1993) 'Atmospheric ozone: a global or local issue? coverage in Canadian and U.S. newspapers', *Canadian Journal of Communication* 18: 81–7.

Dobell, Rod, Fenech, Adam, Smith, Heather A. and Lutes, Mark (1993) 'The Issue of Climate Change in Canada', Toronto: Contribution #D.1 Version 3 to the Project on Social Learning in the Management of Environmental Risk.

ECO (1994) 'JI: Southern NGO Statement', *ECO NGO Newsletter*, Geneva INC 4, Issue 3, 11 February.

Government of Canada (1994) *Canada's National Report on Climate Change: Actions to Meet Commitments Under the United Nations Framework Convention on Climate Change*, Ottawa.

Haraway, Donna (1991) 'Situated knowledges: the science question in feminism and the privilege of partial perspectives', in *Simians, Cyborgs, and Women: The Reinvention of Nature*, New York: Routledge.

—— (1992) 'The promises of monsters: a regenerative politics for inappropriate/others', in Lawrence Grossberg, Cary Nelson and Paula Treicher (eds) *Cultural Studies*, New York: Routledge.

Hart, David M. and Victor, David G. (1993) 'Scientific elites and the making of us policy for climate change research', *Social Studies of Science* 23: 643–80.

Hecht, Susanna and Cockburn, Alexander (1992) 'The rhetoric and the reality in Rio', *The Nation* 22 June: 848–53

Holtzner, Burkart (1972) *Reality Construction in Society*, (rev. edn) Cambridge, MA: Schenkman Publishing Co.

Ingram, Helen, Milward, H. Brinton and Laird, Wendy (1992) 'Scientists and agenda setting: advocacy and global warming', in M. Waterstone (ed.) *Risk and Society: The Interaction of Science, Technology and Public Policy*, The Netherlands: Kluwer Academic Publishers.

Jasanoff, Sheila (1993) 'India at the crossroads in global environmental policy', *Global Environmental Change* 3, 1: 32–52.

Jasanoff, Sheila, Markle, Gerald E., Petersen, James C. and Pinch, Trevor (eds) (1995) *Handbook of Science and Technology Studies*, Thousand Oaks: SAGE Publications.

Latour, Bruno (1987) *Science in Action: How to Follow Scientists and Engineers Through Society*, Cambridge, MA: Harvard University Press.

—— (1993) *We Have Never Been Modern*, trans. Catherine Porter, Cambridge, MA: Harvard University Press.

Latour, Bruno and Woolgar, Steve (1986) *Laboratory Life: The Construction of Scientific Facts*, Princeton, NJ: Princeton University Press.

Leggett, Jeremy (ed.) (1990) *Global Warming: The Greenpeace Report*, New York: Oxford University Press.

Lohmann, Larry (1993) 'Resisting green globalism', in Wolfgang Sachs (ed.) *Global Ecology: A New Arena of Political Conflict*, Halifax: Fernwood Publishing.

Lyman, Francesca, with Mintzner, Irving, Courrier, Kathleen and MacKenzie, James (1990) *The Greenhouse Trap: What We're Doing to the Atmosphere and How We can Slow Global Warming*, Boston, MA: Beacon Press.

Marshall Institute (1989) *Scientific Perspectives on the Greenhouse Problem*, Washington, DC: George C. Marshall Institute .

Michaels, Patrick (1993) 'Global warming: facts vs. the popular vision', in David Boaz and Edward Crane (eds) *Market Liberalism: A Paradigm for the 21st Century*, Washington, DC: The Cato Institute.

McKibbon, Bill (1989) *The End of Nature*, New York: Anchor Books.

Moberg, David (1991) 'Environment and markets: A critique of 'free market' claims', *Dissent* Fall: 511–19.

Oppenheimer, Michael and Boyle, Robert (1990) *Dead Heat: The Race Against the Greenhouse Effect*, New York: Basic Books.

O'Riordan, Tim and Jill Jäger (1996) 'History of climate change science and politics', in T. O'Riordan and J. Jäger (eds) *Politics of Climate Change: A European Perspective*, London, Routledge.

Raynor, Steve (1993a) 'Introduction to special issue on national case studies of institutional capabilities to implement greenhouse gas reductions', *Global Environmental Change* 3, 1: 7–11.

—— (1993b) 'Prospects for CO_2 emissions reductions policy in the USA', *Global Environmental Change* 3, 1: 12–31.

Paterson, Matthew (1996) *Global Warming and Global Politics*, New York: Routledge.

Ross, Andrew (1991) *Strange Weather: Culture, Science and Technology in the Age of Limits*, New York: Verso.

Sachs, Wolfgang (1993) 'Global ecology in the shadow of "development"', in Wolfgang Sachs (ed.) *Global Ecology: A New Arena of Political Conflict*, Halifax: Fernwood Publishing.

Schnaiberg, Allan (1993) 'Introduction: inequality once more, with (some) feeling', *Qualitative Sociology* 16, 3: 203–6.

Schneider, Stephen (1990) *Global Warming: Are We Entering the Greenhouse Century?*, New York: Vintage Books.

Shackley, Simon and Wynne, Brian (1996) 'Representing uncertainty in global climate change science and policy: boundary-ordering devices and authority', *Science, Technology and Human Values*, 21, 3: 275–302.

Shiva, Vandana (1993) 'The greening of the global reach', in Wolfgang Sachs (ed.) *Global Ecology: A New Arena of Political Conflict*, Halifax: Fernwood Publishing.

South Asian NGO Summit (1994) 'Globalization with equity – South Asian NGO report', *ECO Newsletter from Climate Talks*, Geneva: INC 9, Issue 3, WEB: en.climate, 11 February.

Standing Committee on Energy, Mines and Resources (1993) *Sustainable Energy and Mineral Development: A Realistic Response to the Environmental Challenges*, Ottawa: House of Commons, January.

Standing Committee on Environment (1993) *Our Planet . . . Our Future – Including a Compendium of Reports of the Standing Committee on Environment with Index*, Ottawa: House of Commons, June.

Star, Susan Leigh and Griesemer, James (1989) 'Institutional ecology, "translations" and boundary objects: amateurs and professionals in Berkeley's museum of vertebrate zoology, 1907–1939', *Social Studies of Science* 19: 387–420.

Timmerman, Peter (1983) 'The question of global climatic change', *Probe Post* December: 13–15.

Tuathail, Gearoid O. and Agnew, John (1992) 'Geopolitics and discourse: practical geopolitical reasoning in American foreign policy', *Political Geography* 11, 2: 190–204.

Victor, David G. (1991) 'Limits of market-based strategies for slowing global warming: the case of tradeable permits', *Policy Science* 24: 199–222.

White, Rodney R. (1992) 'The road to Rio of the global environmental crisis and the emergence of different agendas for rich and poor countries', *International Journal of Environmental Studies* 41: 187–201.

Woolgar, Steve (1988) *Science: The Very Idea*, New York: Tavistock Publishers.

World Commission on Environment and Development (1987) *Our Common Future – The World Commission on Environment and Development*, New York: Oxford University Press.

World Resources Institute (1990) *World Resources 1990–91*, New York: Basic Books.

Wynne, Brian (1992) 'Risk and social learning: reification to engagement', in Sheldon Krimsky and Dominic Golding (eds) *Social Theories of Risk*, London: Praeger.

—— (1993) 'Implementation of greenhouse gas reductions in the European community: institutional and cultural factors', *Global Environmental Change* 3, 1: 101–28.

—— (1994) 'Scientific knowledge and the global environment', in Michael Redclift and Ted Benton (eds) *Social Theory and the Global Environment*, New York: Routledge, 169–89.

9

HOW DO WE KNOW THAT THERE WILL BE TOO MANY PEOPLE?

Nathan Keyfitz

When one visits the island of Java, or reads of hunger in the Sahel, or tries to find a parking spot near Harvard Square, it looks as though there are too many people. If there were fewer the problems experienced in those places would be less acute. This chapter investigates the reliability of appearances as they are interpreted by common sense, but in a particular context: the disagreement between neo-classical economics and ecology on matters of population and environment.

For one discipline – economics – the question whether there are too many people cannot even be understood, let alone answered, without a theory. For another discipline – biology – the question and its answer are staring us in the face, are all around us if we would only look.

Some of the most eminent scholars of our time have supported one of these opposite views of the relation of the rapidly increasing human population to the welfare of its members. Biologists E.O. Wilson, Peter Raven, Paul Ehrlich declare that we are building up to a catastrophe; that perhaps it is already too late to avoid disaster for the planet and hence for the human race. Maurice Strong, a practical man, puts this point of view succinctly when he says: Population must be stabilized, and rapidly. If we do not do it nature will, and much more brutally.[1] No scientific instrumentation, no mathematical theory, is needed; the prospective overpopulation is obvious.

Another distinguished group, that includes economists Gale Johnson, T.N. Srinivasan, and Julian Simon, says that the danger is much exaggerated and certainly does not justify any substantial diversion of resources from the central task of development and economic growth. In fact they find so little cause within economics for disseminating birth control that they have to leave economics altogether and resort to ethics to justify helping people control the size of their families. That people have a moral right to choose the number of their children overrides the economic neutrality of birth control (National Research Council 1986).

The majority of scientists in North America and the world as a whole support the view that population growth is a danger. A recent expression is provided by the Delhi Conference of October 1993, sponsored by some 60 academic institutions, whose membership includes the majority of the world's top scientists. The final declaration of the conference stated that

> The world is undergoing an unprecedented population expansion ....
> In the last decade food production from both land and sea declined relative to population growth .... We need ... universal access to convenient family planning and health services, and a wide variety of safe and affordable contraceptive devices.
>
> (*Population* 1994)

But a scholar scorns to count authorities as any part of the argument on who is right. Neither the overwhelming proportion of scientists telling us that the planet is in danger from overpopulation, nor their distinction, is an acceptable argument.

If we renounce the easy solution of counting scientists and their distinction to find the truth then we have to face the hard way, a decision on the merits. When scientists disagree we have to look into the evidence ourselves to find what we can believe. Economists are in the minority, but they could still be right.

Specific criteria of belief seem to apply to particular problems, and to dominate particular cultures. A recent study by Paul Helm (Helm 1994) argues that no theory of knowledge is complete without standards for accepting or rejecting evidence as belief-worthy. That is fairly obvious, but what makes it interesting is that radically different standards are to be found in different groups. In our case the groups are not primitive cultures but quite the opposite: the highly sophisticated academic disciplines of economics and biology. The two cultures and the societies that carry them are not isolated illiterates, but very literate indeed, living in a time when instant world-wide communication is at the disposal of every member of the two groups. Yet in fact little communication takes place between them. It is prevented by the arcane mutually incomprehensible languages used by each, and by the circumstances of their lives and work.

The dispute between adherents of the two sciences is seriously damaging. Plainly it is in the general interest that both lines of thought be brought to bear on a problem that could have so crucial an influence on the lives of our children and grandchildren. In the present condition of mutual contradiction we cannot have the benefit of both, or even of either one. The two sciences neutralize one another, and so deprives the public of benefits for which it is paying. Moreover the opposing views that are now placed before the public cast doubt on the authority of science.

For biologists there is no more pressing issue facing mankind than the prospective increase of its numbers; for economists that issue could become a problem some time in the future, but for the present is far down the list of priorities. One discipline, economics, is in search of a theory, the other, biology, insists that no theory is needed.

Malthus was conscious of this conundrum. On the one hand, he quotes approvingly Hume who said that 'of all sciences there are none where first appearances are more deceitful than in politics' (ibid.: 575). Malthus had in mind the Poor Laws, that appeared to help the poor, enabling them to survive through hard times, and yet, by permitting reproduction and so increasing the numbers of the poor, led to the very opposite of the apparently benevolent intentions of those who drafted the laws. Reasoning – theory – is needed to surmount the deception of appearances. But gathering data is equally important. Malthus provides many lessons for our own times, in that he knew that appearances can be deceiving, but nonetheless went out and did field work, collected appearances, as it were.

Since the beginning of the nineteenth century population in the world has multiplied more than fivefold, so the disciplinarian descendants of Malthus should be supermalthusians. Instead quite the opposite: the theoretical perspective changed so that the larger population gave less, not more, cause for alarm. The change in the way that economists think about population has overridden the evolution of population itself. What justifies this is the extraordinarily rapid gains of technology taking place in our time. The accelerating population growth as we went from 2.5 billion to 5.7 billion in the last forty years is seen in the light of technology increasing its power to provide food and other necessities even faster. Calculations based on the past are out of date before they are made. Certainly the sheer size of the physical environment does not change as population grows, but the possibilities of extracting what we need from it have indeed increased enormously, and before we put too much effort into limiting population we should take this into account. So goes the argument of neo-classical economics.

Perfectly reasonable, except that there is a possible trap. In altering – some would say deforming – the environment to provide for those extra people we could be creating huge problems for the future. Especially since so much of what we do to the natural environment is irreversible on a human time scale, everything from the need to feed further billions of people to the second law of thermodynamics by which oil can be burned only once. Species destroyed to make room for people cannot ever be recreated. Does that matter? No one can answer that until the web of life is understood much better than anyone now understands it.

Economics up to the 1930s and 1940s taught that the three elements of production were land, labour and capital. Land disappeared from the models about the 1950s with the realization that through technology unprecedented possibilities of substitution were emerging, and synthetics were everywhere.

Jute was being replaced by nylon, natural rubber by synthetic, copper wires for communication by fibreglass, coffee and tea by Coca-Cola, steel by plastic – the list goes on and on. Especially important, new crop varieties could make use of synthetic fertilizers so the factories that produced the latter were substituting for land, and growing times were shortened so that multiple cropping doubled or tripled the farmer's effective acreage. This was reflected in the Coale and Hoover calculations of the effects of population increase in India and Mexico (Coale and Hoover 1958), where land receives only passing mention.

A little later, with the discovery of human capital and its capacity to construct or replace physical capital, the latter also dropped out of the models or took a subsidiary place. There is sense in this, and yet if human capital, together with the people who embody it, is the sole factor of production, then population can expand indefinitely with an always rising standard of living. What makes good sense for the short run produces an absurdity for the centuries ahead.

Thus in considering the effects of present trends we have to project into the future (a) population increase, (b) technological change, and (c) environmental change resulting from (a) and (b). Item (c) is the most difficult of these three, even though (b) is not easy, and (a) has a wide range. To make matters more difficult yet, we also have to know (d) prospective institutional change (regime of production, regulation of the environment, etc.), if we are to forecast, and that could be hardest of all. No policy decision is possible without forecasts (implicit or explicit), and that applies especially to environmental matters.

Little hard evidence either way on the economic side

Economists of this recent period have found it surprisingly difficult to make a connection of theory with empirical data. Two examples of the hardest kind of data available in the literature show the tenuousness of the data-theory connection.

The first example is the simultaneous rise of population increase and economic growth in the eighteenth and nineteenth centuries. Angus Maddison provides a recent set of estimates of growth rates, for sixteen countries now industrialized, over the past millennium and a half (see Table 9.1).

Discussing such data, Simon Kuznets (1973) raises the possibility that the increase of population was what caused the increase in per capita GDP. The possibility is indeed there, but so is its opposite: that the increase in income caused the increase of population, as Malthus would have said. The latter is possible through many causal paths, of which the most likely is the decline in deaths: that with more income people ate better and so could better resist disease.

When countries are compared at a point of time, data sometimes indicate a positive association – the countries that are progressing economically are

179

Table 9.1 Population growth and economic growth rates for sixteen industrialized nations

	Population	Per capita GDP
500–1500	0.1	0.0
1500–1700	0.2	0.1
1700–1820	0.4	0.2
1820–1980	0.9	1.6

those that have the more rapidly growing populations. Yet even if the association was strongly positive, it proves little if we do not have some other evidence of the direction of causation.

Common to both longitudinal and cross-sectional evidence is the simultaneous occurrence of the two conditions of population and economic growth. From what they show, it could indeed be that the growing population is the cause of the economic progress, and this is the side the populationists emphasize. But, say their opponents, it could equally be that the population growth is not a cause but a result. Thus even leaning over backwards and admitting a positive relation shows nothing about cause; most cross-sectional presentations simply show no relation at all and so prove even less.

This ambiguity is of course well-known to economists who concern themselves with population. Ronald Lee gives as his evaluation:

> [T]hese cross-national studies have not provided what we might hope for: a rough and stylized depiction of the consequences of rapid population growth; unless, indeed, the absence of significant results is itself the result.
>
> (Lee 1983, in Kelley 1988: 1701)

Allen Kelley is even less hopeful: '[S]tatistical correlations provide little prima facie information about the size or nature of the net impact of population growth on economic growth' (Kelley 1988: 1701).

A third scholar, Nancy Birdsall, writes of the relation of population on the one side and progress on the other:

> The amount of solid empirical work on the subject is limited, especially for developing countries, partly because the subject is not really a tractable one for quantitative analysis . . . . The only natural experiment available for analysis is human history; cross-section analyses are a poor substitute.
>
> (Birdsall 1989: 24)

Birdsall goes on to explain the difficulty and the way commonly used to get around it:

> [B]ecause population change is both consequence and cause of economic change, its effects are hard to trace . . . . To be tractable, such models require simplifying assumptions: on the substitutability of labour for capital in production, for example, and the rate and sources of technological change.
>
> (Birdsall 1989: 24)

Herman Daly expresses well the substitutability difficulty: when we are trying to get a house built and have no saws we cannot just hire more carpenters. That is unless the carpenters can make saws. If the saws have to be imported from abroad then limited international currency puts a cap on the number of houses that can be built.[2]

It was the limits of capital that underlay the findings of Ansley Coale and Edgar Hoover in their 1958 study (Coale and Hoover 1958), which remained standard doctrine for a good part of a generation. They took it that the increment of population had to be furnished with capital of the same amount as the population already present if per capita income was not to decline. The harm of population increase was in thus subtracting from the capital available for innovation.

Yet that view has now been brushed aside. Geoffrey McNicoll just does not believe it, but neither does he believe in unlimited substitutability: 'What then can be said about the net savings or investment impact of rapid population growth? The answer appears to be very little' (McNicoll 1984 in Kelley 1988: 1716).

And Simon Kuznets, who looked into the matter thoroughly, took a broader view than most: he pointed to clear advantages of population growth, and also to decided drawbacks. But merely having two long lists is not good enough, and what neither he nor anyone else could speak about is the relative importance of the items in the two lists: '[W]e have not tested, or even approximated, empirical coefficients with which to weight the various positive and negative aspects of population growth' (Kuznets 1960 in Kelley 1988: 1686).

Similarly Allen Kelley, an economist who is also a demographer, goes further into the reasons why empirical resolution of the questions is difficult. For one thing we lack a formal model that reveals and measures the economic outcomes of alternative population scenarios, and the problems of constructing such a model are formidable (Kelley 1988). Over the sixty or so years to which the model must apply if it is to be useful for this purpose, institutional change, intractable to modelling, is bound to occur. Even if institutions were fixed the model has to embody feedbacks in which it is impossible to distinguish causes from effects.

When little relation is shown by a weak test

Labour economists Bloom and Freeman state that 'the empirical evidence shows little relation between the growth of population and income per head or related economic variables' (Bloom and Freeman 1988: 58). The data, as Bloom and Freeman interpret them, support a population neutral point of view.

A point of logic here: data that show little relation do not by themselves support anything. When data tell us that there is no sign of a relationship are they telling us that there is no relationship? The English language is ambiguous on this, as Fowler complains. To say no relation is indicated should only mean (and in German does only mean) that there could be a strong relation but it just does not show; English speakers are not, in the usual way of saying this, forced to make a distinction between a weak relation and weak evidence. What they do, to quote Fowler in a different connection, is 'spread a thin layer of negative colouring over the whole of the sentence' (Fowler 1965). To go from little relation is shown to a population neutral policy violates simple logic.

This logical difficulty appears in many places. Goran Ohlin,[3] citing similar data, concluded: 'There was no apparent relationship between population growth and economic growth'. And the US White Paper released on the occasion of the 1984 Mexico City Conference stated: 'The relationship between population growth and economic development is not a negative one'. These writers go on to say we should not worry about population. The environment is implicitly expected to provide an adequate base for the economy however much population and production rise. Any necessary costs of cleanup will be an affordable deduction from the increasing income.

Admittedly the data are not very sensitive, but if the real negative effect of population on economic growth were strong, would it not show through even with weak data? Not necessarily. The negative effect could be every bit as strong as Paul Ehrlich says it is, and it would still not show through on any short-term comparisons.

The distinction between weak relation and weak evidence is important enough to dwell on a little further. Suppose it is the case that population growth seriously prevents economic and every other kind of progress just because the environment will be interfered with. That is of course a long-term effect. Look back thirty years and examine the annual fish catch off the Atlantic coast of North America and Europe. There was steady growth; each year more fish were caught than the year before; there were more boats in the fleet; investment and technology each year reached new peaks. Insofar as that condition was general there would be a positive correlation between population and economic growth.

The economic data gave little hint of the disaster that is upon us. The Grand Banks off the coast of Newfoundland, for centuries providing a livelihood to adventurous fishermen, where many millions of tons of fish have been caught in the course of the centuries, are now fished out, to the point where the Canadian government has had to declare an absolute ban on fishing. Similarly, in the North Sea, French fishermen are in rebellious protest against restrictions that are in their long-term interest. The fear is that once the present fishery is destroyed other species, like dogfish and eels, either commercially useless or much less valued, will take over the vacancy, making impossible the return of the cod and other valued species. Fishermen are desperate over the loss of their livelihood; what are they to do with those ships that they have gone into debt to buy? Better forecasts would have moderated the previous cycle of investment, to the benefit of all concerned.

The situation was indeed forecast, but using fish population dynamics rather than economic models. No stronger case can be made for combining the two kinds of models, something rarely done. (A notable instance where it is done is Dasgupta and Heal (1979). A few other instances are to be found in Dorfman and Dorfman's (1977) excellent collection.)

There are other ways in which correlation can deceive. A survey of hair length in Europe would reveal that individuals with Y-chromosomes almost invariably have shorter hair than those without. The high correlation proves that length of hair is a hereditary sex-linked character? And because it is hereditary nothing can be done about it? Nonsense – it is mere convention that men wear their hair shorter than do women, and the convention could change at any time (Jencks 1992). Such obvious examples can help prevent misleading over-interpretation of statistical relations.

Thus, to provide an encapsulated history of thought on the subject, what started with Malthus came to be bypassed about the middle of the twentieth century when agricultural yields so increased that limits of land could be overlooked: Malthus' food constraints were put aside as technology produced more and more per hectare. Shortage of capital for development was then stressed as the reason for controlling population. Fewer children required less parental expenditure, less community expenditure for schools, less investment for jobs. But perhaps parents work harder because they have more children to support, so savings could even be higher with many children than with fewer? Unfortunately for this theoretical possibility what we see in North America now is record low savings both public and private, and no one argues that the way to encourage savings is to increase the birth rate.

All this shows how wide is the range of theoretical possibilities. So much depends on what variables one chooses to incorporate in the model. Add to that the difficulty of discriminating among models and determining the causal direction by statistical correlation.

Data: the view from biology

Biologists on their side do not develop a theory of the relation of population and welfare and then seek evidence that would prove it right or wrong. The mode of research applied in physics and economics is not typical for biology. In fact most biologists consider that a search for theory and then for evidence relating to that theory wastes precious time, delays action in the face of a pressing problem. Thus the Ehrlichs (Ehrlich and Ehrlich 1990: 13) simply ask 'why isn't everyone as scared as we are?' by the unprecedented growth of population, nearly 100 million each year, and 90 per cent of these the poorest of the earth's inhabitants. They cite case after case where the dangers of excessive growth of already large populations seem obvious to simple unaided observation.

The literature is full of writings by observers just having a look at some particular case and declaring overpopulation on the face of what they see. In Kenya growth of nearly 4 per cent per year will double a population already 25 million in less than the next 20 years, and this in a country where agricultural possibilities are sharply limited by water shortage. When farming is tried and fails, when forests are overexploited so that the desert spreads, that very fact reduces rainfall, and the change could be cumulative and irreversible. The dry countryside depends heavily on the tourists who come to view its wildlife. How are expanding human populations to support themselves when the space they require is taken away by the wildlife that draws the tourists?

Perhaps experts are asked to make recommendations on slowing down deforestation. Seema Agarwal, working in the forests of Burma (renamed Myanmar by its present government), sees deforestation in its dry zone as due to population pressure (Agarwal 1987).

Perhaps it is a matter of the extreme pollution of seacoasts. A Canadian team looking at Indonesia's coasts found that with increasing economic and population growth many estuaries and coastal waters have passed the limits of their absorptive and rejuvenative capacities (CIDA team 1992).

Beyond all these, at given technologies more people produce more carbon dioxide, more CFCs, consume more fish, produce more noxious waste, burn more oil whose transport inevitably pollutes the oceans. The tragedy of the Atlantic fishery has its analogue in Brazilian and other tropical forests, just to mention examples of what happens to so called renewable resources once they start to be drawn down at faster than the sustainable rate. It is not clear how technology is circumventing the ill effects of these catastrophes.

Yet no number of such cases impresses Julian Simon (Simon 1981). For him we are like the prisoners in the cave of Plato's Republic, looking at flat projections that are distorted representations of the reality outside the cave. Appearances are static; by themselves they cannot suggest the possibility that population growth will in and of itself change other relations. What if the growing density of population forces the abandonment of traditional sharing customs, and encourages private ownership in a regime of free enterprise? That possibility, leading to greatly increased efficiency of production, has been described by economist Ester Boserup (Boserup 1981, 1990). An opposite case is Java, where anthropologist Clifford Geertz found that with increasing density and hence with shortages community feeling was strengthened and the traditional culture of sharing became even more dominant (Geertz 1963). Is the general outcome of increasingly dense population free enterprise or shared poverty? Again a clash of disciplines.

The crossover: the disciplines have interchanged positions

Not only do economics and biology differ at any moment of time, but they have exchanged positions since the nineteenth century. I have spoken of Malthus, called a conservative. But his viewpoint was common to economists of all political stripes, including John Stuart Mill, whose concern for the welfare of the masses is unchallenged: 'After a degree of density has been attained, sufficient to allow the principal benefits of combination of labour, all further increase tends in itself to mischief, as regards the average condition of the people' (Mill 1848 in Singer 1970).

To nineteenth-century economists limits of nature and potential shortages were everywhere. Said William Jevons, one of the most distinguished economists of that period: 'It will appear that there is no reasonable prospect of any relief from a future want of the main agent of industry [i.e., coal]' (Jevons 1906: 9).[4]

Furthermore, Darwin states in his *Autobiography*[5] that he transported Malthus' ideas into biology, but he gave the thesis an optimistic twist. In the famous closing sentence of the *Origin of Species* he clearly identifies evolution with progress: '[A]s natural selection works solely by and for the good of each being, all corporeal and mental environments will tend to progress towards perfection' (*Population Growth* 1992). The master of such glowing language was Herbert Spencer.

One can brood on the crossover between biologists and optimists with regard to population and other matters in the nineteenth century, pessimists in the late twentieth; and in both centuries economists the other way around. And during the crossover in the thinking of the disciplines great changes have occurred in the world, among which the fivefold expansion of population stands out. It is understandable that biologists would take into account the population increase, since they are looking at situations, their vision unaffected by theories concerning what underlies the situations. Prospective advances in technology would justify the economic view, except that those whose science is counted on to achieve the advance that would enable the earth to sustain more billions say it may not be possible:

If current predictions of population growth prove accurate and patterns of human activity on the planet remain unchanged, science and technology may not be able to prevent either irreversible degradation of the environment or continued poverty for much of the world.

(*Population Growth* 1992)

very different conclusions on population and welfare come despite
'c agreements. Biologists, like economists, deal with self-seeking,
_so nearly universal in animal behaviour. They call the struggle for
survival what in economics is the market. Adam Smith's invisible hand corresponds to Darwin's and Dawkins' *Blind Watchmaker* (1986). The unguided
and unplanned process of evolution brings a good outcome – what used to be
called the survival of the fittest – in the same way as competition in the market
brings social welfare. For purposes of day-to-day administration, the market
dispenses with Government, natural selection dispenses with God. But such
resemblance in the logic of the two disciplines does not bring agreement on
what counts for us here – the effect on environment of population and
economic growth.

Are things really what they seem?

On the most general level, the dispute here is one between common sense and
science. The contrast has a long history. Thus on the one side we have
Platonism: 'Sense perception is for [Descartes], as it was for the Eleatics, a
source of obscurity, incapable of providing a base for true knowledge', (De
Santillana 1961: 106) and on the other side empiricism, represented by Francis
Bacon,[6] and innumerable, often illiterate, artisans through the ages. Marx
spoke for economists when he said that if things were what they seem to
common sense there would be no need for science. All its findings would be
immediately visible to everyone. Without the Platonic view on the one side
and the Bacon-artisan practical view on the other we would not have had
modern science. Its achievements have in large part been due to a happy
facility for incorporating both. That is what is not present in the debate on
population and environment in our time.

Conclusion

Where the evidence – the data as interpreted by theory – is as weak as we find
it to be on the relation between human population and human welfare we are
thrown back on the evidence of our eyes as interpreted by common sense. For
academics, including the present author, this is disappointing, for what are we
academics good for if we do not command ways of examining questions that
go deeper than what everyone can see with his or her own eyes?

But even worse for academics is having two disciplines not only cancelling
one another out on this particular issue, but undercutting the trust in science
generally, already under pressure in this sceptical *fin de siècle*.

Paul Ehrlich of Stanford is an important and original scientist, an
authority on certain major aspects of evolution, but his writing on population
does not rest on that. When he says that population is building up to a catastrophe he does not ask us to believe him because of his technical knowledge of

bird life. His writing on population contains little biology that the educated man in the street does not know, but it does contain a rich series of concrete cases. Edward O. Wilson, who knows more about ants than anyone else in the world, similarly does not derive his views on the dangers of population growth from that or any theoretical work he has done; we take him seriously because his judgement is derived from looking closely at many ecological configurations involving people and wildlife.

We do not know the answers to these questions concerning human population and human welfare. We are ignorant, that is, except for one thing: there is a finite probability of causing within a generation or two an ecological collapse that is virtually infinite in the magnitude of its consequences for humanity. A finite probability, even if small, multiplied by an infinite cost, equals infinity even if discounted at a finite rate however high, and should therefore be treated as though it is an infinite cost now. The million-year history of humanity in the form to which it has now evolved could come to an end merely to provide living room for one or two generations.

A higher probability attaches to the ecosphere being so disrupted by increased numbers of people and technological straining to provide for them that without any collapse many of the amenities of living are lost. Damaging climate change, increased rates of cancer as the ozone layer thins, restrictions in diet as we lose the ocean fishery, many other disagreeable or dangerous alterations threaten our platform sailing through space. A recent highly authoritative research report analyses dozens of environmental hazards, and estimates the risk of each in the three categories of human health, health of ecosystems, and social welfare. It even introduces a category of 'peace of mind'. For any of the hazards, one supposes in default of other evidence that the risk in each category is greater the greater the population (California Comparative Risk Project 1994).

It is not on any certainty, but instead on the uncertainty, on the risk argument, that we should listen to ecologists as well as to economists, and hope that the warnings of the former will temper the optimism of the latter.

I am grateful to Professor Robert Dorfman of Harvard for making some major corrections to this chapter.

Notes

1   Opening session of the Earth Summit, Rio de Janeiro, June 1992.
2   The substitutability of labour for capital is indeed a crucial aspect of the problem. I once lived in a village in Java where the local carpenter made looms on which the women wove cloth. Local labour physically created the capital with local materials, and as long as this was possible capital could never be short in relation to the labour seeking to earn a living and no one need have been short of clothing, at least not until the population had outgrown its sources of raw materials.

But the substitutability was within the locality; my villagers could not have gone to the electronically controlled looms that have now come to determine the price of cloth in world markets. The moment capital has to be bought outside in exchange for the limited goods that a village or a country can export the situation changes.

3 Unpublished papers of the Friberg Conference, 1990. The same statement is to be found in many other places, including Keyfitz, Nathan (1977). *Applied Mathematical Demography*, New York: John Wiley and Sons, where a scatter diagram fails to show a relation.

4 Jevons, I am informed by John Caldwell, lived and worked in Australia for some 18 years of his career, and was greatly impressed with the disastrous effects of the exhaustion of the gold mines on which at the time so many Australians depended.

5 'In October 1838 . . . . I happened to read for amusement Malthus on population', he says in his *Autobiography*, 'and with the speed with which populations could multiply favorable variations would tend to be preserved and unfavorable ones to be destroyed. The result of this would be the formation of new species'.

6 For Bacon the pure theorists were like spiders; they spun webs of marvellous ingenuity and formal perfection out of their own bodies, but they had no contact with reality (Cranston 1967: 237).

References

Agarwal, Seema (1987) *Scope of Biological Diversity in Burma, with Special Commentary on the Role of Women*, Washington, DC: USAID.

Birdsall, Nancy (1989) 'Economic analyses of rapid population growth', *Research Observer* 4, 1: 23–50.

Bloom, David E., and Freeman, Richard B. (1988) 'Economic development and the timing and components of population growth', *Journal of Policy Modeling* 10, 1: 57–81.

Boserup, Esther (1981) *Population and Technological Change*, Chicago, IL: University of Chicago Press.

—— (1990) *Economic and Demographic Relationships in Development: Essays Selected and Introduced by T. Paul Schultz*, Baltimore and London: Johns Hopkins University Press.

California Comparative Risk Project (1994) *Towards the 21st century: Planning for the Protection of California's Environment.*

CIDA team (1992) *Marine and Coastal Sector Development in Indonesia*, Vol. 1. Hull: CIDA. Reviewed in WRIT, 1993 Directory of Country Environmental Studies: 152.

Cranston, Maurice (1967) 'Francis Bacon', *Encyclopedia of Philosophy Vol. 1*, New York: Macmillan.

Coale, Ansley J. and Hoover, Edgar M. (1958) *Population Growth and Economic Development in Low Income Countries*, Princeton, NJ: Princeton University Press.

Dasgupta, P.S. and Heal, G.M. (1979) *Economic Theory and Exhaustible Resources*, Cambridge: Cambridge University Press.

Dawkins, Richard (1986) *The Blind Watchmaker*, London: Penguin Books.

De Santillana, Giorgio (1961) *The Origins of Scientific Thought*, New York: The New American Library.

Dorfman, Robert and Dorfman, Nancy S. (1977) *Economics of the Environment: Selected Readings*, New York: Norton.

Ehrlich, Paul R. and Ehrlich, Anne H. (1990) *The Population Explosion*, New York: Simon and Schuster.

Fowler, H.W. (1965) *A Dictionary of Modern English Usage*, (revised by Ernest Gowers) New York: Oxford University Press.

Geertz, Clifford (1971) *Agricultural Involution*, Berkeley, CA: University of California Press.

Helm, Paul (1994) *Cambridge Studies in Philosophy: Belief Policies*, Cambridge: Cambridge University Press.

Jencks, Christopher (1992) *Rethinking Social Policy*, Cambridge, MA: Harvard University Press.

Jevons, Stanley (1906) *The Coal Question: An Enquiry Concerning the Progress of the Nations and the Probable Exhaustion of Our Coal Mines*, London: Macmillan.

Kelley, Allen C. (1988) 'Economic consequences of population change in the Third World', *Journal of Ecomomic Literature* 26, 4: 1,685–728.

Kuznets, Simon (1960) 'Population change and aggregate output', in *Demographic and Economic Change in Developed Countries. A Conference of the Universities-National Bureau Committee for Economic Research*, Princeton, NJ: Princeton University Press.

—— (1973) *Population, Capital and Growth*, New York: Norton.

Lee, Ronald D. (1983) 'Economic consequences of population size, structure and growth', *IUSSP Newsletter* 17: 43–59. Quoted in Kelley, Allen C. (1988) 'Economic consequences of population change in the Third World', *Journal of Ecomomic Literature* 26, 4: 1,685–728.

Maddison, Angus (1982) *Phases of Capitalist Development*, New York: Oxford University Press, Table 1.2, page 6.

McNicoll, G. (1982) 'Consequences of rapid population growth: An overview and assessment', *Population and Development Review* 10, 2.

Mill, J.S. (1848) Quoted by S.F. Singer, *Washington Post*, 22 February 1970.

National Research Council (1986) *Working Group on Population Growth and Economic Development, Committee on Population. Population Growth and Economic Development: Policy Questions*, Washington, DC: National Academy Press.

Population Growth, Resource Consumption and a Sustainable World (1992) A Joint Statement by the officers of the Royal Society of London and the US National Academy of Sciences. Sir Michael Atiyah, President of the Royal Society of London and Frank Press, President of the US National Academy of Sciences.

Population: The Complex Reality (1994) A Report of the Population Summit of the World's Scientific Academies. London: The Royal Society.

Simon, Julian L. (1981) *The Ultimate Resource*, Princeton, NJ: Princeton University Press.

Part 4

ENVIRONMENT, GENDER AND DEVELOPMENT

10

THE GENDER AND ENVIRONMENT DEBATE

Bina Agarwal

What is women's relationship with the environment? Is it distinct from that of men? The growing literature on ecofeminism in the West, and especially in the United States, conceptualizes the link between gender and the environment primarily in ideological terms. An intensifying struggle for survival in the developing world, however, highlights the material basis for this link and sets the background for an alternative formulation to ecofeminism, which I term 'feminist environmentalism'.

Some conceptual issues

Ecofeminism

Ecofeminism embodies within it several different strands of discourse, most of which have yet to be spelled out fully, and which reflect, among other things, different positions within the feminist movement (radical, liberal, socialist). As a body of thought, ecofeminism is still evolving, but it carries a growing advocacy. How might ecofeminist discourse feed into the formulation of a Third World perspective on gender and the environment?

Disentangling the various threads in the debate provides us with the following picture of the central ecofeminist argument(s):[1] (1) There are important connections between the domination of women and the domination and exploitation of nature. (2) In patriarchal thought, women are identified as being closer to nature and men as being closer to culture. Nature is seen as inferior to culture; hence, women are seen as inferior to men. (3) Because the domination of women and the domination of nature have occurred together, women have a particular stake in ending the domination of nature. (4) The feminist movement and the environmental movement both stand for egalitarian, nonhierarchical systems. They thus have a good deal in common and need to work together to evolve a common perspective, theory and practice.

In the ecofeminist argument, therefore, the connection between the domination of women and that of nature is basically seen as *ideological*, as rooted in a system of ideas and representations, values and beliefs, that places women and the non-human world hierarchically below men. And it calls upon women and men to reconceptualize themselves, and their relationships to one another and to the non-human world, in nonhierarchical ways.

The idea that women are seen as closer to nature than men was initially introduced into contemporary feminist discourse by Sherry Ortner, who argued that 'woman is being identified with – or if you will, seems to be a symbol of – something that every culture devalues . . . [That something] is 'nature' in the most generalized sense'. Men, by contrast, are 'identified with culture' (Ortner 1974: 72–3). In her initial formulation, the connection between women and nature was clearly rooted in the biological processes of reproduction although, even then, Ortner did recognize that women, like men, also *mediate* between nature and culture.

Ortner has since modified her position which was also criticized by others (particularly social anthropologists) on several counts, especially because the nature–culture divide is not universal across all cultures, nor is there uniformity in the meaning attributed to 'nature', 'culture', 'male' and 'female'.[2] Still, some ecofeminists accept the emphasis on biology uncritically and in different ways reiterate it (e.g. Salleh 1984).

Others such as Ynestra King and Carolyn Merchant argue that the nature–culture dichotomy is a false one, a patriarchal ideological construct which is then used to maintain gender hierarchy. At the same time they accept the view that women are ideologically constructed as closer to nature because of their biology (Merchant 1980: 144).

Merchant, however, in an illuminating historical analysis, shows that in premodern Europe the conceptual connection between women and nature rested on two divergent images that both identified nature with the female sex. The first image, which was the dominant one, identified nature, especially the earth, with the nurturing mother, and culturally restricted the 'types of socially and morally sanctioned human actions with respect to the earth. One does not readily slay a mother, dig into her entrails for gold, or mutilate her body' (Merchant 1980: 2–3). The opposing image was of nature as wild and uncontrollable which could render violence, storms, droughts and general chaos. This image culturally sanctioned mastery and human dominance over nature.

Between the sixteenth and seventeenth centuries, Merchant suggests, the Scientific Revolution and the growth of a market-oriented culture in Europe undermined the image of an organic cosmos with a living female earth at its centre:

> The ancient identity of nature as a nurturing mother links women's history with the history of the environment and ecological change . . . . In investigating the roots of our current environmental dilemma and its connections to science, technology and the economy,

> we must reexamine the formation of a world view and a science that, by reconceptualizing reality as a machine rather than a living organism, sanctioned the domination of both nature and women.
>
> (Merchant 1980: xx–xxi)

Today, Merchant proposes, juxtaposing the egalitarian goals of the women's movement and the environmental movement can suggest 'new values and social structures, based not on the domination of women and nature as resources but on the full expression of both male and female talent and on the maintenance of environmental integrity' (Merchant 1980: xix).

Ecofeminist discourse, therefore, highlights (a) some of the important conceptual links between the *symbolic* construction of women and nature and the ways of *acting* upon them (although Merchant alone goes beyond the level of assertion to trace these links in concrete terms, historically); (b) the underlying commonality between the premises and goals of the women's movement and the environmental movement; and (c) an alternative vision of a more egalitarian and harmonious future society.

At the same time the ecofeminist argument as constructed is problematic on several counts. First, it posits 'woman' as a unitary category and fails to differentiate among women by class, race, ethnicity, and so on. It thus ignores forms of domination other than gender which also impinge critically on women's position.[3] Second, it locates the domination of women and of nature almost solely in ideology, neglecting the (interrelated) material source of this dominance (based on economic advantage and political power). Third, even in the realm of ideological constructs, it says little (with the exception of Merchant's analysis) about the social, economic, and political structures within which these constructs are produced and transformed. Nor does it address the central issue of the means by which certain dominant groups (predicated on gender, class, etc.) are able to bring about ideological shifts in their own favour and how such shifts get entrenched. Fourth, the ecofeminist argument does not take into account women's lived material relationship with nature. Fifth, those strands of ecofeminism that trace the connection between women and nature to biology may be seen as adhering to a form of essentialism (viz. some notion of a female 'essence' which is unchangeable and irreducible).[4] Such a formulation flies in the face of wide-ranging evidence that concepts of nature, culture, gender, and so on, are historically and socially constructed and vary across and within cultures and time periods.[5]

In other words, the debate highlights the significant effect of ideological constructs in shaping relations of gender dominance and forms of acting on the non-human world, but if these constructs are to be challenged it is necessary to go further. We need a theoretical understanding of what could be termed 'the political economy of ideological construction', that is, of the interplay between conflicting discourses, the groups promoting particular discourses, and the means used to entrench views embodied in those discourses. Equally, it is critical to examine the underlying basis of women's relationship with the non-human world at levels other than ideology.

Vandana Shiva's work on India takes us a step forward in this regard. Like Merchant, she argues that violence against nature is intrinsic to the industrial/ developmental model, which she characterizes as a colonial imposition. Associated with the adoption of this developmental model, Shiva argues, was a radical conceptual shift away from the traditional Indian cosmological view of (animate and inanimate) nature as Prakriti, as 'activity *and* diversity' and as 'an expression of Shakti, the feminine and creative principle of the cosmos' (Shiva 1988: 39, 38). In this shift, the living, nurturing relationship between man and nature as earth mother was replaced by the notion of man as separate from and dominating over inert passive nature. 'Viewed from the perspective of nature, or women embedded in nature', the shift was repressive and violent: 'for women . . . the death of Prakriti is simultaneously a beginning of their marginalisation, devaluation, displacement and ultimate dispensability. The ecological crisis is, at its root, the death of the feminine principle' (Shiva 1988: 42).

At the same time, Shiva notes that the violence against women and against nature are linked not just ideologically but also materially. The destruction of nature thus becomes the destruction of women's sources for 'staying alive'. Drawing upon her experience of working with the Chipko movement – the environmental movement for forest protection and regeneration in the Garhwal hills of northwest India – Shiva argues that 'Third World women' have both a special dependence on nature and a special knowledge of nature. This knowledge has been systematically marginalized under the impact of modern science: 'Modern reductionist science, like development, turns out to be a patriarchal project, which has excluded ecology and holistic ways of knowing which understand and respect nature's processes and interconnect-edness as *science*' (Shiva 1988: 14–15).

Shiva takes us further than the Western ecofeminists in exploring the links between ways of thinking about development, and about the impact of devel-opment processes on the environment and on the people dependent upon it for their livelihood. Nevertheless her argument has three principal analytical problems. First, her examples relate to rural women primarily from northwest India, but her generalizations conflate all Third World women into one cate-gory (irrespective of class, caste, race or ethnicity). Hence, implicitly, a form of essentialism could be read into her work, in that all Third World women, whom she sees as 'embedded in nature', *qua women* have a special relationship with the natural environment. This still begs the question: what is the basis of this relationship and how do women acquire this special understanding?

Second, she does not indicate by what concrete processes and institutions ideological constructions of gender and nature have changed in India, nor does she recognize the coexistence of several ideological strands, given India's ethnic and religious diversity. For instance, her emphasis on the feminine prin-ciple as the guiding idea in *Indian* philosophic discourse, in fact relates to

Hindu discourse alone. Moreover, Hinduism itself is pluralistic, fluid, and contains several co-existing discourses with varying gender implications. But, perhaps most importantly, it is not clear how and in which historical period(s) the concept of the feminine principle *in practice* affected gender relations, or relations between people and nature.

Third, Shiva attributes existing forms of destruction of nature and the oppression of women (in both symbolic and real terms) principally to the Third World's history of colonialism and to the imposition of Western science and a Western model of development. Indisputably, the colonial experience was destructive and distorting economically, institutionally and culturally, but it cannot be ignored that this process impinged on preexisting bases of economic and social (including gender) inequalities. For example, pre-British India, especially during the Mughal period, was considerably class/caste stratified, although varyingly across regions (Habib 1984). This would have affected the patterns of access to and use of natural resources by different classes and social groups.

By locating the 'problem' almost entirely in the Third World's experience of the West, Shiva misses out on the very real local forces of power, privilege, and property relations that predate colonialism. What exists today is a complex legacy of colonial and precolonial interactions that defines the constraints and parameters within which and from which present thinking and action on development, resource use, and social change have to proceed. In particular, we need an analysis of the structural causes of environmental degradation, its effects and responses to it. The outline for an alternative framework, which I term feminist environmentalism, is suggested below.

Feminist environmentalism

Women's and men's relationship with nature needs to be understood as rooted in their material reality, in their specific forms of interaction with the environment. Hence, insofar as there is a gender- and class (/caste/race)-based division of labour and distribution of property and power, gender and class (/caste/race) structure people's interactions with nature and so structure the effects of environmental change on people, and their responses to it. Where knowledge about nature is experiential in its basis, the divisions of labour, property and power which shape experience also shape the knowledge based on that experience.

For instance, poor peasant and tribal women have typically been responsible for fetching fuel and fodder, and in hill and tribal communities have also often been the main cultivators. They are thus likely to be affected adversely in quite specific ways by environmental degradation. At the same time, in the course of their everyday interactions with nature, they acquire a special knowledge of species–varieties and the processes of natural regeneration. They could thus be seen as both victims of the destruction of nature, and as repositories of knowledge about nature, in ways distinct from the men of their class. The former aspect would provide the gendered impulse for their resistance and response to environmental destruction. The latter would condition their perceptions and choices of what should be done. (By extension, women who are no longer actively using this knowledge for their daily sustenance, and are no longer in contact with the natural environment in the same way, are likely to lose this knowledge over time, and with it the possibility of its transmission to others.)

In this conceptualization, therefore, the link between women and the environment can be seen as structured by a given gender and class (/caste/race) organization of production, reproduction and distribution. Ideological constructions such as of gender, of nature and of the relationship between the two, may be seen as (interactively) a part of this structuring but not the whole of it. This perspective I term 'feminist environmentalism': in terms of action such a perspective would call for struggles over both *resources* and *meanings*. On the feminist front there would be a need to challenge and transform both *notions* about gender and the *actual* division of work and resources between the genders. On the environmental front there would be a need to challenge and transform both notions about the relationship between people and nature, and the actual methods of appropriation of nature's resources by a few.

To concretize the discussion consider India's experience. The focus throughout is on the rural environment.

Environmental degradation and forms of appropriation

In India (as in much of Asia and Africa) a wide variety of essential items are gathered by rural households from the village commons and forests for everyday personal use and sale, such as food, fuel, fodder, fibre, small timber, manure, bamboo, medicinal herbs, oils, materials for house building and handicrafts, resin, gum, honey and spices (Kerala Forestry Research Institute 1980: 235). Although all rural households use the village commons in some degree, for the poor they are of critical significance given the skewedness of privatized land distribution in the subcontinent.[6] Data for the early 1980s from twelve semiarid districts in seven Indian states indicate that for poor rural households (the landless and those with less than two hectares of dryland equivalent) village commons account for at least 9 per cent of total income, and in most cases 20 per cent or more, but contribute only 1 to 4 per cent of the incomes of the nonpoor (Jodha 1986).

However, the availability of the country's natural resources to the poor is being severely eroded by two parallel, and interrelated, trends – first their growing degradation both in quantity and quality; second, their increasing statization (appropriation by the state) and privatization (appropriation by a minority of individuals), with an associated decline in what was earlier communal. These two trends, both independently and interactively, underlie many of the differential class-gender effects of environmental degradation outlined later. Independently, the former trend is reducing overall availability, and the latter is increasing inequalities in the distribution of what is available. Interactively, an altered distribution in favour of the state and some individuals, and away from community control, can contribute to environmental degradation insofar as community resource management systems may be more effective in environmental protection and regeneration than are the state or individuals. These two trends are the primary factors underlying the class-gender effects of environmental change. Several intermediary factors impinge on these primary ones, the most important of which are the following: the erosion of community resource management systems resulting from the shift in 'control rights' over natural resources away from community hands,[7] population growth, and technological choices in agriculture and their associated effect on local knowledge systems. These also need to be seen in interactive terms.

Forms of environmental degradation

Although there is as yet an inadequate data base to indicate the exact extent of environmental degradation in India and its cross-regional variations, available macro-information provides sufficient pointers to warrant considerable concern and possibly alarm. Degradation in India's national resource base is manifest in disappearing forests, deteriorating soil conditions, and depleting water resources. Satellite data from India reveal that in 1985–7, 19.5 per cent of the country's geo-area was forested and declining at an estimated rate of 1.3 million hectares a year (Government of India 1990). Again, by official estimates, in 1980, 56.6 per cent of India's land was suffering from environmental problems, especially water and wind erosion. Unofficial estimates are even higher. In some canal projects, one-half the area that could have been irrigated and cultivated has been lost due to waterlogging (Joshi and Agnihorti 1984), creating what the local people aptly called 'wet deserts'. The area under periodic floods doubled between 1971 and 1981, and soil fertility is declining due to the excessive use of chemical fertilizers. Similarly, the availability of both ground and surface water is falling. Groundwater levels have fallen permanently in several regions, including in northern India with its high water tables, due to the indiscriminate sinking of tubewells – the leading input of the Green Revolution technology (Bandyopadhyay 1986; Dhawan 1982). As a result, many drinking water wells have dried up or been rendered unusable. In addition, fertilizer and pesticide runoffs into natural water sources have destroyed fish life and polluted water for human use in several areas (Centre for Science and Environment 1986).

The process of statization

In India, both under colonial rule and continuing in the postcolonial period, state control over forests and village commons has grown, with selective

199

access being granted to a favoured few. To begin with, several aspects of British colonial policy have had long-lasting effects (Guha 1983). First, the British established a state monopoly over forests, reserving large tracts for timber extraction. Second, associated with this was a severe curtailment in the customary rights of local populations to these resources, rights of access being granted only under highly restricted conditions, with a total prohibition on the barter or sale of forest produce by such right holders. At the same time, the forest settlement officer could give considerable concessions to those he chose to so privilege. Third, the colonial state promoted the notion of 'scientific' forest management which essentially cloaked the practise of encouraging commercially profitable species, often at the cost of species used by the local population. Fourth, there was virtually indiscriminate forest exploitation by European and Indian private contractors, especially for building railways, ships and bridges. Tree clearing was also encouraged for establishing tea and coffee plantations and expanding the area under agriculture to increase the government's land revenue base. In effect these policies (a) severely eroded local systems of forest management; (b) legally cut off an important source of sustenance for people, even though illegal entries continued; (c) created a continuing source of tension between the forestry officials and the local people; and (d) oriented forest management to commercial needs.

Post-Independence policies show little shift from the colonial view of forests as primarily a source of commercial use and gain. State monopoly over forests has persisted, with all the attendant tensions, as has the practice of scientific forestry in the interests of commercial profit. Restrictions on local people's access to non-timber forest produce have actually increased, and the harassment and exploitation of forest dwellers by the government's forest guards is widespread (Chand and Bezboruah 1980; Swaminathan 1982).

The process of privatization

A growing privatization of community resources in individual (essentially male) hands has paralleled the process of statization. Customarily, large parts of village common lands, especially in northwest India, were what could be termed 'community-private', that is, they were private insofar as use rights to them were usually limited to members of the community and therefore exclusionary; at the same time they were communal in that such rights were often administered by a group rather than by an individual.[8] Between 1950 and 1984, Jodha's (1986) study shows a decline in the size of village commons ranging between 26 and 63 percentage points across different regions. This is attributable mainly to state policy acting to benefit selected groups over others, including illegal encroachments by farmers, made legal over time; the auctioning of parts of commons by the government to private contractors for commercial exploitation; and government distribution of common land to individuals under various schemes which were, in theory, initiated for benefiting the poor but in practice benefited the well-off farmers. For 16 of the 19 districts covered, the share of the poor was less than that of the nonpoor (Jodha 1986: 1177–8). Hence the poor lost out collectively while gaining little individually.

The erosion of community resource management systems

The statization and privatization of communal resources have, in turn, systematically undermined traditional arrangements of resource use and management. The documentation on this is growing, but even existing work reveals systems of water management, methods of gathering firewood and fodder, and practices of shifting agriculture which were typically not destructive of nature.[9] Some traditional religious and folk beliefs also (as noted) contributed to the preservation of nature, especially trees or orchards deemed sacred (Gadgil and Vartak 1975). Basically, where traditional community management existed, as it did in many areas, *responsibility for resource management was linked to resource use* via local community institutions. Where control over these resources passed from the hands of the community to those of the state or of individuals, this link was effectively broken.

In turn, the shift from community control and management of common property to state or individual ownership and control, has increased environmental degradation.[10] As Daniel W. Bromley and Michael M. Cernea note, 'the *appearance* of environmental management created through the establishment of government agencies, and the aura of coherent policy by issuance of decrees prohibiting entry to – and harvesting from – State property, has led to continued degradation of resources under the tolerant eye of government agencies' (1989: 25).

Property rights vested in individuals are also no guarantee for environmental regeneration. Indeed, individual farmers attempting tree planting for short-term profits have tended to plant quick-growing commercial trees such as eucalyptus, which can prove environmentally costly.

Population growth

Excessive population growth has often been identified as the primary culprit of environmental degradation. And undoubtedly, a rapidly growing population impinging over time on a limited land/water/forest base is likely to degrade the environment. However, political economy dimensions clearly underlie the *pace* at which this process occurs and *how the costs of it are distributed*. The continuing (legal and illegal) exploitation of forests, and the increasing appropriation of village commons and groundwater resources by a few, leave the vast majority to subsist on a shrinking natural resource base. Added to this is the noted erosion of community resource management systems which had enforced limitations on what people could and did take from communal resources, and which could perhaps have ensured their protection, despite population pressure (Bromley and Cernea 1989: 25).

Population growth can thus be seen as exacerbating a given situation but not necessarily as its primary cause. It is questionable that interventions to control population growth can, in themselves, stem environmental degradation, although clearly, as Paul Shaw argues, they can 'buy crucial time until we figure out how to dismantle more ultimate causes' (1989: 7).

What adds complexity to even this possibility is that in the link between environmental degradation and population growth, the causality can also run in the opposite direction. For instance, poverty associated with environmental degradation could induce a range of fertility-increasing responses – reduced education for young girls as they devote more time to collecting fuel, fodder and so on, leading to higher fertility in the long-term, given the negative correlation between female education and fertility; higher infant mortality inducing higher fertility to ensure a given completed family size; and people having more children to enable the family to diversify incomes as a risk-reducing mechanism in environmentally high-risk areas. These links are another reminder that it is crucial to focus on women's status when formulating policies for environmental protection.

Choice of agricultural technology and erosion of local knowledge systems

Many of the noted forms of environmental degradation are associated with the Green Revolution technology adopted to increase crop output. Although dramatically successful in the latter objective in the short run, it has had high environmental costs in the long run, such as falling water tables due to tubewells, waterlogged and saline soils from most large irrigation schemes, declining soil fertility with excessive chemical fertilizer use, and water pollution with pesticides. Moreover, the long-term sustainability of the output increases achieved so far itself appears doubtful. Deteriorating soil and water conditions are already being reflected in declining crop yields.[11] Genetic variety has also shrunk, and many of the indigenously developed crop varieties (long-tested and adapted to local conditions) have been replaced by improved seeds which are more susceptible to pest attacks. The long-term annual growth rate of agricultural production in India over 1968–85 was 2.6 per cent, that is, slightly *lower* than the pre-Green Revolution, 1950–65, rate of 3.08. Crop yields are also more unstable (Rao *et al.* 1988). All this raises questions about the long-term sustainability of agricultural growth, and more generally of rural production systems, under present forms of technology and resource management in India, and indeed in South Asia.

The choice of agricultural technology and production systems cannot be separated from the dominant view of what constitutes scientific agriculture. The Green Revolution embodies a technological mix which gives primacy to laboratory-based research and manufactured inputs and treats agriculture as an isolated production system. By contrast, organic farming systems, now rapidly being eclipsed, are dependent on maintaining a balance between forests, fields and grazing lands. More generally, over the years, there has been a systematic devaluation and marginalization of indigenous knowledge about species-varieties, nature's processes (how forests, soils, and water are formed and sustained interrelatedly), and sustainable forms of interaction between people and nature. These trends are not confined to countries operating within the capitalist mode. Similar problems of deforestation, desertification, salination, recurrent secondary pest attacks on crops, and pesticide contamination are emerging in China (Glaeser 1987).

What is at issue here is not modern science in itself but the process by which what is regarded as 'scientific knowledge' is generated and applied and how the fruits of that application are distributed. Within the hierarchy of knowledge, that acquired via traditional forms of interacting with nature tends to be deemed less valuable.[12] And the people who use this knowledge in their daily lives – farmers and forest dwellers, and especially women of these communities – tend to be excluded from the institutions which create what is seen as scientific knowledge.

The problem here is only partly one of economic inequalities. Underlying the divide between the scientists/professionals (usually urban-based) and the rural users of innovations (including user-innovators) whose knowledge comes more from field experience than from formal education, are also usually the divides between intellectual and physical labour, between city and countryside, and between women and men.

Class-gender effects

We come then to the class-gender effects of the processes of degradation, statization and privatization of nature's resources, and the erosion of traditional systems of knowledge and resource management. These processes have had particularly adverse effects on poor households because of the noted greater dependency of such households on communal resources. However, focusing on the class significance of communal resources provides only a partial picture – there is also a critical gender dimension, for women and female children are the ones most adversely affected by environmental degradation.

The reasons for this are primarily three-fold: first, there is a pre-existing gender division of labour. It is women in poor peasant and tribal households who do much of the gathering and fetching from the forests, village commons, rivers and wells. They also bear a significant responsibility for family subsistence and in many female-headed households are the sole economic providers. Second, there are systematic gender differences in the distribution of subsistence resources (including for health care and food) within rural households, as revealed in anthropometric indices, morbidity and mortality rates, and the low female/male population ratios (Agarwal 1986a). Third, there are significant inequalities in men's and women's access to the most critical productive resource in rural economies, viz. agricultural land, and associated production technology (Agarwal 1988). Women also have a systematically disadvantaged position in the labour market (Agarwal 1984, 1986a; Bardhan 1977).

Given their limited rights in private property resources such as agricultural land, rights to communal resources such as the village commons have always provided rural women and children (especially those of tribal, landless, or marginal peasant households) a source of subsistence, *unmediated by dependency relationships* on adult males. For instance, access to village commons is usually linked to membership in the village community and therefore women are not excluded in the way they may be in a system of individualized private land rights. This acquires additional importance in regions with strong norms of female seclusion (as in northwest India) where women's access to the cash economy, to markets, and to the marketplace itself is constrained and dependent on the mediation of male relatives. (Agarwal 1989; Sharma 1980).

It is against this analytical backdrop that we need to examine what I term the 'class-gender effects' (the gender effects mediated by class) of the processes of environmental degradation, statization and privatization. These effects relate to at least six critical aspects: time, income, nutrition, health, social-support networks and indigenous knowledge. Each of these effects is important across rural India. However, their intensity and interlinkages would differ cross-regionally, with variations in ecology, agricultural technology, land distribution and social structures, associated with which are variations in the gender division of labour, social relations, livelihood possibilities and kinship systems. Although a systematic regional decomposition of effects is not attempted below, all the illustrative examples are regionally contextualized.

On time

Because women are the main gatherers of fuel, fodder and water, it is primarily their working day (already averaging ten to twelve hours) that is lengthened with the depletion of and reduced access to forests, water and soils. Firewood, for instance, is the single most important source of domestic energy in India (providing more than 65 per cent of domestic energy in the hills and deserts of the north). Much of this is gathered and not purchased, especially by the poor. In recent years, there has been a severalfold increase in firewood collection time. In some villages of Gujarat, in western India, even a four- to five-hour search yields little apart from shrubs, weeds and tree roots which do not provide adequate heat (Nagbrahman and Sambrani 1983; Swaminathan 1984).

Similarly, fodder collection takes longer with a decline in the village commons. As a woman in the hills of Uttar Pradesh (northwest India) puts it:

When we were young we used to go to the forest early in the morning without eating anything. There we would eat plenty of berries and wild fruits . . . drink the cold sweet (water) of the *Banj* (oak) roots . . . . In a short while we would gather all the fodder and firewood we needed, rest under the shade of some huge tree and then go home. Now, with the going of the trees, everything else is gone too.

(quoted in Bahuguna 1984: 132)

The shortage of drinking water has exacerbated the burden of time and energy on young women and young girls. Where low-caste women often have access to only one well, its drying up could mean an endless wait for their vessels to be filled by upper-caste women, as was noted to have happened in Orissa.[13] A similar problem arises when drinking water wells go saline near irrigation works (Agarwal 1981).

In Uttar Pradesh, according to a woman grassroots activist, the growing hardship of young women's lives with ecological degradation has led to an increased number of suicides among them in recent years. Their inability to obtain adequate quantities of water, fodder and fuel causes tensions with their mothers-in-law (in whose youth forests were plentiful), and soil erosion has compounded the difficulty of producing enough grain for subsistence in a region of high male outmigration (Bahuguna 1984).

On income

The decline in gathered items from forests and village commons has reduced incomes directly. In addition, the extra time needed for gathering reduces time available to women for crop production and can adversely affect crop incomes, especially in hill communities where women are the primary cultivators due to high male outmigration. For instance, a recent study in Nepal found that the substantial increase in firewood collection time due to deforestation has significantly reduced women's crop cultivation time, leading to an associated fall in the production of maize, wheat and mustard which are primarily dependent on female labour in the region. These are all crops grown in the dry season when there is increased need for collecting fuel and other items (Hotchkiss and Kumar 1988). The same is likely to be happening in the hills of India.

As other sources of livelihood are eroded, selling firewood is becoming increasingly common, especially in eastern and central India. Most 'head-loaders', as they are called, are women, earning a meagre 5.50 rupees a day for twenty kilograms of wood (Bhaduri and Surin 1980). Deforestation directly impinges on this livelihood source as well.

On nutrition

As the area and productivity of village commons and forests fall, so does the contribution of gathered food in the diets of poor households. The declining availability of fuelwood has additional nutritional effects. Efforts to econo-mize induce people to shift to less nutritious foods which need less fuel to cook or which can be eaten raw, or force them to eat partially cooked food which could be toxic, or eat leftovers that could rot in a tropical environment, or to miss meals altogether. Although as yet there are no systematic studies on India, some studies on rural Bangladesh are strongly indicative and show that the total number of meals eaten daily, as well as the number of *cooked* meals eaten in poor households, is already declining (Howes and Jabbar 1986).

Although these adverse nutritional effects impinge on the whole house-hold, women and female children bear an additional burden because of the noted gender biases in intrafamily distribution of food and health care. There is also little likelihood of poor women being able to afford the extra calories for the additional energy expended in fuel collection.

On health

Apart from the health consequences of nutritional inadequacies, poor rural women are also more directly exposed than are men to waterborne diseases and to the pollution of rivers and ponds with fertilizer and pesticide runoffs, because of the nature of tasks they perform, such as fetching water for various domestic uses and animal care, and washing clothes near ponds, canals and streams (Agarwal 1981). The burden of family ill-health associated with water pollution also falls largely on women who take care of the sick. An additional source of vulnerability is the agricultural tasks women perform. For instance, rice transplanting, which is usually a women's task in most parts of Asia, is associated with a range of diseases, including arthritis and gynaecological ailments (Mencher and Saradamoni 1982; United Nations Development Program 1979). Cottonpicking and other tasks done mainly by women in cotton cultivation expose them to pesticides which are widely used for this crop. In China, several times the acceptable levels of DDT and BHC residues have been found in the milk of nursing mothers, among women agricultural workers (Wagner 1987). In India, pesticides are associated with limb and visual disabilities (Mohan 1987).

On social support networks

Social relationships with kin, and with villagers outside the kin network, provide economic and social support that is important to all rural households but especially to poor households and to the women.[14] This includes recip-rocal labour-sharing agreements during peak agricultural seasons; loans taken in cash or kind during severe crises such as droughts; and the borrowing of small amounts of food stuffs, fuel, fodder, and so on, even in normal times. Women typically depend a great deal on such informal support networks, which they also help to build through daily social interaction, marriage alliances that they are frequently instrumental in arranging, and complex gift exchanges (Sharma 1980; Vatuk 1981). Also the social and economic support this represents for women in terms of strengthening their bargaining power within families needs to be recognized, even if it is not easy to quantify.[15] These networks, spread over a range of nearby villages, cannot be reconstituted easily, an aspect ignored by rehabilitation planners.

Moreover for forest dwellers, the relationship with forests is not just functional or economic but also symbolic, suffused with cultural meanings and nuances, and woven into their songs and legends of origin. Large-scale deforestation, whether or not due to irrigation schemes, has eroded a whole way of living and thinking. Two close observers of life among the tribal people of Orissa in eastern India note that 'the earlier sense of sharing has disappeared . . . . Earlier women would rely on their neighbours in times of need. Today this has been replaced with a sense of alienation and helplessness . . . the trend is to leave each family to its own fate' (Fernandes and Menon 1987: 115). Widows and the aged are the most neglected.

On women's indigenous knowledge

The gathering of food alone demands an elaborate knowledge of the nutritional and medicinal properties of plants, roots and trees, including a wide reserve knowledge of edible plants not normally used but critical for coping with prolonged shortages during climatic disasters. An examination of household coping mechanisms during drought and famine reveals a significant dependence on famine foods gathered mainly by women and children for survival. Also, among hill communities it is usually women who do the seed selection work and have the most detailed knowledge about crop varieties.[16] This knowledge about nature and agriculture, acquired by poor rural women in the process of their everyday contact with and dependence on nature's resources, has a class and gender specificity and is linked to the class specificity and gendering of the division of labour.

The impact of existing forms of development on this knowledge has been twofold. First, the process of devaluation and marginalization of indigenous knowledge and skills, discussed earlier, impinges especially on the knowledge that poor peasant and tribal women usually possess. Existing development strategies have made little attempt to tap or enhance this knowledge and understanding. At the same time, women have been excluded from the institutions through which modern scientific knowledge is created and transmitted. Second, the degradation of natural resources and their appropriation by a minority results in the destruction of the material basis on which women's knowledge of natural resources and processes is founded and kept alive, leading to its gradual eclipse.

Responses: state and grassroots

Both the state and the people most immediately affected by environmental degradation have responded to these processes, but in different ways. The state's recognition that environmental degradation may be acquiring crisis proportions is recent and as yet partial; and, as we have seen, state developmental policies are themselves a significant cause of the crisis. Not surprisingly, therefore, the state's response has been piecemeal rather than comprehensive. For instance, the problem of deforestation and fuelwood shortage has been addressed mainly by initiating tree planting schemes either directly or by encouraging village communities and individual farmers to do so.[17]

However, most state ventures in the form of direct planting have had a high failure rate in terms of both tree planting and survival, attributable to several causes – a preoccupation with monocultural plantations principally for commercial use, the takeover of land used for various other purposes by the local population, and top-down implementation. Hence, in many cases, far from benefiting the poor these schemes have taken away even existing rights and resources, leading to widespread local resistance. Also, women either do not feature at all in such schemes or, at best, tend to be allotted the role of caretakers in tree nurseries, with little say in the choice of species or in any other aspect of the project. Community forestry schemes, on the other hand, are often obstructed by economic inequalities in the village community and the associated mistrust among the poor of a system that cannot ensure equitable access to the products of the trees planted.

Ironically, the real 'success' stories, with plantings far exceeding targets, relate to farm forestry, with the better-off farmers in many regions seeking to reap quick profits by allotting their fertile crop land to commercial species, such as eucalyptus. As a result, employment, crop output, and crop residues for fuel have declined, often dramatically (Chandrashekar *et al.* 1987; and Shiva 1988).

As some environmentalists have rightly argued, the predominantly commercial approach to forestry, promoted as 'scientific forestry', is reductionist – it is nature seen as individual parts rather than as an interconnected system of vegetation, soil, and water; the forest is reduced to trees, the trees to biomass (see, among others, Shiva 1987).

But should we see people in general and women in particular as victims of environmental degradation caused by ill-conceived top-down state policies? The emergence of grassroots ecology movements across the subcontinent (and especially in India) suggest otherwise. These movements indicate that although poor peasant and tribal communities in general, and women among them in particular, are being severely affected by environmental degradation and appropriation, they are today also critical agents of change. Further, embodied in their traditional interaction with the environment are practices and perspectives which can prove important for defining alternatives.

The past decade, in particular, has seen an increasing resistance to ecological destruction in India, whether caused by direct deforestation or by large irrigation and hydroelectric works, such as the Narmada Valley Project covering three regions in central India, the Koel-Karo in Bihar, the Silent Valley Project in Kerala (which was shelved through central government intervention and local protests in 1983), the Inchampalli and Bhopalpatnum dams in Andra Pradesh (against which 5,000 tribal people, with women in the vanguard, protested in 1984), and the controversial Terhi dam in Garhwal. Women have been active participants in most of these protests.

However, women's participation in a movement does not in *itself* represent an explicit incorporation of a gender perspective, either in theory or practice, within that movement. Yet such a formulation is clearly needed. Feminist environmentalism as spelled out earlier in this paper is an attempt in this direction.

To restate in this context, feminist environmentalism seeks to provide a theoretical perspective that locates both the symbolic and material links between people and the environment in their specific forms of interaction with it, and traces gender and class differentiation in these links to a given gender and class division of labour, property and power. Unlike, say, Gandhism and Marxism, feminist environmentalism is not a perspective that is consciously subscribed to by an identifiable set of individuals or groups. However, insofar as tribal and poor peasant women's special concern with environmental degradation is rooted in this material reality, their responses to it, which have been articulated both in complementary and oppositional terms to the other ideological streams, could be seen as consistent with the feminist environmentalist framework.

The Chipko movement is an interesting example in this respect.[18] Although it emerged from the Gandhian tradition, in the course of its growth it has brought to light some of the limitations of an approach that does not explicitly take account of class and gender concerns.

The movement was sparked off in 1972–3 when the people of Chamoli district in northwest India protested the auctioning of 300 ash trees to a sports goods manufacturer, while the local labour cooperative was refused permission by the government to cut even a few trees to make agricultural implements for the community. Since then the movement has not only spread within the region but its methods and message have also reached other parts of the country (Appiko in Karnataka is an offshoot).[19] Further, the context of local resistance has widened. Tree felling is being resisted also to prevent disasters such as landslides, and there has been protest against limestone mining in the hills for which the villagers had to face violence from the contractors and their hired thugs.

Women's active involvement in the Chipko movement has several note-worthy features that need highlighting here. First, their protest against the commercial exploitation of the Himalayan forests has been not only jointly with the men of their community when they were confronting nonlocal contractors but also, in several subsequent instances, even in opposition to village men due to differences in priorities about resource use. Time and again, women have clear-sightedly opted for saving forests and the environment over the short-term gains of development projects with high environmental costs. In one instance, a potato-seed farm was to be established by cutting down a tract of oak forest in Dongri Paintoli village. The men supported the scheme because it would bring in cash income. The women protested because it would take away their only local source of fuel and fodder and add five kilometres to their fuel-collecting journeys, but cash in the men's hands would not neces-sarily benefit them or their children.[20] The protest was successful.

Second, women have been active and frequently successful in protecting the trees, stopping tree auctions, and keeping a vigil against illegal felling. In Gopeshwar town, a local women's group has appointed watchwomen who receive a wage in kind to guard the surrounding forest, and to regulate the extraction of forest produce by villagers. Twigs can be collected freely, but any harm to the trees is liable to punishment.

Third, replanting is a significant component of the movement. But in their choice of trees the priorities of women and men don't always coincide – women typically prefer trees that help fulfil their responsibilities for fuel and fodder, while the men prefer commercially profitable species.[21]

Fourth, Chipko today is more than an ecology movement and has the potential for becoming a wider movement against gender-related inequalities. For instance, there has been large-scale mobilization against male alcoholism and associated domestic violence and wasteful expenditure. There is also a shift in self-perception. Women have stood up in public meetings of the move-ment and forcefully addressed the gathering. Many of them are also asking: why aren't we members of the village councils?

Fifth, implicit in the movement is a holistic understanding of the environ-ment in general and forests in particular. The women, for instance, have constructed a poetic dialogue illustrating the difference between their own perspective and that of the foresters (from Shiva 1988):

Foresters: What do the forests bear?
                           Profits, resin and timber.

Women (chorus):   What do the forests bear?
                           Soil, water and pure air,
                           Soil, water and pure air,
                           Sustain the earth and all she bears.

In other words, the women recognize that forests cannot be reduced merely to trees and the trees to wood for commercial use; that vegetation, soil and water form part of a complex and interrelated ecosystem. This recognition of the interrelatedness and interdependence between the various material components of nature, and between nature and human sustenance, is critical for evolving a strategy of sustainable environmental protection and regeneration.

Although the movement draws upon, indeed is rooted in, the region's Gandhian tradition which predates Chipko, women's responses go beyond the framework of that tradition and come close to feminist environmentalism in their perspective. This is suggested by their beginning to confront gender and class issues in a number of small but significant ways. For instance, gender relations are called into question in their taking oppositional stands to the village men on several occasions, in asking to be members of village councils, and in resisting male alcoholism and domestic violence. Similarly, there is clearly a class confrontation involved in their resistance (together with the men of their community) to the contractors holding licences for mining and felling in the area.

At the same time, ecology movements such as Chipko need to be contextualized. Although localized resistance to the processes of natural resource appropriation and degradation in India has taken many different forms, and arisen in diverse regional contexts, resistance in which entire communities and villages have participated to constitute a movement (such as Chipko, Appiko and Jharkhand) has emerged primarily in hill or tribal communities. This may be attributable particularly to two factors: the immediacy of the threat from these processes to people's survival, and these communities being marked by relatively low levels of the class and gender differentiation that usually splinter village communities in South Asia. They therefore have a greater potential for wider community participation than is possible in more economically and socially stratified contexts. Further, in these communities, women's role in agricultural production has always been visibly substantial and often primary – an aspect more conducive to their public participation than in many other communities of northern India practising female seclusion.

In emphasizing the role of poor peasant and tribal women in ecology movements, I am not arguing, as do some feminist scholars, that women possess a specifically feminine sensibility or cognitive temperament, or that women *qua women* have certain traits that predispose them to attend to particulars, to be interactive rather than individualist, and to understand the true character of complex natural processes in holistic terms.[22] Rather, I locate the perspectives and responses of poor peasant and tribal women (perspectives which are indeed often interactive and holistic) in their material reality – in their dependence on and actual use of natural resources for survival, the knowledge of nature gained in that process, and the broader cultural parameters which define people's activities and modes of thinking in these communities. By this count, the perceptions and responses of men belonging to hill or tribal communities would also be more conducive to environmental protection and regeneration than those of men elsewhere, but not more than those of the women of such communities. This is because hill and tribal women, perhaps more than any other group, still maintain a reciprocal link with nature's resources – a link that stems from a given organization of production, reproduction and distribution, including a given gender division of labour.

At the same time, the positive aspects of this link should not serve as an argument for continued entrenchment of women within a given division of labour. Rather, they should serve as an argument for creating the conditions that would help universalize this link with nature, for instance by *declassing* and *degendering* the ways in which productive and reproductive activities are organized (within and outside the home) and how property, resources, knowledge and power are distributed.

Conclusion

The Indian experience offers several insights and lessons. First, the processes of environmental degradation and appropriation of natural resources by a few have specific class-gender as well as locational implications – it is women of poor, rural households who are most adversely affected and who have participated actively in ecology movements. 'Women' therefore cannot be posited (as the ecofeminist discourse has typically done) as a unitary category, even within a country, let alone across the Third World or globally. Second, the adverse class-gender effects of these processes are manifest in the erosion of both the livelihood systems and the knowledge systems on which poor rural women depend. Third, the nature and impact of these processes are rooted interactively, on the one hand, in ideology – (in notions about development, scientific knowledge, the appropriate gender division of labour, and so on) and, on the other hand, in the economic advantage and political power predicated especially, but by no means only, on property differentials between households and between women and men. Fourth, there is a spreading grassroots resistance to such inequality and environmental destruction – to the processes, products, people, property, power and profit-orientation that underlie them. Although the voices of this resistance are yet scattered and localized, their message is a vital one, even from a purely growth and productivity concern and more so if our concern is with people's sustenance and survival.

In particular, the experiences of women's initiatives within the environmental movements suggests that women's militancy is much more closely linked to family survival issues than is men's. Implicit in these struggles is the attempt to carve out a space for an alternative existence that is based on equality not dominance over people, and cooperation with and not dominance over nature.

Indeed, what is (implicitly or explicitly) being called into question in various ways by the movements is the existing development paradigm – with its particular product and technological mix, its forms of exploitation of natural and human resources, and its conceptualization of relationships among people and between people and nature. However, a mere recognition that there are deep inequalities and destructiveness inherent in present processes of development is not enough. There is a need for policy to shift away from its present relief-oriented approach toward nature's ills and people's welfare in which the solution to nutrient-depleted soils is seen to lie entirely in externally added chemical nutrients, to depleted forests in mono-culture plantations, to drought starvation in food-for-work programmes, to gender inequalities in ad hoc income-generating schemes for women, and so on. These solutions reflect an aspirin approach to development – they are neither curative nor preventative, they merely suppress the symptoms for a while.

The realistic posing of an alternative (quite apart from its implementation) is of course not easy nor is it the purpose of this paper to provide a blueprint. What is clear so far are the broad contours. An alternative approach, suggested by feminist environmentalism, needs to be *transformational* rather than welfarist – where development, redistribution and ecology link in mutually regenerative ways. This would necessitate complex and interrelated changes such as in the *composition* of what is produced, the *technologies* used to produce it, the *processes* by which decisions on products and technologies are arrived at, the *knowledge systems* on which such choices are based, and the class and gender *distribution* of products and tasks.

For instance, in the context of forestry programmes, a different composition of the product may imply a shift from the currently favoured monocultural and commercial tree species to mixed species critical for local subsistence. An alternative agricultural technology may entail shifting from mainly chemical-based farming to more organic methods, from monocultural high-yielding variety seeds to mixed cropping with indigenously produced varieties, from the emphasis on large irrigation schemes to a plurality of water-provisioning systems, and from a preoccupation with irrigated crops to a greater focus on dryland crops. A change in the decision-making processes would imply a shift from the present top-down approach to one that ensures the broad-based democratic participation of disadvantaged groups. Indeed, insofar as the success stories of reforestation today relate to localized communities taking charge of their environmental base, a viable solution would need decentralized planning and control and institutional arrangements that ensure the involvement of the rural poor, and especially women, in decisions about what trees are planted and how the associated benefits are shared. Similarly, to encourage the continued use and growth of local knowledge about plants and species in the process of environmental regeneration, we would require new forms of interaction between local people and trained scientists and a widening of the definition of 'scientific' to include plural sources of knowledge and innovations, rather than merely those generated in universities and laboratories.

The most complex, difficult, and necessary to transform is of course the class and gender division of labour and resources, and the associated social relations. Here it is the emergence of new social movements in India around issues of gender, environment, democratic rights, and especially the formation of joint fronts between these movements on a number of recent occasions, that point the direction for change and provide the points of hope.

Indeed, environmental and gender concerns taken together open up both the need for re-examining, and the possibility of throwing new light on, many long-standing issues relating to development, redistribution and institutional change. That these concerns preclude easy policy solutions underlines the deep entrenchment of interests (both ideological and material) in existing structures and models of development. It also underlines the critical importance of grass-roots political organization of the poor and of women as a necessary condition for their voices to be heeded and for the entrenched interests to be undermined. Most of all it stresses the need for a shared alternative vision that can channel dispersed rivulets of resistance into a creative, tumultuous flow.

In short, an alternative, transformational approach to development would involve both ways of *thinking* about things and ways of *acting* on them. In the present context it would concern both how gender relations and relations between people and the non-human world are conceptualized, and how they are concretized in terms of the distribution of property, power and knowledge, and in the formulation of development policies and programmes.

It is in the failure to explicitly confront these political economy issues that the ecofeminist analysis remains a critique without threat to the established order.

Notes

This is a substantially abbreviated version of the paper entitled 'The Gender and Environment Debate: Lessons from India', which first appeared in *Feminist Studies*, 18(1), Spring 1992, pp. 119–158.

1 See especially King (1981, 1989, 1990), Salleh (1984), Merchant (1980), Griffin (1978), and various articles in Plant (1989), and Diamond and Orenstein (1990). Of course, not every strand in these arguments is necessarily subscribed to by each of these authors. Also see discussions and critiques by Zimmerman (1987), Warren (1987), Cheney (1987), and Longino (1981).
2 See the case studies, and especially the introductory essay in MacCormack and Strathern (1980); see also Moore (1989).
3 In some of her later work (e.g. King 1990), King does mention the need for such a differentiation, but does not discuss how this recognition would affect her basic analysis.
4 For an illuminating discussion of the debate on essentialism and constructionism within feminist theory, see Fuss (1989).
5 See case studies in MacCormack and Strathern (1980).

6 It is estimated that in 1981–2, 66.6 per cent of landowning households in rural India owned 1 ha or less and accounted for only 12.2 per cent of all land owned by rural households (Government of India 1987). The distribution of operational holdings was almost as skewed (Government of India 1986).

7 I prefer to use the term 'control rights' here, since what appears critical in this context is less who owns the resources than who has control over them. Hence, for instance, the control of state-owned resources could effectively rest with the village community.

8 However, the degree to which the village community acted as a cohesive group and the extent of control it exercised over communal lands varied across undivided India: it was much greater in the northwest than elsewhere (Baden-Powell 1957).

9 On traditional systems of community water management see Sengupta (1985), Leach (1967) and Seklar (1981). On communal management of forests and village commons, see Guha (1983), Gadgil (1985), and Moench (1988). On firewood gathering practices, see Agarwal (1986b, 1987). Firewood for domestic use in rural households was customarily collected in the form of twigs and fallen branches, which did not destroy the trees. Even today, 75 per cent of firewood used as domestic fuel in northern India (and 100 per cent in some other areas) is in this form.

10 Also see the discussion in Dasgupta and Maler (1990).

11 Under some large-scale irrigation works, crop yields are *lower* than in the period immediately prior to the project (Joshi and Agnihotri 1984).

12 Also see Marglin (1988).

13 Personal communication, Chitra Sundaram, DANIDA (Delhi), 1981.

14 These are apart from the widely documented patron–client types of relationships.

15 See Sen (1990) for a discussion on the bargaining approach to conceptualizing intrahousehold gender relations, and Agarwal (1990) for a discussion on the factors that affect intrahousehold bargaining power.

16 Among the Garo tribals of northeast India in the early 1960s, Burling (1963) found that the men always deferred on this count to the women, who knew of some 300 indigenously cultivated rice varieties. In Nepal even today it is women who do the seed selection work among virtually all communities (Acharya and Bennett 1981).

17 For a detailed discussion on these schemes and their shortcomings, see Agarwal (1986b).

18 Among the many writings on the Chipko movement, see especially Bandyopadhyay and Shiva (1987), Shiva (1988), and Jain (1984).

19 I understand there have also been cases of people hugging trees to protect them from loggers in the United States, although they appear to have no apparent link to Chipko.

20 There is a growing literature indicating significant gender differences in cash spending patterns, with a considerable percentage (at times up to 40 per cent) of what men earn in poor rural households typically going toward the purchase of items they alone consume (such as liquor, tobacco, clothes, etc.), and much of what the women earn going toward the family's basic needs. For examples from India, see especially Mencher (1988).

21 This gender divergence has also been noted elsewhere, as in Rajasthan (Brara 1987).

22 See also Longino (1987).

References

Acharya, Meena and Bennett, Lynn (1981) 'Women and the Subsistence Sector in Nepal', World Bank Staff Working Paper No. 526, Washington DC.

Agarwal, Bina (1981) 'Women and Water Resource Development', mimeo, Institute of Economic Growth, Delhi.

—— (1984) 'Rural Women and the High Yielding Variety Rice Technology in India', *Economic and Political Weekly*, Review of Agriculture, March.

—— (1986a) 'Women, Poverty and Agricultural Growth in India', *The Journal of Peasant Studies*, 13(2).

—— (1986b) *Cold Hearths and Barren Slopes: The Woodfuel Crisis in the Third World*, London: Zed Books.

—— (1987) 'Under the Cooking Pot: The Political Economy of the Domestic Fuel Crisis in Rural South Asia', *IDS Bulletin*, 18 (1).

—— (1988) 'Who Sows? Who Reaps? Women and Land Rights in India', *The Journal of Peasant Studies*, 15 (4).

—— (1989) 'Women, Land and Ideology in India', in Haleh Afshar and Bina Agarwal (eds) *Women, Poverty and Ideology: Contradictory Pressures, Uneasy Resolutions*, London: Macmillan.

—— (1990) 'Social Security and the Family', *The Journal of Peasant Studies*, April.

Baden-Powell, B.H. (1957) *The Indian Village Community*, New Haven, HRAF Press.

Bahuguna, Sundarlal (1984) 'Women's Non-Violent Power in the Chipko Movement', in Madhu Kishwar and Ruth Vanita (eds) *In Search of Answers: Indian Women Voices in Manushi*, London: Zed Books.

Bandyopadhyay, Jayanta (1986) 'A Case Study of Environmental Degradation in Karnataka'. Paper presented at a Workshop on Drought and Desertification, India International Centre, Delhi, 17–18 May.

Bandyopadhyay, Jayanta and Shiva, Vandana (1987) 'Chipko', *Seminar*, no. 330, February.

Bardhan, Kalpana (1977) 'Rural Employment, Welfare and Status: Forces of Tradition and Change in India', *Economic and Political Weekly*, 25 July, 2 July and 9 July.

Bhaduri, T. and Surin, V. (1980) 'Community Forestry and Women Headloaders', in *Community Forestry and People's Participation Seminar Report*, Ranchi Consortium for Community Forestry, 20–22 November.

Brara, Rita (1987) 'Commons Policy as Process: The Case of Rajasthan, 1955–85' *Economic and Political Weekly*, 7 October.

Bromley, Daniel W. and Cernea, Michael M. (1989) 'The Management of Common Property Natural Resources', World Bank Discussion Paper, no. 57, Washington, DC: World Bank.

Burling, Robins (1963) *Rensanggri: Family and Kinship in a Garo Village*, Philadelphia: Pennsylvania University Press.

Centre for Science and Environment (1986) *The State of India's Environment: A Citizen's Report, 1985–86*, Delhi: Centre for Science and Environment.

Chand, Malini and Bezboruah, Rita (1980) 'Employment Opportunities for Women in Forestry', in *Community Forestry and People's Participation – Seminar Report*, Ranchi Consortium for Community Forestry, 20–22 November.

Chandrashekar, D.M., *et al.* (1987) 'Social Forestry in Karnataka: An Impact Analysis', *Economic and Political Weekly*, 13 June.

216

Cheney, Jim (1987) 'Ecofeminism and Deep Ecology', *Environmental Ethics*, 9 (2).

Dasgupta, Partha and Maler, Karl-Goran (1990) 'The Environment and Emerging Development Issues', paper presented at a conference on Environment and Development, WIDER, Helsinki, September.

Dhawan, B.D. (1982) *Development of Tubewell Irrigation in India*, Delhi: Agricole Publishing Academy.

Fernandes, Walter and Menon, Geeta (1987) *Tribal Women and Forest Economy: Deforestation, Exploitation and Status Change*, Delhi: Indian Social Institute.

Fuss, Diane (1989) *Essentially Speaking*, New York: Routledge.

Gadgil, Madhav (1985) 'Towards an Ecological History of India', *Economic and Political Weekly*, Special No., November.

Gadgil, Madhav and Vartak, V.D. (1975) 'Sacred Groves of India: A Plea for Continued Conservation', *Journal of the Bombay Natural History Society*, 72 (2).

Glaeser, Bernhard (ed.) (1987) *Learning From China? Development and Environment in Third World Countries*, London: Allen and Unwin.

Government of India (1986) National Sample Survey Organisation, *37th Round Report on Land Holdings – 1, Some Aspects of Operational Holdings*, Report No. 331, Dept of Statistics, Government of India.

—— (1987) National Sample Survey Organisation, *37th Round Report on Land Holdings – 1, Some Aspects of Operational Holdings*, Dept of Statistics, Government of India.

—— (1990) *Forest Survey of India*, New Delhi: Ministry of Environment and Forests.

Griffin, Susan (1978) *Women and Nature: The Roaring Within Her*, New York: Harper and Row.

Guha, Ramachandra (1983) 'Forestry in British and post-British India: a historical analysis', *Economic and Political Weekly*, 29 October.

Habib, Irfan (1984) 'Peasant and Artisan Resistance in Mughal India', McGill Studies in International Development no. 34, Centre for Developing Area Studies, McGill University.

Howes, Michael and Jabbar, M.A. (1986) 'Rural Fuel Shortages in Bangladesh: The Evidence from Four Villages', Discussion Paper 213, Sussex, England: Institute of Development Studies.

Jain, Shobhita (1984) 'Women and People's Ecological Movement: A Case Study of Women's Role in the Chipko Movement in Uttar Pradesh', *Economic and Political Weekly*, 13 October.

Jodha, N.S. (1986) 'Common Property Resources and Rural Poor', *Economic and Political Weekly*, 5 July.

Joshi, P.K. and Agnihotri, A.K. (1984) 'An Assessment of the Adverse Effects of Canal Irrigation in India', *Indian Journal of Agricultural Economics* 39: 528–36.

Kerala Forestry Research Institute (1980) *Studies in the Changing Patterns of Man–Forest Relationships for Ecology and Management*, Trivandrum.

King, Ynestra (1981) 'Feminism and the Revolt', *Heresies*, No. 13, pp. 12–16.

—— (1989) 'The Ecology of Feminism and the Feminism of Ecology', in Judith Plant (ed.) *Healing the Wounds: The Promise of Ecofeminism*, Philadelphia: New Society Publishers.

—— (1990) 'Healing the Wounds: Feminism, Ecology and the Nature/Culture Dualism', in Irene Diamond and Gloria Orenstein (eds) *Reweaving the World: The Emergence of Ecofeminism*, San Francisco: Sierra Club Books.

Kumar, Shubh and David Hotchkiss (1988) 'Consequences of Deforestation for Women's Time Allocation, Agricultural Production and Nutrition in Hill Areas of Nepal', Research Report 69, Washington DC: International Food Policy Research Institute.

Leach, Edmund R. (1967) *Pul Eliya – A Village in Ceylon: A Study of Land Tenure and Kinship*, Cambridge: Cambridge University Press.

Longino, Helen E. (1981) Book Review in *Environmental Ethics*, 3 (4), Winter.

—— (1987) 'Can There be a Feminist Science?', *Hypatia*, 2 (3), Fall.

MacCormack, Carol P. and Strathern, Marilyn (eds) (1980) *Nature, Culture and Gender*, Cambridge: Cambridge University Press.

Marglin, Stephen A. (1988) 'Losing Touch: The Cultural Conditions of Worker Accommodation and Resistance', in Frederique A. Marglin and Stephen A. Marglin (eds) *Knowledge and Power*, Oxford: Oxford University Press.

Mencher, Joan (1988) 'Women's Work and Poverty: Women's Contribution to Household Maintenance in Two Regions of South India' in Daisy Dwyer and Judith Bruce (eds) *A Home Divided: Women and Income in the Third World*, Stanford, CA: Stanford University Press.

Mencher, Joan P. and Saradamoni, K. (1982) 'Muddy Feet and Dirty Hands: Rice Production and Female Agricultural Labour', *Economic and Political Weekly,* 28 December.

Merchant, Carolyn (1980) *The Death of Nature: Women, Ecology and the Scientific Revolution*, San Francisco: Harper and Row.

Moench, Marcus (1988) 'Turf and Forest Management in a Garhwal Hill Village' in Louise Fortmann and John W. Bruce (eds) *Whose Trees? Proprietary Dimensions of Forestry*, Boulder: Westview Press.

Mohan, Dinesh (1987) 'Food vs Limbs: Pesticides and Physical Disability in India', *Economic and Political Weekly*, 28 March.

Ortner, Sherry (1974) 'Is Male to Female as Nature is to Culture?', in Michelle Z. Rosaldo and Louise Lamphere (eds) *Women, Culture, and Society*, Stanford, CA: Stanford University Press.

Rao, C.H. Hanumantha, Ray, S.K. and Subbarao, K. (1988) *Unstable Agriculture and Drought*, Delhi: Vikas Publishing House.

Salleh, Ariel Kay (1984) 'Deeper than Deep Ecology: The Eco-Feminist Connection', *Environmental Ethics*, 16, Winter.

Seklar, David (1981) 'The New Era of Irrigation Management in India' photocopy, Ford Foundation, Delhi.

Sen, Amartya S. (1990) 'Gender and Cooperative-Conflict', in Irene Tinker (ed.) *Persistent Inequalities*, New York: Oxford University Press.

Sengupta, Nirmal (1985) 'Irrigation: Traditional vs. modern', *Economic and Political Weekly*, Special No., November.

Sharma, Ursula (1980) *Women, Work and Property in North-West India*, London: Tavistock.

Shaw, Paul (1989) 'Population, Environment and Women: An Analytical Framework', paper prepared for the United Nations Fund for Population Activities (UNFPA), Interagency Consultative Meeting, New York, 6 March.

Shiva, Vandana (1987) 'Ecology Movements in India', *Alternatives* 11: 255–72.

—— (1988) *Staying Alive: Women, Ecology and Survival*, London: Zed Books.

Swaminathan, Srilata (1982) 'Environment: Trees versus Man', *India International Center Quarterly*, 9 (3 and 4).

United Nations Development Program (1979) 'Rural Women's Participation in Development', Evaluation Study no. 3 (June), New York: UNDP.

Vatuk, Sylvia (1981) 'Sharing, Giving and Exchanging of Foods in South Asian Societies', photocopy, University of Illinois at Chicago Circle, October.

Wagner, Rudolf G. (1987) 'Agriculture and Environmental Protection in China', in Bernhard Glaeser (ed.) *Learning From China? Development and Environment in Third World Countries*, London: Allen and Unwin.

Warren, Karen J. (1987) 'Feminism and Ecology: Making Connections', *Environmental Ethics*, 9 (1), Spring.

Zimmerman, Michael E. (1987) 'Feminism, Deep Ecology and Environmental Ethics', *Environmental Ethics*, 9 (1), Spring.

11

WOMEN, ENVIRONMENT AND DEVELOPMENT
From Rio to Beijing

Bonnie Kettel

Introduction

This chapter examines the institutional and collegial links that constitute the international 'women, environment and development' (women, environment and development policy frameworks and actors – WED) policy milieu, the issues and events that have called them into being and encouraged their continued vitality, and the new debates and contributions that are presently emerging from collaboration and action within this domain. In particular, the chapter highlights the contributions of an 'expert advisory group' that was mobilized by the Women's Environment and Development Organization (WEDO, in New York), to provide an alternative perspective on emerging WED policy issues in preparation for the Fourth World Conference on Women held in Beijing in September 1995.[1] The diverse viewpoints held – typically very strongly – by women from a variety of contexts and regions in the South and the North have generated intense and very direct internal debate, as well as a significant level of external solidarity in the face of what is perceived by many WED analysts and activists – regardless of their personal background and particular viewpoint – as a world-wide crisis of regional and gender inequity and environmental destruction.

The world of WED

The contemporary WED policy milieu consists of seven interactive 'circles' of participation and action:[2]

- the international institutions and agencies of the larger United Nations system, including the United Nations Development Fund for Women (UNIFEM, in New York);

- bilateral donor institutions such as the Canadian International Development Agency (CIDA), the comparable institutions of donor countries such as Sweden (SIDA), Denmark (DANIDA), Norway (NORAD), and the multilateral Development Assistance Committee of the Organization for Economic Cooperation and Development (DAC/OECD);
- various international and regional research centres and programmes such as the International Development Research Centre (IDRC, in Ottawa), the Women, Environment and Development Network (WEDNET), the Ecology, Community Organization and Gender (ECOGEN) project at Clark University (Thomas-Slayter *et al*. 1991), the Both Ends Working Group on Women and Environment in Amsterdam (Both Ends 1992), and the Centre for Environment, Gender and Development (ENGENDER) in Singapore;
- international NGO's such as the International Women's Tribune Center (IWTC, in New York), WEDO and WorldWIDE (World Women in Defense of the Environment, in Washington DC);
- national governments, especially in the Southern countries;
- national level NGO's such as the Green Belt Movement in Kenya (Maathai 1994); and
- local women's environmental action groups in the South and the North such as the Chipko movement (Saidullah 1993) and the Love Canal Homeowners Association (McIntosh 1993).

Although WorldWIDE, which is an international network of women 'concerned about environmental management and protection', was founded in 1982 (WorldWIDE 1991), much of the concern about women and environment policy issues within this larger institutional milieu was sparked five years later by the publication in 1987 of the report of the World Commission on Environment and Development (The Brundtland Commission), *Our Common Future* (Kettel 1993).

In May 1989, the Women's Foreign Policy Council, established by the Women USA Fund, an American-based non-profit educational organization, held an all-day briefing on 'Women and the Environmental Crisis' in Washington, DC. The origins of WEDO, which is co-chaired by Bella Abzug, a former United States congresswoman, lie in that event. Since that time, international participation in WEDO has greatly expanded, and in 1995, there were also co-chairs from Brazil, Guyana, Norway, Egypt, Kenya, Nigeria, Costa Rica, India, and New Zealand (WEDO 1995a).

By 1990, the attention of the relevant UN agencies, the donor institutions and the international NGO's was increasingly focused on preparations for the forthcoming United Nations Conference on Environment and Development (UNCED), which was held in Rio de Janeiro in 1992 (DAC/OECD 1990). During the preparatory period, prior to this conference, WEDO organized the 'World Women's Congress for a Healthy Planet', which was held in Miami in 1991. The culmination of this phase of policy activity is represented in two documents: the visionary *Women's Action Agenda 21*, which was the outcome of the 'World Women's Congress' (WEDO 1992a), and Chapter 24 of *Agenda 21*, the global plan of action adopted in Rio de Janeiro (UN 1992). The chapter, which is titled 'Global Action for Women Towards Sustainable and Equitable Development', is the most comprehensive official WED policy document currently available.

Since 1992, research, analysis and policy formulation with regard to WED have entered a new phase. There is now an emerging body of critical analysis of the WED perspectives and approaches to policy intervention developed in relation to the Rio Conference. In addition, Chapter 24 has encouraged some new work on policy formulation with WED relevance (see, for example, CIDA 1995). In this context, the contributions of the WEDO expert advisory group are illuminating; they illustrate the concerns being raised by WED analysts and activists with a personal and institutional history of participation in WED policy issues prior to, during, and after UNCED. Many of the members of the WEDO 'expert advisory group' also have a direct involvement in NGOs working on WED or WED-related issues at the local community or national levels in a variety of regional contexts, including many Southern countries, the 'transition' countries of Eastern Europe, and various communities in the North. For this reason, their ideas are informed not only by their participation in policy intervention activities, but more importantly, by their direct day-to-day experience of women and environment issues 'on the ground'.

WED analysis and policy: a historical overview

Although WED policy formulation, as such, certainly begins with *Our Common Future* (WCED 1987), scholarly research and policy analysis dealing with WED issues has a much longer history. This is certainly the case with issues such as women and land tenure (Rogers 1980; Lewis 1981), women's access to energy, particularly to fuelwood (Agarwal 1986; Cecelski 1986), and to forest products generally (Hoskins 1979; Fortmann and Rocheleau 1985). There is also an important body of relatively early work on women's access to water, especially to clear, potable water (INSTRAW 1989), and to the impact of desertification on women (Monimart and Brah 1989), as well as some early work on women's involvements in livestock production (Dahl 1987).

However, much of this work is organized by natural resource sectors; it deals with women and wood, or women and water, but not with women and the natural environment as a broader arena for human use, management and protection. One of the earliest research papers dealing with these broader concerns is Baxter's study of women and environment issues in Sudan (Baxter 1981). The Environment Liaison Centre International, which is based in Nairobi, also held an early workshop dealing with broader WED issues

(ELCI 1985). However, from the point of view of policy formulation, the impact of this early sectoral work was limited. A careful look at the *Forward Looking Strategies for the Advancement of Women*, the platform of action which was adopted at the Nairobi End-of-Decade Conference on Women in 1985, tells the tale (UN 1985). The *Forward Looking Strategies* did call for women to participate more fully in national ecosystem management and control of environmental degradation (Kettel 1995b). However, until *Our Common Future*, WED was generally unrecognized as a broader policy concern (Kettel 1993).

It is also important not to overrate the significance of *Our Common Future* as a basis for WED policy formulation. The Report, which set forward a new policy framework for sustainable development – 'development that meets the needs of the present without compromising the ability of future generations to meet their own needs' – dealt with issues which were considered to have specific relevance to women on only six pages. By comparison, Africa, which was recognized by the Brundtland Commission as a continent 'in crisis', was indexed on over fifty pages (WCED 1987: 43, 388–400).

In this context, two books published in 1988 by Irene Dankelman and Joan Davidson, and Vandana Shiva, had a considerable impact. Dankelman and Davidson's *Women and Environment in the Third World* was empirically documented, and its main argument – that environmental destruction has a disproportionate impact on women – was presented in an easily accessible manner. The relevance of the book to policy formulation for 'women and development', which had been a concern of donor institutions such as CIDA for some time (Rathgeber 1990), was immediately apparent. Furthermore, the book also made clear that there could be few meaningful institutional efforts towards policy formulation or intervention for sustainable development without the participation of women, especially at the local level.

Vandana Shiva's book, *Staying Alive: Women, Ecology and Development*, had a less immediately apparent, but ultimately more visionary policy impact. Dankelman and Davidson still understood the natural environment as a list of natural resource sectors, but Shiva's vision was broader, and far more critical. Her argument was that 'maldevelopment' and environmental destruction are an inevitable outcome of the 'masculine' view of nature that emerged along with the 'patriarchal project' of modern science (1988: 14, 15). In making this assertion, Shiva was drawing on much earlier work that had already revealed the historical interrelationship between patriarchy, science and the 'death of nature' (Merchant 1980). But it was Shiva who linked this analytic discourse to the emerging Third World feminist critique of the mainstream development paradigm that had dominated policy and intervention since the 1960s. This critique had been set forward just a few years earlier in Gita Sen and Caren Grown's equally visionary book, *Development Crises and Alternative Visions: Third World Women's Perspectives* (1985).

The overall impact of the work by Dankelman and Davidson, Shiva, and

Sen and Grown, was to make *Our Common Future* look grossly inadequate as a basis for WED policy formulation. While it is certainly true, therefore, that the Brundtland Commission report set off a great deal of new WED research and policy analysis, one of the motivations for that new level of effort in the WED policy community was recognition of the document's deficiencies. It was in this context that the WEDNET initiative was designed and launched (Rathgeber and Kettel 1989; Kettel 1995a). WEDNET was an IDRC funded research network that documented women's indigenous knowledge of natural resource management through ten different projects in eight African countries. Also, in the years immediately surrounding UNCED, some significant new research and policy analysis did begin to emerge (Clones 1991; Agarwal 1992; Ahooja-Patel 1992; Commonwealth Secretariat 1992; Jacobson 1992; Ofusu-Amaah and Philleo 1993). In October 1992, just after the Rio Conference, the coordinators of a number of research and policy networks that were dealing directly with WED issues also met for the first time in Amsterdam (Both Ends 1992).

In the midst of all this burgeoning work, the dominant concern within the WED policy milieu in the early 1990s was to make a cogent impact on the official platform of action that would emerge from Rio.[3] Much of the critical policy intervention in relation to the conference took place at the Third Preparatory Committee Meeting (PrepComm) in August of 1991. At the outset of the planning process, women were largely absent from the UNCED Secretariat, from the official delegations sent by participating governments, and on the International Facilitating Committee for the NGO Forum (WEDO 1992b: 9). Even at the Earth Summit itself, only 15 per cent of the official delegates and advisors were women (Steady 1993: 29).

The absence of women was all the more ironic and unacceptable given the newly established international network of women activists, scholars and policy analysts that had emerged out of the Nairobi End-of-Decade Conference on Women in 1985. In response to the exclusion of women from the PrepComm process, WEDO organized a 55 member 'International Policy Action Committee' (IPAC), which met for the first time in October 1990. At the Third PrepComm in Geneva, members of this committee, together with an ad hoc group of diverse participants, from a variety of NGO's and the larger policy community, successfully lobbied the official delegates to accept UNCED decision 3/5. This decision directed the UNCED Secretary-General to 'ensure that women's critical economic, social and environmental contributions to sustainable development' were addressed 'as a distinct cross-cutting issue in addition to being mainstreamed in all the substantive work and documentation' then in preparation (WEDO 1992b: 3). At the Fourth PrepComm, in March 1992, much of the success of the Third PrepComm was jeopardized by a dispute between the United States delegation and the G77 group of developing countries. The United States delegation had moved to delete all references to 'overconsumption' in the North from the draft platform of action. The G77 delegates responded with the threatened deletion of all references to family planning and population growth. This was a complex, multi-layered, and largely male-oriented episode, which is discussed more fully elsewhere (Kettel 1996). For our purposes, what is interesting about this debate is the reaction it provoked in the UNCED women's caucus. The caucus issued an immediate protest statement, held two meetings with the head of the G77 and other concerned governments, and organized a plenary session of governmental and non-governmental representatives 'at which women presented their views' on family planning, reproductive choice and population issues in general (WEDO 1992b: 4).[4] The consequence of this multi-faceted intervention was that the language with regard to women's reproductive rights was strengthened throughout the official draft of *Agenda 21*. Thanks to the work of the WEDO–IPAC group, and the ever-expanding women's caucus, Chapter 24 was largely in place by the end of the Fourth PrepComm. Additional references to women's issues and concerns were also included throughout the final platform of action.

However, in the midst of all this success, one key issue was left unresolved in the UNCED process: the provision of financing for international and national WED initiatives. The lack of WED financing was actually a symptom of a much larger problem: the overall unwillingness of the Northern countries to support environmental protection in the South. Most of the minimal financing for *Agenda 21* that was committed in Rio de Janeiro was to be channelled through the World Bank (Rich 1994: 261–2), an institution many would regard as intrinsically hostile to the aims of WED.

The final version of *Agenda 21* left the financing of WED initiatives entirely up to the 'international community', i.e., the donor institutions, and the supportive political will of national governments (UN 1992). The probable cost estimate that Chapter 24 put forward was also minuscule (Carroll-Foster 1993). The total annual cost of implementing Chapter 24 was estimated by the UNCED Secretariat at some $40 million US dollars, a ludicrously small sum which suggests that the Secretariat was hesitant to recommend a larger, but more realistic amount. Instead, Chapter 24 meekly suggested that 'actual costs' would depend on the specific WED strategies that national governments decided to implement.

As a result of this inadequacy in Chapter 24, one of the key WED policy imperatives in the immediate post-Rio period involved the crucial issue of donor commitment to WED funding. Without such donor involvement, few national governments in the South are likely to take on the equity objectives of Chapter 24 (Kettel 1993). In addition to this pragmatic concern, the critique of existing WED policy frameworks and approaches is also vital. A decade after *Our Common Future* was published, most WED researchers and policy analysts would undoubtedly agree that a great deal of relevant analytic work remains to be done (Kettel 1995a and 1995b).

There is also a vibrant concern to protect – and advance – the policy breakthroughs that were achieved in Rio. In the pre-Beijing period, these successes, and those established later at the International Conference on Population and Development (ICPD) in Cairo, 1994, were threatened by some very powerful and committed antagonists. In this context, critical reflection on the Rio experience, and the epistemological and political foundations for WED policy intervention, became all the more important.

Critical reflections on the UNCED experience

Since 1992, scholars and policy analysts have begun to consider the significance of the Rio experience for WED, and for the larger WED policy milieu. Opinions about the relevance and success of the WED interventions at Rio vary (see van den Hombergh 1993). Sabine Hausler offers a negative assessment. The Earth Summit, she suggests, was a 'failure of global proportions'. For the most part, according to Hausler, it simply gave new life to mainstream goals within the new rhetoric of sustainable development. 'Marginal actors', including women, indigenous peoples and citizens' groups generally, were not able, in her view, to change the 'parameters of discussion'. Instead, WED lobbying efforts served only to legitimize what was essentially a process of co-optation of the voices of the marginalized, especially through the incorporation of the language of alternative development and gender awareness into mainstream development discourse (1994: 146–7). She suggests that the inclusion of women and women's environmental concerns in various preparatory documents, and in *Agenda 21*, was largely an exercise in hypocrisy, a mere stratagem on the part of actors such as the Business Council for Sustainable Development and the World Bank to make these documents more broadly acceptable (1994: 151). She argues, therefore, that 'one of the most important tasks is to continue to make visible the ways in which the strategies of power operate and their increasing sophistication' (1994: 148).

Hausler's plea for the continued importance of critical analysis in the WED policy milieu is cogent. When the words are elegant, but donor institutions and national governments are not prepared to pay for WED action, what, at the end of the day, has been accomplished? The World Bank's institutional contributions to debt accumulation and environmental degradation in the South offer little hope of a sudden, profound transformation in that institution's overall outlook and policy (Rich 1994).

Despite the criticisms, I believe that the WED interventions at Rio were worthwhile, and that the existence of official policy documents with improved WED language is a necessary, *but certainly not sufficient*, step towards a more humane, equitable, and environmentally responsible approach to donor funding and action. Official documents such as Chapter 24 of *Agenda 21* offer a vital basis for the evaluation and public critique of inappropriate action and inaction on the part of donor institutions and national governments. This, in my view, is their primary – indeed, perhaps their only – utility. It is important, too, as Hausler also points out, that the UNCED process undermined the 'stalemate of opposition between women from the North and the South' and demonstrated the tremendous willingness of 'women involved in WED issues . . . to work together with women from other cultural and political backgrounds' (1994: 150).

However, as Braidotti, Charkiewicz, Hausler and Wieringa comment, 'the WED movement so far has been carried on mainly by women leaders and professional women from educated, middle-class backgrounds working in development agencies, scientific institutions, environmental, consumer and reproductive rights movements'. This is a significant limitation, which will have to be overcome if we want to formulate 'practical proposals' for the future (Braidotti *et al.* 1994: 179–80). As they suggest, 'one of the main tasks ahead is how to carry to the grassroots level what has happened at UNCED and, together with the women working on that level, develop concrete strategies for pro-environmental change'.

The WEDO advisory group: voices from the regions

In the fall of 1993, WEDO commissioned a draft[5] 'platform of action' dealing specifically with WED issues as an alternative to the official platform, which was then in preparation for the Fourth World Conference on Women in Beijing. Early in 1994, the draft was distributed to the participants in WEDO's large informal network of WED 'advisors' who were asked by WEDO to review the draft platform, and to identify any significant concerns that they felt had been incorrectly or inadequately addressed. A revised version of the draft platform (WEDO 1994) was also discussed at an open meeting organized by WEDO during the March 1994 PrepComm for the Beijing Conference.

The draft was intended to build on the *Women's Action Agenda 21*, and to move the policy debate forward by highlighting concepts and issues which had not been part of the framework of discussion during UNCED.[6] In order to establish a novel point of departure, the draft used the term 'resourcism'[7] defined as an organizing outlook on the natural world that places profits, technology and men's interests at the centre of the development paradigm (see also Kettel 1993; Stamp 1989). The draft identified three post-UNCED 'critical areas of concern': inequality in women's access to environmental health and health care; inequality in women's access to information and participation in the promotion of healthy and sustainable communities; and inequality in women's sharing of power in community, national and international decision-making. Throughout, the draft attempted to identify links of common interest between women in the South and the North, especially with regard to the three critical areas of concern.

Many in the advisory group found the term 'resourcism' provocative, still inadequately defined, but potentially revealing. Numerous points of refinement were offered on details in the text. For our purposes, however, what is important is not what the participants in the advisory group liked – or what they were prepared to tolerate – about the draft, but what they felt was inadequately expressed or missing.

Throughout the responses, there was a prevailing concern to encourage and increase women's equitable participation in decision-making in a variety of arenas, and at all levels (see below). One of the most predominant specific concerns was recognition of the issues that are important to indigenous women. Beatriz Schulthess[8] made an urgent plea for 'the need to break down social and cultural barriers', and to support recognition, rather than assimilation of indigenous women, pointing out that:

> If we want to be catalysts for a fundamental change we have to learn how to interact with women who maintain their own culture . . . we can not continue to interact only among women who learned how to function under the standards set by a dominant male oriented and western society.

Similarly, Aroha Te Pareake Mead commented that 'there are perspectives and issues which are unique to indigenous women'. She offered the example of the sacred sites established by Maori women to bury the placentas of their children. These sites allow women to return 'the fruits of birth to the mother of all births'. Yet 'no national or international instrument recognizes the right of indigenous women to declare 'sacred sites' based on customary rights'.

Many advisors also highlighted the vital importance of reaching women at the local, grassroots level, and especially of identifying issues that are of direct concern to women in the South. One of these was women's access to land, including both private property (especially inherited land), as well as access to common property resources. Stress was also placed on the importance of women's access to informal and formal education. One advisor contributed a copy of the Workshop Recommendations from the 'First Regional Workshop on Women and Environment at Grass-Root Level' held in Kampala in 1990 (The Uganda Women Tree Planting Movement 1990). This vibrant document, which offers a detailed collective reflection of WED issues at the local African level, has a preamble which states that 'the root cause of our African environmental problems is ignorance aggravated by poverty'. However, as the preamble also asserts, 'this lack of resources can be attributed to huge expenses by governments on buying arms to sustain civil war in Africa which in turn leads to creation of refugees living in very unfavourable conditions'.

The emphasis in many of the comments on the lives of women in the South was on the global factors that limit women's access to opportunity, information, income, and basic needs such as health and education. Perdita Huston drew attention to 'the entire global context and structure of the multilateral institutions, which so gravely affect women's livelihood and well being'. Maria Onestini also commented that:

> Women's agenda must be expanded to be outside the home (or the community which is a small extension beyond the home) . . . . Particularly since the globalization of markets, political systems, and of course environmental affairs tend to imply that decision-making is done less and less at the micro level . . . and more done at these macro levels.

Various advisors drew attention to global inequities in terms of trade, flows of aid, accumulation of debt, and distribution of toxic waste, all of which disproportionately affect women in the South. María Eugenia Penón rejected the use of the term 'resourcism' to address these issues. As she said, 'we know we are talking about the capitalism in its present form and liberal economics. Why not call it by its real name?' Several highlighted the negative role of the Bretton Woods institutions – especially the International Monetary Fund and the World Bank – and the transnational corporations. The impact on women and children of structural adjustment programmes, and the resulting withdrawal of national governments from the provision of basic services, was also a topic of concern.

There was an emerging awareness, especially on the part of advisors from the North, that women outside of the developing countries are also being affected by the impact of globalization and environmental destruction. Health, and environmental health in particular, was the arena for much of this discussion. Miriam Wyman commented that 'while there is no doubt that the lot of women in the South is more difficult than that of women in the North, I think it is important to indicate that women everywhere bear the brunt of . . . resourcism'. Health conditions in the workplace were a particular concern. As Natalia Mirovitskaya pointed out: 'the problems of female occupational health remain practically outside the mainstream of medical research'.

Other advisors also cited the lack of scientific and technological research addressed to women's needs and interests, especially with regard to energy. But Ruth Lechte pointed out that there is also a great need for increased scientific literacy on the part of people – men and women – everywhere. As she said: 'we have found in the Pacific that while local people know WHAT happens in their environments given certain actions, they do not know WHY'.

Ending militarism and the armaments trade was also a critical concern. Advisors stressed the importance of increasing women's participation in public decision-making as an essential avenue for overcoming militarism and warfare. Alicia Barcena felt that the participation of women in the multilateral financial institutions and regional development banks was 'crucial'. Rosina Wiltshire also highlighted the significance of women's participation in international trade negotiations, and the need to ensure that 'ethical and equity concerns' were reflected in these agreements.

In a related vein, Simone Bilderbeek made an eloquent plea for recognition of the relationship between women and biodiversity, arguing that

> the relation between women and nature should not only be elaborated in terms of health and resources, but also in spiritual terms . . . . Women need biodiversity, not only to feed us, to provide us with medicines, energy and construction materials, but also because we need beauty around us, we need the spiritual power of nature . . . . Biological and cultural diversity . . . are essential elements of the quality of our lives, communities and societies.

Although the draft platform was intended to deal with issues relevant to *women*, varied concerns were expressed about *gender* inequity in relations between women and men world-wide. As Joni Seager commented: 'inequality is absolutely the meta-concern'. Women's participation in decision-making was central to this discussion. Beatriz Schulthess pointed out that what is necessary is the 'participation of women from all backgrounds and cultures at all levels'. Other advisors also suggested that what gender equity with regard to WED requires is an increased level of gender-sensitivity on the part of women who achieve decision-making authority, as well as the open inclusion of men as participants in a shared global quest.

The crucial policy question which emerges from the WEDO advisors' comments is how the new, more just, and environmentally respectful development paradigm they represent can be furthered and implemented in the post-UNCED setting. What lies underneath most of these written responses is a shared global ethic based on *caring*: on respect and concern for women and men in all the world's regions and cultures, and the well being of the natural environment on which we all depend.

One policy document presently in existence fully incorporates this 'caring' approach to the human and global future as a central element: the *Women's Action Agenda 21* (WEDO 1992a). The relevance of this document, and the more recent comments of the WEDO advisors, is not surprising. 'Care' is a human and environmental responsibility that has been assigned – almost universally – to women in a myriad of social and cultural contexts across the planet. The pursuit of modernity, and the debacle of post-modernity, have left this responsibility more and more in women's hands (Kettel 1993, 1995a). Translating women's experience of care into appropriate policy and effective action is central to the new, more just and environmentally respectful WED paradigm that the WEDO advisors outlined.

WED and the donor community

Northern donor institutions could play a vital role in furthering WED goals through policy formulation and funding for initiatives in keeping with the parameters of gender equity and environmental sustainability established in the *Women's Action Agenda 21*. Effective incorporation of Chapter 24 – which reflects some of the perspective of the Women's Action *Agenda 21* – into detailed WED policy and funding guidelines would be a very useful first step. It is instructive, therefore, to look at the present state of WED policy formulation and action within the donor institutions.

A recent external evaluation of CIDA's Women in Development (WID) policy framework revealed that CIDA and NORAD were commonly mentioned as the two donor agencies 'that have most influenced UN organizations regarding WID' by knowledgeable colleagues in a variety of multilateral development organizations (CIDA 1993a: 9). Throughout the UNCED process, the Canadian delegation strongly supported the inclusion of Chapter 24 in *Agenda 21* (Carroll-Foster 1993). Together with the delegations from Australia, New Zealand, and the Scandinavian countries, the Canadian delegation at UNCED played an important role in ensuring the impact and success of the work of the women's caucus and the WEDO–IPAC lobbying effort.

The new CIDA policy framework for 'Women in Development and Gender Equity' has as its first objective 'to encourage, respond to and support initiatives within and among developing countries in order to: increase women's participation in economic, political, social and environmental decision-making processes' (1995: 1). This new policy framework is a formal document, which has been subjected to the relevant approval processes, and is intended to apply to 'all CIDA activities'.

The new WID/Gender Equity framework builds on two previous documents, an interim policy on *Women in Development*, and CIDA's *Policy for Environmental Sustainability*, both of which were adopted in 1992. It also reflects the results of the external evaluation of the WID policy framework in effect from 1984 to 1992 (CIDA 1992a and 1992b, 1993a). The evaluation team found that, although CIDA had established a reputation as a progressive and enlightened WID donor, after 1990 momentum had been lost: WID-specific projects, and their total budgets dropped 'precipitously'. Ironically, that decline was in part due to CIDA's increased attention to new policy arenas, specifically 'human rights', 'good governance' and 'environmental impact', all of which are centrally relevant to WED (CIDA 1993a: 4). The evaluation report stressed the importance of integrating the WID policy with these other 'cross-cutting' policy imperatives (CIDA 1993a: 13).

The evaluation report also noted that while the 1992 interim WID framework encouraged 'policy dialogue' – often in the interest of improved approaches to gender equity in CIDA funding – this also meant that traditional 'women-only projects' were increasingly neglected. However, no clear means for operationalizing the new approach at the country programme level were established (CIDA 1993a: 5–7). To overcome these dilemmas, the evaluation team also called for the future allocation of 'appropriate resources' to WID. As they commented: 'for WID to be part of the mainstream of CIDA's work, the scale of resources devoted to WID must be more than . . . peripheral' (1993: 14).

The new CIDA WID/Gender Equity framework does attempt to respond to the concerns raised in the evaluation report. To what extent the new policy framework will facilitate greater WED relevance and funding at CIDA remains to be seen. Although CIDA has not outlined a set of detailed WED policy guidelines, a number of institutional attempts have been made to interpret the relevance of WED for CIDA's WID programming. These include, *inter alia*, a WED information kit (CIDA 1993b), and a review of the implications of Chapter 24 (CIDA 1993c: 37–9). This informal document listed six specific objectives for improved WED sensitivity in CIDA activities, and also recommended the strengthening of links between the WID and Environment policy development units 'in order to enhance CIDA capacity to address Agenda 21'.

The 1995 CIDA policy framework is certainly a progressive document. It moves far 'beyond the . . . emphasis on women as agents and beneficiaries to an emphasis on gender equity and women's empowerment' (1995: 2). 'Gender' and 'gender equity' receive detailed conceptual attention in the text, which points out the meaning and significance of the term 'gender' (see below), and stresses that equity 'calls for the differential treatment of groups in order to end inequality and foster autonomy'.

Ironically, however, the CIDA WID/Gender Equity policy framework was put forward at a time when the word 'gender' was itself under attack in the UN policy formulation process. In the months preceeding the Fourth World Conference on Women in September 1995, the attention of WEDO, and other key actors in the WED policy milieu, was focused – for a time almost entirely – on protecting the use of this one word, and all the policy gains its use reflected, in the platform of action that would emerge from Beijing.

Facing the gender backlash: the Beijing meeting

In 1995, twenty years after the First World Conference on Women in Mexico City, some of the most patriarchal institutions and nations on the planet were beginning to notice that male privilege in decision-making at all levels was being eroded by the UN policy process, and by the continuing efforts of the larger international women's movement. The 'backlash' began in Cairo, in September 1994, at the International Conference on Population and Development (ICPD) meeting, and continued into the World Summit on Social Development meeting in Copenhagen in March 1995. In Cairo, a coalition of delegates led by the Vatican adopted a series of adversarial positions with regard to women's reproductive rights and opportunities. In spite of these efforts, the women's caucus, again with the support of the larger women's movement and sympathetic national delegations, was able to ensure that women's participation, concerns, and rights were central to the final Cairo plan of action. Those fundamental principles of gender equity were again reaffirmed, and for the same reasons, at the Social Summit. However, at the final PrepComm for the Beijing conference, which took place in April 1995, a renewed, even stronger, attempt was made to undermine these successes.

Much of the official work at UN PrepComms centres on the process of drafting the platform of action. Delegations can indicate their opposition to the preliminary draft, which is prepared by the Conference Secretariat, by insisting that particular words and phrases be 'bracketed' as unacceptable. All bracketed elements in the draft must be reviewed and rejected, amended, or accepted, either at the PrepComm, or at the Conference itself. Normally, the goal of the Secretariat and the government delegations is to have as little of the draft as possible bracketed immediately prior to the Conference.

At the April 1995 PrepComm, a coalition of delegations, including the Vatican, Guatemala, Honduras, Ecuador, Sudan, Benin, Malta, Libya and Egypt, succeeded in bracketing approximately 40 per cent of the draft platform (WEDO 1995a: 8). The most contentious of these interventions was led by the Guatemalan delegation, which called for the bracketing of the term 'gender' throughout the text. This word, which refers to the social and cultural construction of men and women's statuses, roles and influence, became the focal point for the policy confrontation that was building in the months immediately prior to Beijing.

In April 1995, the PrepComm Chairperson ruled that gender – a word included in UN platforms of action at least since UNCED – could not be bracketed. However, she also set up a working group to seek 'a common understanding of the word gender within the context of the document' (WEDO 1995a: 9). What was really at issue in this definitional debate was the future of male privilege in decision-making. For the 'anti-gender' delegations, male privilege appeared to constitute a biologically inherent – one might say God-given – aspect of human life, which no mere policy document should attempt to transform. On the other hand, if, as the international women's movement had been asserting since Mexico City in 1975, male privilege in decision-making – no matter how pervasive – is merely social and cultural, then it could be challenged and transformed. The debate over the word gender, therefore, was ultimately about whether the world should be run by men, for men, or whether the world could be run by men and women, for people everywhere (see also Kettel 1995c).

In the end, the term gender was used throughout the platform of action. Furthermore, the Beijing platform not only calls for gender equity; it also calls for gender *equality* in national and international decision-making, and in women's access to economic resources, including land, credit, inheritance, natural resources and technology. As a WEDO analysis points out, 'equality can be measured; equity and dignity are more difficult to define, judge and measure and are open to cultural relativism' (WEDO 1995b). The use of the term 'equality' was a step forward that many WED activists could not have envisioned in April 1995. Furthermore, environment was recognized as one of twelve critical areas of concern in the Beijing platform, and at the meeting, 90 governments offered specific follow-up commitments in relation to particular aspects of the document (WEDO 1995c).

In some measure, these outcomes were the result of the activities of the women's 'linkage caucus', which was facilitated by WEDO. The primary goal of the linkage caucus was to ensure that gains for women which had been won at UNCED, and later at Cairo and Copenhagen, were not lost, and indeed, were furthered, in successive UN policy documents. In Beijing, the linkage caucus included 1,320 NGO representatives from 73 countries (WEDO 1995c: 5).

In spite of the gains made in Beijing, as the editorial in the December 1995 WEDO newsletter says, 'Utopia is not within sight'. However, in the words of Bella Abzug:

> We did not get everything that we want . . . . But it is the strongest statement of consensus on women's equality, empowerment and justice ever produced by the world's governments. It's a vision of a transformational picture of what the world can be for women as well as men, for this and future generations.
>
> (WEDO 1995c: 1–2)

Reflections on the future of WED

As the comments of the WEDO advisors reveal, gender equality in decision-making at all levels is an essential element in a larger quest for a more secure and sustainable future. The WEDO 'experts' also insisted that a central role in establishing and implementing a gender-sensitive WED agenda must be played by those women whose lives have been most affected by maldevelopment and environmental destruction in the past. The voices of these women, and not the voices of organized male privilege, are those that must be heard.

There is also, as the WEDO advisors recognized, an important continuing role for research and critical analysis in documenting and assessing what can be done, how those specific objectives can best be fulfilled, and by which institutions and actors. Participatory approaches to these efforts are critical, but there is also likely to be a continuing role for the efforts of scholars and policy analysts working in a variety of institutional settings. The donor institutions, such as CIDA, also have a vital role to play through continued efforts at formulation and implementation of gender-sensitive WED policy and programming. However, without the continued interest and participation of the global WED policy community – especially through direct intervention in the policy formulation process – in the view of the WEDO advisors, nothing of any significance will actually happen. Indeed, as the experience of the April 1995 PrepComm suggests, much could be lost.

Although WED centres on women's environmental interests and needs, particular WEDO advisors stressed that we also need to find new approaches for the participation of men in support of the larger WED agenda. There has, in the past, been great openness in the WED policy realm with regard to participation and debate, and a notable willingness on the part of WED activists, researchers and policy analysts to extend respect and friendship to others involved in the same larger quest. If we want to maintain openness and willingness to work collectively as a basis for effective WED policy intervention, then as various WEDO advisors make clear, we are going to have to care about nurturing diversity, enthusiasm and assertiveness.

The contributions of the WEDO advisory group offer an example and an agenda for that kind of effort in caring and acting collectively, as do the interventions of the women's caucus at UNCED, and the women's linkage caucus in Beijing. We should not be calling for *less* of this kind of effort: we should, in fact, be calling for *more*: more policy intervention, more funding, and more collective participation and action for a genuinely sustainable and equitable future.

Notes

1   The research on which this paper is based was funded by the Women's Environment and Development Organization (WEDO), by a York Sabbatical Leave Fellowship, and by a Research Grant from the Social Sciences and Humanities Research Council of Canada (SSHRCC). I was commissioned by WEDO to write and revise the draft 'platform of action' discussed in the paper in the fall of 1993. The York Sabbatical Leave Fellowship provided me with a research assistant, Lois Dellert, who synthesized all of the responses to the draft during the summer of 1994. The SSHRCC Research Grant (410–93–1184) provided the involvement of another research assistant, Barbara Muirhead, who carried out a great deal of the background research with regard to the critical reflections on WED discussed in the paper. My thanks to Lois and Barbara for their support and critical commentary.

2   My policy involvement in WED issues dates back to 1988, when I became the Canadian Coordinator for WEDNET (the Women, Environment and Development Network), a large-scale research initiative that has documented women's indigenous knowledge of sustainable resource use in eight African countries. (WEDNET was funded by the International Development Research Centre, and headquartered at the Environment Liaison Centre International in Nairobi. An extensive discussion of the WEDNET initiative may be found in Kettel 1995a.) In the years since, I have contributed to WED policy formulation as a researcher (Kettel 1995b), as the background author of relevant discussion papers, and as an unnamed professional consultant. As a result of these varied involvements, I have

a broad personal awareness of the complex links that exist between institutions and actors at the international, national and even local levels with regard to WED policy and action.

3   Since the 1975 First World Conference on Women, the United Nations Conference process has generated a rationale, a forum, an arena of debate and collaboration, and a sense of growing strength and well-being on the part of the international women's movement. The World Conferences on Women – Mexico City (1975), Copenhagen (1980), Nairobi (1985), and Beijing (1995) – have been central to this process and experience.

4   Anyone who has not participated in caucusing and lobbying at a United Nations PrepComm might well have difficulty in appreciating the enormity of the effort involved in the WED interventions at the Third and Fourth PrepComms, and the policy implications – and collective emotional significance – of their success. Effective policy intervention in the context of UN PrepComms and Conferences requires detailed and ongoing analysis of relevant draft documents, daily caucusing, constant collective vigilance and assertiveness, persistent lobbying, and a transformative ability to endure boredom, tension, apathy and fatigue. Successful policy intervention also requires significant back-up in the form of detailed documentation. Much of the official aspect of this task fell to Filomena Steady, who was appointed as the WED specialist in the UNCED Secretariat. In order to support her official activities, Steady organized an important pre-UNCED symposium on 'The impact of environmental degradation on women and children' in Geneva in May of 1991 (Steady 1993).

5   I was commissioned to write the draft that eventually was published as WEDO 1994.

6   While the draft platform is not the focus here, it did establish a framework of discussion to which the advisors were asked to respond. As a result, the draft may certainly have shaped, and limited, some of the resulting commentary. However, the advisors were in no way compelled to accept the parameters the draft established, and a few rejected it either entirely, or for the most part.

7   This term was borrowed from Neil Evernden and John Livingston. In their work, 'resourcism' is revealed as a culturally derived worldview – now predominant in the Northern countries – in which nature is recognized merely of a multiplicity of 'resources' destined for human use in an endless, world-wide quest for financial gain (see Evernden 1984).

8   Each of the authors quoted here has kindly granted permission for my use of their comments in this paper.

References

Agarwal, Bina (1986) *Cold Hearths and Barren Slopes: the Woodfuel Crisis in the Third World*, London: Zed Books.

—— (1992) 'The Gender and Environment Debate: Lessons from India', *Feminist Studies* 18, 1: 119–58.

Ahooja-Patel, Krishna (1992) *Linking Women with Sustainable Development*, Vancouver: The Commonwealth of Learning.

Baxter, Diana (1981) *Women and the Environment*, Sudan Institute of Environmental Studies Research Paper No. 2, Khartoum: University of Khartoum.

Both Ends (1992) *Report of the Meeting of Coordinators of International Networks on Women, Environment and Development*, 8–10 October 1992, Amsterdam: Both Ends.

Braidotti, Rosa, Charkiewicz, E., Hausler, S. and Wieringa, S. (eds) (1994) *Women, the Environment and Sustainable Development: Towards a Theoretical Synthesis*, London: Zed Books.

Carroll-Foster, Theodora (ed.) (1993) *A Guide to Agenda 21: Issues, Debates and Canadian Initiatives*, Ottawa: IDRC.

Cecelski, Elizabeth (1986) *Energy and Rural Women's Work: Geneva 21–25 October, 1985*, Technical Cooperation Report, Geneva: ILO.

CIDA (Canadian International Development Agency) (1990) *Compendium of Readings for the Environment and Women Session, June 20–1 1990*, Women in Development Directorate Hull: CIDA.

—— (1992a) *Women in Development: a Policy Statement*, Hull: CIDA.

—— (1992b) *CIDA's Policy for Environmental Sustainability*, Hull: CIDA.

—— (1993a) *Gender as a Cross-Cutting Theme in Development Assistance: an Evaluation of CIDA's WID Policy and Activities, 1984–1992*, Executive Summary, Hull: CIDA.

—— (1993b) *Women and the Environment Information Kit*, Women in Development Directorate Hull: CIDA.

—— (1993c) *CIDA's Friendly Guide to Agenda 21*, Environment Policy and Assessment Division, Hull: CIDA.

—— (1995) *CIDA's Policy on Women in Development and Gender Equity*, Hull: CIDA.

Clones, Julia (1991) *Women's Crucial Role in Managing the Environment in Sub-Saharan Africa*, Africa Region, Women in Development, Poverty and Social Policy Division Technical Note, Washington, DC: World Bank.

Commonwealth Secretariat (1992) *Women, Conservation and Agriculture: A Manual for Trainers*, London: Commonwealth Secretariat.

DAC/OECD (Development Assistance Committee/Organization for Economic Cooperation and Development) (1990) *Focus on the Future: Women and Environment*, London: International Institute for Environment and Development.

Dahl, Gudrun (1987) 'Women in Pastoral Production: Some Theoretical Notes on Roles and Resources', *Ethnos* 52 (I–II): 246–79.

Dankelman, Irene and Davidson, Joan (1988) *Women and Environment in the Third World: Alliance for the Future*, London: Earthscan.

ELCI (Environment Liaison Centre International) (1985) *Women and the Environmental Crisis*, Report of the Proceedings of the Workshops on Women, Environment and Development, 10–20 July 1985, Nairobi: ELCI.

Evernden, Neil (1984) 'The Environmentalist's Dilemma', in Neil Evernden (ed.) *The Paradox of Environmentalism*, Faculty of Environmental Studies, Toronto: York University.

Fortmann, Louise and Rochleau, Dianne (1985) 'Women and Agroforestry: Four Myths and Three Case Studies', *Agroforestry Systems* 2: 253–72.

Hausler, Sabine (1994) 'Women and the Politics of Sustainable Development', in Wendy Harcourt (ed.) *Feminist Perspectives on Sustainable Development*, London: Zed Books.

Hoskins, Marilyn (1979) *Women in Forestry for Local Community Development: A Programming Guide*, Office of Women in Development, Washington, DC: USAID.

INSTRAW (International Research and Training Institute for the Advancement of Women) (1989) *Women, Water Supply and Sanitation: Making the Link Stronger*, Santo Domingo: INSTRAW.

Jacobson, Jodi (1992) *Gender Bias: Roadblock to Sustainable Development*, Worldwatch Paper 110, Washington, DC: Worldwatch.

Kettel, Bonnie (1993) 'New Approaches to Sustainable Development', *Canadian Woman Studies* 13, 3: 11–14.

—— (1995a) 'Gender and Environments: Lessons From WEDNET', in Rae Blumberg, C. A. Rakowski, I. Tinker and M. Monteon (eds) *Engendering Wealth and Well-Being*, Boulder, CO: Westview.

—— (1995b) 'Key Pathways for Science and Technology for Sustainable and Equitable Development', in *Missing Links: Gender Equity in Science and Technology for Development*, Ottawa: IDRC and UNIFEM, pp. 27–53.

—— (1995c) 'Putting Women and the Environment First: Poverty Alleviation and Sustainable Development', unpublished ms, Faculty of Environmental Studies, Toronto: York University.

—— (1996) 'Putting Women and the Environment First: Poverty Alleviation and Sustainable Development', in A. Dale and J. Robinson (eds) *Achieving Sustainable Development*, Vol. 1. Vancouver: University of British Columbia Press, pp. 160–81.

Lewis, Barbara (1981) *Invisible Farmers: Women and the Crisis in Agriculture*, Office of Women in Development, Washington, DC: USAID.

Maathai, Wangari (1994) *A New Partnership for Development: Agenda for Development, the Experience of the Green Belt Movement*, Statement at the UN World Hearings on Development, Nairobi: National Council of Women of Kenya.

McIntosh, Sue (1993) 'On the Homefront: In Defence of the Health of Our Families', *Canadian Woman Studies* 13, 3: 89–93.

Merchant, Carolyn (1980) *The Death of Nature: Women, Ecology and the Scientific Revolution*, New York: Harper and Row.

Monimart, Marie and Brah, M. (1989) *Femmes du Sahel: la Desertification au Quotidien*, Club du Sahel, Paris: Editions Karthala.

Ofusu-Amaah, Waafas and Philleo, Wendy (1993), *Women and the Environment: An Analytical Review of Success Stories*, Washington, DC: WorldWIDE.

Rathgeber, E. and Kettel, B. (eds) *Women's Role in Natural Resource Management in Africa*, Manuscript Report 238e, Ottawa: IDRC.

Rathgeber, Eva (1990) 'WID, WAD, GAD: Trends in Research and Practice'. *Journal of Developing Areas* 27, 7: 489–502.

Rich, Bruce (1994) *Mortgaging the Earth: The World Bank, Environmental Impoverishment, and the Crisis of Development*, Boston, MA: Beacon Press.

Rogers, Barbara (1980) *The Domestication of Women: Discrimination in Developing Societies*, London: Tavistock.

Saidullah, Jawahara (1993) 'Children of the Himalayas: the Message of Chipko', *Canadian Woman Studies* 13, 3: 84–8.

Sen, G. and Grown, C. (1985) *Development Crises and Alternative Visions: Third World Women's Perspectives*, New York: Monthly Review Press.

Shiva, Vandana (1988) *Staying Alive: Women, Ecology and Development*, London: Zed Books.

Stamp, Patricia (1989) *Technology, Gender and Power in Africa*, Technical Study 63e, Ottawa: IDRC.

Steady, Filomena (1993) *Women and Children First: Environment, Poverty and Sustainable Development*, Rochester, VT: Schenkman Books.

Thomas-Slayter, Barbara, Rocheleau, D., Shields, D. and Rojas, M. (1991) *Introducing the ECOGEN Approach to Gender, Natural Resources Management and Sustainable Development*, Worcester, MA: Clark University.

UWTPM (Uganda Women Tree Planting Movement) (1990) *First Regional Workshop on Women and Environment: Workshop Recommendations*, Kampala: UWTPM.

UN (United Nations) (1985) *The Nairobi Forward-Looking Strategies for the Advancement of Women*, New York: United Nations.

—— (1992) *Agenda 21*, New York: United Nations.

UNIFEM (United Nations Development Fund for Women) (1995) *Putting Gender on the Agenda: A Guide to Participating in UN World Conferences*, New York: UNIFEM.

van den Hombergh, Heleen (1993) *Gender, Environment and Development: a Guide to the Literature*, Institute for Development Research Amsterdam, Utrecht: International Books.

WCED (World Commission on Environment and Development) (1987) *Our Common Future*, Oxford: Oxford University Press.

—— (1992a) *Official Report: World Women's Congress for a Healthy Planet*, New York: WEDO.

—— (1992b) *News and Views*, May–June 1992, New York: WEDO.

—— (1994) *Environment and Development*, Expert Advisory Group on Environment and Development, New York: WEDO.

—— (1995a) *News and Views*, June 1995, New York: WEDO.

—— (1995b) *Turn the Words into Action! Highlights from the Beijing Declaration and Platform for Action*, November 1995, New York: WEDO.

—— (1995c) *New and Views*, December 1995, New York: WEDO.

WorldWIDE (World Women in Defense of the Environment) (1991) 'Interview with Joan Martin Brown', *WorldWIDE News* 9, 2: 1, 7–8.

12

THE GOOD-NATURED FEMINIST

Ecofeminism and democracy[1]

Catriona Sandilands

The title of this paper is inspired by a recent billboard advertisement from the New Brunswick Ministry of Tourism: 'New Brunswick: You'll Love Our Good Nature'. This text is accompanied by a picture of a panoramic landscape, a sweeping view from atop a forested ridge down into an apparently limitless, ever-so-green, somewhere between 'rugged' and 'pastoral' valley. In the foreground of the picture we see the backs of a very young, very white, very heterosexual couple. They are obviously tourists, judging by the tailored, spotless shorts and expensive camera equipment; they are most likely urbanites who have fled from the daily grind of commuting, office towers, and executive weight rooms to come and experience the grandeur of nature.

There's nothing terribly unusual about this picture. Similar versions of nature grace not just tourist brochures, but postcards, opening shots of wildlife documentaries, Group of Seven exhibition posters, Sierra Club calendars, even ads for products ranging from Pine Sol to Kitchen Aid refrigerators. Nature, here, is devoid of human beings. There is no sign of humanity in the green and endless vista. There are no farms, no clear-cuts, no telltale smudges in the distance to indicate a pulp-mill or a town. Nature, here, is the absence of humanity, the place 'where no one has gone before', the *obverse* of civilization.

Perhaps this perspective is most strongly indicated by the presence, in the foreground, of our eco-tourist couple. They are *not* part of nature in this advertisement; they *watch* nature, having come from civilization. The couple, here, represents the human gaze upon nature. And we, the viewers of the ad, are invited to take up this gaze. We, like them, are to take our place in the foreground, in order to watch the pristine wilderness unfold before us, here, literally, at our feet, for our voyeuristic pleasure.

240

This is not an unusual representation of nature, this view by which nature becomes commodity. What is interesting about this particular advertisement is, instead, the *double entendre* invoked by the text: 'New Brunswick: You'll Love our Good Nature'. At the same time as we have a typically human-less, panoramic nature represented by the picture, another nature, one with a very human face, enters into our consciousness from offstage. That nature is the specifically good nature of the 'we' invoked in the text: New Brunswickers.[2] Lurking in the background, we find the good-natured Atlantic Canadian. We have the stereotypical small town, the warm, friendly, community-oriented citizen, the craft store staffed by women in handwoven shawls who sell painstakingly detailed quilts and preserves from their own kitchens (and often Robert Bateman prints and pottery from British Columbia, but that doesn't seem to matter much). We have, in New Brunswick's 'good nature', another commodity: the *gemeinschaft*, a historical and (supposedly) ongoing maritime hospitality that has, presumably, provisioned our eco-tourist couple for their journey into the wonders of the wilderness that New Brunswick has, of course, carefully preserved along with its homemade jam.

It is no accident that I saw this ad on the Gardiner Expressway in Toronto: imagine the harried commuter stuck in traffic, and her response to the possibilities of 'another world, far away'. It is clear that both of the natures produced in this advertisement are tourist commodities, parts of a display carefully orchestrated to attract central Canadian and US tourists to the region, to bolster a flagging economy previously reliant on resource-extraction (they must have done a lot of retouching in the ad to eradicate all traces of forestry). *As* a commodity, however, the juxtaposition of an airbrushed wilderness with home-cooking at the local bed and breakfast, is not designed to speak about the lives of local inhabitants, but, rather, speaks to a supposition of desire.

To take another look at our white, middle-class, heterosexual, Tilley-outfitted couple, we see that the desire represented in the ad is that of the urbanite. Specifically the fantasy represented/constructed centres on the supposed alienation of contemporary urban life. We, the urban middle class – or so scribes characterizing the *zeitgeist* of the 1990s tell us – are disconnected. If the 1980s represented a flurry of 'unnecessary' consumerism, then the 1990s herald a desire to return to simpler times. If the 1980s gave birth to the 'me' generation, to rampant individualism, power breakfasts, and a general orgy of excess, then the 1990s trend toward 'cocooning' and 'family values' is supposed to put us back on the road to health, simplicity and sanity.

In this cultural context, the message of environmentalism, that we are disconnected from nature, has gained a particular kind of currency. Think also of the New Age movement: what we really lack, some say, is a deep sense of 'community'. Valuable though these insights may be in another context, our New Brunswick travel ad shows us just how easily such desires are packaged as commodities. What sells in this ad is the construction of New Brunswick as some sort of repository of these simpler, better times, of what life used to be like for our predecessors, or, more specifically, for the predecessors of what is now the white, urban middle class, at whom the ad is directed. These simpler times show humans in harmony with nature and with each other: nature is in its place, carefully and lovingly preserved, and community is in its place (you can read 'family values' here as well, if you like), equally cherished for its spiritual and emotional nourishment.

Here, in this ad, both the land and its inhabitants are artifacts, museum-pieces, impossible representations of a way of life – or, to use the trendy, shallow word, 'lifestyle' – that certainly doesn't exist now, and probably never did. Nature still exists untouched, something to be marvelled at rather than exploited; community values have also yet to be clear-cut and replaced by the parking lots of urban isolation and selfishness. Perhaps most importantly, the two are seen naturally to go together.

So what does any of this have to do with ecofeminism or with democratic environmental politics more generally? Surely a tourist poster, part of a consumer-oriented, hegemonic order, and a radical social movement explicitly critical of that order, belong to different spheres of social life? The representations of nature and *gemeinschaft* going on in the advertisement not only form part of the context in which ecofeminism appears as a social movement, but also illustrate some of the problems ecofeminism has had in producing a critical and transformative political project. Specifically, ecofeminism has tended to rely on fairly conservative notions of nature and community in its formulations of resistance; these representations are bound up with equally conservative representations of women.

Such problems are not, of course, unique to ecofeminist politics; although particular understandings of women and nature are formed, in ecofeminism, with reference to a specific political agenda, the problem of challenging hegemonic representation is important for critical social movements as a whole as part of a democratic project. Thus, social movements in general, and ecofeminism in particular, need to pay attention to how their oppositional politics challenge – or fail to challenge – dominant discourses, here, dominant discourses surrounding women, nature, and community. This type of challenge may form part of a political practice for ecofeminism and for critical social movements generally. Beginning at a grassroots level, the proliferation and reinscription of discourses is clearly part of a specifically *democratic* politics, and is thus a vital moment in environmentalist (and other) challenges to a profoundly homogenizing and anti-democratic world order.

Ecofeminism: an overview

The term 'eco-feminisme' was coined in 1974 by French feminist Françoise d'Eaubonne to refer to the movement by women necessary to counteract environmental devastation. To d'Eaubonne, and to other ecofeminists after her, women as a group were fundamental to the project of ecological restoration because, in d'Eaubonne's words, no other group 'was so directly concerned at all levels' with nature (1980: 67). Women, engaged in the work of reproduction, nurturance, and the sustenance of life, were more keenly *aware* of processes of nature, of the cycles of life, theirs and others. And women's insights into these natural processes would, thus, point the way out of a male-constructed, male-dominated environmental catastrophe.

In North America, this type of representation resonated in at least two ways. First, it spoke to the struggles of women such as Lois Gibbs, then president of the Love Canal Homeowners' Association. This group was in large part responsible for the New York State government's 1978 declaration of the site as a health emergency. Gibbs, like other mothers in the area, was concerned about the recurrent health problems of her children. When the New York State health department began to intervene, Gibbs and others became suspicious; they collected evidence of cancer, crib deaths, a *75 per cent* miscarriage rate, children crippled with brain damage and physical deformations. They circulated petitions. They demanded explanations. They organized a 500-member community group, held rallies and demonstrations, and used every means possible to make the hitherto secret Love Canal toxic waste dump a *national* problem; eventually, they forced the State to evacuate the worst-hit areas and to provide compensation to home-owners.[3]

In this case, ecofeminism provided a sort of conceptual framework in which to locate, and through which to connect, such struggles *by* mothers over the health of their children (Gibbs, for example, admitted to becoming a feminist as a result of her struggles). Women, mothers, through their responsibility for child care and healthcare, were the first to perceive signs of contamination. In this view, women's reproductive responsibilities brought them in closer touch with nature, and especially what happens when 'nature goes wrong'. A recent statement from the Ontario Advisory Council on Women's Issues shows this perspective clearly:

> Women's concern for the natural environment is rooted in our concern for the health and well being of our family and community . . . .Because we have traditionally been mother, nurse and guardian for the home and community, women have been quick to perceive the threat to the health and lives of our families and neighbours that is posed by nuclear power proliferation, polluted waters, and toxic chemicals.
>
> (Ontario Advisory Council 1990: 3)

At the same time, ecofeminism spoke to debates going on in the feminist movement. In the 1970s, ideas about nature, and women's supposed connections to it, were hotly debated within North American radical feminism. The nature debate focused around reproduction; in radical feminism, analyses of

243

the origins of patriarchal oppression centred on women's responsibility for child care, women's association with material necessity, women's exhibited closeness to nature. Men, en route to transcendent, disembodied culture, were seen to degrade these aspects of women's existence, to *control* women through their bodies, through their fertility, through the very association of women with the body, birth, and nature.

In this formulation, the 'to welcome or renounce connections to nature' debate was about female biology. Some radical feminists – Sherry Ortner (1974), Shulamith Firestone (1970) – advocated some form of renunciation of biology for women, as a way of breaking free of the tyranny of the body en route to full participation in culture, in the rational, in the abstract, in the mind, alongside men. Others – Mary Daly (1978), Susan Griffin (1978) – advocated a celebration of biology, a delight in processes of reproduction and life sustenance, as a way of transforming male culture itself. The devalued aspects of life, those qualities possessed by women because of their lifegiving, reproductive capacities, were seen as the basis of an oppositional, transformative culture for women, in explicit rejection of the hegemony of 'male' destructive qualities.

What ecofeminism offered this polarized debate was a way out.[4] Rather than simply play along with biological determinism, ecofeminists such as Ynestra King suggested that women could, in fact, claim *both* culture and biology in a transformative strategy for women and nature. She wrote, in 1981, that women:

> stand on the biological dividing line. We are the less rationalized side of humanity in an overly rationalized world, yet we can think as rationally as men and perhaps transform the idea of reason itself. As women, we are a naturalized culture in a culture defined against nature
>
> (1981: 15)

Thus, King and other ecofeminists rejected the idea that women are, in fact, closer to nature than men in some essential, biological way. Instead, the *positioning* of women in particular social roles and activities, the *representation* of women as natural creatures, has created, for women, the ability to see both sides, as it were: to be cultured, but to live that culture through a series of experiences always already touched by nature. Such formulations both located women's specific struggles over nature in some sort of theoretical and political context, and rendered nature a terrain of struggle in a non-biologically reductionist, feminist transformative project. As King later wrote, 'although the nature – culture dualism is a product of culture, we can consciously choose not to sever the woman–nature connection . . . [and] can use it as a vantage point for creating a different kind of culture and politics' (1989: 23).

Ecofeminism and discourse on 'women' and 'nature'

It is, thus, fair to say that ecofeminism collected and reshaped certain ecological struggles in its quest to move radical feminism beyond a biologically determinist impasse. Women are not 'naturally more natural' than men; rather, women have been *socially* positioned, in patriarchal societies, in a way that fosters a unique understanding of nature and natural cycles. This unique knowledge needs to be preserved and fostered, as it forms not only the basis of women's present participation in ecological struggles, but a template for a future, harmonious, ecological society.

In order to understand the production of this knowledge, ecofeminism has sought to explain the relations producing a situation in which women are positioned as closer to nature than men. Although there is, currently, quite a variety of different ecofeminisms – some focused on object relations (a North American inflection of psychoanalysis) à la Nancy Chodorow and Carol Gilligan, others more oriented to an analysis of the sexual division of labour[5] – perhaps the most influential current explaining the social construction of women and nature as 'connected' focuses on the ways in which their relations have been produced historically. Specifically, this analysis has us focus on the location of women and nature in a series of binary, hierarchical dualisms.

Beginning with the Greeks, this story goes, and carried on through Judeo-Christian traditions, the world has been divided into two halves: man/woman, culture/nature, white/black, reason/emotion, mind/body, etc. The lower half of each duality is viewed as inferior, as the polar opposite of the upper half. Thus, nature is the absence of culture, emotion the absence of reason, etc. Perhaps most importantly, each lower half only has value insofar as it serves the needs of the upper half. Here, nature only has value as a 'resource', as the raw material for culture, and woman only has value insofar as she serves man, as wife, as mother, as sexual object. Here, women and nature are not Others in their own right, but exist as negative reflections of the valued male character, as objects, as resources.[6] Thus, the solution to our ecological crisis involves the recognition of the value of the subaltern pole, its affirmation as a vital component in a balanced view of human/non-human life, and the dissemination of its characteristics among a wider range of people as a movement in the direction of integration, holism, and non-dominating social/natural relations.

There is, however, a variety of limitations to this account. Most obviously, where are capitalism and colonialism in this trans-historical account of dualism? In response to such problems, a variety of ecofeminist authors – Mary Mellor (1992), Carolyn Merchant (1989), Bina Agarwal (1992) – have produced 'socialist' ecofeminist analyses, and have pointed to the specificity of women's struggles over nature in decolonizing countries. But even in many of these accounts (particularly Mellor's), there is a problem, to borrow the language of poststructuralism, of 'essentialism'. Ecofeminism may not be biologically reductionist, but it *is* often essentialist; its constructions of women and nature, even in some of the most sophisticated accounts, are based on claiming a very limited notion of 'identity' for women and nature, and are based on finding some *specificity* for feminism in relation to ecological struggle (and vice versa). Women and nature are constructed, in ecofeminism, *through* their particular connection; this particularity can be named 'difference', and is a very limiting, and ultimately ineffective, political representation.[7]

The problem of difference is inherent in ecofeminists' reliance on dualism as an analysis of power and oppression. If, their logic goes, male separation from nature, or men's control of reproduction, or patriarchal constructs consigning women and nature to a lesser status, are the source of the problem, then the solution – in some form – centres on the creation of alternatives based on this subaltern experience. To King, women can and should choose not to 'sever the woman/nature connection'. To Mellor, 'a feminist green socialism must be underpinned by the values that have hitherto been imposed upon women: altruism, selfless caring, the desire to help other people realise their potential' (1992: 237).[8] Here, women's specificity vis à vis nature is, somehow, the form of subaltern experience which reveals oppression; this is, thus, a feminist politics based on women's difference. Here also, it is the specificity of nature, as that which is oppressed by culture, that is seen to be the object to be revealed in women's struggles over nature; this is, thus, a politics based on women's ability to recognize nature's difference (implied: men's inability). And these differences are seen to be a question of identity: women's identity gives them a privileged vantage-point on things natural, given their social position in nature, or on the margins of male-defined culture, or even as an oppressed group empathizing with another's experience of oppression.[9]

Judith Plant, an ecofeminist and bioregionalist from British Columbia, offers an excellent example of this logic:

> Historically, women have had no real power in the outside world, no place in decision-making and intellectual life [a debatable point in and of itself]. Today, however, ecology speaks for the Earth, for the 'other' in human/environmental relationships, and feminism speaks for the 'other' in female/male relations. And ecofeminism, by speaking for both the original[!] others, seeks to understand the interconnected roots of all domination as well as ways to resist and change.
>
> (1990: 156)

This statement gives the impression that liberation, for both women and nature, relies on the ability of a social movement to foster the speech of oppressed groups. But not any speech will do: what needs to emerge, in order for liberation to proceed, is speech emanating from the very aspects of life which are oppressed, devalued, and exploited in (patriarchal) society and culture: the 'difference'. Thus, in ecofeminism women are encouraged to speak about their connections to nature; conversely, one could argue that nature speaks, or becomes spoken, at that moment where it appears as part of *women's* experience and knowledge. Thus, both nature and women become reduced to the points where the two, supposedly, connect: other arenas, places where women may be cultured or where nature may be outside the realm of women's experiences, are not the points about which ecofeminists feel compelled to speak.

Furthermore, even in those ecofeminist narratives that stress the importance of capitalism, and sometimes especially in accounts that attempt to deal with racism,[10] this subaltern speech takes the form of a reversal. If patriarchy has abstracted and elevated the rational, then the speech that needs to be spoken is of the irrational (called 'mystery', for example). If science is hegemonic, then spirituality must be revalued as a necessary component to human existence. If the problem has been an over-enthusiastic focus on market life, then the modes of living associated with families are the key to our salvation. There is the pervasive sense that patriarchal, anti-nature social relations have elevated one side of human/natural existence at the expense of the other; that Other must be spoken, revalued, reintegrated into human activity (if not given primacy over all other modes of activity) if destructive relations are to be challenged.

Unfortunately, reversal has the effect of reifying the very dualism seen to be the cause of the problem. The aspects of women that are emphasized in ecofeminism share a great deal in common with those aspects of femininity idealized in contemporary white, western, middle-class discursive ideals: care, nurturance, connectedness to others, body awareness, etc. Ironically, perhaps, 'womanhood' in ecofeminism tends to resemble closely the denigrated female other of so-called masculine ideals; it's just that its value has been altered. Complexity and contradiction seldom appear as crucial features.

Similarly, just as that which is not male becomes the desired speech of oppressed womanhood, so too does that which is not culture become the natural state from which we came and to which we must aspire. Nature, here, acts to represent all that is wrong with civilization. As patriarchal culture is individuated, nature is an interconnected web. As masculine ideology emphasizes rationality, nature is mysterious. And, not surprisingly, many of the attributes associated with femininity also come to characterize nature: nature is defined in terms of stereotypical femininity because contemporary culture is the manifestation of all that is quintessentially male.

Were this moment of reversal part of an ironic or deconstructive strategy, were it somehow part of a process of exposure by which the arbitrariness of the social constructions of women and nature are pointed out, then it would be reasonable to consider it a valuable political tool. As it stands, ecofeminism does successfully point to the ways in which certain aspects of human/natural existence are excluded from dominant representations of worth, value, and even possibility: it critiques ideology, in the classical sense. But this oppressed womanhood, and this particular construction of nature, are not meant ironically: beyond male ideology lies the truth, and the truth lies in the subaltern identity. For women to discover a way of being that is free from patriarchal domination – part of both the process and the eventual goal of ecofeminism – an oppositional, women's identity needs to be reclaimed from patriarchal thought, celebrated, and affirmed. Similarly, if human/nature relationships are to be restored, a new human identity, one based on experiences of continuity with nature, must also be rediscovered and integrated into a new, non-oppressive code of behaviour.

So what we have is a politics which is based on the production of a new identity – or, more accurately, on the revaluation of an old one – this one caring, connected, and respectful of nature. Does this sound a little bit familiar? Let me offer you another quote, this one from Carolyn Merchant:

> Historically, the rise of capitalism eroded the subsistence-based farm and city workshops in which production was oriented toward use-values and women and men were economic partners [really?]. The result was a capitalist economy dominated by men and a domestic sphere in which women's labour in the home was unpaid and subordinate to men's labour in the marketplace. Both women and nature are exploited by men as part of the progressive liberation of humans from the constraints imposed by nature. The consequence is the alienation of women and men from each other and both from nature.
>
> (1990: 153)

This passage provides, as it were, the final piece of the puzzle. Not only does ecofeminism play within a hegemonic series of constructions of women and nature, but it also looks back to a 'simpler, better time' in which women and nature were not exploited. Although Merchant's golden age is rather more recent than the neolithic yearnings of other ecofeminists, we see the same discursive construction going on: the past, somewhere, embodied not only community, meaning *gemeinschaft*, but a better life for women and nature as integral aspects of the community's idyllic functioning.

The desire for community expressed in ecofeminism is also manifest in a version of politics that would have the home, the family, restored to some central place in social value (without, it seems, questioning the forms of power that appear in contemporary families). Indeed, the 'home' metaphor is used to describe what our new being in nature is supposed to look like – the earth as a home, a place that shelters and sustains us, a place where we can 'be' without artifice, a place where, if we pay close attention to those who love us, we learn new values and behaviours. Time and time again, for example, we are told that *oikos*, the Greek root of 'eco', means 'home'. Thus home – not accidentally women's sphere – is the metaphor for nurturance, caring, and connection, the shape of our ideal eco-community.

248

Thus, there are three crucial elements: community, women, and nature. In combination, the three share a remarkable similar series of idealized traits. But none, of course, actually exists. The representations are, like our fictional, good-natured New Brunswickers, a matched set of museum pieces. The representations speak of reified desire, not of the complex and contradictory discourses through which women, nature, and community are produced and negotiated. The representations are not, most importantly, created as ironic fictions by critical social movements themselves, but are aspects of the hegemonic discourses that critical social movements are and should be trying to dislocate. Thus, here, ecofeminism fails to challenge the very relations it has set out to critique. There is no challenge in a series of idealized and reified representations that is not only already *present* in hegemonic discourses, but that is *explicitly* bought and sold as a discursive commodity in travel brochures.

Perhaps ecofeminism has not simply bought, lock, stock, and barrel, those discourses that happen to be available on the market. On the other hand, a mere reversal is insufficient as a political strategy, precisely because it fails to challenge the relations by which the discourses became hegemonic in the first place. To take up a hierarchical discourse and simply turn it on its head does nothing to alter the discourse itself, or to question the power relations in which the discourse makes sense. Ecofeminists' desire – for the obverse of patriarchal, alienated culture, for a nurturant femininity, for a pristine nature – ends up taking the same form as an advertisement for a bygone way of life, a tourist desire, and not by accident. Both representations of desire are constructed within a hegemonic discourse, and ecofeminism, by failing to challenge the tenets of that discourse, falls prey to the same reifications, the same simplifications, the same projections of Otherness that we saw in our good-natured travel poster.

Destabilization: ecofeminism and democracy

One of the most important moments in environmental politics – indeed, in any purportedly democratic social movement politics – involves challenging the relations of power embedded in dominant discourses. In any democratic environmentalism, it is vital to resist the ability of hegemonic representations to define, categorically, humans' relations to nature and to each other. To create alternatives, to think beyond the definitions of sense and reality that appear in a hegemonic version of common sense, it is important to challenge and displace the order that underscores such dominant representations.[11]

In this view, destabilization and democratization work in tandem. The moment at which a hegemonic truth is revealed to be partial and incomplete is the moment at which other discourses may be revealed or produced more forcefully. It is certainly the case that we are constantly subject to multiple and contradictory discourses – of women, of nature, and of community, for example – but it is also the case that the (public) contestation of such categories produces an increased proliferation of responses, and from a wider range of points in social life. Thus, in the moment of destabilization there is the potential for greater democracy. At the same time, democracy is often (not always) transgressive; insofar as representational spaces are opened through a democratic desire for public contestation, the ability of a single term to quilt an order among a variety of constructions becomes more difficult. To paraphrase Sheldon Wolin, 'democracy is the nightmare of hegemony'. In the process of proliferation, then, destabilization becomes more likely, but only if the hegemonic term is shown to be partial and incomplete.

Despite their best intentions, most ecofeminists have not shown hegemonic discourses around women, nature, and even community to *be* partial and incomplete. They have, instead, worked largely *within* the limits of dominant discourses, and have simply played with the values attached to their various constitutive elements. They have continued to homogenize what needs to be creatively torn apart. And they are not alone in doing so; many other critical social movements, likewise focused around a subaltern, oppositional identity, have also taken up an idea of Otherness, and have produced from it a politics which gives ironic legitimacy to the relations constructing that otherness in the first place. Analytically, this strategy is inadequate, as it fails to examine the social and political processes that create identity.

Politically, another series of questions emerges. The construction of the subaltern, emphasizing as it does certain aspects of life as fundamental to an identity, inevitably constricts the expression or creation of others. In the creation of ecofeminism, for example, politics has been defined in terms of a particular constellation of issues that affect women as women, or nature as experienced *by* women (and a very particular group of women at that). Much as ecofeminists might argue that *everything* is, potentially, an ecofeminist issue, it is as a result of this particular construction of identity politics that many other environmental groups can safely marginalize potentially valuable ecofeminist insights.[12]

Identity politics, like the one ecofeminism tends to be bogged down in, cannot rise to the challenge of democratic social transformation. What is necessary is, instead, a destabilization of the relations and discourses producing identity. Such a project includes both an active and specific challenge to the reifications of women and nature and community produced in hegemonic discourses, and a self-conscious democratization of discursive possibilities, here, although there are certainly other methods, through a reappropriation of local knowledges (variously defined).

Despite their inadequacies, the Greens have shown some interesting promise in the direction of democratization and destabilization. A large part of Green politics, on paper at least, focuses on the creation and empowerment of local knowledges of nature and community. While we can still see elements of the 'unspoiled wilderness' in some Green proposals, their actions and political platforms centre on a version of nature that specifically includes humanity. Similarly, one of the most interesting features of Green politics is its local definition of community. The Greens, in Ontario at least, are fundamentally concerned with re-inscribing on politics a variety of different meanings of community.[13] Perhaps in part because so many Greens are themselves urbanites, this community does not resemble the *gemeinschaft*. It is based, instead, on principles of local decision-making, local production and consumption, and local planning. All of these broadly communitarian principles are located in an agenda of showing how they need to be specifically produced through the geographies and ecosystems of the particular area itself.

Thus, nature is specified locally; it includes not just sweeping vistas, but everyday human/environment interactions. It focuses not on 'man [*sic*] in the wilderness', but on developing alternative ways of living in, and thinking about, the environment as part of a reformulation of what it means to be human. That reformulation is also contingent on inventing new forms of community, not somehow mourning a state of grace destroyed by capitalism, but building institutions to promote a democratic, responsive sense of belonging and empowerment, for an urban context just as much as – although differently from – rural settlements.

Here, there is a construction of the local as not just one small point in a global homogeneity, but as a centre for the production of meaning itself. The local, here, is not an instance in some wider plan, but is the seat of the process of definition. More importantly, perhaps, there is a profound recognition of the necessity of democratization, a sense that broad principles – sustainability, but even democracy itself – are to be constructed at a local level, by the community itself, however that community may be defined and organized. Although one can certainly see elements of the desire for connection displayed in the New Brunswick travel poster in this political agenda, the politics itself does not sell us a political tourist destination. Rather, it shows that nature and community are, potentially, part of everyday life, but *not* attainable within the confines of existing, hegemonic constructions of either, and *not* attainable without a struggle that challenges the operations of hegemonic discourse itself: to totalize, reify, commodify, and disempower. The community that the Greens offer could not be placed on an expressway billboard at least in part because it would not make sense in dominant discourses; its challenge to hegemonic constructions of nature and community are such that there could be no reified Other to whom our travel desires are directed. Who knows what their 'good nature' would look like? The diffusion of discourse, the claiming and legitimating of multiple, local knowledges, is, in this context, a democratic act.

In short, the Greens' agenda of reformulating nature and community is a destabilizing challenge to hegemonic discourses, and it is so because of its primary focus on democratization. We cannot specify what nature and community would look like outside a process of empowering different, local groups to define them for themselves. Here, destabilization proceeds *through* democratization; different, and perhaps radically transgressive, meanings of nature and community appear from the grassroots, from local concerns. And this in explicit rejection of a social order that seeks to wrest control of these discourses from the local, to turn unformulated desire into mass commodity, to reproduce hegemony by archaeologizing nature and community. Thus, the act of proliferation, the democratization of meaning itself, is a profound challenge.

The feminist problem, perhaps ironically, is where the local meets its Waterloo. There is a tendency in the Greens toward a reification of the local to mean the geographic. In a sense, the Greens – like many bioregionalists – are moving toward a version of community that considers place as *the* primary representation of belonging; in so doing, they are slipping into the terrain of identity politics. This is one reason why the Greens find it so difficult to include feminist politics in any thoroughgoing manner; to do so would be to call into question the idea of the local in a relatively unsettling way: place does not guarantee democracy after all, and small doesn't necessarily mean feminist.[14] It would also suggest that the destabilization of hegemonic discourses of community and nature might also necessitate the destabilization of discourses on women, something that the Greens are ill-prepared to do, but a process in which they must begin to engage if their version of community is to respect and foster the heterogeneity it must.

For ecofeminists – who are certainly better prepared than the Greens to destabilize discourses on women – a central project must be democratization. This process requires inclusion, an opening of discursive spaces for a wider proliferation of voices than are represented at present. But it also requires a rethinking of the central tenets of identity politics more generally, away from a project based on the reification of identity as the basis for a master-narrative of oppression and redemption, and toward a project of fostering conflicting views, working through the tensions among a variety of situated knowledges of nature, and refusing to reify any single one as the ideal toward which all should strive, in all contexts.

Democracy, here, is local, partial, and always already in process. While it does not *guarantee* a critical rethinking of the category women, the specification and empowerment of local knowledges (again, variously defined), has the potential to challenge the hegemonic representations of women, and their relations to nature, that are so prevalent in contemporary social and political life. To truly challenge these representations suggests abandoning the solidity of identity in favour of the diffusion of discursive power and its regrounding in local, democratic constitutions. Women, as an overarching collectivity, or even as a series of voices with a common, gendered referent, may not exist at all.[15] In fact, it may be that the category women, like community, offers more in its transgression of certainty than it does in its grounding as an essence or position.

It is this disruptive potential that must be emphasized in ecofeminist politics. The process of inviting and strengthening local knowledges is, in the final instance, one of ecofeminism's greatest strengths as a politics of resistance. Writes Lee Quinby:

> Ecofeminism as a politics of resistance forces us to question the categories of experience that order the world and the truths we have come to know, even the truths of our radical politics, by confronting us with the truths of other women and men, differently acculturated, fighting against specific threats to their particular lands and bodies.
>
> (1990: 126–7)

For ecofeminists, the process of breaking free of limiting hegemonic constructs thus means disrupting their very discursive foundations. It means seriously challenging our own good nature, and working toward the construction of local knowledges of women that cannot be sold back to us as totalizing, homogenizing, and fundamentally disempowering representations. It means fostering alliances – conflictual though they may be, in many cases – among these local struggles and local knowledges to resist and subvert the conditions in which these representations make sense. And perhaps, above all, it means living with the fact that a democratic politics has us call our common sense into profound question.

Notes

1 This paper was written in 1993. Although its central argument is still valid and relevant, it bears mention that ecofeminist theory, green politics and my thinking on both have shifted since then. In particular, many ecofeminists have shifted since then. In particular, many ecofeminists have addressed precisely the questions of essentialism that I raise, although others still seem quite comfortable to reassert their inherently good natures.

2 The 'us' could, in fact, include both human and non-human provincial residents: imagine 'good-natured' bears, moose, squirrels.

3 See 'Action from Tragedy: Women at Love Canal and Three-Mile Island', *Heresies* 4, 1, Issue 13, 1981.

4 Of course there are many other ways out, among them, deconstruction. For an excellent example, see Joan Scott (1988) 'Deconstructing Equality-versus-Difference: Or, the Uses of Poststructuralist Theory for Feminism', *Feminist Studies* 14, 1.

5 For a discussion of different currents in ecofeminism, and of the proliferation of ecofeminisms that emerged in the 1980s, see my forthcoming book, *The Good-Natured Feminist: Ecofeminism and Democracy*, Minneapolis: University of Minnesota Press, chapters one and three. On object relations, see Nancy Chodorow (1978) *The Reproduction of Mothering: Psychoanalysis and the Sociology of Gender*, Berkeley, CA: University of California Press. On the sexual

division of labour and the creation of women's 'difference', see Hartsock, Nancy (1983) 'The Feminist Standpoint: Developing the Ground for a Specifically Feminist Historical Materialism', in Sandra Harding and Merrill B. Hintikka, *Discovering Reality: Feminist Perspectives on Epistemology, Metaphysics, Methodology, and Philosophy*, London: D. Reidel.

6 Of course, this is what Simone de Beauvoir said, although with an orientation to a rather different political project than ecofeminism's. See *The Second Sex*, New York: Alfred A. Knopf, 1952.

7 Some of my critiques of ecofeminism's 'essentialism' are laid out more fully in the forthcoming book.

8 The particularly alarming thing about this view of 'feminism' is that it comes after a relatively thorough analysis of the intricate workings of capital in the creation of environmental domination.

9 Agarwal is one of a growing number of authors who write on ecofeminism (she intentionally rejects the label in favour of 'feminist environmentalism') to question the unity of the category women. A number of the articles in Greta Gaard's anthology *Ecofeminism: Women, Animals, Nature* (Philadelphia: Temple University Press, 1993) also do this. Even in these pluralized accounts, however, there is a strong sense that the basis of women's struggles over nature has to do with a particular, oppressed, and identifiable set of experiences *in* nature.

10 There is a particularly difficult tendency in ecofeminism to suggest that women in the 'Third World' are somehow closer to nature than other women (usually phrased as a question of labour), and that aboriginal peoples are particularly good repositories of natural knowledge. Few of these attempts at inclusion pays significant attention to the specific conditions in which environmental degradation takes place, or to the effects of colonization and imperialism on supposedly traditional knowledges.

11 For an excellent, destabilizing reading of nature in political discourse, see Shane Phelan (1993) 'Intimate Distance: The Dislocation of Nature in Modernity', in Jane Bennett and William Chaloupka, *In the Nature of Things: Language, Politics, and the Environment*, Minneapolis: University of Minnesota Press. For an equally wonderful reading of gender, nature, and the demise of organic dualism, see Donna Haraway (1990) 'A Manifesto for Cyborgs: Science, Technology, and Socialist Feminism in the 1980s', in Linda Nicholson, *Feminism/Postmodernism*, New York: Routledge.

12 For example, during my work with the Ontario Greens, women activists expressed to me time and time again their dissatisfaction not only with ecofeminism but with the ways it was wielded in Green politics. What happened in the Greens was a reduction of feminism to ecofeminism, a process by which feminism was subsumed into already-existing Green discourses of priority, necessity, and possibility. Feminism appears in the Greens (in my experiences) mostly as some sort of state-ment about nurturance or connection – as an accessible and unproblematic identity – ignoring, among other things, the problems of systemic women's poverty, or the sexism of electoral politics, or the disproportionate effects of defor-estation on women in some communities. Feminism has never, as a result, seriously informed the Ontario Greens' political strategies: discourses around valuing nurturance came to stand in for serious discussion of gender issues. In the Greens, ecofeminism is thus a very different thing from feminist ecology: it became an iden-tity at the expense of political discussion, transgression, and even democracy. I would argue that this kind of problem cannot be attributed simply to phenomenal sexism in the Greens (although such an attribution would not be without cause).

13 At least, they were. As I describe in my paper 'Ecology as Politics: The Promise and Problems of the Ontario Greens' (in W.K. Carroll, *Organizing Dissent: Contemporary Social Movements in Theory and Practice*, Toronto: Garamond, 1992),

there was a 'split' between those Greens focused on grassroots transformation and those Greens concerned with electoral politics. The 'electoralists' seem to have won, and the 'grassrooters' moved on to other movements, but that is another story.

14 A serious rethinking of the home metaphor might also appear, given that homes are not particularly safe places for many women, and given that divisions of domestic labour are far from equitable.

15 On this point I am supported by the considerable legacy of feminist poststructuralism. See in particular Denise Riley (1988) *Am I That Name? Feminism and the Category of 'Women' in History*, Minneapolis, MN: University of Minnesota Press.

References

Agarwal, Bina (1992) 'The gender and environment debate: lessons from India', *Feminist Studies* 8, 1: 119–58.

Daly, Mary (1978) *Gyn/Ecology: A Metaethics of Radical Feminism*, Boston, MA: Beacon Press.

D'Eaubonne, Françoise (1980) 'Feminism or death', (orig. 'Le feminisme ou la mort', 1974), translated and excerpted in Elaine Marks and Isabelle de Courtivron (eds) *New French Feminisms: An Anthology*, Amherst, MA: University of Massachusetts Press.

Firestone, Shulamith (1970) *The Dialectic of Sex: The Case for Feminist Revolution*, New York: Bantam Books.

Griffin, Susan (1978) *Woman and Nature: The Roaring Inside Her*, San Francisco: Harper and Row.

King, Ynestra (1981) 'Feminism and the revolt of nature', *Heresies* 4, 1 (issue 13): 12–16.

—— (1989) 'The ecology of feminism and the feminism of ecology', in Judith Plant (eds) *Healing the Wounds: The Promise of Ecofeminism*, Toronto: Between the Lines.

Mellor, Mary (1992) *Breaking the Boundaries: Toward a Feminist Green Socialism*, London: Virago.

Merchant, Carolyn (1980) *The Death of Nature: Women, Ecology, and the Scientific Revolution*, San Francisco: Harper Collins (repr. 1989).

—— (1990) 'Ecofeminism and feminist theory', in Irene Diamond and Gloria Feman Orenstein (eds) *Reweaving the World: The Emergence of Ecofeminism*, San Francisco: Sierra Club Books.

Ontario Advisory Council on Women's Issues (1990) *Women and the Environment*, Toronto, October.

Ortner, Sherry (1974) 'Is female to male as nature is to culture?', in Michelle Zimbalist Rosaldo and Louise Lamphere (eds) *Women, Culture, and Society*, Stanford, CA: Stanford University Press.

Plant, Judith (1990) 'Searching for common ground: ecofeminism and bioregionalism', in Irene Diamond and Gloria Feman Orenstein (eds) *Reweaving the World: The Emergence of Ecofeminism*, San Francisco: Sierra Club Books.

Quinby, Lee (1990) 'Ecofeminism and the politics of resistance', in Irene Diamond and Gloria Feman Orenstein (eds) *Reweaving the World: The Emergence of Ecofeminism*, San Francisco: Sierra Club Books.

Part 5

CONSUMPTION: WORK AND AFFLUENCE

13

OVERCONSUMPTION

Paul L. Wachtel

The conventional wisdom conceives an antithesis between economic development and ecological sustainability. As the former concept has been primarily conceived, there is indeed such an antithesis. The image of a billion Chinese, a billion Indians, and billions of others throughout Africa, Asia, and Latin America living in the way that North Americans and Europeans now live is an ecological nightmare. How then to prevent environmental catastrophe in a way that does not preserve injustices and reflect a 'roll up the drawbridge' mentality? The answer lies in North Americans examining *our own* way of life and our own assumptions, which have been so seductive to those in the Third World and have in large measure shaped their aspirations as well as our own.

In a host of largely unexamined ways, the economies of North America, Europe and other highly industrialized parts of the world have operated on the assumption that the sense of well-being depends crucially both on the quantity of goods and services available to the population and on the rate at which that quantity is growing. It is easy to understand how such an assumption could hold sway. There certainly are ways in which our lives seem to be enriched by the panoply of goods and services available to us. And yet, there is little indication that our lives are fuller or happier than those of our parents' or grandparents' generation, who, in fact had much 'less'.

There are multiple reasons for this failure of economic growth to yield an increased sense of well-being, but many of them come down to the fact that there are largely unacknowledged *side effects* to our growing material wealth. One of the few things that *laissez faire* economists have got right is that there is no such thing as a free lunch. There are *costs* to what we get, and we fool ourselves when we pretend that there are not. Where economists begin to go wrong is in forgetting that growth too has costs – *high* costs – as does the so-called free market. Moreover, those costs are not reflected in the price of goods or services produced within the growth-oriented system, thus misleading us about the price we are paying.

In part, this is taken into account by economists under the rubric of *externalities*. But there are several limitations to addressing the difficulty in those terms. Perhaps most immediate is that externalities is a concept that is more often honoured in the abstract than seriously addressed in the way our economy is run. Even in economists' own terms, the degree to which our prices and policies reflect the costs which transactors try to externalize is rather minimal. Externalizing and socializing costs while privatizing and internalizing gains is virtually the explicit mandate of the corporate CEO, and in this respect at least they are quite successful.

But even if the prevailing notions of externalities were taken much more seriously than they are, they would not be sufficient to enlighten us about the true costs of our way of life. For one thing, externalities are usually discussed in terms of the externalized cost of a particular transaction or class of trans-actions—for example, when a factory dumps its waste into a nearby river or into the air, thus artificially keeping the price of its product low because the cost of disposing of the waste is paid neither by the factory nor by those who buy its products but by all of us. That cost might be reflected in increased medical bills resulting from air or water pollution, lost work days in *other* factories and industries due to illnesses produced by the first plant's waste, increased cleaning bills for clothes soiled by soot, loss of tourist dollars resulting from the river becoming unswimmable, and a host of other costs paid by nonparticipants in the transaction between the factory and its customers.[1]

But there are many other kinds of externalities that are undescribed or underestimated because of the ideological biases of 'free-market' economic analysis. There is a strong prejudicial inclination in such analyses toward examining transactions as freely made choices between conscious participants whose decisions are relevant only to their own well being, not to others'. It is from this vantage point that there appears to be an intimate connection between capitalism and freedom (e.g., Friedman and Friedman 1980; Hayek 1944). But this is a distorting lens through which the world as it actually exists can scarcely be glimpsed. In the real world of massive outputs and massive influence by massive firms operating within a powerfully interlocking system of social and economic influences, most of us have relatively *little* choice about the basic circumstances of our lives. We can 'choose' to buy product A instead of product B and, in principle, not to buy at all. But even these choices (especially the latter) are constrained by the consequences of the very system that purports to be the guarantor of our freedom.

To offer a concrete example, in interviews I conducted a number of years back exploring the psychological dimensions of attitudes about money and possessions, parents frequently stated they felt 'helpless' about saying no to their children when the children insisted on buying sneakers at prices the parents felt were absurd. For each family, the fact that all the other kids at school were also buying absurdly expensive sneakers left their own kids feeling like outcasts if they did not do the same. Thus, they were *not* really free to choose. The other kids' purchases – in standard economic thinking simply a matter between the purchaser and the seller – had powerful externalities; they virtually forced the as yet uninitiated child and his parents to spend the money too.

Economists don't like to consider the impact of my purchase or my income on you. They prefer the myth that each transaction is a private matter, benefitting both parties to the transaction and impacting on nobody else. It apparently makes the theory neater and the mathematics easier. But if the distortions introduced by these simplifications do not fatally impair economists' ability to make predictions about various quantitative measures of production and distribution, they generate thoroughly misleading conclusions about well-being or the good life.

One of the relatively few economists to take seriously the impact of people's choices and economic activities on each other has been Robert Frank. Frank notes that 'in setting up formal models of economic behaviour, economists almost always assume at the outset that a person's sense of well-being, or utility, depends on the absolute quantities of various goods he consumes, not on how those quantities compare with the amounts consumed by others' (Frank 1985: 33), but that in the real world, in contrast to the models of economists, 'abundant evidence suggests that people do in fact care much more about how their incomes compare with those of their peers than about how large their incomes are in any absolute sense'. He notes with pleasure Mencken's definition of wealth as 'any income that is at least one hundred dollars more a year than the income of one's wife's sister's husband' (ibid.: 5).

Frank points out how, as a consequence of this powerful comparative dynamic, we work longer hours than we really desire to (see also, in this regard, Hunnicutt 1988; Schor 1991), we take risks with our health, and we abuse the environment. In the tautological worldview that dominates mainstream economics in our society, this cannot happen; we always work exactly the amount we want to, take exactly the risks we desire, and buy precisely the kind and quantity of goods we truly want. The very fact that we bought the goods and worked the hours is in itself taken as evidence that that must be what we really want.

Moreover, not only is this what we want but it is also, *mirabile dictu*, what will most benefit us. There is no room for mistakes in this model, and no conflict or self-deception. Economists, with their extraordinarily rationalistic models, are the Western world's last pre-Freudians. Further, the output of the economic system – whatever it might be and whatever consequences non-economists might notice regarding human welfare – is virtually unconditionally endorsed by the assumption that human beings are rational utility maximizers who know their needs with great precision and by the additional assumption, noted by Frank as well as many others, that the greater the quantity of goods we buy the greater our 'utility'. It is not that there is *evidence* for this; it is a matter of definition. This set of questionable assumptions treated as if they were facts is bolstered by a pseudodemocratic rhetoric in which the economist professes not to inject his or her values into the discourse, preferring to let the people speak through their own autonomous decisions. Those who question whether what we produce and buy is really good for us may thereby be dismissed as 'elitists' and 'social engineers' who attempt to substitute their judgments and values for the people's freely arrived at choices.

A key element in this intellectual shell game – and one that bears especially on how our mainstream economic ideas contribute to environmental degradation – is the concept of 'revealed preferences'. In this hyper-behaviouristic view, the way to know what people want and what they value is to observe how they act. Now it is certainly not irrelevant to observe how people act. But the inferences to be drawn from observations of how people spend their money are much more complex and tricky than most economic analyses take into account. Frank (1985), for example, has argued insightfully and persuasively that many analyses of so-called revealed preferences give a highly misleading picture of what people really want because they do not take into account the way in which the very operations of the market, which exclude *collective* decisions, force people into choices that resemble the Prisoner's Dilemma. Israeli economist Shlomo Maital has wittily depicted the model guiding most economic analysis as positing an 'exacting consumer matching subjective value and objective price right at the precipice of his budget line, along which he or she skates with Olympian precision' (Maital 1982: 147). As he notes, such a model is at best 'far-fetched'.

The very way economists pose their questions about what people's preferences are reveals a bias toward buying and producing more goods that parallels the way in which the system itself pushes us toward choices that, in their sum, impoverish our lives as we, purchase by purchase, think we are enriching them.

Thus, in attempting to present a sober and balanced approach to determining just how much production we should sacrifice for how much abatement of pollution, Lester Thurow makes the following suggestion:

> Imagine that someone could sell you an invisible, completely comfortable facemask that would guarantee you clean air. How much would you be willing to pay for such a device? Whatever you would be willing to pay is what economists call the *shadow price* of clean air ....
> Such a facemask cannot be purchased, but any pollution control program that can give us clean air for less than this price is a programme that is raising our real standard of living.
>
> (Thurow 1980: 108)

Implicitly, of course, Thurow is saying that if clean air costs *more* than this 'shadow price' it is *not* worth it, its benefits do not exceed the costs in lost production. Here once again, we see what *looks like* a highly democratic and sensitive analysis; the economists' bias toward defining well being in terms of having more goods to buy is obscured. If it turns out that the analysis reveals that *x* amount of pollution control is not worth it, it is because *the people* have spoken, the people have revealed their preferences. But the answers we get depend on the questions we pose to people, and, for a variety of reasons, 'what would you be willing to pay?' is a question likely to bias the answer toward more goods and less clean air.

Of course, if the mask were very inexpensive, then the question becomes easy and trivial. Few would not spend a few cents to breathe cleaner air. But implicit in Thurow's posing of the question is the more difficult question of what we should do if the price were rather high. In this case, far from simply revealing our true preferences or providing an accurate accounting of the real costs and benefits from the point of view of the people who might endure or enjoy them, the response to the question posed in this form is likely to illustrate how irrational human beings can be when important life issues are squeezed into the Procrustean calculus of dollars and cents. Let us suppose, for example, that each mask cost $5,000. I can readily imagine hesitating to spend the $20,000 it would cost to protect my family of four. I can even imagine some of the sentences that might masquerade in my head as sober thoughts: 'They probably wouldn't really work'. 'How much difference would it make?' 'Is pollution really such an immediate threat after all?'

Does this, then, reveal that the 'shadow price' of clean air is clearly less than $5,000 per person, that if it took as much as $5,000 per capita to achieve the goal we would not want it? At first glance, it might seem so, especially since, as someone who has taken the trouble to write publicly about the need for more emphasis on the quality of the environment and less on material goods, I may be reasonably supposed to put a higher value on clean air than most people do. Do I, then, complain about pollution in the abstract, but prove unwilling to back up my professed views with hard currency? I think not. Rather, what is illustrated by the conflicted response I have candidly offered is the irrational overvaluation of money that pervades the lives of almost all of us, an irrationality from which, unfortunately, I am not exempt.

Why do I say that my likely response to the question Thurow poses is irrational, rather than simply a truer or deeper reflection of what I really want than my abstract musings might lead me to expect? Could it not be, as the viewpoint of the economist implies, that the pocketbook reveals our true preferences and values more accurately than mere words? The basis for my contention becomes clearer if we put Thurow's question in a different form, a form that advocates of economic growth conveniently leave out: *How much money would I be willing to take in return for letting someone blow polluted air into my child's face every day?*

This question is logically equivalent to Thurow's as a basis for determining the 'shadow price' of clean air. It too tells us what the economic exchange value of clean air is to us. But it would elicit a quite different response from me, as it would, I believe, from most people. From the vantage point of this latter question, the benefits of clean air may seem to be virtually infinite. There is *no* amount of money I would take in free exchange in return for any significant dirtying of my children's lungs.

Now, to be sure, it is true that my response might be different if my children were starving and the money were needed to feed them. Clean air, under those circumstances, might be viewed as a luxury I could not afford. Tragically, there are many people in the world who do face the equivalent of such a trade-off, and they do decide – quite rationally – that dire economic necessity requires being less finicky about the niceties of ecological purity. But the middle class, and even the working class, of North America, Europe, and other developed parts of the world are by no stretch of the imagination in such circumstances, and it is a peculiar definition of rationality that endorses their choosing as if they were. Thinking about life's trade-offs in the terms suggested by Thurow's phrasing of his question may indeed lead such people to exhibit habits of thought more suited to a society characterized by severe deprivation. But our vulnerability to such confusion should not be confused with an informed expression of our true desires *or* our true interests. The posing of questions in ways that pull from us our most impulsive response, or that rely on the specious lure of numbers, should require informed consent. When fully apprised of the import of the question, and offered alternative ways to think about it, the determination of the 'shadow price' becomes less shadowy.

Misperceptions of goods and satisfaction

The fallacies that lead us to produce and to buy more than is good for us or for the environment we depend on to sustain our lives are not the exclusive property of economists. The ways we pose questions *to ourselves* also lead us to do a poor job of representing our own interests and our true needs. The accelerating rush toward production – bear in mind that even in the recession of the early 1990s we produced considerably more than we did a decade before – has certainly built upon a desire for 'more' that is widespread throughout the population. But what few of us seem to realize is that the 'more' we achieve at this point yields us little in the way of enduring satisfaction. Indeed, few even realize that we do have more; the widespread nostalgia for the 'good old days' of prosperity in the 'affluent' 1950s and 1960s seems not to be accompanied by a recognition of how much more most Americans have now than their counterparts did then.[2]

One need not rely solely on impressions in documenting this point. Taking the United States as a case example, there is systematic evidence both that most Americans have much more now and that they are not more satisfied as a consequence. Consider, for example, the results of a series of surveys taken over several decades charting the perceived sense of well-being of the American population; the percentage of people describing themselves as very happy on those surveys peaked in 1957 (Campbell 1981). Interestingly, this is just about the time John Kenneth Galbraith finished his highly influential book, *The Affluent Society* (Galbraith 1958). Let us therefore consider how that earlier period of perceived affluence compares to our present more troubled times in terms of the goods and services the economy actually poured out. The differences provide little comfort for those who claim that an increasing output of material products has much to do with human welfare. *After* correcting for inflation, we still find that every man, woman, and child in the United States now has about $1.50 for every dollar their equivalents had back when Americans felt they lived in the affluent society, a 50 per cent increase in real spendable income. (Of course, not every man, woman, and child has shared equally in the growth – indeed, that is a significant part of what is wrong with how growth-oriented, market economies are organized – but, as the figures below make quite clear, the higher level of material affluence in the United States today – in times perceived as economically troubled – than in times perceived as ones of prosperity and satisfaction is evident through most of the population). Compared to the late 1950s, when the *experience* of satisfaction and prosperity were considerably higher than today, the actual increases in America's wealth are prodigious: for example, twice as many homes have their own washing machines; five times as many have dryers to go with them; three times as many have freezers; five times as many have air conditioning; and more than *nine* times as many have dishwashers.[3]

To this must be added the large number of things most middle-class Americans now have that didn't even exist back then – VCRs, computers, CD players, microwave ovens, Walkmen, even the 'Air Jordans' my interviewees felt unable to deprive their children of. As one looks at the full picture of the stock of goods that has become standard in American life, and compares it to what was standard – or even luxurious – in the time of John F. Kennedy, it is remarkable both how little we have to show for all of it in the way of satisfaction and how little we even realize that we do have so much more.

Other lines of evidence similarly point to the failure of increases in purchasing power and of stocks of goods to provide the expected increase in experienced well-being. In international comparisons, there is little indication that societies with high levels of material output are any happier or more satisfied than societies whose output is much lower (Easterlin 1973, 1974). Where consistent differences are evident, they are more likely to be *within* any given society and to involve the influence of the comparison processes noted by Frank. Such wealth-related influences on perceived well-being, to the degree they exist, do not point to growth as a solution; growth can raise the level of affluence of the society as a whole (which seems to make little difference in perceived well-being) but it *cannot* increase the number of people in any given percentile.

If one turns to the role of economic growth and well-being *within* a given society, the findings similarly provide little comfort to advocates of growth. In one study (Duncan 1975), for example, housewives in Detroit were asked, 'How do you feel about your standard of living – the kind of house, clothes, car, and so forth you can afford on your household's income?'. The question was asked repeatedly over a sixteen-year period when the average income of families in the area increased over 40 per cent (*after* correcting for inflation and taxes), yet the percentage of respondents who described themselves as satisfied did not increase at all. Studies done cross-sectionally rather than longitudinally similarly find no increment in satisfaction attributable to higher income. Indeed, in one study, conducted in Wisconsin, reported satisfaction was *higher* in a part of the state that was less economically developed, and it *dropped* when greater industrial development came to the area (Wilkening and McGranaham 1978).

The vicious circles of the growth way of life

Why *is* it that growth has yielded us so little in enduring satisfaction? Why do we not experience ourselves as enjoying a higher standard of living than the previous generation when in fact we have so much more? To explicate fully the ironies and psychological contradictions of our emphasis on economic growth would require considerably more space than is available here (see Wachtel 1989 for a detailed account). A brief sampling can at least provide the general outlines of the vicious circle in which we are caught. To begin with, it must be noted that the entire dynamic of a growth-oriented economy absolutely *requires* discontent. If people begin to be satisfied with what they have, if they cease to organize their lives around having still more, the economy is in danger of grinding to a halt.

Part of the problem, of course – the most obvious part – can be traced to advertising. The very purpose of modern advertising is to generate desires and discontents; if an ad can make you feel your life is not complete without product X, it has done its job. But ads are not the only source of this phenomenon. The entire society is structured to lead us to define our aspirations in terms of products, and new products are constantly coming on the market. Moreover, this tendency is exacerbated considerably by another set of psychological factors. A variety of studies conducted under the rubric of *adaptation-level theory* (e.g., Helson 1964), as well as research conducted from related paradigms, has demonstrated that our judgments about an experience are shaped very largely by our level of expectation. In a growth-oriented society, our expectations are continually being raised, and so our adaptation level – the level against which we compare new experiences – keeps rising. Only what is above the new standard even gets noticed. Satisfaction becomes like the horizon; it looks a clear and finite distance away and potentially reachable. But as you approach it, it continually recedes, and after much effort you are no closer than you were when you began.

So part of why producing more and more goods doesn't satisfy our cravings is that our standards keep changing, both for reasons adumbrated by psychologists and for reasons recognized by economists such as Frank and Easterlin. But there are other reasons as well for the ambiguous and sometimes even paradoxical relationship between material goods and the sense of well-being. Many of the ways we gear up for growth actually *undermine* some of the more fundamental sources of satisfaction and well-being, leaving us feeling more insecure and less satisfied than we were before. Freedman, summarizing the results of a number of major studies of the sources of happiness, concluded that '[o]nce some minimal income is attained, the amount of money you have matters little in terms of bringing happiness. Above the poverty level, the relationship between income and happiness is remarkably small' (Freedman 1978: 136). What does matter, based on these studies, are things like love, friendship, being part of a community, being committed to or part of something larger than oneself. But it is precisely these things that a way of life organized around growth and market transactions impairs. The expectations, assumptions, and arrangements those of us in the industrialized world live by lead us to sacrifice a great deal, both individually and collectively, for the sake of maintaining the economic system at a higher and higher level of output (which, we are told, is the only way it can be maintained at all).

To begin with, we work too hard as we strive to be able to afford the larger and larger package that defines a standard way of life, and we make our work lives less and less pleasant as we, societally, forget that the workers from whom we wish to extract greater and greater productivity are *ourselves*, and as more and more of us feel the insecurity of corporate efforts, within the same frame of reference and same value system, to become 'lean and mean'. And all too often, we attribute all the hours of work not even to the wish to get ahead or to 'make it', but simply to the need to 'make ends meet'. For most Americans, there is relatively little sense of economic amplitude, simply the experience of trying to keep up with the treadmill. Yet what the figures cited just above (comparing present purchasing power and present stocks of goods with those prevailing in an earlier time of perceived prosperity) should make clear is that the definition of 'making ends meet' keeps changing. What not too long ago would have defined a fairly luxurious upper-middle-class standard of living now feels to most Americans like just making ends meet.[4] The air conditioning, dishwasher, television set, VCR, and so forth that once were signs of luxurious living are now experienced as necessities. They provide no special sense of pride or satisfaction. They become background, of significance only if they are absent; as our threshold for satisfaction rises, our threshold for deprivation lowers.

One might say that this is a sign of progress and certainly there *is* something salutary about the fact that we no longer regard as luxuries such items as running water or a refrigerator, that we are committed to the idea that no one in our society should be without them. But as the definition of necessity keeps evolving, we need to notice two things: that the sense of well-being or satisfaction does not increase in the same way and that the earth is groaning under the strain.

The century-long march toward shorter working hours has virtually ground to a halt. Although there has begun to be some movement toward shorter working hours in Western Europe, throughout most of the industrial world (including Europe) we remain largely fixated on the 35- or 40-hour week. Indeed, in the throes of our ever-increasing 'needs', many of us, especially in North America, are working longer hours today than we did a while back – or at least those of us who have a job; because one consequence of our failure to reduce working hours as productivity keeps increasing – and it does keep increasing, despite the peculiar language so commonly in use of referring to a decrease in the rate of *increase* as 'declining productivity'[5] – is that maintaining employment at high levels becomes more and more difficult. The only way to do it within the present set of assumptions is – hardly surprisingly – via growth. And so the system maintains itself by chewing its own tail: we must grow in order to keep people working, and we must keep people working the 35 or 40 hours a week we have labelled as 'full time'[6] – rather than taking some of the fruits of increasing productivity in leisure, which would reduce working hours and spread the work to more people – because if we took it in leisure we wouldn't grow. The logic is both impeccable and utterly circular. For if we took our dividends in leisure, we wouldn't *need* to grow to keep people working (nor, of course, would we place as great a strain on the ecology).

But it is not just long – and stressful – working hours that maintain the sense of deprivation. Our economic assumptions also conflict with what we know about the need for community and human solidarity. Organizing so much of the life of our society around competition takes its toll, as does our emphasis on a mobile work force. Whether it be the individual's search for a 'better' job – where better is defined in strictly monetary terms, with the impact on a family of uprooting itself pushed aside – or the impact of the closings of plants and offices in the managers' search for greater 'efficiency', or the playing out of the societal game of 'upgrading' one's house periodically if one can, a large portion of the 1 out of 5 Americans who move each year do so as part of how we collectively play the game of seeking economic growth. This uprooting, along with the long and stressful work hours, has a significant negative impact on family life, community, and friendships. The impact on the sense of community of frequent moves scarcely needs to be spelled out. Our ties to community *and* to friends become thinner when we know that we – and if not, our friends or neighbours – are likely to move before too long. Family life suffers too from the stress of two parents working long, inflexible hours (another consequence of placing the firm's 'efficiency' over other values), or from the strains of single parenthood in a society that provides little assistance with day care or (again) flexible work hours – and whose high divorce rate is probably not unrelated to the other strains discussed here.

The ways we attempt to deal with the stresses and losses this way of life brings about end up compounding our difficulties still further. The web of painful ironies in which most middle-class North Americans are caught derives from the fact that the very system that creates the strong sense of deprivation offers itself as a means of assuaging it. Rather than addressing the real sources of our discontent, we purchase goods and services, barely noticing that the goods and services we have *already* purchased have not done the trick.

The silver lining in the gloomy picture?

What I have said thus far may seem to present rather negative a picture. It is a picture filled with self-deceptions, dissatisfactions, foolish chasings after things that are not good for us. But in an important way it is an *optimistic* picture. For it suggests that we are not *inherently* on a collision course with ecological disaster; that our happiness does not in fact depend on the activities that are doing such harm to the earth and to the future prospects of our children and grandchildren.

Advocates for the environment have made the error of couching most of their appeals in terms of sacrifices we must make for the good of the environment or our children's future. Not surprisingly, however, people are not eager to hear sombre messages about the need to 'tighten our belts'. Denial and delay are the natural response, while the earth continues to deteriorate so that even more stringent restrictions become necessary to undo the damage. When, in contrast, it is understood that much of our sense of deprivation is due not to insufficient growth (with still more prodigious growth as the cure) but to the very things we have done to ourselves in pursuing the chimera of growth itself, a different reaction and a different course of action suggests itself.

What we who are concerned about the environmental consequences of our present way of life need to do is to consider the ecology of human satisfaction. We need to understand better what makes people feel good about themselves and about their lives and how our present way of life fails on that count as much as it does from an environmental vantage point. We need, moreover, to present an image of an alternative, an alternative in which our extraordinary technological advances do not result in the Hobson's choice of overwork or unemployment but in which rather the fruits of our capacity to produce what we need in less time are taken in leisure. We need to spell out in detail what a way of life would look like in which our rewards came in more time for friends, family, reading, painting, or sports rather than in the gadgets around which we have defined our aspirations but which much evidence indicates do not really enrich our lives. We need to consider alternative modes of economic organization so that global competition does not reduce us to the lowest common denominator and so that scientific and technological progress can be channelled toward improvements in our health and well-being rather than toward the quick buck and the quick thrill. There is, indeed, a great deal to be done, and many difficult questions remain. But it is already a significant step in the right direction when we understand that we have been barking up the wrong tree. There is by now abundant evidence that the tree of growth is not the tree of satisfaction. While there is still a forest out there, it is time for us to shift our gaze and free ourselves from our obsession with growth.

Notes

1   There are still other costs – even more important costs – that are not well measured in dollar and cents terms at all. To be sure, there are economists who believe that even the most precious and intangible elements of living and loving can be given a price tag and that we can make more rational and sensible trade-offs thereby; indeed, one economist, Gary Becker, has even won a Nobel prize for such efforts. A brief chapter cannot detail why such exercises are more a symptom of our problems than a useful tool in solving them, one way in which the value we are judged to impute to clean air by economistic methods can easily be distorted. Calculating the value of love is still a bit stickier.

2   On the other hand – and this bears directly on the central point of this chapter – there *is* a sense in which those earlier times were more prosperous: if one thinks of prosperity not in terms of the meaningless totals that a striving after growth point us toward, but as a sense of comfort, of being pleased with what one has, and of feeling secure about the future, then yes, there *is* a way in which those earlier times were more prosperous.

3   Indeed, these figures are for *percentages* of homes with these items. Since the population grew during that period, the increase in the absolute number of homes with these items was even larger.

4   This refers here specifically to Americans because the data most readily available comes from the United States. But there is little reason to think that the conclusions would be any different in any of the other advanced industrial societies.

5   'Declining productivity *growth*' is, of course, what is usually being referred to when the term 'declining productivity' is introduced into discourse about trends in the economy. The latter, highly misleading term, however, is exceedingly common, and its use offers a revealing glimpse into the ways that assumptions of growth penetrate our psychology and distort our perceptions.

6   By the standards of the nineteenth century, *most* people today work only part time. Even a bare minimum of historical perspective makes it unambiguous that definitions of 'full time' and 'part time' are utterly relative, but we seem to have narrowed our vision so that the 40-hour week seems to many North Americans virtually God-given.

References

Campbell, A. (1981) *The Sense of Well-Being in America*, New York: McGraw-Hill.

Duncan, O.D. (1975) 'Does money buy satisfaction?', *Social Indicators Research* 2: 267–74.

Easterlin, R. (1973) 'Does money buy happiness?', *The Public Interest* (Winter): 1–10.

—— (1974) 'Does economic growth improve the human lot? Some empirical evidence', in P. David and M. Reder (eds) *Nations and Households in Economic Growth*, Stanford, CA: Stanford University Press.

Frank, R.H. (1985) *Choosing the Right Pond: Human Behavior and the Quest for Status*, New York: Oxford University Press.

Freedman, J. (1978) *Happy People*, New York: Harcourt Brace Jovanovich.

Friedman, M. and Friedman, R. (1980) *Free to Choose*, New York: Harcourt Brace.

Galbraith, J.K. (1958) *The Affluent Society*, Boston, MA: Houghton Mifflin.

Hayek, F. (1944) *The Road to Serfdom*, Chicago, IL: University of Chicago Press.

Helson, H. (1964) *Adaptation Level Theory*, New York: Harper and Row.

Hunnicutt, B. (1988) *Work Without End: Abandoning Shorter Hours for the Right to Work*, Philadelphia, PA: Temple University Press.

Maital, S. (1982) *Minds, Markets, and Money*, New York: Basic Books.

Schor, J.B. (1991) *The Overworked American: The Unexpected Decline of Leisure*, New York: Basic Books.

Thurow, L. (1980) *The Zero Sum Society*, New York: Basic Books.

Wachtel, P.L. (1989) *The Poverty of Affluence: A Psychological Portrait of the American Way of Life*, Philadelphia, PA: New Society Publishers.

Wilkening, E.A. and McGranaham, D. (1978) 'Correlates of subjective well-being in northern Wisconsin', *Social Indicators Research* 5: 211–34.

14

WORK IN A SUSTAINABLE SOCIETY

Robert Paehlke

Introduction

The leading divergence between the short-term interests of global capitalism and the interests of many people, especially younger people, centres on a significant reduction in average work time – and the equitable sharing of access to work. Unfortunately global capitalism may well have a majority of Canadians on its side (unwilling to reduce their present level of access to full-time, life-long work opportunities).

Structural unemployment has grown rapidly throughout the rich nations over recent decades (see Tables 14.1 and 14.2 below). The time for such initiatives as limitations on overtime, the four-day week, and/or an even stronger push for early (or early partial) retirement schemes has clearly arrived. Such measures are overdue on: (1) social grounds (e.g., hopelessness has become a cultural norm within a generation that has had – for more than a decade now – few opportunities for meaningful or even permanent work at a living wage); (2) economic grounds (e.g., unmanageable deficits are in part the result of public costs related to high unemployment); and (3) environmental grounds (e.g., political pressures to continue to extract resources at unsustainable levels from the underemployed and those fearful of falling into that abyss).

The political challenges associated with any new approach to work time distribution are, however, daunting. There is little evidence that the above-mentioned costs of inaction are widely and fully understood and appreciated.

Table 14.1 shows average unemployment rates for each of the seven major OECD nations from 1965 through 1988. The figures for 1989–93 continue the upward trend that is so clearly indicated in the data below. The central point here is that the trend toward structural unemployment is not so much a matter of temporary or uneven dislocation as an historically rooted and widespread problem. Rising unemployment is simply not particular to one or any group of rich nations and it is not a phenomenon of recent years alone. Nor is it simply a result of a 'recession'.

Table 14.1 Average unemployment rates for the seven major OECD countries

	1965–9	*1970–4*	*1975–9*	*1980–4*	*1985–8*
United States	3.7	5.3	6.9	8.2	6.4
Japan	1.2	1.3	2.0	2.4	2.7
Germany	0.9	0.9	3.5	5.7	6.5
France	1.8	2.6	4.9	8.0	10.3
Great Britain	1.7	3.1	5.4	10.3	10.5
Italy	5.5	5.7	6.8	9.0	10.3
Canada	3.9	5.7	7.3	9.8	9.1
Average	2.8	3.5	5.2	7.6	8.0

Source: McBride 1992

Table 14.1 clearly shows that a pattern of rising levels of unemployment has been deep and long. The pattern also holds more recently for five of the G7 nations. The two exceptions are the United States and Great Britain which have shown modest improvement when comparing 1985–8 with 1994–6. In the other five unemployment levels have continued to rise until now, especially in Germany. OECD figures show the average unemployment rates for 1994–6 to be: Canada, 9.9 per cent; United States, 5.7 per cent and falling; Japan, 3.1 per cent and rising; France, 12.1; Germany, 8.5 per cent; Italy, 11.8 per cent and rising; Britain, 8.9 per cent and falling. It would appear that some wealthy nations can reduce unemployment by increasing the proportion of part-time workers and by cutting social programmes and wages for the unskilled. What is less clear is if similar changes in other nations would lower their rates without leading to a renewed rise in unemployment in the United States and the United Kingdom. That is, is total wage capacity within the wealthy nations a zero-sum game, given globalization and the digital revolution?

Nor is the phenomenon limited to the G7 nations alone. Nine other rich nations (Australia, Austria, Belgium, Finland, Netherlands, Norway, Spain, Sweden, and Switzerland) show a similar pattern. Furthermore, the pattern holds across a wide variety of approaches to social policy, scales and patterns of governmental services, levels and patterns of debts and deficits, political cultures, levels of public enterprise, levels of privatization, and so forth. Table 14.2 presents data for these nine nations in summary and in combination with the seven (G7) from Table 14.1.

Generally, the worst of the economic and social burden associated with this seemingly inexorable shift has been borne by several groups. The hardest-hit groups include those nearing, but not yet at, early retirement age. Such persons frequently find it very difficult to return to the work force when their

Table 14.2 Average unemployment rates

	1965–9	1970–4	1975–9	1980–4	1985–8
9 Nations	1.8	2.0	3.9	6.5	7.0
16 Nations	2.3	2.7	4.5	7.0	7.4

Source: McBride 1992

positions are 'downsized'. Especially affected are the young who are now frequently forced to chose between accumulating an absurd array of university degrees (and debt) or serving in the rapidly growing legions who are employed on a temporary and/or part-time basis at or near the legal minimum wage without any of the once-normal benefits. The absence of any employment security is increasingly the situation facing a substantial minority of society in many rich countries. It is also increasingly the expected situation of the large majority of society, especially that of the young. But this is only one of many social, economic, and environmental implications of the new high unemployment societal norm.

Many of the most visible social effects of high unemployment are widely understood and need not be detailed here. These include increases in family break-up and male violence, alcoholism, crime, illness, depression, and suicide. On the positive side, and less discussed but very important as well, are the potentials for improved family life associated with moderate reductions in work time, especially for parents of young children (so long as such work opportunities are available at a reasonable approximation of a living wage, with a reasonable level of employment security, and with some family benefits).

Employers frequently find, for example, that overall productivity is enhanced if employees are allotted a number of hours per month for family business including the care of sick children. This is one (very modest) basis on which work time reductions could be allocated. Such an allocation would recognize both that the rise in unemployment levels is related to the expanding entry of females into the labour force and that there is no turning back on that front. In the present context where both parents of young children now normally work the stress on all family members, especially perhaps women, is considerable.

Even a modest reduction in the work week (to, for example, four 8-hour instead of five 7-hour days) would go a very long way in sustaining and supporting families. Almost all families presently face enormous emotional challenges closely linked to the limited time which now exists for meaningful family life. The cost to society of a rise in family breakdown is clearly enormous. One need not be a mindless advocate of a return to some alleged past era of 'family values' to grant that the family dissolution rate throughout most rich nations represents a tragic loss. Gender relations characterized by mutual recriminations may well be in large part the result of the total working hours added to most family's existence over recent decades. Family break-up (especially without a radical shift in court attitudes to male or joint custody) generally now restores the gender-based division of domestic obligations. Moreover, we have created a world where the best division of labour open to the remaining intact families with young children (given the high cost of institutional child care) is a life where one partner works a full-time night shift or 32-hour weekend job while the other deliberately works the opposite pattern in order to control the cost of child care. There are now many such noble partnerships, and in many ways such arrangements may be better than the alternatives presently available, but it could be characterized as a gender-equitable version of the family life of a nineteenth-century coal mining family. Surely we can now imagine a better world.

Economically, the costs of not adjusting work time to share work on a more equitable basis are also considerable. Were unemployment eliminated and employment security enhanced through the redistribution of access to work time it would seem likely that police costs, health care costs, family services costs, welfare costs, unemployment insurance costs would decline. So too would the need for many other social services. Other adjustments in work patterns could be made at the same time with an eye to spreading the impact on infrastructural services (public transportation, roads, and electricity demand, for example). As well, hourly productivity in a four-day week would in all probability be higher than in a five-day week. These economic benefits are not inconsiderable.

On the other hand, the effects of more equitably sharing work time on total governmental tax revenue might be neutral, or even marginally negative. Sales tax income would likely rise as the newly employed would, on average, have a higher marginal propensity to spend than the presently employed. However, income tax receipts might decline as the marginal tax rate for the newly employed would be lower on average than that of the presently employed whose incomes would presumably decline by something quite near to the amount earned by the newly employed. Most analysts would assume that wages would decline proportionately with the fewer hours worked, but – given positive productivity effects – a case can be made that employers and employees should split the gained difference and lessen the decline in wages. If this possibility were to result from sector by sector negotiations (or if it were legislated) governmental revenues could actually rise. Given, then, that governmental costs would decline significantly, it is fair to conclude that the overall effect on governmental budget deficits would be positive and there is a possibility that the result would be strongly positive.

Environmentally, there are several possible, generally positive, effects. First and foremost, pressures to extract resources beyond sustainable levels, or to allow polluters to engage in job blackmail with equanimity in the name of employment opportunities, would decline (Grossman and Kazis 1991). Second, there could be significant environmental improvements associated with the evening of time-related burdens on infrastructure (lowered electricity peak times mean fewer power plants need be constructed). There could also be a moderate downward pressure on GNP since government borrowing and spending would decline and total wages might also decline slightly at least in the short-term as incoming employees would be paid less on average than are present employees, especially when paid at overtime rates. This latter effect would likely be temporary as full employment would drive wages upwards (this of course is one reason neither capital nor government has pressed for changes in work time distribution). These GNP effects would be small and it is not clear that GNP effects would be necessarily positive environmentally.

A larger environmental question is: in what ways would spending patterns and habits be altered, what would the old spenders cut out and what would the new spenders emphasize? More important perhaps unemployment and employment insecurity increase the political, economic, and social pressure to pollute and to extract resources non-sustainably. Nonetheless the impacts associated with post-industrial human play could be as environmentally problematic as is industrial-age work (and as is the involuntary absence thereof). The environmental impacts of recreational pursuits will be treated in the fourth and final section of this chapter. The human ambivalence regarding freedom from labour will be explored in section three. Suffice it to say here that in the long run, if and when work time were significantly reduced, it is possible that the environmental impacts associated with increased leisure time would be as significant as those associated with employment – at the least reduced impacts are not automatically associated with increased leisure as some earlier analysts have suggested.

There are larger questions to be considered as well. Work is a principal source of individual identity and meaning and has been a core element of social structure through all of history in nearly every variety of socio-economic system. The weakening or radical alteration of work and employment patterns (especially if society were eventually to go beyond steps like reductions in overtime or the wider use of the four-day week) could prove to be a very great challenge. Moreover, reducing governmental debts and deficits could accelerate unemployment levels above those which might be shared equitably without massive political resistance from the employed (since most public expenditures are employment intensive). These are not questions which can be resolved in a short chapter (nor do I know the answers), but they will be addressed at least tangentially.

Looking backwards from a globalized political economy

Looking back on the extensive jobs/environment literature of the 1970s has, in recent years, become increasingly instructive. This exercise can help us to understand both the general evolution of the economy and the extent to which environmental problems and unemployment problems can no longer be resolved independently. The general conclusions drawn in the early jobs/environment literature were accurate, but the full dimensions of the employment/environment relationship were not then fully understood. That is, it is true that many environmental initiatives do, if adopted, result in additional rather than diminished employment opportunities, but the extent to which employment pressures promote and encourage political pressures in opposition to environmental protection was grossly underestimated. Nor could the jobs/environment analysts of the 1970s have foreseen the complex ways in which these anti-change and anti-environmental pressures would manifest themselves by the 1990s.

Specifically, the jobs/environment analyses of the 1970s demonstrated that recycling was more labour-intensive than disposal in most cases (Pearce and Walker 1976). It was also shown that both energy conservation initiatives and solar and other forms of renewable energy were more labour intensive than were 'hard path' energy megaprojects (Brooks 1978; Kennedy 1978: 34–5). Organic agriculture also embodies more work time per unit of output than does more conventional 'industrial' agriculture. As well it takes more employees to clear transmission line rights-of-way by mechanical than by chemical means and there is a great deal of labour in reforestation efforts. Other 1970s studies showed, rather surprisingly, that public transportation was not only more energy efficient, but at least as labour intensive as a relatively more automobile-dominated transportation system (Hannon and Puelo 1974). Both a mandatory requirement of refillable beverage containers and pollution abatement legislation were shown to be net generators of employment (Bailes and Gudger 1974; Chandler 1984). A jobs/environment programme advanced by the US Sierra Club in 1978 also included railroad construction, improvements to national parks, urban parks and city core revitalization efforts (Goldstein and Sage 1978).

That some environmental initiatives could threaten some jobs was never denied. The broad claims implicit in the jobs/environment literature as a whole were that the net effects on employment of the full array of environmental protection initiatives were not just negative as was commonly presumed at the time, but were probably positive in net terms. As well it was suggested that there were numerous policy opportunities available to governments that would simultaneously ameliorate environmental damage and enhance employment opportunities. Few governments took up very many of these challenges to intervene in such ways.

Since the 1970s global economic integration has proceeded at a pace that

277

was not fully anticipated by many analysts at the time that the conclusions of the jobs/environment literature were put forward. Nor did they anticipate the extent to which, and the speed with which industrial service and managerial jobs could be eliminated by new technologies. By the 1990s we had arrived at a point where nearly everyone (rich or poor) had become economically insecure. Headquarters managerial staff are now nearly as vulnerable as low-wage, low-skill service and industrial workers. As well, the future of employment in the public sector in Canada, Sweden, and many other rich nations is now as uncertain as employment in the private sector. Further, globalization would appear to now assure that whatever contractions of employment occur in one rich trading nation will soon also likely occur – in the name of competitiveness and opportunity – in most, if not all, such nations. Compounding the new levels of job insecurity in the rich nations is the accelerating drift of labour-intensive manufacturing and other forms of employment to the increasingly skilled workers within poorer nations.

This multifaceted transformation places the jobs/environment literature in a context which largely overshadows its particular findings. The job losses and gains owing to environmental initiatives are relatively small compared to those associated with changes in international competitiveness, or compared to the impacts of the new forms of economic and employment rationalization. Unfortunately, rationalization – or downsizing as it has come to be called – is now widely accepted as inevitable while the employment risks associated with environmental protection are frequently taken to be optional luxuries which we can no longer afford. Almost any 'optional' additions to production costs are now routinely rejected by industry, government, and society at large as a threat to 'our' national position within the global marketplace.

As well, any job losses other than rationalization-related losses are seen by some – particularly, of course, the incumbents in those jobs – as unacceptable even if there are net employment gains overall. In the present context it would seem to be an easy matter for those job incumbents and/or their employers to gain a sympathetic public hearing. In addition, it seems an increasingly easy matter for governments to absolve themselves of any responsibility to generate employment by any means other than by 'improving our international competitiveness' through tax cuts to industry, harmonized limits to environmental and other forms of regulation, and wage reductions in both the public and private sectors.

Thus, in summary, one might identify six differences between the 1970s and the 1990s context within which society understands the relationship between employment and environmental protection. The first three of these points are offered by way of summary of the preceding discussion; the remaining three will require some further discussion below. The six differences are:

1   There has been and will continue to be an on-going transfer of manufac-
    turing employment to poorer nations particularly notably in recent years
    to Mexico, China, Southeast Asia and India.
2   There has been and will continue to be a wide and perhaps accelerating
    rationalization and automation of manufacturing, service, management,
    and communications employment.
3   Public sector debts and deficits will likely necessitate hiring freezes and/or
    employment reductions across the public sector in many nations for at
    least the next decade.
4   The collapse of sustainability of some renewable resources has already
    resulted in significant employment losses in some traditional extractive
    industries and it is probable that there will be more cases of this in the
    future.
5   'Green' products, including pollution abatement, are now widely touted
    as an economic growth opportunity, but in most cases the former would
    replace existing products.
6   In many industries and within the public sector employees are working
    longer hours to improve a plant's or a firm's 'competitiveness', to allow
    employers to avoid the cost of benefits packages to additional employees,
    or simply to help to avoid the effects of future downsizing come the next
    recession or rationalization.

The latter three of these items are worth exploring further before we return
our attention to the central question of this inquiry – the redistribution of
available work opportunities.

In the 1970s many environmentalists warned of a coming collapse of the
resource base of industrial society, sometimes in the most alarmist possible
tones (Catton 1980; Heilbroner 1974). The collapse of industrial society itself
was presumed by many 1970s environmentalists to be imminent. Over the
coming decades this perspective was widely rejected as apocalyptic and indeed
the case was frequently erroneous in its particulars or simply overstated. Most
resources – even fossil fuels – would appear to have held up and pollution has
not led directly to either the widespread collapse of industrial society, or to the
transformation of that society despite Bhopal and Chernobyl. However, we
have now already witnessed the complete collapse of one of the world's
greatest renewable resources – the Atlantic fishery. The coming decades will
likely witness at least the temporary decline in availability of another – the
coastal forests of the Pacific Northwest.

The employment losses in each of these cases are massive on a local scale
and 'softened' only by the preceding rapid rationalization and automation of
extractive capacity within these industries. (The demise of the resource is, of
course, not unrelated to the efficiency with which it can now be extracted.
Lower costs of production help to assure high rates of use in the case of wood
products and rising health-related demand for fish led to a willingness to

ignore the decline in catches as prices rose and profits remained high.) Surprisingly the demise of these resources has not led to a return to an assertive and apocalyptic environmentalist rhetoric in the style of the 1970s. This is a reflection, at least in part, of the extent to which the tone of contemporary discourse has been truly transformed by the ideology and reality of economic globalization.

The sustainable development dialogue of the late 1980s and early 1990s has also played an important role in this changed perspective on the relationship between environment, economy and employment. The environmentalism of the 1970s was at its core an argument for the end of excessive materialism and a need for zero economic growth. Not all environmentalists then agreed with the limits-to-growth argument that pollution problems and resource shortfalls would soon lead to a collapse of industrial society, but most would have been astonished by the tone of the contemporary debate. Green products are seen by some as a means of restoring economic growth and sustainable development as a means of keeping the global economy on an even keel. Economy and environment seem sometimes to have been transformed from 'protagonists' to 'partners', a truly astonishing ideological shift! Is 'green' now a basis for resistance to industrial products or merely new type of industrial product? Clearly it can be both.[1]

One greets this transformation in environmental thought with mixed feelings. The growth in GNP per se never was at the heart of all environmental problems. Barry Commoner was (and is) right in many instances – the core problem is that most technological and economic choices are based exclusively on a short-term profit calculus. However, on the other hand, GNP growth is neither necessary for, nor important to, the amelioration of environmental problems within the rich nations of the world and, moreover, GNP growth may well (but yet might not) prove to be part of the multi-faceted challenges to sustainability which the planet as a whole faces. (See Wachtel, 'Overconsumption', in this volume.) The rich nations can and should rapidly decouple economic growth from both the expansion of resource extraction and from the proportion of the population that must be employed 40 hours per week, fifty weeks per year or anything near to that amount. The former could slowly decline as a result of rising energy and materials taxes (perhaps in part in the place of income and payroll taxes) and the latter must very soon be maintained through work time redistribution (rather than unemployment, welfare and spreading poverty).

But in some industrial sectors we are moving in the opposite direction on both fronts. We have increased extraction from our forests and, in the face of high rates of unemployment, some industrial sectors are seeing both increases in overtime for hourly employees and accelerating hours of work for salaried employees. The high unemployment context and the ideology of global competitiveness makes employees and governments alike reluctant to question the right of employers to elect these (or for that matter any) options. Only a renewal of consideration of the relationship between environmental protection (including sustainability) and employment – a consideration which is not afraid to have doubts about competitiveness and economic growth as the highest possible goals for a society – can resolve the central contradictions of the 1990s and beyond. The thinker who has come the closest to seeing the way to resolve these contradictions is André Gorz.

André Gorz and the *Liberation from Work*

Gorz's greatest contribution to the discourse of the late twentieth century lies in his recognition of the truly historic and liberatory character of the now declining necessity for work and wage labour. A reading of Gorz reveals an understanding of unemployment that is less a temporary failure of capitalism than a measure of an utterly transformational achievement of human ingenuity. We are potentially on the eve of nothing less, in Gorz's view, than the beginning of the end of the need for human wage labour. We need only to come to understand the possibility as such and to see through the transformation.

In *Paths to Paradise: On the Liberation from Work*, and in his earlier *Farewell to the Working Class: An Essay on Post-Industrial Socialism*, Gorz argued that if productivity increases were transferred primarily to work time reductions (rather than to profits and/or to wage increases) work time could be radically reduced in a matter of a few decades. He asks readers to

> imagine that society were to distribute yearly productivity gains in the following way: a third in the form of greater purchasing power, and two thirds in the form of additional free time. With an annual increase in productivity of 5 per cent – easily achieved in the past – the length of the working week would fall from 40 to 35 hours over a period of four years . . . . A 20-hour week could be achieved in 20 years . . . and, if we take vacations and public holidays into account, would amount to a yearly total of barely 900 hours.
>
> (Gorz 1982: 135–6)

Gorz went on to note that 900 hours was equivalent to five months of the year at then-present work rhythms (which are roughly equal to the present work rhythms of those who now remain employed on a full-time basis). Thus it would be possible that most people might come soon to have seven months of the year off, enough that many individuals could begin to define themselves in terms of their 'leisure' as opposed to their 'work' activities.

Gorz concurred with the argument of a group working with Jacques Delors to the effect that the freeing of time in this manner would lead 'almost automatically to calling the productivist socio-cultural model into question' (Gorz 1982: 137). The Delors group, writing in 1980 and in the tradition of

French socialism, was even then groping for a way to preserve some clear meaning and distinctive position for left politics. The striking ways in which the world has since changed would seem to have rendered their and Gorz's visions of the future simultaneously both more necessary and less possible. Capitalism seems less able now than then to achieve full employment even at prosperous points in the business cycle, but it is more politically entrenched than ever. It is almost impossible now to envision a politics which could achieve anything like Gorz's attribution of one-third of productivity gains to increased employee earnings and simultaneously two-thirds to increased leisure time.

However, given the costs of high unemployment for both state and society it is perhaps plausible to imagine a future politics wherein some significant proportion of productivity gains would go to reduced work time with the remainder divided between labour and management in the 'usual manner'. Alternatively, reductions in work time could perhaps be introduced with corresponding reductions in weekly or monthly income (as would be the case with the elimination of mandatory or even voluntary overtime). Earnings per hour would continue to increase (or decrease) as they otherwise might have done (except that full employment would assert its own upward pressures).

In the present political context, or anything like it, it is difficult to imagine the achievement of anything more favourable to labour than possibilities of this sort. On one level this latter assertion is simply an admission that the 'revolutionary' imagination has, at least for this author, faltered in the face of the contemporary political and economic realities. On another level it might be argued that (however it is achieved almost on whatever terms) rapidly declining work time, if accompanied by a renewed hope for full employment and an equitable distribution of work, is profoundly revolutionary in itself. Such a transformation would be as fundamental as the more equitable distribution of access to goods and wealth that Marx and so many other good souls dreamt of before Marxism. From an environmentalist perspective one can appreciate this more fully – therein there are real collective and long-term limits to individual and short-term human material gains. Time becomes the most valuable commodity.[2]

It may be the case that labour will not in very many contexts enthusiastically accept reduced work time in the place of the on-going maximization of wage increases. Nor are private sector employers likely to often and voluntarily pay the costs of sharing available work from their profits. Historically there has been no evidence of any such inclinations in either camp, with or without high levels of popular concern for the unemployed, for the environment, or regarding governmental deficits. Neither capitalists nor workers have very often imagined such matters to be their particular concern or responsibility.

Only the environmental movement has considered the relationship between employment and sustainability in either environmental or economic terms.

Lately, however, some governments and leaders have begun to see connections between high unemployment, rising deficits, and the growth of governmental services and expenditures. However they rarely consider the environment or the concerns of the economically vulnerable within the deficit-cutting solutions which they then put forward. Supports for the unemployed, public services, and public sector employment must be cut, full stop. It is as if the sudden absence of a welfare state could somehow in itself create more employment opportunities than have existed for decades.

On the other hand neither environmentalists, nor trade unions, nor left intellectuals have rushed to embrace the model adopted by the NDP in Ontario during the recession of the early 1990s of reducing work time in the public sector as an alternative to cutting jobs. Nor has there been much by way of an update, appreciation, or critique of Gorz's work. It is time perhaps for both. As regards the first matter, equally distributed reductions in work time across the public sector with proportionate wage reductions are a good means of partially rectifying governmental deficits. Such cuts should be balanced by cuts to private sector subsidies and increases in corporate taxes. Reduced work time in the public sector (achieved to avoid layoffs where they would otherwise be nearly certain) may then generate pressure to limit overtime (and even reduce the work week) and thereby stimulate hiring within the private sector. Despite some labour union support for reduced overtime as a route to more jobs, generally the view stated here is wildly out of favour within progressive circles in general and public sectors, including university faculty unions, in particular. Nonetheless, it would seem to be a politically plausible route to full employment and the environmental benefits of such a change.

In summary, there are four problems with Gorz's case, primarily matters which have arisen since he made his argument. First, as noted, the demise of state socialism and the rise of globalization have radically enhanced the relative power of capital. This all but eliminates the prospects for appropriating a large proportion of capital's 'share' of productivity gains to the cause of work time reductions (with no loss in income). Second, Gorz did not focus sufficiently on the multiple social and psychological functions of work and employment in modern societies. Third, Gorz overestimated the potential for labour enthusiasm for the undertaking he was putting forward. Fourth, Gorz failed to consider the potential for environmental impacts which might be associated with increased free time.

Work and employment serve many functions, all socially and ideologically conditioned, but some with real roots very near to the core of the modern human character. Modern society has been structured around employment and the modern personality around work. Gorz has perhaps underestimated the challenge associated with any attempt to shift employment and work to a secondary social role. It is not only 'employers' who will resist and be fearful of change. Many workers will simply opt to take supplementary employment as soon as the time is freed to make it possible. Extra money would not be the only motivation. Self-definition is for many rooted in employment position. Further, sociability is initiated and achieved primarily within the workplace. As well, personal confidence and security are undermined for many by the absence of a secure source of at least potentially rising income. These latter realities in particular can (and will and even must) change with time but the change will not transpire so easily, one suspects, as Gorz would have it.

Following from the above – and from the relative weakness of organized, not to mention unorganized, labour within the contemporary political context – is a limit to the enthusiasm of presently employed persons for involuntary work time reductions. If perceived as imposed such measures will be resisted, especially perhaps by the young who have already been forced to delay entry into the labour force. The best prospects for change may lie among the relatively economically secure (older) workers. Voluntary (or quasi-voluntary) work time reductions come most frequently in the form of earlier retirement dates (through buyout packages, early partial retirement, and voluntary early retirement options). Such shifts need not necessarily be in conflict with the coming demographically induced shortfalls in governmental pension funds – early partial retirement (e.g., at 55) could be tied to modest delays in full retirement (to 67 or even 70). The partial retirement period could be funded privately (through RRSPs and/or employer pension funds) and governmental pension payments could be reserved for the period of full retirement.

There are a variety of other possibilities, but some would seem to be more widely acceptable than others. Early retirement, even with some loss in lifetime income, might be an easier sell than shorter work weeks with proportionate reductions in income. While a shift from 40 to 35 hours per week or from 35 to 32 hours, with proportionate or partially proportionate wage reductions, could roughly achieve full employment, few in North America have yet advanced such options. But by contrast the so-called four-for-five adjustment (where four years salary is spread over five years with every fifth year off) wherein work is shared to avoid layoffs (or simply to allow for regular leaves-of-absence) are quite popular. Also rapidly gaining in frequency of use are the often exploitative arrangements for contract work, temporary work and part-time work. In these latter cases, change may well not come in the form of Gorz's vision of labour militancy and enthusiasm for reduced work weeks for all, but legislation requiring proportional benefits might make this option palatable for some.

Finally here, Gorz's assumption was that most persons would spend their leisure in environmentally desirable or at least in environmentally benign activities: growing and preparing food on a small scale, doing crafts, writing novels, and so forth. However, play can be as environmentally problematic as work. Some would spend their new leisure racing about in off-road vehicles and speed boats, or touring in motor homes. One wonders, for example, if people would not do more recreational travelling and burn more fuel than they would in moving back and forth to work. If so, environmental impacts might well increase and such increases might only be limited to the extent that incomes actually declined. Even increased wilderness 'appreciation' can be highly problematic environmentally. None of these negative outcomes is necessary, but the point is that Gorz's picture of environmentally benign leisure inclinations is not automatic – both work and play can have significant environmental costs.

Gorz's views in these matters were conceived apparently during an extended trip to North America where he lived among environmentally oriented young people for a time. Such attitudes and habits may well come to prevail for a majority, especially if governmental policies encourage appropriate adjustments. However, these changes will require a continuation and an acceleration of the cultural transformations of recent decades and will not flow automatically from the availability of more leisure time.

The politics of environmental protection will be increasingly bound up with the politics, culture, and economics of temporal equity and work time reductions. Environmental organizations should more often support measures which promote access to work chances for those denied the opportunity and, equally, all the possible options for persons to voluntarily choose to work less than 'full' time. The particular role that these organizations can play is to be explicit about the relationships between the culture of commodification, the global competitiveness (formerly the Protestant) work ethic, and environmental protection.[3] (See Wachtel, 'Overconsumption', in this volume.)

Conclusion: centrist environmentalism and the politics of temporal equity

The politics of the future can be envisioned as involving an ever-shifting interplay of three closely related, but analytically distinctive, realms – environment, equity (including labour), and economy (the ever-present forces of global capital). In pessimistic moments one might also see a future with but one dominant perspective (global capital), a world wherein the forces of equity and environment in combination could rarely, if ever, prevail on an issue of importance. One might as well assume, then, there are, on the other hand, good reasons to think that the three-dimensional political future is a plausible future, including an economic and social necessity to redistribute continuously an ever-declining amount of work (in order to resolve what once might have been called a contradiction).

This contradiction is central in that it affects all three political dimensions simultaneously – environment, equity and economy. The equity effect is obvious: some have work and income and some do not. The environment is affected because those without work and those insecure in their work will oppose those environmental protection initiatives which threaten or appear to threaten existing or potential employment opportunities. The economy itself is affected because those who do not earn do not produce and do not consume.

Economy-oriented, pro-growth organizations (e.g., the privately owned media) continue to celebrate both globalization and rationalization, largely ignoring the price that is paid in terms of employment and environmental sovereignty. Those same organizations assume as well that it is impossible to threaten resources to the point of disrupting the very functioning of the economy. Sustainable development is a concern of some in positions of power, but it does not – as they interpret it – require more than minor adjustments in the production and consumption patterns that would otherwise obtain.

Moreover, looming and visible apocalypse simply cannot be relied upon by environmentalists. Someone will farm fish when they are otherwise unavailable. When the large trees are all but gone someone will produce particle board and glulam with what remains. As the oil declines someone can gasify coal and the price of nuclear power will seem economically acceptable. The environmentally best future is but the best possible future in the value-laden (and scientifically informed) view of one group of humans – environmentalists. It is only one of several possible futures acceptable to our ever-adaptive species.

The environmentally best future must, then, be sold politically and – herein lies the greatest challenge – achieving that future may well involve serious economic trade-offs for both capital and labour. Moreover, some futures which now seem to be environmental nightmares may come to seem not all that bad in time. In lieu of wild nature humans could learn to love, perhaps nostalgically, a computer-stored virtual nature, complete with the smells, but without the actual dangers and discomforts. There would also be zoos, food farms, seed farms, tree farms, and frozen egg and sperm vaults, and a few parks for those more adventurous and scientifically and horticulturally inclined. What, economically, are we humans prepared to give up to leave adequate space for a viable wild nature? How can we muster the collective will to avoid what seems at times an almost inevitable natureless future?

Despite the extreme challenge facing environmentalists, it is nonetheless possible that the best chance for the political success of environmental values is through some form of ideological centrism – a view self-consciously both distinct from and 'between' that of capital and that of labour. In a world dominated by capitalist ideology such a view might well look to many much like 'moderate progressive environmentalism' (Paehlke 1991). But there is a subtle difference which – if anyone notices – might be seen as a half-step toward the centre of the old political (left–right) spectrum, if anyone could any longer understand what it meant.

This half-step would allow environmentalists to suggest that equity advocates and economy (capital) advocates may have much in common. Capital and labour (and their allies) may remain defined by their differences, but their commonalities could leave an important ideological opening for green politics. Both capital and labour seek to maximize their share in short-term yields from the process of economic production. Both seek to minimize their inputs to and to maximize their removals from the public treasury. Both strongly favour maximizing economic growth in order to advance these combined goals. A centrist version of environmentalism might, then, consistently, and with effect in some political contexts, advocate: (1) balanced governmental budgets, even public debt paydowns; (2) balanced limits on both profits and wages in the name of environmental protection; and (3) the maintenance of some social, environmental, and educational spending on the grounds that they provide employment with minimal environmental impacts.

In general such an approach would provide a moral and moderate opposition to the inclination on all other fronts to a get-it-all-and-get-it-now (instant gratification at all costs) approach to life. This latter view has defined the politics – both left and right – in the post-Second World War period, but it has offended many people other than environmentalists. The doubtful would include many traditional conservatives, some religious persons and organizations, some advocates of community and family values, anarchists, some democratic socialists, and many advocates of the welfare state. What has been lacking is a clearly articulated perspective toward which a variety of concerned individuals might be drawn, a perspective which goes beyond matters of purely environmental concern.

One possible key to the success of this distinctive (centrist) approach to environmentalism and political economy is rooted in the equitable distribution of work (the 'politics of time', as Gorz characterized it). Such a concern draws environmental thinking toward social and economic considerations in a consistent way – it provides a potential appeal in the realms within which humans lead their everyday lives. But it does so in relatively nonmaterialist terms, and it establishes a variety of benefits – social, economic, and environmental – which do not require (nor do they utterly exclude) economic growth. The equitable distribution of available work can be integrated – most importantly – with the reduction of many burdens currently imposed by the present on the future. This integration can be achieved in several ways and its achievement would establish a link to the ideological heart of environmentalism: sustainability.

First, the equitable distribution of work lessens the unemployment burden implicitly imposed by the old on the young. Second, the equitable distribution of work lessens the pressure from the unemployed and the fearful to impose environmental and sustainability costs in the name of employment opportunities for the desperate and fearful. These connections are obvious, but there are others. For example, the equitable distribution of work could be achieved in part through a shift from payroll to resource extraction taxes thus encouraging new employment relative to overtime and simultaneously encouraging investment in recycling and energy efficiency. In this way resource sustainability and employment opportunities are clearly and deliberately linked. Similarly work redistribution can be linked to deficit and debt reduction, another key means by which the present imposes costs on the future. The challenge here is to achieve public sector work time reductions which do not simply pass the costs through to undermining the stability of pension systems in the long-term to provide disproportionate benefits to an earlier generation in yet another way.

In this and other ways the meaning of sustainability itself is radically broadened and placed at the centre of environmental advocacy. Interestingly sustainability could also in a similar manner acquire meanings which might be favoured by some advocates of the perspective of capital. Payroll taxes are widely unpopular in such circles and seen as a threat to corporate sustainability. Moreover, were it the case that work time reductions were widely accepted as better than layoffs and even desirable in their own right, resistance to technological innovation and productivity improvements would diminish. Further, to the extent that at least some employment opportunities were available to all the cost of and even the need for social programmes would be reduced. The potential attendant moral climate should find favour in such circles, perhaps offsetting the rise in the collective and individual bargaining power of employees.

Finally two considerations remain – a glimpse at the potential political appeal of a politics of time, and a concluding note on the environmental risks associated with increased leisure time. Europe is the locus of some beginning experiments with work time reduction and Green parties there have led the way with consistent advocacy of change. In France and Germany some large industries have instituted reduced work weeks. In Norway public opinion polls suggest quite wide support, as the analysis of Tor Traasdahl of the economy–environment NGO *Framitiden i vare hender* (FIVH – the future is in our hands) indicates:

> Several studies have been carried out in order to ascertain the willingness of full-time employees in Norway to reduce working hours (by 10 per cent) and wages (by 3–7 per cent). An average of 50–62 per cent (slightly higher among women than men) answered 'yes', on the condition that the 'sacrifice' could reduce the number of idle hands. So our strategy now is (as it becomes more and more evident that economic growth in an already highly efficient economy cannot solve the unemployment problem) to link reduced purchasing power with more leisure time and the need for more jobs. If this equation can be reasonable [sic] solved in theory, the political potential for realizing it in practice seems quite promising.
>
> (Traasdahl 1994: 32)

The political key may lie in simultaneously shifting both production and consumption patterns. FIVH, for example, advocates schemes to share automobile ownership widely – a change which could in itself reduce an urban family's total expenses by up to 10 per cent overall. More durable goods, investments in household energy efficiency (lighting, appliances, and insulation, for example) and a reduced emphasis on highly processed and industrially prepared foods all also reduce living costs in the long-term and lower environmental impacts simultaneously. Additional free time would tend to make attending to such changes more manageable. The small reductions in income that according to FIVH are widely acceptable would render such changes in consumption more necessary. The risk is that the combination of such shifts in consumption and the greater availability of time could lead to other environmentally problematic consumption activities.

The solution is not sharper downward shifts in income as might have been advocated by 1970s environmentalists. These are widely unacceptable politically and unnecessary environmentally. A broader knowledge and public understanding of the environmental life cycle costs of various consumption activities (more research and public education) is part of the solution, as are shifts in tax burdens toward more environmentally problematic products and behaviours. But most important may be the selective provision of environmentally mindful public services. Ontario has established community-based 'green-ups' which provide services to improve the efficiency of energy and water use, waste reduction, and other services. New York State has provided outright improved insulation and weather stripping for a high proportion of low-income households. The Norwegian Society for the Conservation of Nature/Friends of the Earth Norway offers the following crucial suggestion: 'provide for a reduction in leisure travel through [the] sound planning of leisure activities in the local community' (Bank 1994: 27).

What is needed is a comprehensive alternative vision – alternative to a globalized system driven by consumption and profit alone. One cornerstone of such a vision could be employment security and another could be expanding free time. Another is the view that consumption of whatever goods unimpeded individual whim might seek cannot be sustained for anything but a small minority of humans and we should not continue to imagine that any of us (even hard-working intellectuals) are so entitled. One simply must hope that this alternative vision will come to be widely understood and that collective ways will be found to meet human needs in new, less materially intensive ways. The declining material expectations of young Canadians and others elsewhere is perhaps the beginning of a transformation of the nature of need itself. Any willingness on their (and our) part to adapt can and should be encouraged by more secure work opportunities, and the time necessary to learn how to play in new ways.

Notes

1 This ambivalence turned into the open in the form of serious internal struggles within the Canadian environmental organization Pollution Probe which publicly endorsed the particular 'green products' of the major grocery chain Loblaws. Many felt that Probe's manner of proceeding in this instance undermined the integrity and credibility of the organization and the environmental movement generally. Others felt that it forced that movement to 'live in the real world' and to accept that better products and processes are important and sufficient and that environmental perfection is impossible. Within Probe the anti-endorsement group prevailed.

2 On a modest scale and perhaps unconsciously this has been the approach of – dare one say it in a publication originating within Ontario – the New Democratic Party (NDP) government of Ontario which, in its so-called and widely unpopular social contract, has traded days off for wage reductions within its public sector. This approach, while unpopular in the extreme, is notable in that it has been a money-for-time trade which has allowed the government to reduce public sector wage costs sharply with a minimum of employee layoffs. Clearly this initiative is not the successful quasi-revolutionary struggle of labour-power that Gorz had envisioned but the outcome is not so different, on a small scale, in environmental, social, and economic terms. This is especially true if one allows for the fact that general (and public sector) productivity has not increased by anything like the 5 per cent rate that Gorz assumed (assuming that one could measure public sector productivity with any accuracy). The politics of time may look very different than Gorz had envisioned, but that is not necessarily something to lament without qualification.

3 Environmental intellectuals need to develop further and make central the germane ideas of, for example, William Leiss in *The Limits to Satisfaction*, Alan Durning in *How Much is Enough?*, and Paul Wachtel in *The Poverty of Affluence*.

References

Bailes, Jack C. and Gudger, Charles M. (1974) *The Economic Impact of Oregon's Bottle Bill*, Corvallis, OR: Oregon State University Press.

Bank, Helene (1994) 'Everyday environmental protection: thinking globally – acting locally', in William M. Lafferty (ed.) *Steps Towards Sustainable Consumption: A Presentation of Selected Norwegian Initiatives*, Oslo: Prosject Alternativ Framtid.

Brooks, David B. (1978) *Economic Impact of Low Energy Growth in Canada*, Ottawa: Economic Council of Canada.

Catton, William R. Jr. (1980) *Overshoot: The Ecological Basis of Revolutionary Change*, Urbana, IL: University of Illinois Press.

Chandler, William U. (1984) *Materials Recycling: The Virtue of Necessity*, Washington, DC: Worldwatch Institute.

Durning, Alan (1993) *How Much Is Enough?: The Consumer Society and the Future of the Earth*, New York: W.W. Norton.

Goldstein, Neil B. and Sage, Samuel H. (1978) 'The Sierra Club's Job Package: an environmental works program', *Nation* 226: 146–8.

Gorz, André (1982) *Farewell to the Working Class: An Essay on Post-Industrial Socialism*, London: Pluto Press.

Grossman, Richard H. and Kazis, Richard (1991) *Fear at Work: Job Blackmail, Labour and the Environment*, Philadelphia, PA: New Society Publishers.

Hannon, Bruce and Puleo, F. (1974) *Transferring from Urban Cars to Buses: the Energy and Employment Impacts*, Urbana, IL: Centre for Advanced Computation, University of Illinois.

Heilbroner, Robert L. (1974) *An Inquiry into the Human Prospect*, New York: W.W. Norton.

Kennedy, Edward M. (1978) 'Energy and Jobs', *Public Power* 37: 34–5.

Leiss, William (1976) *The Limits to Satisfaction*, Toronto: University of Toronto Press.

McBride, Stephen (1992) *Not Working: State, Unemployment, and Neo-Conservatism in Canada*, Toronto: University of Toronto Press.

Paehlke, Robert (1991) *Environmentalism and the Future of Progressive Politics*, New Haven, CT: Yale University Press.

Pearce, D.W. and Walker, I. (1976) *Resource Conservation: Social and Economic Dimensions of Recycling*, New York: New York University Press.

Traasdahl, Tor (1994) '*Homo consumens*: man as consumer', in William M. Lafferty (ed.) *Steps Towards Sustainable Consumption: A Presentation of Selected Norwegian Initiatives*, Oslo: Prosject Alternativ Framtid.

Wachtel, Paul (1994) *The Poverty of Affluence*, Philadelphia, PA: New Society Publishers.

15

ECOLOGICAL POLITICS IN CANADA[1]

Elements of a strategy of collective action

Laurie E. Adkin

This was a merchant who sold pills that had been invented to quench thirst. You need only swallow one pill a week, and you would feel no need of anything to drink.
'Why are you selling those?' asked the little prince.
'Because they save a tremendous amount of time', said the merchant. 'Computations have been made by experts. With these pills, you save fifty-three minutes in every week'.
'And what do I do with those fifty-three minutes?'
'Anything you like . . .'
'As for me', said the little prince to himself, 'if I had fifty-three minutes to spend as I liked, I should walk at my leisure toward a spring of fresh water'.

> Antoine de Saint Exupéry, *The Little Prince* (1943)

Paradigms of social change

In greatly simplified terms, we may distinguish in contemporary political thought two opposing approaches to the understanding of social change. The first, with roots in Marxism, maintains a conception of collective subjects, or actors, who at particular historical conjunctures become capable of self-conscious identity as well as political mobilization around a far-reaching critique of the nature of their society and an agenda of alternatives. The post-Marxist variant of this approach is found in new social movement (NSM) theory. NSM theorists, while arguing (for reasons which cannot be explained here) that the industrial working class no longer constitutes such a collective subject, nevertheless hold to the conception of a social movement. In this view of a social movement, the actors must have a discourse which identifies fundamental social antagonisms, as well as what is at stake in the possible outcomes.[2] This involves adopting *normative stances* regarding the desirable directions of social development which inform the social movement's vision of a better world, and its concrete proposals for the reform of economic, social and political institutions. Second, a social movement defines a *collective identity* linking many different actors to a shared interpretation of societal-level conflicts. Most NSM theorists have identified the ecology movements of Western Europe as movements which embody – at least in nascent forms – the elements of the long-awaited new social movement.

The second approach to social change in essence argues that the conditions for the formation of a new social movement – as defined above – no longer exist in the 'post-modern' era. Such concepts are throwbacks to modern grand narratives (including Marxism) which seek to provide 'total' explanations of the origins, dynamics and telos of historical eras and social formations. They seek to reduce the immensely varied phenomena of societies to a small number of 'central' meanings or to a single logic. The second approach rejects such 'totalizing' and 'reductionist' claims. It argues that social identities have become more than ever particularist and differentiated. The implicit national framework of social movement building has also been called into question by processes of capitalist globalization. Moreover, the impulse to construct social movements rests upon universalizing assumptions about human nature and human needs. Upon examination we find that all such assumptions are discursively constructed, historically and culturally specific, often eurocentric, phallocentric, and so on. In a word, the search for a new social movement – the successor of the workers' movements of the nineteenth century – is not only an exercise in nostalgia, but also inherently reductionist and exclusive in relation to the plethora of social identities and experiences.

The implications of this second approach for a theory of social change seem to be that politics will henceforth consist of the localized and relatively unconnected struggles of identity or interest groups. The pessimistic view is that this represents a victory for technocratic, capitalist elites who have succeeded in simultaneously centralizing economic and knowledge-based forms of power, while decentralizing and weakening popular democratic bases for decision making and solidarity. The optimistic view is that social actors are merely adapting to the new realities of the globalization of capitalism, as well as to technological changes. Developments such as the 'decentring' of the nation-state as a focus of political strategy, and the decline of socialist class discourse, correspond to the emergence of new self-conscious subjects as represented by all kinds of cultural and political protests. At both local and global levels, these subjects are transforming our conceptions of politics, democracy, and social change.[3]

This chapter explores the possibility of constructing a social movement in Canada today, as well as the relationship of ecology to such a project, taking into account the arguments of the 'second approach' outlined above. Ecology encompasses a complex conception of human/nature relationships as 'interdependent', as integral to life (human, other species, and planetary) and individual and social well-being (or as fundamental to the explanation of the crises of these). Through its principles of harmony or equilibrium, respect for others/differences, mutual recognition, prudence, and the promotion of understanding and co-existence rather than domination, ecology constructs a human–nature relationship which contradicts the instrumental re\la\tionality of modern societies. Since nature is not 'out there', but integral to being human, its crisis is symbolic of our crisis as human beings. In André Gorz's words, for ecologists the 'defence of nature' stems from the defence of the life-world.[4] But can the subject of *ecology as a social movement* be constructed as a kind of naturalized humanity, facing an enemy defined as technocratic, bureaucratic, and capitalist rationality? Is this not a new version of humanism, making universal claims about human nature and happiness, only in a less anthropocentric guise? Nor can it be taken for granted (as much NSM theory implicitly does) that social movements must be organized as resistances to *national* states, implying a national level mobilization, a national–popular collective identity, and an imagery of 'the state' as the central locus of power. Neither can it be assumed that contemporary social movements will be characterized by the relatively stable collective identity and political forms, or by the longevity of cultural values and practices which were associated with the nineteenth- and twentieth-century socialist movement.

Although certain assumptions of NSM theory need to be revised in light of recent developments, I believe that we can identify the kinds of conflicts to which social actors sharing similar environments are responding, and the possibilities for making linkages among their struggles. Moreover, we can argue for the necessity of such projects on the radical democratic grounds proposed by such theorists as Chantal Mouffe (Laclau and Mouffe 1985; Mouffe 1988, 1990). That is, a struggle is 'radical'/ radicalized insofar as it does not seek the emancipation of one collective subject via the subordination of another, but instead recognizes the multiple subjectivities of individual actors and their common stakes in changing social relations of domination and exploitation.[5] In her essay 'Radical Democracy: Modern or Postmodern?', Mouffe argues for a post-modern political philosophy:

> in which judgement plays a fundamental role that must be conceptualized appropriately so as to avoid the false dilemmas between, on the one hand, the existence of some universal criterion and, on the other, the rule of arbitrariness. That a question remains unanswerable by science or that it does not attain the status of a truth that can be demonstrated does not mean that a reasonable opinion cannot be formed about it or that it cannot be an opportunity for a rational choice . . . . To assert that one cannot provide an ultimate rational foundation for any given system of values does not imply that one considers all views to be equal . . . . It is always possible to distinguish between the just and the unjust, the legitimate and the illegitimate,

but this can only be done from within a given tradition, with the help
of the standards that this tradition provides.

(Mouffe 1993: 14–15)

Mouffe is concerned to rearticulate existing elements of the liberal democratic tradition, 'no longer viewing rights in an individualist framework but
rather conceiving of "democratic rights"' which 'while belonging to the individual, can only be exercised collectively and which presuppose the existence
of equal rights for others' (1993: 18–19). The linking of diverse democratic
struggles 'requires the creation of new subject positions that would allow the
common articulation, for example, of antiracism, antisexism and anticapi-
talism' (ibid.: 18). To this list, we may add 'antiproductivism', or opposition to
the instrumental exploitation of nature, or other conceptions of ecology.
Ecological struggles and identity, when articulated to these other (race,
gender, class) subject positions, are inevitably transformed. As Mouffe argues:

it is not a matter of establishing a mere alliance between given interests but of actually modifying the very identity of these forces. In
order that the defence of workers' interests is not pursued at the cost
of the rights of women, immigrants, or consumers, it is necessary to
establish an equivalence between these different struggles. It is only
under these circumstances that struggles against power become truly
democratic.

(Mouffe 1993: 19)

In the discussion of radical democratic, counter-hegemonic 'philosophy',
strategy, or discourse, ecology as an 'identity' or 'subject position' is strikingly
absent. In these respects, ecology presents particular difficulties. Those
Greens who do hold to the idea of a counter-hegemonic social movement have
had difficulty defining a *collective subject*; nature is not a social actor. Who,
then, does 'ecology' defend? Against what? And how are these actors' needs
and struggles connected to a particular (ecological) construction of nature?
The ways in which the interests of diverse collective subjects are related to an
ecological model of human–nature relationship need to be elaborated.
Ecology must become as much a discourse about specific societal relations as
it is about relations between humans and nature.

Developing a normative stance: 'the hidden side of my philosophy'

Imbedded in the radical democratic project to connect and to advance particular struggles are assumptions about these struggles' legitimacy and
desirability. (We have some criteria for labelling certain struggles 'progressive'
or 'alternative', and others 'regressive' or 'status quo'.) The democratization

of political and economic decision making is implicitly viewed as the necessary *precondition* for the realization of such needs. What kinds of needs (both individual and societal), as well as democratic demands (problematizing the limitations of liberal conceptions of equality and citizenship rights), can a counter-hegemonic movement express today? How would this construction of needs not be merely defensive or nostalgic (reassertions of threatened identities or privileges) while at the same time building on contemporary experiences of fragmentation and alienation, and upon our philosophical traditions (of equality, citizenship, community, individual rights, etc.)? These questions become more urgent daily, as global capitalist strategies and the policies of neo-liberal elites create ever more complex layers of inequality and differentiation, and as right-wing populist parties mobilize support for patriarchal and xenophobic agendas.

A counter-hegemonic ecological discourse must be articulated to real experiences of deprivation and alienation, but without homogenizing such experiences. We must look for the ways in which different subject positions may have stakes in a common philosophical and political discourse. This requires that we identify certain experiences *as* deprivation or alienation, and that from this interpretive stance we make an argument about the necessary conditions for (and the possibility of) human happiness. This will be mainly an argument about *the conditions for a plurality of choices and alternatives*, rather than about the ideal type 'emancipated individual'. However, such a project entails claiming knowledge about what these conditions are, and claiming to be able to explain unhappiness by their absence.[6] All critical intellectual praxis rests upon conceptions of human needs, or of human nature, which are discursively constructed. We cannot, therefore, do without such conceptions, and it seems to me that the interpretive project is legitimate so long as we remain self-reflexive, critical, and open regarding our assumptions and our objectives. We need not claim that our interpretations represent universal experiences or goals in the sense that we can define happiness for every individual. However, we can speak from our local knowledges of needs which may be realized only through the democratization of social decision making and a more inclusive agenda of alternatives.[7]

The question, then, is how may we construct the collective identity of a social movement? We might start with a discussion about our human relational needs, the experiences and needs of our bodies, and our associations with nature.[8] What we have to attend to, in searching for connections among our struggles, are the very experiences that – as social critics/interpreters – we have been conditioned to ignore or to exclude from our analyses. This involves stepping back from formalistic and scholastic categories to a space of self-reflection and dialogue with others. Struggling with the problem of where and how to take a political stance, bell hooks says:

Before I could consider answers, I had to face ways these issues were intimately connected to intense personal emotional upheaval regarding place, identity, desire . . . . My response was simply that when you hear the broken voice you also hear the pain contained within that brokenness – a speech of suffering; often it's that sound nobody wants to hear.

(hooks 1990: 146)

What we need to acknowledge are the ways in which, in Julia Kristeva's words, 'pain is the hidden side of my philosophy, its mute sister' (1989: 4). Retrieving her voice may be the precondition of our liberation.

Listening to the voices of a whole range of subjects tells us that their experiences of pain and alienation are intimately linked to the issues of time, work, and security of subsistence. The dominant model of work – particularly in North American societies – offers the great majority of the population one of two conditions: material deprivation (unemployment or casual employment) or spiritual deprivation (meaningless and stressful full-time employment in an extremely competitive labour market). As both health statistics and the popular preoccupation with the body as the war zone of social ills are making manifestly clear, both of these conditions make us sick. While employment entails alienation, unemployment entails marginalisation, particularly in a culture which blames and criminalizes the victim. Under these circumstances, unemployment can hardly be called 'freedom from work', or leisure, and indeed, neo-liberal regimes like the macho, Thatcherite Conservatives of Alberta are doing everything possible to make unemployment one hell deeper than the minimum wage.

Why should ecologists make theirs the problems of time and work (or freedom and security)? How are proposals for security of subsistence based on shorter work hours and the redistribution of income linked to the goals of ecology?[9] The argument has been made most persuasively by Alain Lipietz, in his ongoing work on alternatives for a new historical compromise based on the principles of autonomy, solidarity, and ecology. In essence, an economy based on the growth of free time, rather than on the ever-growing production and consumption of commodities, would curb the insatiable exploitation and destruction of nature, while allowing individuals more opportunities to transform their relationships to one another, to a previously objectified and alienated nature (including other species), and to their urban environments. Countering the logic of neo-Taylorism and global competition also provides a strategy for solidarity with the exploited populations of the Third World and for limiting resource pillage and environmental destruction. What Lipietz and others are proposing is a gradual transformation of the logic and values underpinning the organization of work, the mode of consumption, the welfare state, and global inequalities.

The issues of work and time are integral to *diverse experiences* of alienation

297

and deprivation: to struggles for gender equality – for the emancipation of both women and men from an oppressive sexual division of labour; to struggles against racism; and to the modern splits between body and mind, and between humankind and nature. For example, unemployment/economic crisis/fiscal deficit and other such elements are being articulated to the presence of visible minorities by means of a racist construction of the latter as competitors with the supposed (more entitled) majority for jobs, as welfare scroungers or as criminals. A counter-hegemonic discourse about unemployment would associate unemployment with the logic of capitalist accumulation and global competition, and with productivism, and would argue for alternatives including liberation from work, and security of basic needs for all. It would not only speak to, but alter, the ways in which groups are differentiated socially and spatially, situated in hierarchized relations. Thus work and time are crucial discursive objects of struggles to define an alternative logic of societal development. These struggles begin from statements about human needs which resonate with many different individuals. A partial list of such needs/rights includes:

- the freedom to choose where to live
- basic security of subsistence
- meaningful work and creativity
- time for relationships, time for both sexes to care for children and parents (versus the current segregation of generations from one another, and the super-burdening of women as care-givers)
- time to enjoy a diversity of activities
- time for experiences which restore our relationships with communities and with nature.

André Gorz observes that, in Europe, a growing belief in the necessity to reduce work – to liberate time for a multitude of other activities – 'cuts across all classes and levels of society including the working class and the governing segment of the ruling class' (1993: 66). Further: 'For a very large majority, work – whatever its level of complexity – involves skills that are too specialized, and cultural resources that are too impoverished, to supply meaning to their lives' (ibid.: 67).[10] In Canada, such realizations are dawning even in sectors of business and government; proposals for the statutory reduction of work time have issued from the Canadian Ministry for Human Resources Development (HRDC) since 1994. The Canadian Autoworkers Union has proposed the reduction of work time as a strategy for reducing unemployment and social inequalities (CAW 1993).

The crisis of time, happiness, and nature is expressed by individuals describing their daily experiences, as well as by collective actors (e.g., women's and environmental organizations, unions, senior citizens' coalitions), and is attributed by them to the neo-Taylorist, productivist, and neo-conservative agendas of corporations and governments. While the degree to which such agendas have been implemented varies from one province to another in Canada (its most extreme forms presently being in Alberta (Adkin 1995) and Ontario), there are general similarities in the predominant patterns of work, social inequalities, urban and environmental problems, and so on, which make possible the linking of particular experiences to a collective strategy of resistance and change.

Experiences of deprivation and alienation, which, when named, reveal repressed needs and desires, are central to the discourse of radical and plural democracy. For in the end, what prevents these needs and desires from being realized, are hierarchies of power and relationships of domination (based on class, race, gender, and privileged knowledges).[11] It is the monopolization – as well as the criteria – of decision-making by political, bureaucratic, economic, and technocratic elites which prevent alternative social choices from being seriously considered. This is not to disregard the importance of 'consent', 'compensation', or defence of privilege in sustaining the hegemony of industrial and consumer capitalism, patriarchal sexism, racism, and the domination of nature. But the consequences of neo-liberal economic restructuring, entailing the attempt to shrink drastically the realm of the political (to re-privatize decisions about the model of development), have deepened the democratic contradictions of liberal-productivism rather than creating the foundations for a new and stable historical compromise.

Voices for change: questions for ecology

'If this were a democracy, we would be working six-hour days.'

Lloyd Axworthy, the then minister of Human Resources Development Canada (HRDC), reported to the Canadian Federation of Labour annual convention in May 1994 that: 'The fastest-growing area of the economy last year was in the amount of overtime'. He estimated that '50 to 60 per cent of Canadians are working more than the standard 40 hour week' (Axworthy 1994). A document produced by the HRDC in October 1994 put this in the context of pressure on families, stating that in 64 per cent of families with children under 13 years of age, both parents work more than 40 hours a week (HRDC 1994d: 2). Figures on blue collar industrial workers indicate that one in five are working 8 hours or more a week in overtime (Jackson 1994). Some hourly paid workers in manufacturing are working up to 70 hours a week without overtime pay (even where this violates provincial labour laws) (Berto 1993). Salaried employees typically work 50- or 60-hour (or more) weeks (O'Hara 1993).

The dominant model of work is also implicitly gendered, built as it is on the assumption of 'one human being at work for, say 40 hours a week (plus commuting and possibly overtime) with a partner available full-time for domestic tasks' (Sassoon 1987: 160). With the growing participation of women in wage-labour, the tension between the assumption of a traditional sexual division of labour and the reality of people's lives is widening the fractures in what Anne Showstack Sassoon calls the male model of work:

> [A] whole series of contradictions between paid work, welfare state services and social needs are becoming clear because of the constraints which derive from the inflexible organization of formal jobs . . . .[T]he domestic sphere, the world of work, the welfare state are all organized as if women were continuing a traditional role . . . . These changes in women's lives have produced conflicts in different spheres of social life which derive from the choices women make in which the need and desire to *combine* having children and to remain in the labour force structures their lives.
>
> (Sassoon 1987: 160)

Figures provided by the Conference Board of Canada (1994) and the Vanier Institute of the Family (1994) illustrate some of these changes and conflicts.[12] From 1967 to 1986, the percentage of families with two-income earners grew from 34 to 62. (This trend corresponds to declining real family incomes in Canada since the 1970s.)[13] In 1990, three-quarters of families earning between $25,000 and $45,000 depended on two incomes. Almost 60 per cent of Canadian women were in the labour force, compared to 39 per cent in 1967. Over half of women with children under 6 years of age were in the labour force. Yet other norms have been slower to change: employed women spend approximately twice as much time doing unpaid household work as their male counterparts (Barr 1993: 24), and in 1993 the average working woman (working full-time) earned 70 cents for every dollar earned by a man. The Vanier Institute concludes:

> The overall Canadian average income and the two-earner average income are not so far apart, which indicates that by working at a paid job, most married women are replacing the losses to inflation and taxes, and making possible any slight increase in the average family's income. They are not providing affluence or luxury. Women tend to earn less than men doing comparable work. They are also more likely to be found in part-time jobs, or so-called 'female ghetto' jobs. Considering the likelihood that many women are working part time at jobs with little or no career potential, it is clear that their primary motivation is bound up with the economics of the family. More simply, one income is not enough to sustain a family.
>
> (Vanier Institute 1994: 12)

As is the case in England, described by Sassoon, a model of work which is utterly out of synch with the realities of women's participation in the labour force, continues to be underpinned by state social policy. The Conference Board of Canada reports:

> Finding affordable, reliable and high quality child care presents a difficult challenge for contemporary parents, especially if they are low- or middle-income earners. Indeed, the average cost of unsubsidized centre based child care in Canada ranges from approximately $330 to $450 per month. Moreover, unexpected events (such as the illness of a child or the cancellation of a babysitter) often force working parents to look for last-minute assistance. As well, Canada's available daycare spaces can hold only 14 per cent of children potentially in need of care, which means that employees are often forced to use ad hoc and short-term techniques to provide for their children's well-being.
>
> (Conference Board 1994: 5)

Not surprisingly, a 1989 Conference Board study found that: (1) More than one-quarter of employees who provide care to children find it 'difficult' or 'very difficult' to balance work and home responsibilities; (2) More than one-third of parents report that they experience 'a lot' of or 'moderate' stress or anxiety because of their child care duties; (3) 41 per cent of working mothers in the federal public service have considered quitting their jobs because they feel they do not have enough time with their children (Conference Board 1994: 5). All fully employed professional women face this trade-off between work and family, leading some to postpone (or decide against) having children, and others to leave jobs which demand 60 hours of work per week and more (Lax 1994).[14]

Women with children are in general more likely to seek part-time work because of their domestic roles. In 1989, 31 per cent of women in the paid labour force held a 'non-standard' job (part-time, part-year and temporary) compared to 16 per cent of men (HRDC 1994d: 2). A study by the Canadian Labour Congress found that, in 1992, one half of the women in the paid work force held part-time jobs (Gooderham 1993).[15] By 1994, in the wake of massive cutbacks in the public sector, 69 per cent of all part-time workers in Canada were women, and 34 per cent of those women indicated that they would prefer full-time work (Status of Women Canada 1997). Part-time ('flexible') work in services continues to be poorly paid, which is part of the explanation for the statistic that women occupy 72 per cent of the ten lowest-paid occupations in Canada. Forty per cent of women between the ages of 25 and 44 (the group most likely to have pre-school age children in the household) who were working part-time in 1993 wanted to work full-time (HRDC 1994c: 2).

Those women who continue to try to 'do it all' cope with enormous stress. The HRDC reports that women between the ages of 15 and 44 report severe stress at two times the rate of men, linked to the fact that working women are still assuming two-thirds of household responsibilities (HDRC 1994d: 2). In a 1992 survey by Quebec's *Le Magazine Affaires Plus* of 4,000 readers, 45.4 per cent of respondents said they felt stressed by the demands of their professional, family, and marital lives. Sixty-three per cent said they would compromise career advancement to devote more time to their personal, marital, or family lives. Fifty-two per cent said they would consider a less demanding job in order to preserve their family and personal lives (Duhamel 1993).[16] According to HRDC, 'stress-related disorders due to overwork cost Canadian business an estimated $12 billion a year' (HRDC 1994d: 1). Thus for those living in two-income earner families, the conditions in which the choice to have children is made result in anxiety, guilt, and exhaustion, summed up in the cry: *not enough time – too many demands!* The dominant model of work intensifies family conflict, punishes the body, and obstructs the efforts of women and men to eliminate sexism.

Married couples with children constitute only 48 per cent of families in Canada, however. Eleven per cent of families are led by a female lone parent. The Vanier Institute observes:

> Nowhere is the problem of the working parent more acute than in lone-parent families, which are the most likely to be poor. Unlike the more affluent, they have difficulty affording child care, or purchasing labour – and time – saving homes and appliances. More than 1.2 million of Canada's children live in families with incomes below poverty lines. Children living with a lone-parent mother are five times more likely to live in poverty than those living with two parents.
> (Vanier Institute 1994: 13)[17]

Female single parents with children between the ages of 3 and 5 have an unemployment rate of over 20 per cent. Given the typically low wages of 'women's' jobs, having to pay for child care would likely leave the family more impoverished than if the mother were to remain on welfare.[18]

The particular conflicts posed to women by the dominant model of work and sexual division of labour are moreover not restricted to the demands of child care and labour force participation. Women are also the primary care givers for elderly, disabled, or infirm relatives.[19] A 1993 report predicts that by the year 2000, 77 per cent of employees will have some type of responsibility for elderly relatives ('Eldercare' 1993). The World Bank recently estimated that by the year 2030, 30.2 per cent of Canada's population will be over 60 years old (IBRD *Averting the Old Age Crisis*, October 1994. Figures cited in 'Worldwide aging crisis feared', *The Globe and Mail* 4 October 1994, A1).

The model of work also structures our physical environment. The Fordist model of large urban agglomerations of full-time workers (the suburbs-encompassing megalopolis) structured the development of housing, transportation, land-use, services, and so on. It typically located concentrations of workers and their families far from 'natural experiences', both spatially and culturally.[20] The predominant directions of post-Fordist restructuring – including among other things the penetration of commodity relationships into more and more spaces of the life-world, the elimination of pauses by new technologies of communication and transportation, and the 'disaggregation' of urban environments[21] – have not served to dissolve the boundaries between the mind and the body, women and men, generations, town and country, and between humans and nature. More than ever, commodity relationships seem to determine the limits, the timing, and the contents of our natural experiences.

Albert Borgmann makes an interesting distinction between 'real' and 'hyperreal' experiences in the post-modern era, using as an example the possible conditions of a ski trip.[22] In the 'real experience', one goes to the mountains, discovering their grandeur and expanse, and experiencing one's continuity with the natural world (for Borgmann this approximates a *spiritual* experience). He contrasts this with the experience of going to a constructed ski hill within an enormous dome in a Japanese city. The climate and snow conditions will be perfectly controlled and predictable. One will book one's ski time assured that one will have perfect snow. Yet the dome is not continuous with its world; it lacks the 'commanding presence' of the mountains. Insofar as it is 'artificial', therefore, the experience is 'hyperreal', devoid of the spiritual and natural dimensions of the real. In the first case, time is 'irregular', unmanageable; it cannot be 'programmed'. One must wait for the next snowfall, or one must take one's chances that the snow conditions might be less than perfect. In the second case, time is part of the package – the experience of consumption. If one has enough money, one never has to wait. It is not a relationship with nature that determines when one skis, but a commodity relationship. At the same time, access to 'real' or 'spiritual' experiences of nature is contingent upon having the means (time and money) to travel to the mountains. It is thus an option more attainable for some social groups than for others. Moreover, the encroachment of recreational 'development' means that such wilderness sites are shrinking in number and size, and are subjected to ever-greater pressure from the human species.

Liberal productivism is related in another important way to the hidden side of my philosophy. That is, the necessity to go to where the jobs are (or to suffer unemployment) entails for many individuals a very painful loss of their historical identities, and of their belonging in families and communities – as a kind of exile. The mobility and 'multiple rootedness' which is sometimes regarded by post-modern theorists as emancipatory (entailing richness of experience and adventure), is in fact the specific experience of those privileged enough to have real choices – including the luxury of return. The majority of the migrants, however, speak in terms of *not having any choice* – of rupture, loss and exile.

Again, it is important to identify the different ways in which deprivation and alienation are experienced from different subject positions. For most professionals, and 'middle strata' workers who are full-time employed, the keenest sense of deprivation is around *time* (the scarcity of free time), and this is compounded by the 'demands' of co-habitation, parenthood, and the gender roles reproduced by the society. For these groups, the crisis is that life is consumed by the black hole of work – referring to activity that is experienced as meaningless, alienating, unrecognized, or unrewarded, or – simply – exhausting and excessive.

The direction of economic and social restructuring is intensifying this crisis for many individuals. One has only to think about the pressure on nurses in hospitals where the permanent staffs have been greatly reduced, to be partially replaced by casual nurses who are not unionized, and work without contracts. Their daily responsibilities and stress increase as the necessary conditions for them to do their jobs crumble away.[23] Although cut-backs in health spending are creating an immediate crisis of accessible and adequate health care, the effects are also being felt in the social services and in education. Social service workers who administer welfare benefits and other government services are constantly faced with the inadequacy of their budgets to meet the needs of the clients.

In all of these occupations, there is no reasonable balance between work, pleasure, leisure, self-directed activity, time for relationships, or the needs of the body. Neo-liberal policies are worsening all of these conditions, and deepening the alienation and frustration of working life. On the other hand, an equally powerful fear of losing the security of that monthly direct deposit – of entering the grey zone of jobs without benefits, pensions, or increments, or no jobs – keeps most people locked into the cycle.

For the unemployed and the partially or occasionally employed (categories which disproportionately include youths,[24] single mothers, women, racial minorities in certain parts of the country, indigenous peoples,[25] persons with disabilities[26]) the 'crisis' is the constant threat of material deprivation, further marginalization, and criminalization by public authorities. And the working poor – the category that some governments are trying so hard to expand by slashing social security and eliminating the minimum wage – really have the worst of all worlds: no time, no money. 'Flexibility' for many categories of workers simply means 'employer flexibility' to lay-off, fire, sub-contract jobs. Such 'flexibility' was always greater regarding the employment of women, and the neo-liberal restructuring of the conditions of work has been called by some the 'global feminization of labour'.

Any movement for social change must name these experiences and demonstrate the stakes that their subjects have in a common programme of reforms. The (exploitative, racist, sexist) norms of work in our society, and the treatment of humans as expendable and mobile factors of production entail profound alienation and loss. What is lost is the possibility to develop depth and continuity in relationships – relationships which constitute our identities and our belonging. What is lost is the possibility of experiencing ourselves in a variety of environments from the position of traveller or explorer, rather than that of vagrant or exile. In very few occupations today is work experienced as sufficiently meaningful and rewarding to compensate for its alienating and stressful aspects, including the routinization and compartmentalization of life activities. Nor do state systems of social welfare compensate for the forms of depersonalisation and exclusion experienced by the unemployed and the working poor. Moreover, a system of production and consumption whose logic is the ever-expanding circulation of commodities cannot compensate for its alienation of nature and its destruction of the natural environment.

For all of the subjects whose needs and identities are negated by these experiences, interests may be constructed in the egalitarian redistribution of productivity gains (in the forms of more jobs, more free time, guaranteed basic income, salary gains for the poorest paid groups), involving legislated and negotiated changes in work norms, and far-reaching reforms of the welfare state. The construction of such linkages will require both a radical, pluralist democratic discourse, and a discourse about the conditions for happiness. The potential for such a project was neatly summed up in the declaration of an Edmonton taxi driver: 'If this were a democracy', he said, 'we would be working six-hour days. We would be talking about family time, about happiness'.

More free time, or more consumption? Ecology and 'the destructive identity between freedom and happiness'

A Latin American friend once said of North American society that it functioned 'like an ant hill'. Despite North America's reputation abroad for 'free spirits', 'rugged individuals' and 'liberated women', when it comes to the dominant rhythms and patterns of life here, my friend's analogy was quite apt. 'Americanism' and 'Fordism' – as the title of Gramsci's famous essay suggests – were in important ways virtually synonymous. This is the home of Taylorism and neo-Taylorism.[27] North American cities are designed as continuous circuits connecting the factory to the mall to the household (via the automobile, of course). Whether it is in McDonald's or on the freeway, time is of the essence, and patience is short. One is meant to keep moving on this circuit. As foreigners often observe, in North America, 'people live to work', and the compensation is consumption.[28]

Among such 'foreigners', of course, was Herbert Marcuse; the paradox of a society which sees itself as very 'liberal' but which is at the same time very conformist and regimented, was explained by Marcuse in terms of a psycho-social theory of surplus repression (the answer to Henry Ford).[29] Indeed, the bourgeois ideology – so deeply internalized by the North American working class – that increasing consumption of *things* supplies greater happiness, is a neglected aspect of the common opposition of workers to environmental conservationist discourse. While the production sphere of capitalist accumulation is a well-documented structural cause of conflict (jobs/economic growth versus the environment/conservation), the importance of the equivalence 'consumption equals happiness' for the continual growth of capitalism tends to be treated in an overly simplistic and reductionist manner. 'Over-consumption' is not – as some environmentalists argue – the product of 'human greed' but a *compensation* for the deprivations imposed on individuals by the dominant model of development. Purchasing things becomes a substitute for having time or for having meaningful relationships, e.g., fast food as a substitute for preparing a meal to be shared with others; a gift to make up for absence; an expensive car 'to be somebody'; new clothes to 'feel better'. Mass culture is packaged to fit rigidly compartmentalized leisure time, and functions to pacify consumers.[30]

It is important to remember that our consumption norms and our uses of 'free' time have been delimited and conditioned by the terms of the labour we perform; they are not, therefore, completely 'free' choices, since alternative choices are not possible.[31] Moreover, individuals' preferences adapt over time to their environments; changes in preferences may lag behind changes in available options, but lifestyle choices are not written in stone (or as some environmentalists and neo-classical economists would have it – in human nature). Compensation is essential to the disciplining and moulding of individuals *as* workers in this society. It is therefore all the more important that environmentalists not be heard as ascetics, seeking to *intensify* deprivation by withholding (through authoritarian means if necessary) compensations. Instead, ecologists must speak directly to experiences of deprivation, and be heard as defenders of both security of subsistence and happiness of being.[32] Ecology, in other words, must become a language of desire.

Neither is 'over-work' simply a product of 'human greed'. The long hours of North American workers are a rational response to employers' predominantly neo-Taylorist strategies for the maximization of profits. High unemployment and declining real incomes[33] – despite productivity increases made possible by new information technologies – have increased the pressure on workers to accept overtime and even unpaid hours of work, and to hold more than one job at a time. Juliet Schor, author of a major study of work in the United States, shows that the average work week lengthened between 1969 and 1987. In 1987, the average employed person was working 163 hours longer in a year (or about one month) than two decades earlier:

> Moonlighting is now more prevalent than at any time during the three decades for which we have statistics . . . . The main impetus behind this extra work is financial. Close to one-half of those polled say they hold two jobs in order to meet regular household expenses or

pay off debts. As one might expect, this factor has become more compelling during the 1980s, with the disappearance of stable positions that pay a living wage and the increase of casual and temporary service sector employment.

A second factor, operating largely on weekly hours, is that Americans are working more overtime. After the recession of the early 1980s, many companies avoided costly rehiring of workers and, instead, scheduled extra overtime. Among manufacturing employees, paid overtime hours rose substantially after the recession and, by the end of 1987, accounted for the equivalent of an additional five weeks of work per year.

(Schor 1991: 29, 31)

United States data (like the Canadian figures cited above) indicate that despite the difficulties of making ends meet, many workers would choose to exchange additional future income for more free time.[34]

Certainly habits of work and leisure are ingrained as well in the particular 'work ethics' of different cultures and labour movements, as well as in gender, class and racial ideologies which construct sexual divisions of labour. The choice of freedom over the forms of compensation offered by post-Fordist societies will not be an automatic or universal one. What is involved is *a cultural struggle to transform values while at the same time making alternative choices structurally possible*. The very complex task of activists seeking to build a social movement is to link discursively the kinds of needs which many subjects are expressing to democratic principles (both egalitarian and pluralist), to arguments about the conditions for happiness, and to concrete proposals for change.[35] To borrow a phrase from Marcuse, the potential of ecology as a social movement lies in establishing (what is for liberal-productivism and patriarchy) 'the destructive identity between freedom and happiness' (1966: 51).

Frontiers of Canadian political ecology

Ecologists, too, as a predominantly white, middle-class movement, accept various compensations and enjoy the privileges of their positions *vis-à-vis* indigenous peoples, persons of colour, and Third World peoples. Weaving the kind of discourse about needs and alternatives sketched above will also require Canadian ecologists to challenge the dominant constructions of civilization/nature which make meaning of the experiences of indigenous peoples, subordinated racial groups, and Third World peoples, and in so doing, challenge the forms of their own complicity in relationships of domination.[36] In this section I wish to open a conversation about one dimension of this discursive project: the possible articulations of ecology and indigenous people's struggles for self-determination.

307

Critical discourses deconstruct what is perhaps the most profound symbolic code of modernism: the relationship between humankind and nature (which, in modern terms, is expressed as the phallocentric and eurocentric subject – object relation of *western/white/man to nature/woman/colonized peoples*). The concepts of human, culture, civilization, science, and progress are all defined in *opposition* to (inferior) 'nature'. Challenging these ways of thinking confronts deep resistance from those groups which have stakes in the privileges of dominant knowledges. Thus, on one hand, ecologists', feminists', and indigenous peoples' critiques of modernization are commonly dismissed as purely anti-modern (or 'utopian'), and indigenous peoples serve symbolic functions in modernizing discourses about the human–nature relationship – about 'progress' and 'civilization'. On the other hand, elements of indigenous peoples' struggles (e.g., for the preservation/regeneration of traditional values and ways of life, or for self-determination) may be articulated to modernizing discourses, thereby dissolving the radical, counter-cultural critiques imbedded in these struggles. Moreover, ecologists may be complicit in the continuing domination of indigenous peoples by virtue of their absence, or silence, in confrontations between modernizers and indigenous groups. These are enormous and important problems to which I cannot do justice here. In the following paragraphs I offer interpretations of two cases as representative of the possibilities for counter-hegemonic or assimilating constructions of indigenous peoples' struggles.

Indigenous peoples are symbolically positioned by the discourse of modernization between civilized/urban/developed/modern/society, and nature/wilderness. That is, they are located on the frontier of the dominant paradigm. Now this frontier could have a number of associations,[37] but the one that predominates is almost entirely negative: beyond the frontier is immiseration, deprivation, marginalisation – in a word, the status of an outcast. Why? Because indigenous peoples have refused *progress*; they have refused assimilation into the modern world. They function, in other words, as the proof that there is *no alternative* to the choices offered by modernity (i.e., the choice between material or spiritual deprivation). The 'spiritual values' of indigenous peoples are viewed by the majority of the white population as a religion with few adherents, while the 'spiritual reality' is equated with such phenomena as teenage drug abuse and suicide, alcoholism, and the abuse of women and children. Utopian beliefs in reciprocal, respectful relations with nature, the dominant group concludes, yield only material and spiritual disaster. Hence the only 'realistic' path is to manage the unavoidable processes of objectification, exploitation, and commodification of nature in as 'sustainable' a way as possible.

The above modern interpretations of native 'difference', as well as the potential antagonism between indigenous conceptions of traditional values and modernization, are illustrated in particularly dramatic form by the 'stand-off' (between natives and the Canadian army) at Kanehsatake (also known as

Oka, Quebec) in 1990.[38] The opposition of members of the Kanienkehaka (Mohawk) Nation and the Haudensosaunee Six Nations Iroquois Confederacy to the extension of a golf course onto land claimed as native ancestral ground, was constructed by the native actors as a defence of traditional spiritual values and of their land against the ceaseless encroachment of money-making 'development'. Donna Kahenrakwas Goodleaf writes:

> In March 1990, the Kanienkehaka people of Kanehsatake . . . discovered that the mayor of Oka, Jean Ouellette, along with his councillors had hired a developer to construct an additional nine-hole golf course and some condominiums to increase the community's tax revenues. The construction would result in the deliberate destruction and desecration of the ancient sacred burial grounds of Kanehsatake and the destruction of the pine trees. . . .
>
> Current struggles by Indigenous peoples are not only against the state and multinationals, but, as Winona LaDuke (1982) states, against a state of mind based on conquest, that believes the land and all peoples are expendable in the name of 'progress' and 'Western civilization'.
>
> (Goodleaf 1993: 225–40)

The tactics used by the natives, including barricades at Kahnawake and Kanehsatake and the blockade of the Mercier Bridge connecting many commuters to Montreal, provoked widespread frustration and even violence on the part of the inconvenienced white population (the infamous stoning of the cars that were evacuating women, children, and elderly persons from the reserve). The armed defence of native territory against work crews, the Quebec security police, and – eventually – the Canadian Armed Forces was criminalized by the Quebec and federal governments' discourse. Media coverage of the struggle increasingly ignored the role of Mohawk women as negotiators and spokespersons, while focusing on the 'Rambo' images of some of the male warriors.

There were civil disobedience actions in solidarity with the Kanienkehaka on the part of indigenous groups across the country (Goodleaf 1993). The most significant demonstrations of non-indigenous support for the Kanienkchaka took the forms of the Oka Peace Camp (organized by indigenous and non-indigenous people), and participation in support groups in eastern Ontario which were collecting food and medical supplies for transportation to the beseiged communities of Kahnawake and Kanehsatake. In the wake of the 'Oka Crisis' the discourse of indigenous peoples' political organizations has become more militant, drawing upon the resistance of the Mohawks for symbols of heroism, for lessons regarding the tactic of civil disobedience and use of the media, and to strengthen a collective identity based not only on shared experiences of marginalization but on determined resistance.

Many elements of indigenous peoples' struggles for the conditions in which to create different relationships between humans and nature are also found within the counter-cultural discourse of ecofeminism. For example, Goodleaf calls upon 'all peoples' to 'broaden their narrow concept of liberation and go beyond the human to a vision rooted in a spiritually- and politically-based worldview of Indigenous peoples that encompasses the four-legged, the waters, the air, the earth – all things which support the sacred web of life' (ibid.: 241). Kahn-Tineta Horn, also from Kahnawake, explains that in 'our [Kanienkehaka] mythology, the women were created first, and came from the earth. We bring forth life, and we also are the anchor of the society, so the men get their energy from their association with women' (Horn 1991: 38). Yet it is anti-colonial discourse (not eco-feminist) which provides the dominant interpretation of indigenous women's and men's struggles against white European supremacy.

The 'Oka Crisis' did not forge new solidarities among indigenous women and men, white feminists, and ecologists. Many indigenous women question the utility of seeking alliances with white, middle-class feminists who 'appear to share a presumption in common with the patriarchs they oppose, that they have some sort of inalienable right to simply go on occupying our land and exploiting our resources for as long as they like' (Jaimes and Halsey 1992: 332, cited by Goodleaf 1993: 240). Canadian environmental organizations seemed equally absent from the battlefield at Oka, and relations between non-native environmentalists and native groups remain tentative. The possibilities for a convergence of values and objectives among indigenous peoples, feminists, and ecologists have yet to be fully developed in Canada. Yet in the context of a relationship between colonized and colonizers, white middle-class ecologists are not simply positioned in some neutral zone, and bear a greater responsibility to develop solidaristic linkages with indigenous women and men.

A second possible articulation of indigenous peoples' 'traditional values' and demands for self-determination which should be of concern to ecologists is illustrated by the responses of some members of the Meadowlake Tribal Council [MTC] to the proposal by Atomic Energy Company of Canada Ltd. to locate a nuclear waste burial site on land belonging to 8,500 Cree and Dene people in northwestern Saskatchewan.[39] The outcome of AECL's search for a deep ('Precambrian shield') burial site crucially concerns anti-nuclear activists everywhere, since the *de facto* moratorium on the building of new reactors in North America is in part due to the – until now – unresolved problem of the disposal of radioactive spent fuel and debris from decommissioned reactors. A site in Saskatchewan (or elsewhere on the shield) could open the way for a new phase of nuclear industry growth, with radioactive waste from distant places being shipped to Canada for disposal.[40]

The Executive Director of the MTC, Ray Ahenekew, has argued in favour of allowing the AECL to survey Council land by constructing the nuclear waste burial site as an opportunity for native self-government and economic development. The 'educational' video produced by the MTC (consisting largely of interviews with AECL scientists) states that the 'storage facility' will provide 600 full-time jobs for native people, plus another 500 jobs for people in businesses providing goods and services for the 'industry'. Opponents of the site are identified by Ahenekew as 'do-gooders' (read: 'environmentalists') and Europeans; he does not refer to 'internal' opposition from other elders, though this exists.[41] The opponents are constructed as new colonizers, trying to dictate developmental choices to indigenous peoples. In this way, the interests of native peoples in self-determination become linked to the choice of nuclear waste acceptance; the 'ally' of native autonomy becomes the AECL; and the 'enemy' becomes organizations like the Canadian Coalition for Nuclear Responsibility. The *raison d'être* for native self-government shifts from being an *alternative* kind of development, based on an organicist, intersubjective relationship with nature, to being *economic development tout court*, summed up in Ahenekew's statement: 'Making good profits – that's what economic development is all about for first nations peoples'.[42] *Et voilà*, modernization in the service of cultural difference and autonomy.

But how to get around the antagonism between 'traditional native values' as they have been defined and validated by the political discourse of native peoples, and the dominant values of modernization? This is a difficult trick to perform, but the modernizers of the MTC make some interesting attempts. First, conflictual associations are 'disappeared'. For example, in the video, the potential site of the nuclear waste burial is referred to not as 'ancestral ground' (as it likely would be if defence of ownership were at stake), but as 'Precambrian shield' (a scientific/geological term with no traces of cultural and spiritual identity). The word 'nuclear' – with its connotation 'radioactive' – is avoided, and replaced by 'spent fuel' – suggestive of something benign and used-up. Indeed, the latter association becomes clearer with Ahenekew's construction of 'spent fuel' as equivalent to something like 'old bones' having a place in an organicist cycle of life:

> Hunters always leave a piece of an animal that they kill. We take uranium out and we don't leave anything but a hole in the ground. So it falls within that category – it [nuclear waste burial] puts something back. What are you going to put back? Spent fuel maybe. The future will tell.

The future will tell, indeed, how indigenous peoples' discourses about autonomy, traditional values, and human–nature relations are articulated to either radical, counter-cultural or modernizing discourses.

Conclusions

In claiming that our visions are *not* (as the so-called 'realists' would say) 'mere idealism', but rather, yearnings for a utopia that is historically possible, ecologists are involved in a highly complex engagement with the institutions and the symbols of the dominant rationality. The engagement has been critical and deconstructive, seeking to problematize what was normal, to make visible what was invisible, to validate what was disregarded. Yet ecology faces the challenges both of confronting its own modern limitations and privileges, and of offering medium-term alternatives which 'realistically' speak to the widely shared experiences of communities of individuals (and not merely in abstract terms about better management of 'the economy' or 'the environment'). These tasks imply the need for a normative, interpretive stance which can articulate diverse subject positions to a common agenda for social change. In other words, a collective identity for ecology as a social movement cannot be constructed in the absence of a discourse about experiences which are spatially, temporally, and culturally located.

The task of critical intellectuals is neither to defend universal, totalizing theory, nor to adopt a fashionable, relativist 'politics of difference',[43] but rather to make those connections that will help us to 'collectively build effective theories of experience' (Haraway 1990: 215). As Rosalind O'Hanlon and David Washbrook argue in their critique of the apolitical implications of some deconstructionist theory, a strategy of collective action requires a 'theory about experience as the medium through which resistances emerge and are crystallized or about the conditions under which the subordinate can become active agents of their own emancipation on the basis of this experience' (O'Hanlon and Washbrook 1992: 152). Ecologists can link a particular 'theory of experience' to a political discourse of radical and plural democracy. However, to do so, ecology must learn to speak in the many tongues of its mute sister, which reveal human capacities for joy as well as the necessity of the liberation of nature.

Notes

1 This essay has benefited from the comments of David Bell, Radhika Desai, Malinda Smith, and Susan Smith, and is the product of countless conversations. Special thanks to Juan Ormeño for the analogy of the ant hill.

2 The criteria I employ here are adapted from the work of the French sociologists who in the 1970s and 1980s were grouped around Alain Touraine (1978, 1980), in the Centre d'Analyse et d'Intervention Sociologique, ENESS, Paris. The German sociologist, Klaus Eder (1993), elaborates this conception of a social movement in his work on counter-cultural and radical political movements.

3 For such an 'optimistic' view, see W. Magnusson and R. Walker, 'Decentering the state', *Studies in Political Economy* 26 (Summer 1988).

4 '[The ecological movement] was born originally out of a spontaneous protest against the destruction of the *culture of the everyday* by the apparatuses of economic and administrative power. By "culture of the everyday" I mean the

whole self-evident collection of intuitive knowledge of vernacular know-how (in the sense given to this term by Ivan Illich), the habits, norms and modes of conduct that enable individuals to interpret, to understand, to assume responsibility for the way they inhabit the world that surrounds them' (Gorz 1993: 57).

5 Let me emphasize that this is not a position of 'relativism' *vis-à-vis* all social interests and rights claims. The radical and plural democratic project proposed by Mouffe and others calls for the construction of social *antagonisms*, entailing the identification of 'the enemy'. Certain interests are simply incompatible, e.g., a system of production based on capitalist accumulation cannot be made compatible with workers' freedom from exploitation.

6 Kenneth Gergen (1991) and Albert Borgmann (1992) try to show how the post-modern world can be emancipatory for individuals, if we can come to terms with letting go of traditional conceptions of self, or if we can revalidate the natural and the spiritual in the new spaces opened up by the critique of rationalism. But whether enrichment is the outcome for individuals, or suicide, clearly depends on a great deal of social context. The extent to which the post-modern era will be one of new freedom or of new domination (based on the control of information and technology, hyper-commodification, etc.), is being determined by struggles on many fronts.

7 I recognize that the boundaries, in this formulation, between universal-humanist and particularist discourses about needs are less than clear. I do not as yet see a way to reconcile the conflicting positions of the 'anti-humanist' deconstructivists and those seeking to elaborate a post-Western, post-humanist conception of the human (e.g., Lazreg 1988; Mohanty 1989). The only strategy which seems to be available for those who continue to believe in the conscious agency of social subjects, and in the necessity of something called a 'social project' is a kind of 'working outward' from a plurality of discursive sites, in keeping with the imagery of a web of inter-relations.

8 Feminist theorists, engaged with post-modernism, have shown how the Cartesian separation of mind and body as well as the privileging of mind (consciousness) over body (sensual experience) has led, in western thought, to the 'construction of rationality upon the exclusion of the senses – whose organ of experience is the body'. Philippa Rothfield (1990), rejecting what she terms the 'anti-humanism' of some post-structuralist thought, argues that subjectivity may be reconceptualized by listening to the body.

9 Strategies to reverse the processes of social exclusion include proposals for the reduction of work time, redistribution of income among categories of workers, and some form of basic income and/or government subsidies to a sector of socially useful employment. Most of the Green parties of Europe have become advocates of such proposals, not only on solidaristic social grounds, but also because of the anticipated anti-productivist effects of such policies. Claus Offe summarizes some of the key arguments regarding the links between ecology and the basic income proposal, in the essay 'A non-productivist design for social policies', (1992). Specific proposals are not evaluated here, where the focus is to establish the common stakes of different social actors in the general values and objectives underlying such proposals. For discussions of proposals for the reduction of work time, basic income, and so on, I refer the reader to: Alain Lipietz (1992, 1993, 1996); David Purdy (1994); Philippe van Parijs (1992). In *Crisis and Choice in European Social Democracy*, Fritz W. Scharpf argues that the most feasible short-term strategy for the left in Europe today is a redistribution of income within the working class in the forms of work time and income (1991: 274). This requires that the left fight for 'solidaristic ideals'. Lipietz makes a similar argument: '[T]he new logic encourages the use of money from solidarity to make it multiply in socially

313

useful tasks: paying unemployed people, or rather giving financial help to self-managed agencies of unemployed people, to rehabilitate rundown social housing, enhance and enrich the environment, and help people in their own homes' (1992: 109).

10 There will, of course, be opposition to mandatory limits on overtime, the adoption of a four-day week, or other such proposals, particularly from the manufacturing sector employers using neo-Taylorist strategies to compete in the 'North American Free Trade' environment. According to the chief economist for the Canadian Manufacturers' Association, manufacturers cannot afford to hire more workers because: 'Prices for manufactured goods have remained relatively flat since 1989, wages have gone up, and costs of benefits and other employee-related costs are steadily increasing' (Jayson Myers, quoted in *The Globe and Mail* 11 December 1993). We are confronted here with the limitation of any purely national conception of strategy, a point also emphasized by Scharpf (1991) in relation to full employment options.

11 Charles Taylor arrives at similar conclusions: 'The politics of resistance is the politics of democratic will-formation. As against those adversaries of technological civilization who have felt drawn to an elitist stance, we must see that a serious attempt to engage in the cultural struggle of our time requires the promotion of a politics of democratic empowerment. The political attempt to reframe technology crucially involves resisting and reversing fragmentation' (Taylor 1991: 118).

12 Neither report correlates any of its data to racial or ethnic variables, (and only some of the survey results differentiate between male and female respondents). As a consequence, the racial and ethnic dimensions of poverty, family structure, employment, and so on, are rendered invisible.

13 In both Canada and the United States, real income has been declining since the 1970s (HRDC 1994b; Schor 1991: 80).

14 Job insecurity and downward pressure on family incomes have also been linked to an increasing number of abortions among women in their thirties. See 'Abortion rate increase linked to recession', *The Globe and Mail* 4 October 1994, pp. A1, A7. Another 'strategy' for more affluent professional women/mothers has been to employ 'nannies' who are often poorly paid recent immigrants.

15 The 'pushing out of full time work' phenomenon affecting women with families is evident in Alberta, where the province's economy has been undergoing radical neo-liberal restructuring under the Conservative Provincial Government. There was an increase in the unemployment rate among women aged 15 to 24, from 11.9 per cent in January 1993 to 13.3 per cent in January 1994. The rate for women overall increased in the same period from 9.1 to 9.8 per cent. The number of full-time jobs filled by women decreased by 4,000, while part-time positions grew by 12,000. See 'Tory women doing "mighty fine"', *Edmonton Journal*, 8 March 1994, A5.

16 A survey of medical doctors in Alberta, made by Decima Research in 1993, showed that 52 per cent have experienced clinical depression, and over half say they experience 'a fair amount of stress'. See 'Income doesn't equal professional happiness for Alberta's doctors, national survey shows', *The Edmonton Journal*, 29 October 1993, A8.

17 The Vanier Institute reports that 2.5 million people use food banks each year in Canada. Over 40 per cent of these are children (1994: 16). According to National Council of Welfare figures cited in HRDC (1994c: 1), 90 per cent of families composed of a female lone-parent and two children under seven years of age are classified as 'low-income'.

18 This fact – of considerable concern to the present architects of social security reform – is indicative of the unremunerated value of women's domestic labour. Statistics Canada reports that in 1992, the value of unpaid work (and two-thirds of

women's work is unpaid) to the Canadian economy was $318.8 billion, or 41.4 per cent of GDP (HRDC 1994c: 2).

19 The Conference Board reports that 'as a result of declining fertility and a large but temporary increase in birth rates after the Second World War, 20 per cent of Canadians will be over the age of 65 by the year 2021' (1994: 4). A survey of 7,000 employees done by the Conference Board in 1990 found that '16 per cent provided some form of support for elderly, disabled or infirm relatives. Of these, nearly two-thirds of those primarily responsible for this care were women compared with approximately one-quarter who were men' (MacBride-King 1994).

20 The consequences of the Fordist work model for the natural environment, and for other species, are enormous, and cannot be adequately discussed here. Michel Aglietta describes the transformation of the conditions of existence of the wage-earning class, which underlies the transition to the intensive regime of accumulation (1987: 79–87, 151–179). This entails a 'radical separation between town and country' (Ibid: 79) and the virtually total dependence of the majority of the population on commodified sources of food. In the advanced capitalist countries this includes the massive commodification of animals for human consumption. The assembly-line production of meat, moving from the country-side to the cities, is particularly horrific.

21 For a discussion of the concept 'disaggregated city' and of (post-Fordist) 'complex cities' as sites of new social movements, see Kling 1993.

22 This example was used during a seminar given by Mr Borgmann at the University of Alberta, in November 1993.

23 An obstetrics nurse told me that five full-time nurses were fired from her department in 1994, following budget cuts, leaving five fewer nurses to care for the same patient load. The Nurses Association of Alberta reported that 2, 000 nurses had been laid off between 1993 and the end of 1994. A doctor complained to me that after months of specialists' team work on a patient, the individual was discharged from the hospital, only to learn that out-patient treatment was no longer available. The doctor said that, as a result, months of treatment and recovery would be undone.

24 According to the HRDC:

> In 1993, there were approximately 420,000 young people in any given month who were unemployed and actively looking for work. That's an unemployment rate of almost 18 per cent for those 15 to 24 years of age – much higher than the national average of 10.1 per cent for 25 to 54 year-olds. Young Canadians were particularly hard hit by the recent recession. They experienced a disproportionate share of job losses, and their participation rate fell from 70.2 per cent in 1989 to 63.3 per cent in 1993 . . . . Almost half of the youths not in school or the labour force in 1992 were women with children.
>
> (HDRC 1994e)

25 HRDC provides figures for registered Indians living on reserves in 1991: 32 per cent of working age registered Indians were employed, but only 17 per cent of young registered Indians living on reserves were employed. This may help to account for the migration of young native persons to the cities. Unfortunately, the Ministry does not give figures for the unemployment and social assistance rates of young natives living off the reserves. According to Status of Women Canada (1997), 1993 statistics showed that 28 per cent of visible minority women and 33 per cent of aboriginal women lived in a 'low-income' situation.

26 The HRDC (1994a) reports that more than two-thirds of persons with disabilities had employment income of less than $10,000 in 1989.

27 For a description of neo-Taylorist responses to the Fordist crisis, see Lipietz (1992), and Schor (1991: 80–1, 139–57).

28 Certain experiences of deprivation and alienation are particularly intense in North America, although perhaps they will grow in Europe, given the terms of economic union (the homogenization of work norms, the pressure toward greater 'labour mobility'). Workers do in fact work longer hours in the United States than in Europe (although the work week in the United Kingdom is approaching that in the United States – see below). Even following the recession of the 1980s, unions in Europe were more successful in advocating reduced work time as an egalitarian means of redistributing productivity gains and reducing unemployment. Schor cites figures to show that weekly hours have continued to fall in Europe, while they have increased in the United States. IG Metall in Germany won a 35-hour work week for its members in the 1980s, setting a new standard for bargaining throughout the economy. Vacation hours have also risen in collective agreements negotiated in Europe. Statutory vacation periods range from three weeks (in the Federal Republic of Germany in 1988) to five weeks in Austria, Finland, France, Luxembourg, and Sweden. Most of the other EC member countries had four-week statutory holidays (Schor 1991: 81–2).

The famous exception in Europe is that other bastion of neo-liberalism, the United Kingdom. A Eurostat survey in 1990 showed that full-time workers in Britain were working an average 43.7 hours per week, compared to 39.9 hours in Japan, and the 'Europe 12' average of 40.4 hours (Hicklin 1995: 8). Hicklin also cites research findings that 'excessive overtime is now commonplace for almost half the workforce', and that 44 per cent of workers surveyed report being 'exhausted' when they return home. Moreover, 'Britain, alone in Europe, sets no minimum wage, guaranteed paid holiday, or maximum working week' (Ibid: 9), and the Tory government contested the EU directive on working times which sets a *maximum* limit of 48 hours per week.

29 In his last public lecture before his death, Marcuse argued:

> In democratic societies, introjection (along with the forces of law and order, ever ready and legitimate) suffice to keep the system going. Moreover, in the advanced industrial countries, affirmative introjection and a conformist consciousness are facilitated by the fact that they proceed on rational grounds and have a material foundation. I refer to the existence of a high standard of living for the majority of the privileged population, and to a considerably relaxed social and sexual morality. These facts, to a considerable extent, compensate for the intensified alienation in work and leisure which characterizes this society. In other words, conformist consciousness provides not only an imaginary compensation but also a real one. This militates against the rise of a radical character structure.
>
> (Marcuse 1992: 32)

30 People who have put in a full day at work, plus commuting, and some domestic tasks, do not have much energy (or time) left over to pursue active, interactive, or self-creative uses of leisure time. The fact that the three industrialized countries with the longest work hours – Japan, the former USSR, and the United States – also have the longest hours of television viewing is suggestive of a link between work exhaustion and passive forms of leisure. See *The Gallup Report* 248 (May

1986), p. 8, and; F.T. Juster and F.P. Stafford, 'The allocation of time: empirical findings, behavioral models, and problems of measurement', Working Paper, Institute for Social Research, University of Michigan, February 1990, p. 9, table 2, cited in J. Schor (1991), p. 217, fn. 39. A study of sexual behaviour within two-income families would probably also confirm a syndrome predicted by Marcuse, called: 'I'm too tired to have sex; pass the remote-control'. Meanwhile, television-watching has replaced conversation in parent–children relations, according to recent research by the Institute for Social Research, University of Michigan, and the International Association for the Evaluation of Education Achievement, cited in Pepper Schwartz, 'Hey, is there anyone home?' (New York Times News Service), reprinted in *Victoria Times Colonist* 25 February 1995, C1, C3.

31 As Schor and Lipietz, among others, point out, there are many things that we would like to do which require more than an hour or an afternoon, or even a weekend. We postpone such activities, or never develop the skills to engage in them (e.g., music, or carpentry) because our compartmentalized bits of leisure rule them out.

32 Paul Wachtel (this volume) argues for an 'ecology of satisfaction', at the same time observing that environmentalists in the United States are not making these kinds of connections. He cited surveys of *middle-class* households in the United States which show that commodities are decreasingly associated with happiness, and give grounds for predicting that decreased work time would not result in increasing consumption of things (see also: Wachtel 1989). These findings are not surprising, given that – as new social movement theorists like Klaus Eder (1993) have observed – it is the new middle class which, though in many ways materially privileged, defends ideas of 'the good life' that are critical of productivism and modernization.

33 Figures cited above show that the real wage has been declining in Canada. The average wage of US workers peaked in 1973. Since then it has declined to its mid-1960s level (Schor 1991: 80).

34 Schor cites survey data from 1978 and 1989 studies: Fred Best, *Exchanging Earnings for Leisure: Finding of an Exploratory National Survey on Work Time Preferences* (Washington, DC: United States Employment and Training Administration 1980); Robert Half International, 'Family time is more important than rapid career advancement: Survey shows both men and women support parent tracking', (San Francisco, 28 June 1989). For data on European workers' attitudes, see Daniel Yankelovich *et al. The World at Work* (New York: Octagon Books, 1985).

35 Union strategies are going to be crucial to the outcomes of struggles around work and leisure. Juliet Schor argues that the United States 'no longer possesses a culture of resistance to long hours or a political movement to press for government reforms' (1991: 81), since the demand of the nineteenth-century labour movement for more leisure was virtually extinguished from the agenda of the American unions following the Second World War. Schor contrasts this situation to the strategies adopted by workers' movements in Europe.

36 Representations of Third World peoples serve similar symbolic functions for the discourse of modernization. 'Developmental' discourse identifies poverty with nature, and the satisfaction of human needs with modern civilization (it also typically depicts 'the Third World' as predominantly rural, ignoring the interesting contradiction that between the cities and the countryside, and within the cities, great wealth and modern, 'advanced' sectors co-exist with enormous poverty). I am referring here to the very prevalent views in western societies today (and among neo-classical economists and Third World elites) that, e.g., famine is a result of an inability to master nature technologically, or of individuals to control their fertility, or simply the 'backwardness' of certain peoples on the continuum of human civilisation . . . . Nature, in other words, becomes a link in a chain of equiv-

alences which associates such diverse elements as 'lack of contraceptives', 'a subsistence logic of production and consumption', or 'lack of modern technology', but which always arrives at places like 'poverty', 'high infant mortality', and even, 'ecological disaster'. Discourses which articulate 'nature' and 'subsistence' to the sustenance and nurturing of life, self-sufficiency, and egalitarian social practices are seldom heard. (One recent neo-classical take on nature/technology/Third World development may be found in the C.D. Howe Institute publication, *The Environmental Imperative: Market approaches to the Greening of Canada* (1990) (edited by G. Bruce Doern. See Richard Lipsey, 'Report and Comments').

37 Alanis Obomsawin's film *Kanehsatake: 270 Years of Resistance* (1993) permits a number of native voices to speak regarding the meanings of this frontier.

38 There are numerous other examples of conflicts between governments, corporate interests, and non-native workers, on one hand, and native bands, on the other, centred around resource exploitation and hydro-electric dam construction. Environmentalists have positioned themselves in various ways in such conflicts.

39 This story was presented in a CBC Radio documentary produced by Bob Carty and broadcast 20 November 1994, on the programme 'Sunday Morning'.

40 These concerns have been stated in various submissions by the Canadian Coalition for Nuclear Responsibility (CCNR) to the Federal Environmental Review Panel on the Nuclear Waste Management and Disposal Concept (Canadian Coalition for Nuclear Responsibility, 1995, 1996, 1997), which are available on the CCNR's website at: http://www.ccnr.org. In a 20 November 1994 interview broadcast on CBC Radio, the president of the CCNR, Gordon Edwards, said that in the 1980s the AECL had proposed to 'rent space' in a disposal site to exporters from other countries, in order to make the project economically feasible. Given the huge estimated cost of the geological burial method ($13 billion in 1996) (CCNR 1996: 2), it has been asked how such a project will be financed. If the idea is to make money by 'renting space', then, like the Detroit incinerator's 'energy (and profits) from waste' logic (Adkin and Alpaugh 1988), there may be an impetus to generate nuclear waste indefinitely.

41 Other elders interviewed by Carty expressed reservations about the siting of a nuclear waste disposal facility on their land. In presentations made to the Federal Review Panel on Nuclear Waste Management and Disposal Concept, aboriginal spokespersons emphasized their concerns that their peoples had not been adequately included in the review process, and had not been given the necessary means to make expert assessments or even to be represented at the hearings. See Federation of Saskatchewan Indian Nations *et al.* (1995); and presentations made to the Review Panel's public hearings in March 1996 by: Regional Grand Chief Gordon Peters, Union of Ontario Indians; Gerry Fontaine, Sagkeeng First Nation; Deputy Grand Chief Brian Davey, Nishnawbee-Aski Nation; Vice-Chief Allen Adams, Federation of Saskatchewan Indians; and Assembly of Manitoba Chiefs; and Andrew Orken, legal advisor to the Quebec and Labrador Region of the Assembly of First Nations and the Grand Council of the Crees (of Quebec). The transcripts of these presentations may be obtained from the website of the Canadian Environmental Assessment Agency at: http://www.ceaa.gc.ca.

42 The Meadowlake Tribal Council has an annual budget of about $23 million. The Council owns a saw mill, and has forestry and trucking operations.

43 For an excellent critique of the apolitical nature of 'politics of difference' (i.e., 'difference' disguises 'antagonism'), see Himani Bannerji, 'But who speaks for us? Experience and agency in conventional feminist paradigms', in Bannerji (1991).

References

Adkin, Laurie (1995) 'Life in Kleinland: Democratic opposition to economic freedom', *Canadian Dimension* (Special Report) (April–May).

Adkin, L. and Alpaugh, C. (1988) 'Labour, ecology, and the politics of conversion in Canada', in Frank C. Cunningham *et al.* (eds) *Social Movements/Social Change* (Socialist Studies Annual 4), Toronto: Socialist Studies Society and Between the Lines.

Aglietta, Michel (1987) *A Theory of Capitalist Regulation: The US Experience*, New York: Verso. (First pub. as *Régulation et Crises du Capitalisme*, Calmann-Lévy, 1976.)

Axworthy, Lloyd (1994) Quoted in Mackie, Richard 'Overtime eats jobs, unions told', *The Globe and Mail* (5 May): A1.

Bannerji, Himani *et al.* (eds) (1991) *Unsettling Relations*, Toronto: Women's Press.

Barr, L. (1993) *Basic Facts on Families in Canada, Past and Present*, Statistics Canada, ct. no. 89–516, Ottawa: Minister of Industry, Science and Technology, (cited in *The Conference Board of Canada*, 1994).

Berto, Fergo (1993) Quoted in 'Long hours driving employees to join unions', *The Globe and Mail* (11 December).

Borgmann, Albert (1992) *Crossing the Postmodern Divide*, Chicago, IL: University of Chicago Press.

Canadian Auto Workers (1993) *Hard Times, New Times: Fighting for our Future, Report to the National Collective Bargaining and Political Action Convention*, Toronto, May 4–7.

Canadian Coalition for Nuclear Responsibility (1997) 'Summary argument on nuclear wastes', submitted to the Federal Environmental Assessment Review Office Panel on the Management of Canada's Nuclear Fuel Waste (18 April).

—— (1996) 'Model brief on nuclear wastes' (no date).

—— (1995) 'Conformity analysis of the lack of conformity of AECL's geological burial concept', submitted to the Federal Environmental Assessment Review Office (8 August).

Conference Board of Canada (1994) *The Work and Family Challenge: Issues and Options*.

de Saint Exupéry, Antoine (1943) *The Little Prince*, New York: Harcourt, Brace and World Inc.

Duhamel, Pierre (1993) 'Tout pour le travail, rien pour la famille', *Le Magazine Affaires Plus*, March: 11–20, cited in *The Vanier Institute of the Family* (1994).

Eckersley, Robyn (1992) *Environmentalism and Political Theory: Toward an Ecocentric Approach*, New York: State University of New York Press.

Eder, Klaus (1993) *The New Politics of Class (Social Movements and Cultural Dynamics in Advanced Societies)*, London: Sage Publications.

'Eldercare: the next wave in work and family programs', in *Canadian HR Reporter* (July 1993), cited in the *Conference Board of Canada* (1994).

Federation of Saskatchewan Indian Nations, The Assembly of Manitoba Chiefs, The Assembly of First Nations of Quebec and Labrador, The Grand Council of the Crees (of Quebec) (1995) 'Joint First Nations' submission to the Federal Environmental Review of the Nuclear Fuel Waste Management and Disposal Concept:

Conformity and Adequacy Analysis of the Proponent AECL's Environmental Impact Statement' (August).

Gergen, Kenneth J. (1991) *The Saturated Self: Dilemmas of Identity in Contemporary Life*, New York: Basic Books.

Gooderham, M. (1993) 'Fewer women's jobs, CLC says', *The Globe and Mail* (4 June).

Goodleaf, Donna Kahenrakwas (1993) 'Under military occupation: indigenous women, state violence, and community resistance', in Linda Carty (ed.) *And Still We Rise (Feminist Political Mobilizing in Contemporary Canada)*, Toronto: Women's Press.

Gorz, André (1993) 'Political ecology: expertocracy versus self-limitation', *New Left Review* 202: 55–67.

Gramsci, Antonio (1971) *Selections from the Prison Notebooks*, trans. and ed. Quintin Hoare and Geoffrey Nowell Smith, New York: International Publishers.

Haraway, Donna (1990) 'A manifesto for cyborgs: science, technology, and socialist feminism in the 1980s', in Linda J. Nicholson (ed.) *Feminism / Postmodernism*, London: Routledge.

Hicklin, Aaron (1995) 'The new slavery', *Scotland on Sunday* (8 January).

hooks, bell (1990) *Yearning: Race, Gender, and Cultural Politics*, Toronto: Between the Lines.

Horn, Kahn-Tineta (1991) 'Beyond Oka: dimensions of Mohawk sovereignty', *Studies in Political Economy* 35: 29–41.

Human Resources Development Canada (1994a) 'Poverty: background facts', October.

—— (1994b) 'The need for social security reform', October.

—— (1994c) 'Women and social security', October.

—— (1994d) 'Work and family: background facts', October .

—— (1994e) 'Youth: background facts', background paper prepared for the Minister's discussion paper *Improving Social Security in Canada*, Ottawa, October.

IBRD (1994) *Averting the Old Age Crisis*, cited in 'Worldwide aging crisis feared', *The Globe and Mail* (4 October): 1A.

Jackson, Andrew (1994) Quoted in Mackie, Richard, 'Overtime eats jobs, unions told', *The Globe and Mail* (5 May): A1.

Jaimes, Annette M. and Theresa Halsey (1992) 'American Indian women: at the centre of indigenous resistance in contemporary North America', in M. Annette Jaimes (ed.) *The State of Native America: Genocide, Colonization and Resistance*, Boston, MA: South End Press.

Kling, Joseph (1993) 'Complex society/complex cities: new social movements and the restructuring of urban space', *Mobilizing the Community* (Urban Affairs Annual Review 41) Newbury Park, CA: SAGE Publications.

Kristeva, Julia (1989) *Black Sun*, New York: Columbia University Press.

Laclau, Ernesto, and Chantal Mouffe (1985) *Hegemony and Socialist Strategy: Towards a Radical Democratic Politics*, London: Verso.

LaDuke, Winona (1982) 'Natural to Synthetic and Back Again', in Ward Churchill (ed.) *Marxism and Native Americans*, Boston, MA: South End Press.

Lax, Joan (1994) Quoted in 'Bar Association is encouraging families to hang on', *The Globe and Mail* (17 October).

Lazreg, Marnia (1988) 'Feminism and difference: the perils of writing as a woman on women in Algeria', *Feminist Studies* 14, 1: 81–107.

—— (1993) *Vert espérance (L'avenir de l'écologie politique)*, Paris: Editions la Découverte.

—— (1992a) *Towards a New Economic Order: Postfordism, Ecology, and Democracy*, Polity Press (trans. of *Choisir L'Audace*, Paris: Editions la Découverte, 1989).

—— (1992b) 'A regulationist approach to the future of urban ecology', *Capitalism, Nature, Socialism* 3, 3: 101–10.

Lipietz, Alain (1996) *La Société en Sablier*, Paris: Editions la Découverte.

MacBride-King, J. (1990) *Work and Family: Employment Challenge of the '90s*, (Report 59–90 Ottawa): The Conference Board of Canada (cited in Conference Board, 1994).

Marcuse, Herbert (1966) *Eros and Civilization: A Philosophical Inquiry into Freud*, Boston, MA: Beacon Press.

—— (1992) 'Ecology and the critique of modern society', *Capitalism, Nature, Socialism* 3, 3: 29–38.

Mohanty, S. P. (1989) 'Us and them: On the philosophical bases of political criticism', *Yale Journal of Criticism* 2, 2: 1–31.

Mouffe, Chantal (1993) *The Return of the Political*, London: Verso.

—— (1990) 'Radical democracy or liberal democracy?' *Socialist Review* 20, 2: 57–66.

—— (1988) 'Hegemony and New Political Subjects: Toward a New Concept of Democracy', in C. Nelson and L. Grossberg (eds) *Marxism and the Interpretation of Culture*, Urbana, IL: University of Illinois Press.

Obomsawin, Alanis (1993) *Kanehsatake: 270 Years of Resistance*, National Film Board of Canada.

Offe, Claus (1992) 'A Non-Productivist Design for Social Policies', in Philippe van Parijs (ed.) *Arguing for Basic Income (Ethical Foundations for a Radical Reform)*, London and New York: Verso.

O'Hanlon, Rosalind and Washbrook, David (1992) 'After Orientalism: Culture, criticism, and politics in the third world', *Comparative Studies in Society and History* 34, 1.

O'Hara, Bruce (1993) Quoted in 'Long hours driving employees to join unions', *The Globe and Mail* (11 December).

Purdy, David (1994) 'Citizenship, Basic Income and the State', *New Left Review* 208: 30–48.

Rothfield, Philippa (1990) 'Feminism, subjectivity, and sexual difference', in Sneja Gunew (ed.) *Feminist Knowledge: Critique and Construct*, London: Routledge.

Sassoon, Anne Showstack (1987) 'Women's new social role: contradictions of the welfare state', in A. Showstack Sassoon (ed.) *Women and the State*, London: Hutchinson.

Scharpf, Fritz W. (1991) *Crisis and Choice in European Social Democracy*, trans. Ruth Crowley and Fred Thompson, London: Cornell University Press (trans. of *Sozialdemokratische Krisenpolitik in Europa*, Frankfurt: Campus, 1987).

Schor, Juliet B. (1991) *The Overworked American: The Unexpected Decline of Leisure*, New York: Basic Books.

Status of Women Canada (1997) 'Statistics on women in Canada' (updated 14 January 1997), Ottawa: http://www.swc.gc.ca.

Taylor, Charles (1991) *The Malaise of Modernity*, CBC Massey Lecture Series. Concord, Ontario: House of Anansi Press.

Touraine, Alain (1978) *La Voix et le Regard*, Paris: Editions du Seuil.

Touraine, Alain, Hegedus, Z., Dubet, F. et Wieviorka, M. (1980) *La Prophétie anti-nucléaire*, Paris: Editions du Seuil.

van Parijs, Philippe (ed.) (1992) *Arguing for Basic Income (Ethical Foundations for a Radical Reform)*, London and New York: Verso.

Vanier Institute of the Family (1994) *Canadian Families*, Ottawa.

Wachtel, Paul (1989) *The Poverty of Affluence: A Psychological Portrait of the American Way of Life*, Philadelphia, PA: New Society Publications.

Part 6

ECOLOGY AND POLITICS

16

IT'S NOT EASY BEING GREEN

Peter Timmerman

The roots of the Green Party in Canada

There has been very little substantial research into the admittedly short history of the Green Party of Ontario and Canada (Lyon 1985; Sandilands 1992; Harries-Jones 1993). At the same time, in a number of countries, there has been a move towards something of a retrospective look at the period that saw the birth of the environmental movement (e.g., Jamison *et al.* 1990). Part of this retrospection is due to a sense that the environmental movement has exhausted some of its initial momentum, and that now is a good time to pause and see where we have been, as a prelude (one hopes) to a new forward impulse (Braile 1994).

The history of the emergence of Green Parties in Europe is now fairly well known. After the final burst of the student's movement in the late 1960s, various issues began to get the attention of the remaining activists, and ecology was one of these, building on the works of Schumacher (1973), the British publication *Blueprint for Survival* (The Ecologist 1972) and others. Under various names, local and regional parties began to spring up, associated initially with 'citizen's initiatives', often around nuclear issues. Italy, Belgium, Holland, and France were among those countries that eventually were able, through various forms of proportional representation, to obtain seats in local and state legislatures. It was, of course, the German Greens who made the biggest impact by winning twenty-seven seats in the federal Bundestag in 1983 with 5.6 per cent of the vote. In Britain, the Ecology Party was founded in 1973 – changing its name to the Green Party in 1986. New Zealand began its Values Party also in 1973.

The idea of a Green Party in Canada was essentially stimulated by the publicity associated with the German Greens, though there were influences from the British experience (e.g., Trevor Hancock, the main spokesman for the Canadian party in its early years had been associated for nine years with the British Ecology Party). The German Green example was, to say the least, something of a poisoned gift to progenitors of Green parties world-wide. It fixed in the minds of many people the idea that the only true model for a

Green Party had to be anarchic, and that this model could somehow get you into power. This ignored some brutal local truths about Germany, including the fact that proportional representation enabled the German Greens to get a legitimate foothold on the national political scene.

In Canada in the late 1970s, before the arrival of the German Green model, there were sporadic individual attempts to run for Parliament on various environmental platforms, with people proclaiming themselves as candidates for ecology and so on. The biggest substantial effort seems to have been a group of people calling themselves 'The Small Party', which got its start one night around a bar at a conference, and subsequently fielded seven candidates in the 1980 federal election. They included such people as Elizabeth May, now Director of the Sierra Club of Canada.

In 1982 and early 1983, a variety of initiatives were undertaken in different parts of Canada to establish Green Parties, especially in British Columbia, Alberta, Ontario, and Quebec. In British Columbia, for example, a first unofficial Green Party candidate, Betty Nickerson, ran in a federal by-election. In what follows, attention is focused on Ontario, partly because that was where the movement towards a national party crystallized.

On 7 May 1983, a group of people met in Peterborough, established the Green Party of Ontario and set about organizing a National Conference for the fall. One of the unforeseen consequences of this first initiative was the decision not to have an interim constitution, but to set up a constitution committee. As a result, constitutionalizing became the focus of intense theoretical and political debate over the next five years, and consumed immense amounts of time, which could have been far more profitably spent. Also occupying substantial amounts of time were the standard minutiae of getting a party going, signing up memberships, getting an office going. There were specific hurdles that had to be overcome: to be an official party in Ontario, for example, you needed to have 10,000 signatures. To qualify as a party at federal level, you needed to run at least 50 candidates, and so on.

On 27 June of that year, a simultaneous press conference was held in Toronto, Ottawa, Vancouver, with contributions from the Montreal chapter, announcing the formation of the National Party. This received widespread coverage. In fact, it was noticeable throughout its early period the Greens got very favourable and extensive media coverage. Many journalists were closet greens.

It will perhaps come as no surprise to those who have participated in similar exercises that the first year or so of this activity, in spite of substantial problems, was a lot of fun, was extraordinarily exhilarating, and a rapid political education.[1] Members of the Party stood on street corners, talked all night, drove or bussed endlessly around the province, made friends for life, and set about remaking the planet.

For better and worse, people were attracted to the Green Party from all over the political spectrum. Some of the people who were the most sympathetic to ecological ideas turned out to be Tory farmers in the backblocks of Ontario. Robert Paehlke, among others, has noted the conservative appeal of many Green ideas, which was complicated by a North American strain of radical individuality that tended to move towards a kind of defensive anarchism (Paehlke 1989). These people tended to favour technological solutions for participatory ills.

Many who gravitated towards the Green Party were people who had been expelled, burned, or turned off by other political parties, or the entire political system. Almost every meeting was therefore haunted with the spectre of paranoia and immense mutual suspicion, lurking under the love of all humankind rhetoric. Bertrand Russell once remarked that alternative schools almost never work, because people send their problem children to them, rather than their normal children. Many Green Party meetings were therapy sessions. Long hours were spent attempting to overcome histories of personal problems, bad group dynamics, and feelings of global helplessness. A 1984 report from the Munich *Sueddeutsche Zeitung* said: 'A caucus meeting of the Green Party is like a group therapy session. But while there is nothing wrong with therapy, what has it got to do with politics?'

The most extraordinary manifestation of this was the first, founding meeting, of the National Green Party, held at Carleton in Ottawa in November 1983. Approximately two hundred people from across Canada had come together. It was an unmitigated disaster. It began appropriately enough. The first speaker, whose name had been drawn out of a hat to ensure fairness, turned out to be a man who was pushing Esperanto as the working planetary language. This immediately outraged the delegates from Quebec, who saw this as a threat to French. (Why it wasn't also considered a threat to English is still a puzzle.) For the next two days, there were accusations and counter-accusations about power plays, about Ontario's dominance or Toronto's dominance over the proceedings, the entire panoply of Canadian internal squabbling; all mingled with calls for world peace and the effort to design a party logo. By the end of the meeting, delegates from across the country were screaming at each other, and were only persuaded by some deft stick-handling on the part of the meeting Chair to agree on the most minimalist structure. Apart from some subsequent heroic efforts, the effort to establish a national party structure was abandoned.

This kind of activity is perhaps common to all parties in their early stages. But sometimes the need for therapy got more serious. Since the Toronto meetings took place quite openly, all sorts of people with all sorts of causes wandered into the room: people with greenback schemes, people trying to get worker's compensation, artists, mystics. The meeting was once confronted by a very frail young man who announced that he had been fasting himself to death as a protest against Canadian defence policy, and was looking for support. The party meeting immediately passed a motion praising his efforts, and then after a break in the meeting, it was belatedly realized that if he died the Greens would have been parties to his death. Since it was known that I had done quite a bit of study of Mahatma Gandhi, I was phoned up and asked if I would go and try and talk the young man out of continuing. It took a very intense and terrifying weekend to get him finally to abandon his fast.

This alienation of people from the political process and from each other was so severe that it constantly overshadowed Party activities. Much of this was fought out over constitutional issues. For example, there was the whole issue of voting. A number of people in the party were somewhat socially impaired Ayn Randians and Skinnerians who were most comfortable dealing with a computer screen, and they were continually attempting to create – this was the 1980s – a referendum system which would hook everyone up to computers so that Party members could vote on all issues, all the time, and would therefore not need to meet. These people have presumably now gone on to the Internet.

There were constant efforts to make sure that no leadership would evolve, no formally agreed upon policy could be developed, and no decisions could be taken above the local level. Much of this involved the vexed question of representation vs. participation. I came away from the Green Party as a strong supporter of the principle of representative democracy. Much of the rhetoric of the Green Party was about love and trust, and yet most people in the Party wouldn't trust anyone who left the room. They were unable to believe that anyone could be trusted to express their views, to consider the alternatives, and to do what was best for all concerned. Delegation was betrayal. Everybody had to be involved in every decision all the time, and that meant it became like trying to organize a bag of kittens.

This was of course a plausible strategy if you wanted to be part of a grass-roots movement rather than a political party, and there was a schizophrenia about what it was people were engaged in doing by joining the Greens. This led to interminable arguments about whether we were a movement disguised as a party, or a party disguised as a movement.

What was most disturbing was the abuse of power associated with the lack of structure. Apart from the fact that the most personable and manipulative people formed power groupings that were unacknowledged and unaccountable, there were a number of incidents in which the most vulnerable people in the party were subjected to real difficulties. These tended to involve commitments of money which went unrecovered and unaccounted for, losses which these people could ill afford.

Eventually, to cut a long story short, the reasonable people who had become involved in getting the party going became increasingly impatient with the lack of progress. In November 1984, six Toronto Greens, three of the chief party officers and three other members (including myself) met and decided that, given the deteriorating situation with regard to funding, membership and activity, something had to be done. The two existing consultation structures, a pseudo-computerized Monthly Mailing and Referendum System (MMRS), and the Ontario Coordinating Committee (OCC) were ineffectual; and their decisions were, in any case, binding on no one. The rump group decided to hold a constitutional drafting meeting at a 'neutral location' (Ancaster in December) and submit the result to a referendum among all Green Party members in Ontario. This was done, and the referendum carried out in January 1985, proposing a decision-making structure which would include representation from each of the local parties across Ontario. After a fairly strident campaign, this referendum was surprisingly successful, and won by an overwhelming majority of the votes cast (though there was only a 25 per cent return rate of the audited ballots).

This was, however, the signal for a minority revolt among various regional members, and a further acrimonious debate ensued. Problems continued, exacerbated by a continuing drop in membership which made the new governing system almost unworkable. In order to satisfy various critics, the quorum for decision making at the provincial level had been set quite high, and it became impossible to achieve a provincial quorum at the new Provincial Delegate Council – again partly because those who had been defeated at the referendum were still actively opposed to an organizational structure.

By this time – 1985 – those who had been involved in the founding of the Party had become burned out and disillusioned with the lack of progress. Within about six months, all of these strong activists left the Party and went on to other tasks. All these people were already working at full-time jobs, and most of them had families. The leadership of the party, which had been held in trust by Trevor Hancock in Toronto, passed to Seymour Trieger of the British Columbia Greens, and essentially the story moved west.[2]

Discussion and conclusions

It is sobering to contemplate the fact that after twenty years of Green political activity, and an astonishing rise in global environmental awareness, no Green Party in an Anglo-Saxon country has succeeded in getting a single person into a federal legislature (there has been more luck in local and regional legislatures such as Tasmania), and no Green Party anywhere that I know of has succeeded in getting more than 25 per cent of the vote in any major legislative contest. The European Green movement is in substantial disarray, with most of the senior figures having abandoned similar efforts to create sustainable political parties; although there has been a substantial resurgence of support in Germany for the Greens. This is, of course, not to suggest that green attitudes and environmental politics have not succeeded, particularly in Europe, in becoming an accepted and powerful part of the landscape.

The questions this situation raises include not only why has the Green Party not succeeded in Canada, but also whether the idea of such a party was, and is, flawed. By far the best discussion on this issue is by Catriona Sandilands in her 1992 article, 'Ecology as Politics: The Promise and Problems of the Ontario Greens'.

To begin with, the first question. There are a number of reasons, some already mentioned, why the Canadian party has not succeeded (thus far). Most obviously, in countries without proportional representation, it is necessary to compromise with certain elements of mass party machinery. This is even truer in Canada now that the entry fee to getting on the ballot was substantially increased in passing last year. There has been a persistent fairly clandestine activity on the part of established political parties to prevent the participation of smaller parties in the political process. Ironically perhaps, this has not stopped the sudden explosion of protest parties and regional parties in Canada, which is a kind of alternative historical norm for this country.

More crucially, a party doomed to 5–10 per cent of the vote, and no likelihood of significant power, has no discipline, because nothing that is said really matters. It is possible to remain pure. Rhetorically, it was always possible to retreat into the idea that Greenery was a movement, and not a party. It was also possible to argue that as long as our ideas got across, it didn't matter if political power was achieved.

The mention of the sudden rise of protest parties in Canada brings to mind the question of why the Greens have not shared in the experience of the Reform Party, or the earlier Social Credit and Creditiste waves. The main answer must be found in the refusal of the Party to accept the structures of a traditional party, including and especially the need for a single leader. The possibility of re-educating the public into a different style of collegial leadership – if such a thing is possible – probably requires day-to-day exposure to such a leadership; which requires an official elected presence to begin with. The European experience with rotating leadership has not been promising.

It was a tenet of most people in the Green Party that single leadership was inherently corrupting and led to autocracy. On the other hand, it seemed within the bounds of feasibility to have very strong powers of recall and review, combined with appropriate consultative mechanisms, that would have overcome many problems associated with abuses of power. The main problem with this kind of suggestion, of course, was that there was a wide-ranging belief that we were in the business of re-inventing politics, and that none of the working methods of other parties could be acceptable to us.

A third problem, particularly in Canada, is that Green politics has been consistently associated with the Left, and many of its roots were, seemingly, in New Left analyses. It was always possible for New Democratic Party supporters to argue that the Green Party would steal their votes; and that the NDP was the best hope for environmentalists in any case.

Although the Greens hoped to be seen as a new alternative to the old politics of Left and Right, with a vision for a total transformation of society, they were unable to escape being labelled as a single-issue party (i.e., environmentalists). If they were occasionally considered to be a multiple-issue party, the other issue was often nuclear disarmament, which made them indistinguishable from parties of the Left. It must be recalled that this period was the height of the Reagan variation on the Cold War. This made it impossible, for example, to have an intelligent debate on what an appropriate defence policy for Canada might look like.

Fourth, the Canadian Green Party suffered by not being very strongly rooted in local and regional government. The German Greens and others had begun locally. In Canada, the national Green Party tended to be based on a foreign example, rather than an indigenous movement even though there was, and is, a very strong environmental movement in Canada. Yet the Green Party was never able to build strong allegiances with the environmental movement. Why was this the case?

For one thing, many of the leaders of the environmental movement were already committed to the NDP. If they were not committed, they tended to be somewhat apolitical or pragmatic. This suggests that they were giving the Green Party a certain period of time to prove its viability before they would consider giving it their support, neither of which in practice materialized. There also emerged a curious kind of environmental politics, which is difficult to describe. A number of environmentalists and their organizations had already begun to move into a relation with government which would be threatened if environmentalism became too identified politically with one party. Rather, environmental issues were to be considered as beyond political labels, or alternatively imbued with a different kind of political authority that would directly threaten the bureaucracies and ministers involved.

Again, it may be that the importation of the Green Party idea was both a catalyst and an obstacle. If the Canadian Green Party had been founded as part of a local or regional struggle (e.g., a 1980s Clayoquot Sound or the struggle over James Bay), or earlier in the process (in the 1970s as opposed to the 1980s), it might have had deeper roots and stronger connections. It is interesting to speculate, for instance, on why the strong political movement around acid rain in the mid-1970s did not generate a political party. The answer might be found in the emerging powerful, but quasi-neutral, alliances formed by the environmental organizations, the government bureaucracies, and the scientists who wanted to resolve that particular issue, and the bulk of the specific future issues that would come along in the 1980s. A new political party would have upset that nexus of mutual influence.

Fifth, the Canadian Party never had a strong enough intellectual and theoretical base from which to work. One of the great failings of the Party – and the difficulty in establishing a national party exacerbated this – was that it was never able to produce a coherent 'greenprint' or original Canadian manifesto around which the various streams of thought and practice could mobilize.

This necessarily raises the question whether such a coherent 'greenprint' was possible. There were – and are – considerable tensions, not to say contradictions, in much of the Green movement, which in its early years was without three basic resources and themes that are, perhaps, now beginning to appear.

One, there was no serious detailed economic–ecologic analysis of both industrial society and its potential alternatives upon which to build. This is now emerging, both through the work of ecological economists, and the efforts of near-mainstream economists like Herman Daly. A book like *For the Common Good* (1994), with all of its flaws, would have provided a much-needed focus for hammering out a cogent party platform.

Two, if every serious political theory should have at its core some model of the human, even the human in society, the Greens had almost nothing original to say about this. Robert Paehlke ends his book on *Environmentalism and the Future of Progressive Politics* (1989) with the caution that the environmental movement 'must remain conscious of its roots in a value-laden appreciation of the human condition'. The term 'value-laden' is ambiguous, but if we look at the kind of thinking associated with political figures like Vaclav Havel, it seems to me that any new politics must come to terms with certain ontological issues raised by our perilous, paradoxical physical situation. If we examine the origins of the modern environmental movement in the early 1960s, there were a number of themes that were quite powerful, of which the drive to eliminate obvious pollution sources was perhaps the most obvious. Another theme, which was present at the outset, but which became buried, involved 'threats to the intimate' associated with the infiltration of radiation, DDT, and other micropoisons into natural and human systems. This theme re-emerged in the late 1980s on a global scale, with the breakthrough of concerns over species loss and ozone depletion into the public consciousness. A focus on an ontopolitical theme like this could have resulted in a much more profound political analysis taking place, one that could have resulted in a new kind of political call to concern.

Lastly Greens had no serious discussion of cultural issues. A naïve Romanticism reigned, as it still reigns among most environmentalists. This was perhaps harmless when coping with the notion of unmediated experience of nature; but it made (makes) the environmental movement vulnerable to certain nineteenth-century assumptions inherent in the entire range of political options currently on offer in the West.

Sandilands (1992) suggests that some of these problems are actually virtues, in the same 'counter-hegemonic' tradition that Adkin (1992) discusses. 'Ecology' becomes then a kind of place-holder, or more specifically a relational matrix within which a number of connections to other social movements, and the local diversity of political actions can be sustained. One problem is that 'Ecology' keeps being degraded or narrowed into 'environmentalism' – a familiar theme to Green activists. Sandilands notes that ecology has so far failed to live up to its 'connective potential'.

One of the problems with the Green Party (and the movement) is that it is too quick to dismiss the richness of what is possible in a refurbished democratic politics that retains forms of representative government, etc. Not everything embedded in a hegemony needs to be abandoned. Greens should support re-use (bricolage?) as well as recycling. It is possible for a time to be part of a political process and still hold parts of it at arm's length, especially if there are ways of ensuring critical self-awareness of how one is being influenced. Gandhi believed that all of human experience was religious, including politics. This seems to me to be a slightly safer belief than that all of human experience is political, especially when politics becomes religion.

A stronger 'ecology' as the enabling metaphor for politics might have focused, as mentioned, on the theme of 'threats to the intimate', which does make some of the links that Sandilands proposes, especially to the women's movement, the discovery of the body as a political site, and the increasing sophistication of the cultural analysis of environmentalism.

But I would like to conclude with my sense of sadness at a lost opportunity, or perhaps an opportunity which has evolved elsewhere, differently, among those who were affected by the early efforts. I would say, for instance, that, Bob Stanfield notwithstanding, Trevor Hancock is the best Prime Minister we never had in this country – of course he is still young enough to try elsewhere.

I came away as something of a grudging advocate for some of the virtues of representative government, but must acknowledge the difficulties associated with the concept of representation in an age where identity is partly defined through rituals of participation, and partly counter-defined by narratives of 'facelessness' and alienation. We need to work on forms of 'representative participation'; and that seems to have been where the more focused Greens were beginning to put their energy towards the end of the process described above. It is a pity that effort remains underappreciated and this approach substantially untried.

For better or worse, there probably was an alternative which was never seriously considered, but which might have produced a somewhat more successful, if compromised, Party. A breakaway 'conservative' Green Party, perhaps with a different name, and with an argued commitment to some kinds of formal structure, strict recall procedures, rotation of offices and the like, might have been able to sustain itself to the point in the late 1980s when a more successful effort would have been possible. It is worth considering whether a purely pragmatic approach for a period of time would have allowed the Greens to take advantage of many of the lost opportunities in the late 1980s, and got us to the point where we could have had enough resources to support a full-scale effort at dismantling the boat that carried us over to a poisoned shore. We might have hopelessly betrayed ourselves, but it might also have been more fun to try. Permanent marginal status is more debilitating than creative – though perhaps counter-hegemonists would disagree. The real issues for environmental politics at the working level involve such issues as trust, entrusting, relationship, and power.[3]

Notes

1 My experience began (on which much of this analysis rests), and was rooted in, the political education I received from the years 1983–7 through my participation in the founding of the Green Party of Canada, more particularly, the Provincial Green Party, and even more particularly, the Metro Toronto Chapter of the Greens. I entered the process as an environmentalist with a social science background, and as someone who had been somewhat political earlier in my life – I had worked at one time for candidates or parties all across the political spectrum. I was convinced, even before I joined the Greens, that none of the major political parties had much to offer by way of grappling with what I saw as a new emerging worldview, and I had hopes that the environment might act as a catalyst or a 'unifying space' for a new way of thinking about the earth.

These remarks sound suspiciously like memory trying to make out that my ideas at the time (1983) were more advanced than perhaps they were. However, without being too autobiographical, I should state that I had been working on global environmental issues for some time already, and two years previously, I had published a book reviewing, in the light of world history, what I called 'Vulnerability, Resilience, and the Collapse of Society' (Timmerman 1981). Also, simultaneously with joining the Greens locally, I had become involved internationally with what was about to evolve into the global 'Sustainable Development of the Biosphere' project. This involved interacting with a number of eminent scientists, including such figures as James Lovelock, whose ideas were just beginning to arrive on the world stage. It was this unique period when I found myself shuttling between the global and the local that propelled me into taking the possibilities of a global ecological and political vision seriously.

2 This part of my story ends. I continued to participate in meetings and activities until about 1989. The Green Party continues to function (perhaps more strongly in provincial parties like the Ontario Greens); and was most recently involved (in 1994) concerning fund raising in support of protestors at Clayoquot Sound. Three years ago, however, I was asked in another capacity to address a meeting of Greens in Scarborough. During discussion, I made some historical remarks about the difficulties we faced during the first few years of the Party, and a number of people were quite horrified by what I said. The reason was that they were still wrestling with the same topics almost ten years later, and the same arguments were still circling through the Party.

3 When I began to write this, I took a look at my own subsequent trajectory, and found that I had become more and more interested in the roots of human concern, in ethics, and in considerations of spirituality. As somebody once said in a different context, I had met in those days with a kind of evil, often most deeply located in myself, and I was never the same again.

References

Some documentation for the paper above derives from my extensive (though incomplete) unpublished files of the activities of the Green Party of Ontario and of its Metro Toronto Chapter from 1983–6. Permission for access and quotation from these files other than for bona fide researchers may have to be cleared with the official Green Party of Canada.

Adkin, Laurie E. (1992) 'Counter-hegemony and environmental politics in Canada', in William K. Carroll (ed.) *Organizing Dissent: Contemporary Social Movements in Theory and Practice*, Canada: Garamond Press.

Bookchin, Murray (1990) *The Philosophy of Social Ecology*, Montreal: Black Rose Books.

Braile, Robert (1994) 'What the hell are we fighting for?' *Garbage* 6, 3: 28–35.

Bramwell, Anna (1989) *Ecology in the Twentieth Century: A History*, New Haven, CT: Yale University Press.

Daly, Herman E. and Cobb, John B. Jr. (1994) *For the Common Good*, (2nd edition), Boston, MA: Beacon Press

Deudney, Daniel (1993) 'Global environmental rescue and the emergence of world domestic politics', in Ronnie D. Lipschutz and Ken Conca (eds) *The State and Social Power in Global Environmental Politics*, New York: Columbia University Press.

The Ecologist (1972) *Blueprint for Survival*, Harmondsworth, Middlesex: Penguin.

Harries-Jones, Peter (1993) 'Between science and shamanism: the advocacy of environmentalism in Toronto', in Kay Milton (ed.) *Environmentalism: The View From Anthropology*, London and New York: Routledge (ASA Monograph No. 32).

Jamison, Andrew, Eyerman, Ron and Cramer, Jacqueline (1990) *The Making of the New Environmental Consciousness*, Edinburgh: University Press.

Lyon, Vaughan (1985) 'The reluctant party: ideology vs. organization in Canada's Green Movement', *Alternatives* 13, 1: 3–8.

Naess, Arne (1989) *Ecology, Community, and Lifestyle*, David Rothenberg (trans. and ed.) Cambridge: Cambridge University Press.

Paehlke, Robert C. (1989) *Environmentalism and the Future of Progressive Politics*, New Haven, CT: Yale University Press.

Reed, Peter and Rothenberg, David (eds) (1993) *Wisdom in the Open Air: The Norwegian Roots of Deep Ecology*, Minneapolis, MN: University of Minnesota Press.

Roussopoulos, Dimitrios I. (1993) *Political Ecology*, Montreal: Black Rose Books.

Sandilands, Catriona (1992) 'Ecology as politics: the promise and problems of the greens', in William K. Carroll (ed.) *Organizing Dissent: Contemporary Social Movements in Theory and Practice*, Canada: Garamond Press.

Schumacher, E.F. (1973) *Small is Beautiful*, London: Blond and Briggs.

Timmerman, Peter (1981) *Vulnerability, Resilience, and the Collapse of Society*, Toronto: Institute for Environmental Studies, EM-1.

17

TOWARDS A SOCIAL ECOLOGICAL POLITICS OF SUSTAINABILITY

Franz Hartmann

Introduction

If asked to define what the phrase ecological politics means, non-specialists might say it had something to do with trying to save the environment by changing government policies so that we could create an environmentally sustainable society. They might refer to campaigns by environmental groups as examples of ecological politics and note that the environmental movement is the spearhead of ecological politics. If pressed to explain what we were saving the environment from they might respond 'humanity', specifically overpopulation, overconsumption, and greed. The decision about whether something will save or further damage the environment would require advice from scientists, who have a good knowledge of how nature works, to determine the environmental impact of a given policy or action.[1]

This 'popular' view shows that ecological politics is actually an extremely complex subject, and involves much more than simply changing government policy. Eco-political actions are premised on a particular view of the causes of environmental problems. These views, in turn, are premised on specific theories of how to understand nature, society and their relationships. This suggests that eco-politics encompasses not just political activity but problem analysis and discussion about social and scientific theories. Nevertheless, most people tend to ignore the problem analysis and theoretical realms of eco-politics. They see eco-political struggle limited to issues concerning government policy.

Nevertheless an increasing number of people are questioning the dominant interpretations of the causes of ecological problems and the social and scientific theories that form the basis of these interpretations. This suggests, therefore, that eco-politics is really a struggle over political action, problem analysis and theory.

Is nature natural?

In trying to develop an understanding of both nature and society, it is necessary to begin with some ontological and epistemological remarks. As Merchant (1980) and Wilson (1992) amongst others have shown, what is considered natural and what constitutes nature changes historically and culturally. They suggest our view of nature has more to do with the society we live in than with any objective 'nature'; in other words, nature is a social construct. However, since at least the nineteenth century it has been claimed that true, objective nature can be discovered using the methods of the natural sciences, most notably accomplished by Charles Darwin in his theory of evolution. In this tradition, the dominant outlook in the natural sciences presents us with a view of nature as separate from society, a machine made up of component parts. One of the many 'discoveries' is that nature is the realm of scarce resources where competition between and amongst species for these resources drives evolution.

However, many theorists note the ontology and epistemology of the natural sciences are so heavily influenced by social factors that to consider the scientific view of nature 'objective' is simply false. For example, Levins and Lewontin (1985) outline the striking similarities in ontological premises of bourgeois theories of society and the natural sciences:

> The social ideology of bourgeois society is that the individual is ontologically prior to the social. Individuals are seen as freely moving social atoms, each with his or her own intrinsic properties, creating social interactions as they collide through space . . . . Inevitably people see in physical nature a reflection of the social relations in which their lives are embedded, and a bourgeois ideology of society has been writ large in a bourgeois view of nature. That view was given explicit form in the seventeenth century in Descartes' *Discours*, and we practice a science that is truly Cartesian.
>
> (Levins and Lewontin 1985: 1)

Like bourgeois ideology, Cartesian science assumes individual, atomistic parts are the building blocks of reality. In order to explore nature we must first reduce it to its component parts, and understand the intrinsic aspect of these parts. Viewed like a clock, nature becomes an assemblage of parts making up the whole (Levins and Lewontin 1985: 1–2).

Worster (1977) makes a similar point in his discussion of how nineteenth-century social forces affected Darwin's theory of evolution.[2] In discussing Darwin's emphasis on savage conflict and competition in nature, Worster (1977) writes:

And it is here that nineteenth-century culture, as well as the Darwin persona, set a direction for the supposedly inviolable world of science. The emphasis Darwin gave to competitive scrambling for place simply could not have been so credible to people living in another place and time. It is absolutely impossible to conceive such a view of nature coming from, say, a Hopi in the American southwest .... Even in the limited realm of nineteenth-century western science, it is striking how much of Darwin's work and the social response to his ideas were the products of the Victorian frame of mind in Great Britain and the United States.

(Worster 1977: 168–9)

The lesson from this critique of the scientific view of nature is that our understandings of nature, and for that matter society, are never neutral. They are the product of given social formations. Ontologically and epistemologically, this leaves us in a potential conundrum. If any claims we make about nature are socially produced, the whole idea of discovering 'natural laws' or living in harmony with nature seems doomed. Put differently, we seem to be incapable of discerning whether what we see in nature is a reflection of an objective nature or social circumstances.[3]

A social-ecological theory of reality

However, this conundrum only remains if we insist on seeing nature and society as ontologically separate and the products of distinct forces. An alternative approach begins by discarding the notion of an objective, separate, knowable nature. In this approach there are no objects called society and nature. Instead, there is a reality which is the product of social and ecological forces. The (built) environment is the physical aspect of reality. Ecological forces include (soil) fertility rates, climate, photosynthesis, respiration, radiation levels, and so on. These forces are the outcome of innumerable relationships amongst all living organisms and their non-organic environment and they guide and limit the actions of organic life and inorganic processes. Social forces are a distinct subset of ecological forces since humans have the ability to form social relations that affect their behaviour and ecological relations. Social forces describe the habits, customs, institutions, laws, ideologies, modes of reasoning, language and so on which guide and limit our actions. These forces are the product of all the social relations we engage in such as class, political, cultural, gender, spatial and sexual relations. Social forces are the outcome of the unique articulation of social relations in time and space.

This suggests social and ecological forces affect one another constantly. For example, if the radiation emanating from the sun should change, it would probably have a dramatic impact on social relations. Or, if people stopped burning fossil fuels and dramatically reduced energy consumption these new social relations would have a significant impact on the climate. As the second example illustrates social forces help shape ecological forces, along with all other organisms. However, this does not suggest we have control over or determine ecological forces. As the first example shows, there are many ecological forces over which people have little, if any, influence.

A social-ecological theory can never be neutral or objective because it is always the product of the forces that are trying to be explained. Therefore any claims about finding 'natural laws' must always be viewed with caution since our interpretation of ecological forces is always through the lens of particular social forces. This approach is in contrast to positivist science which tries to explain one facet of reality (nature) and claims its understanding is not influenced by social factors and, hence, is objective. The new approach is also unlike positivist science in that it does not use a reductionist and atomistic epistemology and ontology. Instead, it relies on a dialectical approach to reality. It is worth outlining – very briefly – this dialectical approach just to get a sense of how fundamentally different it is from the approach used by positivist science.

The dialectical approach is found in the works of Dickens (1992), Levins and Lewontin (1985) and Harvey (1993).[4] Harvey notes the emphasis in dialectical analysis is on relations between, rather than on individual organisms: 'Dialectical thinking prioritizes an understanding of processes, flows fluxes and relations over the analysis of elements, things, structures and organized systems' (Harvey 1993: 34). In fact, the dialectical view suggests change and transformation are the norm. Levins and Lewontin (1985) claim two more principles of a dialectical view are:

> that a whole is a relation of heterogenous parts that have no prior independent existence as parts . . . [and] that in general the properties of parts have no prior alienated existence but are acquired by being parts of a particular whole.
>
> (Levins and Lewontin 1985: 273)

Harvey states: 'The interdigitation of parts and wholes entails the "interchangeability of subject and object, of cause and effect"' (Harvey 1993: 55). It becomes apparent from this very brief overview of the dialectical method that the social-ecological theory of reality has a much different approach than positivist science. The emphasis on relations amongst organisms instead of on individual organisms and the view that an organism is both a whole and part of a larger whole makes the traditional division between society and nature unnecessary. Although still differentiating between distinct types of relationships – social and ecological – the new theory acknowledges that these relationships are part of a larger whole – reality – where they interpermeate one another constantly. Moreover, social-ecological theory removes the false security of objectivity and forces those interested in theorizing about 'nature' and 'society' to acknowledge their social influences. Finally, the theory leads to a different sort of ecological politics. The struggle is over the relationships we are in with humans and non-human agents. We contest not only how to understand these relationships but what they should be and what we can do to reproduce or alter them.

A theory of sustainability

This new theory of reality can help develop an understanding of the crisis of sustainability. Denotatively, sustainability means the capability of reproducing a given arrangement. Commonly, sustainability is usually tied to the concept of development and, in Canada, refers to 'current practices [that do] not diminish the possibility of maintaining or improving living standards in the future'.[5] But this definition is not adequate since there are situations where sustaining one set of relationships may impede sustaining another set of relationships. This means sustainability inherently contains a normative element: when it is invoked, it tells us what particular sets of relationships are of value to the author. For example I would argue that the set of relationships that need to be sustained are as follows:

1   Relationships among humans based on: mutual respect and tolerance; equitable access to food, clothing, health care, shelter and meaningful work; freedom of thought and ability for mental development; democratically determined political and economic decisions.
2   Relationships among humans and other species where the attempt is made to minimize human domination of and impact on other species.
3   Relationships among organisms and their environment which have created the climate, hydrological cycle, radioactive levels, and other environmental conditions (i.e., ecological forces) that we have experienced throughout most of human history.

The social-ecological theory of reality provides us with an insight into this (and any other) definition of sustainability. It suggests my understanding of sustainability – as with everyone else – is both socially and ecologically influenced. It is a product of the class, gender and cultural relations I am part of; and it is influenced by the ecological relations I perceive. Also, it suggests that since my actions will shape, along with other organisms, the physical environment we share, sustainability has no objective status.

This understanding of sustainability illuminates the crisis of sustainability; that is, the impediment of the reproduction of the ecological and social relations just mentioned. The social-ecological theory of reality can also help us understand this crisis. The theory avoids the pitfalls of environmental and social determinisms by requiring an examination of both social and ecological relations.[6] That means, for example, to understand why the burning of fossil fuels at present levels is probably unsustainable, we must explore ecological factors: how the laws of thermodynamics, climatic patterns, and the biological processes of other organisms contribute to environmental conditions that are unsustainable. But as importantly, we must look to social relations to understand the crisis: that means exploring what social processes cause increased fossil fuel burning in the first place. Also, the social-ecological theory of reality suggests that since human actions help create the environment, they can be changed to create a different, sustainable environment.

Since humans cannot now (and probably never will be able to) overcome the laws of thermodynamics or control the earth's climate, the best route to understanding the crisis of sustainability is to focus on social relations. Specifically, this means examining what social processes contribute to the crisis and suggesting ways in which to transform these processes.

The crisis of sustainability in industrial societies

So-called 'modern, industrial' societies are unsustainable because of specific types of ecological and social relations. To begin with, the ecological relations required to provide the material to produce the goods and services needed to 'maintain' these societies are destroying increasing numbers of species and their habitats.[7] In the drive to maximize economic production, economic agents attempt to eradicate, control and transform organisms and environments to meet their economic needs. In addition, the pollution created by the production and consumption of these goods reduces and often destroys the relationships between organisms and their environment and the ability of organisms to reproduce. In sum, the maintenance of present industrial societies requires subjugation of organisms and the production of an environment (both in urban areas and in so-called wilderness) that reflects the needs of a select group of economic agents who wield power and authority. The unintended side effects of the production of an environment based on this domination include global climate change and species extinction.

Therefore, according to my criteria for sustainability, the current set of ecological relationships is unsustainable. In addition, these relationships may be incapable of sustaining the present set of social relations, most significantly influenced by capitalist class relations. This is what James O'Connor (1988) calls the second contradiction of capitalism.

Alongside this ecological unsustainability is a social unsustainability in industrialized societies. The division between the rich and the poor is increasing both in so-called developed and developing countries. High unemployment and under-employment rates, the reduction of social services from the state, lack of access to safe food and water, the reduction of the power of labour unions, and higher tax burdens have swelled the ranks of the poor and reduced the middle class. Meanwhile, wealth has been concentrated in fewer hands. The entrenchment of international free trade via GATT and

341

NAFTA-type agreements, the instantaneous transfer of capital to anywhere in the world, the dismantling of government regulations and welfare programmes have created a global economy that favours the wealthy. Put simply, class inequities are growing.

Linked to these class inequities are also ethnic and gender inequities. In Canada for example, the early 1990s saw women and non-white immigrants increasingly blamed for stealing jobs, abusing welfare services and the many other social 'ills' facing the country. Ironically, these very groups are often the worst-paid and are relied upon to do the dirty work of society. Thus, social relations, like ecological relations, are based on inequity and domination. These tendencies suggest social relations are unsustainable, according to my definition of sustainability.

The social causes of the crisis of sustainability

The practices of industrial societies are from this perspective dependent on unsustainable ecological and social relations. This, of course, raises the question: what are the causes of these unsustainable relations and practices? As we noted above, the social-ecological theory suggests there are ecological forces that contribute to this crisis. Since we generally cannot change them and rely on them for our survival, we must look to the social relations and forces that precipitated the crisis. There are many social factors responsible. They include: a view that domination of people and ecological forces is necessary and acceptable; acting as if society is somehow separate from other organisms and the environment; structuring economic relations and institutions to compel ever-increasing production and consumption of goods and services; and, organizing the economy and the state to maximize the private accumulation of capital via a market economy. All of these causes are related.

Unlike many liberal and Marxist social theorists, Murray Bookchin (1989) argues there is nothing inherent about the human condition that requires human domination of 'nature'.[8] Indeed Bookchin (1989: 44–6) argues the rise of domination within human societies led to human domination of 'nature'. This suggests domination has an important role to play in unsustainability. Domination is about justifying the act of imposing your will onto something external to yourself. Karen Warren argues that for domination to occur there must be an 'oppressive conceptual framework (i.e., a set of beliefs, values, attitudes and assumptions which shape one's world view) that explains, justifies, and maintains relationships of domination' (Warren 1990: 127). The three elements of this framework include:

(1) value-hierarchical thinking, i.e., 'up-down' thinking which places higher value, status, or prestige on what is 'up' rather than on what is 'down'; (2) value dualisms, i.e., disjunctive pairs in which the disjuncts are seen as oppositional (rather than complementary) and

exclusive (rather than as inclusive), and which place higher value . . .
on one disjunct rather than the other . . . ; and (3) the logic of domination, i.e., a structure of argumentation which leads to a
justification of subordination.

(Warren 1990: 128)

As Warren notes, the logic of domination 'involves a substantive value
system, since an ethical premise is needed to permit or sanction the 'just'
subordination of that which is subordinate' (Warren 1990: 127). To concretize
the point, patriarchy requires thinking that: men are different than women;
the apparently distinct qualities of men are somehow better than the distinct
qualities of women; and, the superior qualities of men justify subordinating
women.

The crucial element of domination is therefore moral justification of
subordination activated by some hierarchicalized difference. Without this
moral justification an oppressive conceptual framework would not exist and
domination (at least on a systemic basis) would not be possible. From the
perspective of sustainability, this raises an interesting point.

As Bookchin (1989: 45–6) argues, social systems of domination of 'nature'
have their roots in social structures premised on coercion, command and
obedience. Warren's work indicates these traits are sustained by an oppressive
conceptual framework. This suggests that if moral justification of subordination (or domination) did not exist in a society's conceptual framework, then
systemic domination (through coercion, command and obedience) would not
exist. In other words, if a tenet of the conceptual framework was that no one
had the right to subordinate 'nature' or other people, then it would take away
the present moral justification of actions or thoughts that destroy ecosystems
and force some people into miserable conditions for the sake of others.
Assuming that social relations can exist without subordinating and changing
ecological forces (the major premise of my definition of sustainability), then
one would see a dramatic reduction in unsustainable practices. This suggests,
as Bookchin argues, that the legitimation and practice of domination is a
cornerstone of an unsustainable society.[9]

Another cause of unsustainability is thinking and acting as if society is
somehow separate and independent from other organisms, ecosystems and
the environment (i.e., ecological forces). The dominant views in both the
natural and social sciences accept this approach. That means intellectually we
exclude the examination of the interpermeation between social and ecological
forces. But more importantly, we act in ways that reinforce the society–nature
dichotomy. For example, advocates of 'sustainable development', who appear
to acknowledge at least intellectually the link between humans and the
biosphere, use this concept to further justify what are clearly unsustainable
practices and relations (see Schmidheiny 1992). But this blindness to how
specific actions are detrimental to ecosystems extends to many of us. For

example, most of us acknowledge the dangerous impact the whole economy and culture of cars have on ecosystems. Yet many of us who are in a position to use public transit rely on cars nonetheless for reasons of pure convenience. Therefore, thinking and acting as if we weren't part of and dependent on the biosphere contributes to unsustainability.

This leads to a third cause of unsustainability: the structuring of economic relations and institutions to compel ever-increasing production and consumption of goods and services. This approach to economics is the trademark of industrialized societies[10] and is reflected in our obsession with growing GNPs and productivity.[11] The reason this causes unsustainability were noted above: the more we make and consume, the more resources we use and the more pollution we create. Even taking into account attempts by businesses to become green, market economics dictate they must produce ever more to be considered successful. As long as this impetus for ever-higher production and consumption exists, sustainability will be difficult to achieve.

The final cause of unsustainability I want to discuss is organizing the economy and the state to maximize the private accumulation of capital via a market economy.[12] The ecological critique of capitalist economies has been perhaps one of the few positive growth industries in the last few years.[13] Essential to this critique is that the capitalist mode of production is the main material cause behind the destruction of sustainable ecological and social relations. The drive for accumulation – through maximizing surplus value extraction or profit – necessitates the increased commodification of labour and ecosystems. This process sets up relationships of domination by valuing actions that assist in accumulation and devaluing actions that do not. Therefore, since money can be made by destroying habitat and treating people unequally, domination is justified. Moreover, it assumes organisms and resources can be assigned an exchange value (i.e., a money form). It treats organisms and the environment as separate individual units, and ignores the myriad of relations between them. In addition, since maximizing surplus value is the primary aim in all capitalist economic decisions, an attempt is made to transform all ecological and social relations to assist in accumulation. In other words, value is measured purely in terms of money without regard for other life forms. This has led to ever-increasing destruction of species, habitats and social conditions all in the name of profit and competition.

The state is implicated in this unsustainable process by providing the conditions for private accumulation to occur. A product of various struggles such as class, the state's power is dependent on tax revenues derived through taxation of corporations, people's income and consumption. In other words, the state's power base is dependent on the continuation of a capitalist economy.

To sum up quickly then, the crisis of sustainability has four social causes: the moral justification of domination in our belief systems; actions that ignore our linkage to and dependence on ecosystems; economic institutions and relations compelling ever-growing economic activity; and, capitalist economies. All of these causes manifest themselves in particular types of social relations and forces. As the social-ecological theory of reality notes, these social forces interpermeate ecological forces creating a new set of ecological forces and physical environment. Increasing evidence suggests this new environment and set of ecological forces are impeding human reproduction.

Towards a politics of sustainability

This analysis prompts the question: what do we do to promote sustainability? The social-ecological theory developed here suggests that although the crisis is partially accelerated by ecological factors, it is also social. Other living organisms and the environment will likely not spontaneously change to meet the needs of industrial societies. Instead, humans will have to change their practices. The first step is to identify strategies that – given our analysis – won't solve the crisis. One such strategy is to reform the present system. This is perhaps the dominant strategy advocated by practitioners of eco-politics. However, as the preceding analysis indicates, capitalism requires the continuation of many unsustainable practices. A capitalist society is dependent on: the domination of ecosystems and people; constant economic growth; and neglecting the organism–environment relationship. This suggests making capitalism sustainable is a difficult if not impossible task.[14] Another strategy is simply to replace capitalism with state control of the economy. However, the practices and legacy of the old Soviet Union and China show that domination, economic growth and neglecting ecosystems are not limited to capitalist societies. A third strategy is to use spiritual means. Those who think we can get to a sustainable society simply by spiritual means forget our day-to-day material existence is based on an economic system that is responsible for environmental degradation. In other words, while a spiritualism that acknowledges the importance of ecological forces and human equity may be useful in promoting sustainability, it must be accompanied by a strategy to change our material existence as well.

What, then, is a viable strategy for sustainability? The preceding analysis suggests we must first rid ourselves of the unsustainable social relations, specifically the structures, institutions, beliefs and practices that reproduce them. We must attempt to eradicate domination in all facets of society, develop an economy which is not driven by the constant need for growth and is not controlled by blind market forces. As well, a mind set must be promoted whereby social and ecological forces are seen as always affecting one another. Put simply, we must transform social relations.

The most obvious place to begin is with the institutions and structures which form our social relations. These include the family, the community, cultural institutions, the state and the economy. Within the family, the community and cultural institutions we can challenge systems of domination by treating all people as equals and expect others to do the same. Sexism,

345

racism, classism, homophobia and other attitudes of domination must be replaced with tolerance towards difference *and* a fundamental belief in equity. To accomplish this we must not only rid ourselves of the 'oppressive conceptual framework' identified by Warren, but we must also call on the state to develop social policies that alleviate existing inequalities. Domination must also be impeded in our public institutions such as the state. This can be done most effectively by democratizing the bureaucracy and devolving power to regional governments.[15] Within the economy domination can also be challenged through democratization of the workplace and economic decisions. This would involve establishing community-controlled businesses and production councils to replace international institutions such as transnational corporations and GATT. Bioregionalism (see Sale 1985) and radical municipalism (see Bookchin 1985, 1989, 1990, 1991) speak to this.

The rationale behind democratizing and decentralizing power in both the state and the economy is as follows. The concentration of power sets up a structure for a few to dominate the many. Decentralizing power, on the other hand, makes wide-scale domination by a few much more difficult. In the same way, democratization involves empowering more and more people. It is a decision-making structure where the majority, not the minority, must agree to a specific action. If domination should occur, it would be a result of the majority. As this suggests, decentralizing power and democratization do not guarantee non-dominating behaviour. However, they – at minimum – remove structures in the state and economy that help promote domination. In sum, the first step to sustainability is to create social relations and structures that impede, not promote domination.

The next step is to develop an economy that impedes constant growth and capitalist accumulation while promoting sustainable ecological and social relationships. To accomplish this, economic and state decisions would no longer be made to fuel private capital accumulation. Instead, decisions would be based on meeting social needs in as ecologically sensitive a way as possible. For example, community production councils would decide – in consultation with consumers and local producers – the needs of the community. Then, they would help producers meet these needs in a sustainable fashion.

How do we nurture these structural changes that promote sustainability through concrete political actions? As noted above, we must focus our energies on family, cultural, economic and state institutions since they have such a significant control over our social and ecological relations. We must, effectively, transform these institutions. What follows is a handful of political actions that begin to achieve this goal:[16]

1 Too often political actions have a narrow, single-issue focus. While it is important to have an attainable goal, many political activities treat symptoms instead of causes.[17] One way to alleviate this problem is by making linkages between social justice and environmental problems and their root causes in all

of our political campaigns. For example, if we are campaigning to stop pesticides use in public parks, then we should be speaking about the inequities of
the economic and political systems that encourage and give so much power to
large chemical firms to make money from polluting. That means
campaigning not only for changes in pesticides regulation but also for social
justice issues such as workers' rights. Concurrently, we must call for the
democratization of the state and the economy. This process will help foster
co-ordinated, collective opposition to existing dominating political economic
relations.

2 The best way of democratizing the economy is by supporting locally
controlled businesses (such as cooperatives) and locally produced products
and services. Most depend on community members for their survival and are
therefore quite sensitive to community needs. This is in direct contrast to large
chain stores which only stay in the community as long as a certain profit
margin can be maintained. While changing consumer decisions alone cannot
transform the economy, such actions are nevertheless important. Every time
we buy something we are reproducing a set of economic and ecological relations. When we buy a tomato grown in Mexico from a large grocery store
chain we are reproducing unsustainable, dominating economic activity.
However, when we buy an organic tomato from a local farmer or grow a
tomato ourselves, we are probably reproducing sustainable economic activity
which is not dependent on exploitation. Therefore, the more we support local
businesses, the less we reproduce the current destructive system. Moreover,
this process helps construct alternative economic relations and acknowledges
the importance communities and individuals play in constructing social relations.[18]

3 Kick (or at least minimize) our addiction to goods and services that are
ecologically damaging. We can support ecological procurement policies in the
home, workplace, at our community centres, and for government. Part of this
means re-defining needs and convenience. Many people see giving up uneco-
logical products and services as a sacrifice. This attitude comes from
advertisers who have convinced us consuming a product produced through
human and environmental degradation is both necessary and convenient.
Kicking our addiction to these goods once again stops the reproduction of the
unsustainable, exploitative system.

4 Support local political mobilization in our communities and in other
communities throughout the world. Currently, many groups depend on
provincial and national multi-stakeholder processes instigated by government
as a means towards local political mobilization. While some of these processes
can lead to positive results, they are most often skewed against local groups.
The reason for this is that not everyone at the multi-stakeholder table has an
equal opportunity to influence the process and government policy. As Hoberg
(1993: 322) notes with respect to multi-stakeholder processes set up around
environmental issues, environmental groups have a small fraction of the time,

institutional resources, money and public relations skills that government and corporations sitting at the table do. Moreover, the state uses multi-stakeholder processes to legitimize action (or inaction) that helps reproduce an economic system that works for owners of capital and the state. Finally, multi-stakeholder processes mean the time and skills of community organizers go into fulfilling bureaucratic requirements instead of community empowerment. By minimizing involvement in multi-stakeholder processes, we begin to de-centre the state as the predominant site of political struggle. This allows community members to focus on exchanging skills and knowledge through direct community action, thus promoting real community empowerment. This process builds self-reliance and sustainability. Therefore, nurturing community activism helps minimize the bureaucratization of action, avoids legitimizing the state yet acknowledges that certain state struggles are necessary.

5 We must work together with other local, social change groups in our community and throughout the world. The free trade of ideas, experiences and challenges among ourselves locally and globally means we help develop local self-empowerment on a global basis. Bringing about social change on a global scale does not require large, centralized institutions. This emphasis on local action and global co-ordination of local action can both confront and transcend global political and economic forces.

Conclusion

These last five points are of course just a sampling of what people practising ecopolitics arising out of a social-ecological theory of reality think can move us towards sustainability.[19] This type of eco-politics differs from other types in two fundamental ways. First, it arrives at a different understanding of the impediments to sustainability. Most environmental campaigns see the lack of proper pollution abatement equipment, dirty production methods and externalized environmental costs as the major causes of environmental destruction.[20] In other words, the impediment to sustainability is a technical issue. This type of ecopolitics reproduces the positivist scientific notion that society and nature are mostly separate. Few, if any, connections are made between other social relations and structures and environmental destruction.

In contrast, the ecopolitics presented here is premised on the view that all social relations and structures interpermeate ecological forces (and vice versa) and form the physical environment. Therefore to understand the causes of environmental destruction we must look to a variety of social relations such as class, gender, and culture to see how they contribute to the destruction. When this is done we see that important social relations and institutions depend on domination, endless growth, the separation of society from nature, and market forces.

This leads to the second major difference between the ecopolitics presented here and more traditional versions. Environmental campaigns premised on technical explanations of unsustainability only call for technical changes. Better pollution abatement equipment, cleaner production processes and including the environment in economic calculations are the most frequent goals of environmental campaigns. In contrast, a social-ecological politics calls for transforming the social relations and structures that cause unsustainability. For example, it sees no purpose in simply calling for pollution abatement equipment and leaving intact social relations which support constant growth. This is why all five political actions presented above call for fundamental changes in social relations and the structures that support them. Their goal is to help develop social forces that, when interacting with ecological forces, create a sustainable reality and physical environment.

Finally, and perhaps most importantly, the social-ecological theory and politics presented here provide us with hope. Since humans, like all organisms, both transform and are transformed by their environment, we know our current destructive relations are not permanent. Indeed, we know human agency allows for the possibility of positive change.

Notes

1 I actually posed these questions to a number of friends (admittedly not a representative sample of the population) and they responded as indicated.

2 For a more contemporary discussion of how social forces have constructed various ideologies of nature, see Smith (1984) chapter 1.

3 For example, Murray Bookchin, who rejects the scientific view of nature, develops an epistemology and ontology of nature based on what he calls dialectical naturalism and claims this approach can help us discover an objective nature. Yet, as Eckersley (1989) points out, this view of nature may have more to do with how Murray Bookchin wants to see nature than any real, objective nature. Grundmann (1990) makes a similar comment about ecologists (deep ecologists, bioregionalists, etc.) who claim to have discovered natural laws.

4 This is only a bare outline of their work and thus suffers from over-generalization and gaps.

5 This definition is from the Canadian *Report of the National Task Force on Environment and Economy* quoted in Rees and Roseland (1991: 15).

6 By this I mean it avoids neo-Malthusian arguments as well as arguments by orthodox Marxists who assert ecological crises are purely social constructs.

7 See Lester Brown (1991) for an overview of the impact the world economy is having on the environment.

8 As noted above, the concept of nature has no status in the social-ecological theory of reality. However, its usage cannot be avoided since most people rely on it to describe the relations of non-human organisms, activities and events. Therefore, I use it only when invoked by others.

9 See Eckersley (1992: 148–54) for a critical assessment of what she calls Bookchin's social hierarchy thesis.

10 Soviet-style communist countries were also obsessed with constant growth.

11 On the problems with GNP as a measure of economic and environmental welfare see Daly and Cobb (1989).

12 For an excellent discussion of the capitalist state and economy from a Canadian perspective see Panitch (1977) and Clement and Williams (1989). However, it

should be noted none of these works incorporate ecological forces into their analyses.

13 A sampling of these critiques include: articles within *Capitalism, Nature and Socialism*, Harvey (1993), McLaughlin (1990), Bookchin (1991a), Altvater (1993), Eckersley (1992).

14 See Bell *et al.* (1994), O'Connor (1994), and Brugmann (1994) for a debate on the issue of whether capitalism is sustainable.

15 See Albo, Langille and Panitch (1993) on democratizing the state.

16 I concentrate on political and economic structures since this is my field of interest. There is some excellent work that has been done on this issue. For a sampling of it, see Marcia Nozick (1993) and the 'Sustaining Our Communities Factsheets' produced by the Toronto Environmental Alliance.

17 Within environmental politics in Canada this tendency seems to be the norm. For example, most waste management campaigns organized by environmental groups emphasize reducing packaging size and recycling. The role the accumulation process plays in the production of waste (i.e., accumulation necessitates ever-increasing production and consumption which creates waste) is generally ignored. Although practicing the 3Rs hierarchy (Reduction, Reuse, Recycle) suggests challenging the accumulation process, hardly any campaigns have tackled the issue of how to reduce the production and consumption of unnecessary consumer items. In effect, the campaigns treat the symptom, not the cause of waste production.

18 The potential for sustainable community economic development is staggering. Consider how much money a person spends in a year for just food, clothing, shelter and entertainment and how much of it leaves the community and country. Imagine if the students and faculty of an average Canadian university changed their buying habits and spent half of their money supporting locally controlled businesses and locally produced products. Not only would there be significant job creation, we would reduce our dependence on transnationals and the unsustainable, exploitative economy that helps them.

19 There is much debate surrounding the appropriate sites of ecopolitical struggles, the appropriate social agents to engage in these politics and what the mix between local and global actions should be. See Eckersley (1992) for a good overview of this debate.

20 See Adkin (1992) for an excellent overview of the environmental movement in Canada.

References

Adkin, L. (1992) 'Counter-hegemony and environmental politics in Canada', in William K. Carroll (ed.) *Organizing Dissent: Contemporary Social Movements in Theory and Practice*, Toronto: Garamond Press: 135–56.

Albo, Gregory, Langille, David and Panitch, Leo (eds) (1993) *A Different Kind of State? Popular Power and Democratic Administration*, Toronto: Oxford University Press.

Altvater, Elmar (1989) 'Ecological and Economic Modalities of Time and Space', *Capitalism, Nature and Socialism* 3: 59–70.

—— (1993) *The Future of the Market*, (trans. Patrick Camiller) London: Verso.

Bell, David, Keil, Roger and Wekerle, Gerda (eds) (1994) *Human Society and the Natural World*, Toronto: Faculty of Environmental Studies, York University.

Benton, Ted (1989) 'Marxism and Natural Limits: An Ecological Critique and Recon-struction', *New Left Review* 178: 51–86.

Bookchin, Murray (1985) 'Theses on Libertarian Municipalism', *Our Generation* 16: 9–22.

—— (1989) *Remaking Society*, Montreal: Black Rose.

—— (1990) *The Philosophy of Social Ecology: Essays on Dialectical Naturalism*, Montreal: Black Rose.

—— (1991a) 'The Meaning of Confederalism', *Our Generation* 22: 88–101.

—— (1991b) *The Ecology of Freedom*, Montreal: Black Rose.

Brown, Lester (1991) 'The New World Order', in Lester Brown *et al.* (eds) *State of the World 1991*, New York: W.W. Norton.

Brugmann, Jeb (1994) 'Comparing the Imperatives for Ecosystemic and Capitalist Development', in John P. Clark (1989) 'Marx's Inorganic Body', *Environmental Ethics* 11: 243–58.

Clement, Wallace and Williams, Glen (eds) (1989) *The New Canadian Political Economy*, Kingston: McGill-Queen's University Press.

Clow, Michael (1992) 'Ecological Exhaustion and the Global Crisis of Capitalism', *Our Generation* 23: 1–25.

Daly, Herman and Cobb, John B. Jr. (1989) *For the Common Good*, Boston, MA: Beacon Press.

Dickens, Peter (1992) *Society and Nature: Towards a Green Social Theory*, Philadel-phia, PA: Temple University Press.

Eckersley, Robyn (1988) 'The Road to Ecotopia? Socialism Versus Environmentalism', *The Ecologist* 18: 142–7.

—— (1989) 'Divining Evolution: The Ecological Ethics of Murray Bookchin', *Environmental Ethics* 11: 99–116.

—— (1992) *Environmentalism and Political Theory: Toward an Ecocentric Approach*, Albany, NY: State University of New York Press.

Grundmann, Reiner (1991) 'The Ecological Challenge to Marxism', *New Left Review* 187: 103–120.

Harris, Judith and Alexander, Donald (1991) 'Beyond Capitalism and Socialism: The Communitarian Alternative', *Environments* 21: 29–37.

Harvey, David (1993) 'The Nature of the Environment: The Dialectics of Social and Environmental Change', in Ralph Miliband and Leo Panitch (eds) *Real Problems False Solutions, Socialist Register 1993*, London: Merlin Press.

Hoberg, George (1993) 'Environmental Policy: Alternative Styles', in Michael M. Atkinson (ed.) *Governing Canada: Institutions and Public Policy*, Toronto: Harcourt Brace Jonavich.

Kemp, Penny *et al.* (1992) *Europe's Green Alternative: A Manifesto For A New World*, Montreal: Black Rose.

Levins, Richard and Lewontin, Richard (1985) *The Dialectical Biologist*, London: Harvard University Press.

Martinez-Alier, Juan (1992) 'Ecological Economics and Socialist Economics', *Our Generation* 23: 26–45.

McLaughlin, Andrew (1990) 'Ecology, Capitalism and Socialism', *Socialism and Democracy* 10: 69–102.

Merchant, Carolyn (1980) *The Death of Nature*, San Francisco: Harper Collins.

Nozick, Marcia (1992) *No Place Like Home: Building Sustainable Communities*, Ottawa: Canadian Council on Social Development.

O'Connor, James (1988) 'Capitalism, Nature and Socialism: A Theoretical Introduction', *Capitalism, Nature and Socialism* 1: 11–38.

—— (1989) 'Introduction: Political Economy of Ecology', *Capitalism, Nature and Socialism* 3: 5–14.

—— (1990) 'Socialism and Ecology', *Our Generation* 22: 75–87.

—— (n.d.) 'Red Green Politics–Think Locally, Act Globally: Towards an International Red Green Movement'.

—— (1994) 'The Politics of Sustainability: Remaking Capital or Remaking Nature?, in David Bell, Roger Keil and Gerda Wekerle (eds) *Human Society and the Natural World*, Toronto: Faculty of Environmental Studies, York University.

O'Connor, Martin (1989) 'Codependency and Indeterminacy: A Critique of the Theory of Production', *Capitalism, Nature and Socialism* 3: 33–57.

Panitch, Leo (ed.) (1977) *The Canadian State: Political Economy and Political Power*, Toronto: University of Toronto Press.

Rees, William E. and Roseland, Mark (1991) 'Sustainable Communities: Planning for the 21st Century', in *Plan Canada* 31, 3: 15–24.

Ryle, Martin (1988) *Ecology and Socialism*, London: Radius.

Sale, Kirkpatrick (1985) *Dwellers in the Land: The Bioregional Vision*, San Francisco: Sierra Club Books.

Schmidheiny, Stephan (1992) *Changing Course: A Global Business Perspective on Development and the Environment*, London: MIT Press.

Simon, Thomas (1989) 'Varieties of Ecological Dialectics', in *Environmental Ethics* 12: 211–31.

Smith, Neil (1984) *Uneven Development: Nature, Capital and the Production of Space*, Oxford: Basil Blackwell.

Toronto Environmental Alliance (1994) 'Sustaining Our Communities', A Factsheet Series produced by the Toronto Environmental Alliance.

Warren, Karen J. (1990) 'The Power and Promise of Ecological Feminism', in *Environmental Ethics* 12: 125–46.

Wilson, Alexander (1992) *The Culture of Nature*, Oxford: Blackwell.

Worster, Donald (1977) *Nature's Economy: A History of Ecological Ideas*, Cambridge: Cambridge University Press.

18

ENVIRONMENT RIGHTS
AND DEMOCRACY

Robyn Eckersley[1]

Introduction

Why should the environment movement be at all interested in pressing its claims in the idiom of rights, given that its primary concerns are largely collective in nature? Surely an environmental rights discourse would introduce an unwelcome degree of individual abstraction – not to mention an aggressive and rugged individualism – into the environmental policy debates and detract from what ought to be an overriding emphasis on cultivating civic virtue, social solidarity and community responsibility in tackling ecological problems?

An appropriately formulated body of environmental rights might serve to protect, rather than undermine, the generalizable community interest in environmental protection. In particular, environmental rights may be used to connect democratic and ecological concerns while also addressing some of the shortcomings of current environmental law and administration. While this discussion is primarily concerned with the national and international dimensions of the case for *human* environmental rights, brief consideration will also be given to the case for the 'rights of nature'.

The ecological failings of liberal democracy

According to Ulrich Beck (1992) we are now living in 'the risk society'. That is, the social production and distribution of *wealth* is now increasingly accompanied by the social production and distribution of environmental *risks and hazards*, many of which escape ordinary perception and materialize only after long lead times. Ecological problems such as pollution are the 'piggy-back products' which are inhaled or ingested *with* other things. They are the *stowaways of normal consumption* (Beck 1992: 40). In the jargon of neo-classical economic theory, they are the 'negative ecological externalities' generated by

353

market activity, the unwanted and unintended side-effects of production and consumption.

Ecological problems raise a new layer of challenges to democratic theory and practice. In particular, the ubiquitous, irreversible and transboundary character of many ecological problems has highlighted an increasing lack of correspondence between those who *make* decisions, those who possess the relevant *knowledge*, those who are *responsible* for decisions, and those who are *affected* by them. The challenge for those seeking to reconnect democratic and ecological concerns is to find ways of resisting or minimizing problem displacement – whether across social classes, species, geographical regions, ecological media (water, air), and jurisdictional and administrative boundaries (for a recent discussion of these questions, see Mathews 1996).

The proliferation of environmental laws and agencies over the last three decades seems to have done little to appease public concern over the growing scale, rate and seriousness of many ecological problems. Indeed, there is a growing disquiet among many environmentalists as to whether the regulative principles, institutions and bargaining practices of liberal democracy are adequate to the task of properly managing the risk society (Eckersley 1994 and 1996). These inadequacies arise from:

1   The limited scope of formal representation on behalf of the 'new environmental constituency', namely, future generations, non-human species and persons living outside the territory of the polity ('the representation deficit').
2   The narrow time horizons of political deliberation, which create a pressure for expedient rather than prudent political decisions in relation to many ecological problems ('the time horizon deficit').
3   Limitations in knowledge and understanding of complex ecological problems ('the knowledge deficit').
4   The partisan and competitive bargaining processes of democratic will formation, which are not conducive to the protection of collective interests such as environmental protection ('the political rationality deficit').
5   The compartmentalized and discretionary nature of much environmental law and administration, which impede a concerted and integrated response to ecological problems (the 'implementation deficit').

In terms of representation, the modern liberal democratic state (whether unitary or federal) is organized to represent only the citizens of territorially bounded political communities. Yet the environment movement is concerned to 'represent' the interests of a considerably expanded constituency of 'non-citizens' who cannot vote or otherwise participate in the formal political decision making processes of territorially defined polities, but nonetheless can be profoundly affected by the decisions made in any given polity. This expanded constituency includes all those who suffer the environmental spillover effects – not only particular disadvantaged classes and groups among the citizenry but also noncompatriots, future generations and non-human species.

Even within the territories of liberal democratic states, the 'public interest' in environmental protection fares particularly badly in the competitive political bargaining processes of democratic will formation. Environmental protection largely depends on public interest advocacy that is able to defend long-term generalizable interests rather than short-term particular interests. Sound environmental management demands that decisions be made on the basis of long time horizons and a cautious approach to risk assessment, particularly if the interests of the new environmental constituency are to be considered.

However, in liberal democracies, political decisions are made on the basis of very short time horizons (corresponding, at most, to election periods). Assessing potential ecological risks often requires scientific expertise that is not accessible to the 'layperson', and is often highly contentious within scientific circles. Such scientific controversy and uncertainty tends to generate a 'wait and see' response on the part of decision makers rather than an anticipatory and preventative response in accordance with the precautionary principle.

Liberal democracies presuppose partisan political competition between selfish actors in the struggle for 'who gets what, when and how'. Such partisan competition has increasingly taken a corporatist form, which systematically favours self-interested and well-resourced peak organizations at the expense of poorly resourced, poorly organized and dispersed groups seeking to defend more diffuse, generalizable interests, such as community environmental groups. Corporatist bargaining processes constrain the terms and negotiating margins of political debate in ways that serve special or vested interests over generalizable interests. Moreover, environmental claims are often reduced into a format that is susceptible to compromise; environmental lobby organizations are characterized, like private lobby organizations, as merely pursuing the 'sectional' or 'vested interests' of their members. Such interests must therefore be 'balanced' against the claims of other interest groups in the corporatist negotiations, political compromises, and incremental policy shifts that characterize liberal democracies. The upshot is that the longer-term public interest in environmental protection is systematically traded-off against the more immediate demands of capital, and to a lesser extent, labour. In liberal democracies the urgent, it seems, systematically displaces the important. Decisions which go against this established pattern usually attract intense debate and criticism.

Moreover, many environmental laws confer considerable discretion on both the executive, administrative and judicial arms of government and provide very limited opportunities for public rights of enforcement. The Australian legal system, in particular, is a long way from what Theodore Lowi (1979) has called a 'juridical democracy', that is, government and administration according to clear laws, clear procedures and clear standards of implementation. Such clarity is essential if environmental laws are to be interpreted as in accordance with the wishes of the legislature (rather than in accordance with the guesses or preferences of the bureaucracy or courts).

Finally, there is the added problem of whether the administrative State is institutionally capable of providing a flexible and co-ordinated response to the complex, systemic and increasingly transboundary nature of many ecological problems – problems that throw down major challenges to conventional administration and bureaucratic rationality. Bureaucratic steering systems operate on the basis of problem decomposition, compartmentalization and allocation – a mode of operation that routinely generates problem displacement across bureaucratic 'system boundaries'. Such bureaucratic rationality, it has been argued, is considerably at odds with 'ecological rationality' (Dryzek 1987). These difficulties appear to be compounded in federal systems, such as Australia's, which is made up of nine distinct political authorities (plus local government) with areas of overlapping jurisdiction covering regions of enormous geographic and climatic diversity.

In what ways might an environmental rights discourse overcome these various 'deficits' of liberal democracy in ways that remain consistent with democratic principles?

The general appeal of rights

Before addressing the question of the possible scope and content of environmental rights, there are several general reasons why the environment movement might be interested in representing environmental concerns in the form of rights claims. The general appeal of environmental rights – whether as *citizenship* rights within particular jurisdictions or as a further development of the international *human* rights discourse – is that they promise to provide more *systematic* representation and consideration of the environmental interests of citizens as well as the interests of the 'new environmental constituency' – locally, nationally, regionally and internationally.

At the local and national levels, an appropriately formulated body of substantive and procedural environmental rights has the potential to redress some of the shortcomings of current environmental law and administration, which is largely concerned to accommodate competing interests via cost-benefit analysis rather than uphold environmental values against competing claims. The major innovations to environmental law and administration that took place in the early 1970s (most notably the introduction of environmental impact assessment legislation) have largely followed a utilitarian rather than a rights-based path. Building on the analysis and framework of modern welfare economics, these innovations established new techniques of risk assessment or impact assessment based on cost-benefit analysis, while maintaining tight executive control of major environmental decisions. As Mackay (1994) has shown, although the US Environmental Protection Agency (EPA) was a product of the 'rights revolution', it is not, and was never intended to be, a rights-based agency. This is especially so in Australia, where state and federal EPA legislation confers considerable administrative and ministerial discretion and extremely limited litigation rights on the part of the public.[2]

It is precisely this utilitarian framework of environmental decision making (which ultimately furnishes only 'advice' to the executive) that has made environmental rights seem so attractive to environmentalists. That is, pressing environmental claims as rights is intended to make such claims nonnegotiable – or at least, less negotiable than they currently are. As Stone (1987: 54) points out, '[w]e do not conduct a cost-benefit analysis every time someone claims a right to free speech' because the right to free speech is considered sacrosanct, whatever the cost. It serves to 'trump' competing claims for utility maximization (Dworkin 1984). Similarly, whereas the cost of strict pollution prevention (as distinct from incremental abatement) might outweigh the benefits of clean air and waterways in a utilitarian calculus, such costs could not be used as an adequate defence in an action based on the infringement of an environmental right to clean air and water. The introduction of environmental rights has the potential to alter radically the established framework of decision making in favour of 'the environment' (of course, the same effect can be achieved by legislation that unconditionally prohibits certain ecologically degrading activities, without necessarily conferring legal rights on particular persons or species).

In federal systems and other regions of 'pooled sovereignty' such as the European Community, environmental rights can transcend intergovernmental conflicts and buckpassing by directing attention away from the respective powers of the different tiers of government and towards the rights and obligations of citizens and corporations *vis-à-vis* the state. Moreover, attempts to dilute or override particular rights in one jurisdiction may spawn protests by potentially affected citizens in another jurisdiction. As Courchene and Walsh (1994: 26) observe, 'citizen empowerment with respect to rights is pan-national and, therefore, non-territorial and, by extension, profoundly anti-federal in the traditional sense of federation. In this 'new federalism', the cleavages pit the enshrined-rights interests against the traditional vested interests'. Of course, the extent to which rights may be made to 'trump' competing rights or utility claims in any given jurisdiction is ultimately a function of how they are framed and aligned by the legislature in relation to competing claims, and how they are interpreted by the courts. (For example, in Canada, the 1982 Charter of Rights and Freedoms is an example of qualified rather than supreme rights; such rights may be confined in their operation by the courts in certain circumstances and expressly overridden by the legislature.)

At the international level, the human rights discourse now transcends national, jurisdictional and geographic boundaries and increasingly serves as an important protective buffer against the dynamics of globalization. The inclusion of environmental rights as part of the human rights discourse has the potential to add further moral weight and political legitimacy to environmental concerns, providing an additional form of pressure on governments to take more concerted steps to protect the environment.

The rights and wrongs of rights

Some of these general claims in favour of environmental rights are controversial and, to some extent, question begging. They do not, for example, acknowledge the many powerful critiques of rights waged not only from the conservative and socialist traditions (e.g., Edmund Burke and Karl Marx) but also from within the liberal tradition (e.g., Jeremy Bentham). Despite their many differences, these critics have all challenged the abstract universalist pretensions of the rights discourse and pointed to the apparent conflict or tension it creates between individual and community interests. The objection has already been raised that rights are an unsuitable means of expressing generalizable environmental concern because they are ordinarily tied to individual rather than generalizable interests.

Moreover, 'it is in implementation that the law finally defines itself and the social order of which it is part' (Yeager 1991: 175). And it is now a platitude that the legal system tends to favour those with money, power, education and position. Indeed, it might be said that the environmental rights discourse reflects the middle-class character of the green movement, and that it might be applied by green middle-class radicals in ways that threaten working-class interests (e.g., by forcing the relocation, restructuring or closing down of polluting industries).

There is also the more recent post-modern and feminist objections to the notion of abstract universal rights and to the proclaimed impersonality and impartiality of public law (including the idea that there can be neutral moral adjudicators of rights, such as judges). Here, feminist and post-modern sceptics would argue that any attempt to develop a universal discourse on environmental rights is necessarily imperialistic, ethnocentric and bound to run into trouble, especially when construed as an abstract international discourse. Abstract universal rights, so the argument might run, cannot adequately attend to cultural, geographic and gender *difference*.

There is also the vexed question of how to delineate and define the scope and content of environmental rights in ways that ensure that they are both justiciable and enforceable. Here it is typically argued that it is likely to be very difficult to squeeze all complex environmental conflicts into conventional right–duty relationships that are capable of being recognized and enforced by the judicial system. Nor is the already overburdened judiciary likely to be especially enamoured with the possibility of proliferating lawsuits, involving highly complex and technical questions and multiple parties. In any event, it is frequently argued that judges already have too much political power.

Finally, there is the argument that inflating and overburdening the rights discourse with new environmental claims might actually serve to debase or devalue, rather than strengthen, the existing repertoire of rights.

Yet we shall see that none of the foregoing arguments prove to be fatal to the case for environmental rights, although they do point to significant limitations in over-ambitious attempts to frame all environmental concerns in the language of rights. There is indeed little to be gained from broad generalizations about environmental rights at the national (as distinct from international) level; indeed, one might speculate that problems of justiciability and enforceability are likely to increase in direct proportion to the degree of generality in which new constitutional or statutory environmental rights may be framed.

However, in addressing the question of rights and justiciability, it is important to draw distinctions between moral and legal rights claims. (Moreover, in relation to legal rights, there are important differences between substantive and procedural rights in relation to the environment.) As we shall see, the international human rights discourse is pre-eminently a moral discourse that is necessarily couched in very general terms; moreover, such rights may be protected by nation states without necessarily conferring substantive environmental legal rights on citizens (e.g., they may be protected by general laws). Similarly, the moral argument that species have 'existence rights' may be best implemented by means other than conferring substantive legal rights on species (by, say, conferring certain procedural rights on 'ecological citizens' [Christoff 1996]). Before exploring these crucial definitional and implementation questions, however, let us first explore the general case for an international *human* right to a healthy environment.

Towards international environmental rights?

As we have seen, one of the many appeals of the human rights discourse (not only from the point of view of the environment movement) is that it has become an international discourse transcending national, jurisdictional and geographical boundaries. Whereas citizenship rights attach only to those persons who qualify as citizens of a particular polity, human rights attach to each and every person by virtue of the fact they are human – irrespective of race, creed, gender or language. Once the birthright of the 'sovereign people' and a foundation stone of the liberal democratic state, the rights discourse can now serve as a potent challenge to the sovereignty claims of nation states and subnational political units in federal systems.

The growing human rights consciousness of the post-Second World War era (sobered by the experience of fascism) has recently intensified in the 'new Europe' in the form of a renewed interest in social charters, citizenship rights and now environmental rights. For example, an expert committee chaired by the Dutch government has drawn up a draft 'Charter on Environmental

Rights and Obligations of Individuals, Groups and Organizations', which had been endorsed by the thirty-five countries present at the Bergen Conference on Environment and Development in May 1990 as providing a basis for further international consultation leading up to the Earth Summit in 1992 (Rehling 1991). Although this document did not gain sufficient support for presentation at the Earth Summit, environmental NGOs in Europe have urged that this Charter should remain the basis for lobbying the EC, the Council of Europe, the ECE and the United Nations (Rehling 1991: 153).

Indeed, in a world of increasing economic integration and political fragmentation, particularly in Europe, many minority groups are becoming increasingly dependent on the protection afforded by rights. In terms of the formal recognition of rights, Britain now stands somewhat alone in Europe as the only state that insists that Parliament shall be unhampered by formal constitutional restrictions. In contrast, continental Europe is sceptical towards this defence of an unfettered parliament, preferring written constitutions to this 'tyranny of convenience'. Indeed, two-thirds of European countries have made the European Convention on Human Rights (adopted in 1950 in the aftermath of fascism) part of their domestic law (Dworkin 1990: 18–19).

Despite the many long standing objections to rights, the post-Second World War international human rights discourse has moved well beyond the scope of the American Bill of Rights of 1787 and the 'Declaration of the Rights of Man and the Citizen' proclaimed by the French National Assembly of 1789. Alongside these more traditional political and civil rights (known as the first generation of rights) the 1948 United Nations Universal Declaration of Human Rights and the 1966 International Covenants on Civil and Political Rights and on Economic, Social and Cultural Rights have vindicated a much broader, second generation of human rights. These include a right to 'medical care and necessary social services' (Article 25) and a right to 'protection against unemployment' (Article 23). More controversially, the UN Declaration on the Right to Development (1986) has embodied the aspirations of developing countries (and more recently, Eastern Europe) in a third generation of 'solidarity rights' (which also includes self-determination and nondiscrimination).

These three generations of human rights (civil and political, economic and social, and development/solidarity) reflect a discordant philosophical rights heritage that has been associated with three different political revolutions and associated philosophies: the bourgeois revolution of the late eighteenth century, the socialist revolution of the early twentieth century and the rise of the welfare state, and the anti-colonialist revolution of the post-war years (Marks 1980–1). Would an international environmental rights discourse provide a fourth generation of human rights that might also serve to recontextualize and qualify existing human rights in ways that reflect the late twentieth-century political revolution and philosophy of environmentalism?

Environmental rights are not (yet?) part of the international human rights discourse. Indeed, some observers have scrutinized the 1948 United Nations Declaration and the 1966 International Covenants (on Civil and Political Rights and on Economic, Social and Cultural Rights) and found many rights to carry *anti-ecological biases* (Aiken 1992). For example, both of the Covenants carry provisions which uphold 'the right of all peoples to enjoy and *utilize fully* their natural wealth and resources' (Articles 47 and 25 respectively; my emphasis). Such rights are hardly conducive to the preservation of ecosystems and threatened species.

A few human rights, however, have been found to offer some ecological mileage, such as the right to health in the International Covenant on Economic, Social and Cultural Rights. Indeed, the human right to health has the potential to serve as a proxy environmental right and is likely to serve as a more politically potent environmental right than some of the general and ambitious claims for, say, a 'right to clean air and water'. Generally speaking, however, what are widely called the first, second and third generation of human rights in the 1948 Universal Declaration, the 1966 Covenants and the 1986 Right to Development Declaration are largely 'environmentally impotent' (Aiken 1992: 193).

Nor is there a generally recognized right to an undegraded environment in international law (Pain 1992: 320; Bailey 1993: 100–1). However, talk of international environmental rights has been 'in the wind' for some time. For example, environmental rights are now increasingly finding a home in many formal and informal charters and declarations, including the 1972 Stockholm Declaration, the 1982 UNEP World Charter for Nature (where the language of responsibility replaced that of rights) and the 1992 Rio Declaration.

Indeed, on the road towards Rio, there had been a concerted push towards a much more ambitious document than the Rio Declaration that finally received the imprimatur of the United Nations in 1992. As early as 1987, the influential report of the World Commission on Environment and Development (the Brundtland report) had recommended a set of 'legal principles' for sustainable development, the first two of which read as follows:

Fundamental Human Right

1   All human beings have the fundamental right to an environment adequate for their health and well being.

Inter-generational Equity

2   States shall conserve and use the environment and natural resources for the benefit of present and future generations.

Moreover, in addition to the draft charter on environmental rights initiated by the Bergen conference on Environment and Development (discussed above), environmental rights have also found their way onto the agenda of the UN Commission for Human Rights. An ambitious international 'Draft Declaration of Principles on Human Rights and the Environment' has recently been recommended by the Special Rapporteur on Human Rights and the Environment in her 1994 Final Report to the UN Sub-Commission on Prevention of Discrimination and Protection of Minorities (a subsidiary body to the UN Commission on Human Rights).[3] Although this document is only in draft form, it is likely to serve as a reference point for future discussion of human rights and the environment. The draft declaration effectively recontextualizes established human rights (such as health, welfare and cultural rights) in an ecological context, enshrines protection for cultural minorities (including the right of Indigenous peoples to control their lands and maintain their traditional way of life), restates the principles of inter- and intra-generational equity in relation to resource entitlement, and sets out a wide range of procedural rights necessary for the realization of the substantive rights.

Clearly, in the wake of these initiatives, the move towards an international environmental rights treaty is now no longer unthinkable. Bailey (1993: 104), for example, has proposed a core human right to a sustainable environment as the basis for an international framework convention, which could be followed up with a number of interrelated protocols dealing with specific areas. Such protocols could address such specific matters as the environmental rights of indigenous peoples and human environmental health rights. The protocols would be regarded as particular expressions of a general or core human right to a sustainable environment. Moreover, such rights would attach primarily to communities rather than to individuals and would provide a foundation for broad ecologically sustainable development strategies.

The international human rights discourse is essentially a moral discourse which transcends national boundaries. It is has evolved largely as general principles and standards that are sometimes uncertain in application and by no means uniformly endorsed. The *practical* realization of the noble ideal of human rights depends on the cooperation of nation states and the enactment of appropriate regional, national and local laws. In many cases, the gap between 'heavenly rights theory' and 'earthly rights practice' is vast.

However, the human rights discourse is an evolving discourse and there is an increasingly dynamic interplay between the international, regional and national rights discourses – an interplay which sometimes has an upward ratcheting effect on political expectations as discriminated groups appeal to the higher moral authority of international or regional human rights against discriminatory laws at the local or national levels. Moreover, there is already a wide array of examples of constitutional and statutory environmental rights which would give effect to, or otherwise complement, the proposed international environmental rights.

In the absence of a UN police force to supervise and enforce international human rights, the United Nations has largely relied on the cooperation of states, moral suasion and condemnation to ensure compliance with human rights. Alongside the work of international agencies and committees, there is now a growing array of international non-government aid and environment organizations that are prepared to stand ready to investigate, report and publicize the abuse of environmental rights. As Waldron has observed in the more general context:

> perhaps the greatest achievement of the post-war consensus in this regard is that there is now scarcely a nation on earth which is not sensitive to or embarrassed by the charge that it is guilty of rights-violations. That may not stop the violations in question, but the sensitivity at least provides a foothold for political and international pressure.
>
> (Waldron 1987: 155)

Environmental rights and democratic theory

On what basis might human environmental rights be connected to democratic theory? As moral claims, rights are no longer invoked as something that is God-given or 'natural' (claims which were originally advanced by John Locke in his classic liberal defence of 'natural rights' but later criticized by Jeremy Bentham as 'nonsense upon stilts'). Rather, they are derived from a set of moral principles that ultimately rest on respect for the inherent dignity, value and autonomy of each and every individual. This is also the basic moral principal which underlies the principle of one person/one vote. This idea – a secularization of the Christian idea that each individual human being is of equal spiritual worth before God – has been a powerful driving force in the long struggle for universal suffrage and is now enshrined in the Universal Declaration of Human Rights of 1948.

The rights-based tradition of liberal democratic theory has typically argued that there are certain 'basic' rights of individuals or groups which must not be bargained away by ordinary majorities because they provide the *preconditions* for democracy or are otherwise necessary for effective citizenship (e.g., freedom of speech and association).

Political struggles for further 'democratization' and liberation have often involved struggles for political recognition and *inclusion* via the extension of rights to discriminated groups. In such struggles for recognition, the rights discourse has been used as a means of strengthening democracy, often by way of an 'immanent critique' of traditional liberal democratic ideals. That is, it has been the stark discrepancies between the formal existence of traditional liberal rights and the substantive enjoyment of such rights that has led to the growth of the modern welfare state, and to a widening of the rights discourse to include economic, social and cultural rights. This growth in 'welfare rights' has been justified, in part, as necessary for the proper exercise of the more traditional rights. Moreover, welfare rights are also increasingly recognized as morally valid claims in their own right.

By the same token, environmentalists have a basis for arguing that there are certain environmental rights or interests which should not be traded off in liberal democracies – either on the grounds that such rights provide the long-term *preconditions* for democracy or simply because such rights fulfil basic welfare requirements which ought not to be compromised. On this view, environmental rights must take their proper place alongside welfare rights to form the full complement of *citizenship* rights, since it is only when both welfare and environmental rights are met that individuals are capable of full citizenship. As Benton (1993) has recently showed, the traditional liberal rights discourse has ignored both the 'embodiment' and ecological 'embeddedness' of individuals (both human and non-human). The development of environmental rights might also furnish a further rationale for more substantial social and economic transformations towards ecological sustainability. Such a discourse has the potential to provide a 'protective service' on behalf of both human and non-human life.

But how might this protective service work in the case of the non-human world? Over the last two decades, environmental philosophers have challenged the human-centred philosophical foundations of liberal democratic theory by arguing that not only humans but also non-human species have intrinsic value. The animal rights and environmental ethics debates have drawn attention to the fact that it is not necessary for a being to be a competent moral, rational or linguistic *agent* in order to be a morally worthy *subject*. Many humans (e.g., infants and the intellectually handicapped) do not possess full reason or moral competence, yet they are recognized as possessing certain 'basic rights', which create direct moral obligations on the part of morally competent humans. According to this argument, it is arbitrary and unjust to exclude non-human species from moral consideration when it is clear that they can be harmed from human actions in ways that are not substantially different in kind from human 'moral patients'. The disqualification of non-human animals from moral and legal consideration *simply because they are not human* is therefore exposed as an unwarranted human prejudice, as Human Chauvinism. Moreover, a purely instrumental posture towards the non-human world carries disturbing implications. After all, if our sole reason for protecting nature is simply that it is *useful* to *us*, then there is no basis upon which to resist the technological substitution of nature or argue for the protection of 'useless' species.

Ecologically oriented political theorists have also resisted drawing sharp and morally significant distinctions between humanity and nature. Whereas most political theorists have traditionally focused on what is special or distinctive about human beings, ecologically oriented political theorists have sought to draw attention to the commonalities between human and non-human animals. By replacing the putative human/animal *opposition* (which underpins so much moral and political theory) with an ecological framework based on a set of human/animal *continuities*, Ted Benton (1993) has identified a broad category of bodily needs (e.g., health, nutrition, physical security) and biophysical interdependencies that are essential to the well being of *all* animals. These areas of human/non-human continuity – which Benton encapsulates in the concepts of *embodiment* and *embeddedness* – are seen to be morally significant for all animals (human and non-human). If we are to give moral priority to the autonomy and integrity of the individual (human and non-human), we must accord the same moral priority to the material conditions (including bodily and ecological conditions) that enable that autonomy to be exercised. By widening the circle of moral considerability, humans, both individually and collectively, have a moral responsibility to live their lives in ways that permit the flourishing and well-being of both human and non-human life.

Just as the classical theory of liberal democracy is based on a theory of justice which recognizes the inherent value and dignity of the individual (without which there could be no commitment to democracy) so too a theory of 'environmental democracy' would demand a recognition of the inherent value of all life.

It might appear to follow from these foundational moral arguments that an expanded ethical framework of 'environmental democracy' must necessarily extend to all species individual and/or collective rights to ensure that they are politically and legally 'represented'. However, while certain forms of *legal recognition and protection* of non-human life would necessarily follow from this moral case for 'extended environmental democracy', it does not follow that this recognition and protection must take the form of *legal rights*. As we shall see, an environmental democracy need only demand that the existing citizenry be properly equipped to monitor and uphold public environmental laws enacted for the benefit of both human and non-human life. In short, an environmental democracy would encourage and facilitate 'ecological citizenship' (Christoff 1996).

Indeed, there is an animated debate within environmental philosophical circles concerning the appropriateness of extending rights to non-humans – a debate that was partly fuelled by Christopher Stone's adventurous attempt to extend legal standing to natural entities in response to the common law standing restrictions on public interest litigation by environmental groups (Stone 1974). Critics of non-human rights have pointed out that the rights discourse is essentially a humanist discourse that would anthropomorphize the non-human world in order to include it in a human ethical code (Livingston 1981: 62–3). The language of rights becomes especially strained and ungainly as we move from a consideration of human and human analogous cases (e.g., domesticated and captive animals) to a consideration of entire biotic communities and other ecological entities. Such a humanist discourse cannot possibly do 'ecological justice' (Eckersley 1996: 17–18).

Yet many of these critics have overlooked Stone's distinction between legal *rights* and legal *considerateness* (or recognition), a distinction which is explored and developed in *Earth and Other Ethics* (Stone 1987: 45). That is, any environmental legislation that protects natural entities (e.g., species, wilderness areas) may be said to make such entities legally recognized by the courts (without creating legal *rights* on the part of the entities). According to Stone, any infringement of such laws ought to be actionable by human guardians *on behalf of the natural entity* without the 'human guardian' having to show any personal injury or interest, which is required under the common law rules of standing.

Stone's somewhat ingenious jurisprudence is offered as a basis for broadening the common law standing rules to enable environmentally concerned citizens or specially appointed guardians to seek judicial review of environmental legislation on behalf of natural entities. The reasoning is compelling: if such laws are primarily concerned to protect *non-human* interests, it is both illogical and unreasonable to demand that 'human guardians' wishing to uphold the law for the sake of the non-human interest must demonstrate a *personal* stake in the outcome (e.g., by showing special damage or the infringement of a private right).

In Australia, the common law standing rules have presupposed that any 'implementation deficits' in general laws would be filled by the Attorney-General acting as guardian of the public interest – by taking action *ex officio* or by relation (i.e., granting permission to an individual to bring proceedings in the name of the Attorney-General). Rarely, however, have Attorneys-General exercised their discretion in this way (and their discretion is effectively beyond reproach by the courts). Indeed, as high-ranking members of Cabinet, Attorneys-General have usually been more concerned to legitimate rather than challenge the exercise of State power. Such a state of affairs suggests that the guardianship function might be better served by an ecologically informed and legally empowered citizenry and/or a well-resourced statutory body that is relatively independent of the executive.

Just as it is illogical and unreasonable to demand personal injury on the part of plaintiffs seeking to protect non-human interests (e.g., threatened or endangered species) it is no less illogical and unreasonable for the law to demand a *personal* stake on the part of plaintiffs seeking to uphold any environmental laws enacted for *general* human benefit. Any restrictions on participation and standing in relation to environmental laws should be the exception, not the rule.

But how far should environmental rights be carried? To what extent is it possible – and indeed desirable – to develop and define a body of substantive environmental rights that might serve thoroughly to insulate a delineated set of 'environmental assets' from all potential competing claims? On what basis might a constitution or ordinary legislation rank *a priori* human environmental health rights or certain environmental assets ahead of other human interests? How might such rights be formulated without involving the courts in an assessment of competing utilities?

Linking substantive and procedural rights

The case for substantive, as distinct from merely procedural, environmental rights faces two significant challenges. The first of these relates to the presupposition of a strong political consensus in relation to content and ranking of rights claims; the second relates to the role of the judiciary in environmental decision making.

As we have seen, the appeal of rights claims is that they are not amenable to trade-off. However, to succeed, such claims must attract a strong and continuing political consensus with regard to the inviolability of environmental claims *vis-à-vis* competing claims. While a political consensus might occasionally be possible in relation to *particular* environmental assets, a more systematic, *a priori* ranking of environmental rights and duties is unlikely to attract the necessary political consensus. Indeed, it is precisely the absence of consensus that has led environmental law down a procedural path that has largely been concerned to accommodate interests rather than vindicate particular environmental values. The economic theory of public goods and externalities not only offers a simple (many would argue simplistic) analysis of the problem; it also provides surrogate market techniques for the calculation of environmental preferences for inclusion in cost-benefit analyses, thereby providing a pragmatic accommodation of interests. As Tarlock has argued, welfare economics 'has undermined the development of a theory of environmental rights' (Tarlock 1988: 63).

The second challenge facing those seeking to defend substantive environmental rights concerns the challenge of definition and adjudication. On this question, abstract and general formulations, such as 'a right to clean air and water', are in a similar category to abstract claims for 'a right to employment'. Both are claims are desirable, but it is not always easy to identify those who are responsible for causing the problem of pollution or unemployment. Even in those cases where 'culprits' may be identified, they are likely to be far too numerous to join in legal proceedings. Moreover, plaintiffs are likely to face considerable hurdles in establishing causation and liability and the judiciary cannot make meaningful rulings in the absence of clear and settled standards of adjudication. Indeed, these objections provide the Achilles heel of the case for environmental rights. Again, they also help to explain why environmental law has been more concerned with *assessing risks* rather than establishing causal links between particular activities and actual harm (links which are ordinarily required by courts of law).

However, these two general challenges are not fatal to the case for substantive environmental rights. The strong likelihood of conflict between environmental and other rights ought not to stand alone as an argument against adding environmental rights to the existing rights repertoire if the moral case is otherwise accepted. After all, many existing rights frequently come into conflict (most notably the right of privacy versus the right of freedom of speech), but such conflict is not a good reason for dispensing with either of these important rights; rather, the inevitable clash between rights highlights the need for the ongoing re-evaluation, adjustment and refinement of rights on the part of both the legislature and the courts in response to changing conditions.

Nonetheless, the likelihood of growing conflict between rights does call for a degree of restraint and realism in the selection and formulation of environmental rights claims to minimize conflict and thereby limit the power of the court to assume the role of legislator. One way of ensuring a 'juridical democracy' in relation to environmental rights is to establish clear links between substantive and procedural claims. That is, instead of an abstract and ambiguous 'right to clean air and water', an environmental bill of rights might declare that citizens have a right to ensure that air and water quality is maintained in accordance with the standards set by current environmental laws (standards which would undergo regular public review). In other words, the problems of justiciability and rigidity may be addressed by formulating the *substantive* environmental rights of citizens in terms standards established by democratic (rather than judicial) processes.

To be effective, such substantive environmental rights presuppose the establishment of an associated set of environmental procedural rights, such as rights to know (i.e., access to environmental information, rights to be informed of new proposals), rights to participate in the formulation of policies and standards, rights to object and rights to bring actions against departments and agencies that fail to carry out their duties according to law. Such an interlinked set of substantive and procedural rights would not be calling on the judiciary to make environmental adjudications on the merits by deciding 'how much' or 'what is reasonable'. Rather, they would merely seek to strengthen the supervisory role of the courts to ensure that the state is both more responsive and responsible and that the 'rule of law' with respect to the environment is upheld. Such procedural safeguards would not only help to redress the current underrepresentation of environmental interests but also provide a firmer guarantee of environmental decision making according to law.

Finally, the substantial evidentiary burden of establishing causation and liability on the part of plaintiffs in upholding environment rights could be considerably lessened by adopting the precautionary principle as a procedural rule in cases of potentially serious or irreversible environmental damage. This principle provides that where there are threats of serious or irreversible environmental damage, lack of full scientific certainty should not be used as a reason for postponing measures to prevent environmental degradation. Over the last decade, this principle has appeared in policy statements, international and regional conventions and declarations (e.g., Rio Declaration and the Maastricht Treaty on the European Union) and national legislation. Indeed, the precautionary principle – construed as an evidentiary principle – is perhaps the most important single procedural rule that is likely to resist the inexorable process of environmental problem-displacement. In environmental rights cases, it could be applied to mean that it is enough for a plaintiff in an action to uphold an environmental right to raise a *prima facie* case that there are threats of serious or irreversible environmental damage for the onus to shift to the defendant to prove the negative. No single decision rule is likely to do more to represent the interests of both ecological citizens and the 'new environmental constituency'.

Some of the recommended environmental procedural rights, including broader standing rules *vis-à-vis* public environmental statutes, have already been introduced in some jurisdictions with considerable success. One such example is the Ontario Environmental Bill of Rights (EBR) (Bill 26, 1993), which declares in its preamble that 'the people of Ontario recognize the inherent value of the natural environment' and 'have a right to a healthful environment'. Although the Act does not go on to create any new substantive environmental rights, it creates a range of new participation and litigation rights in relation to a specified range of environmentally significant decisions, the combined effect of which is to increase the opportunity of the public to participate in environmental decision making and bring actions to ensure that the environmental laws of Ontario are upheld. The EBR (which is partly inspired by the more succinct Michigan environmental bill of rights) also establishes an electronic registry containing a computerized database of policies, acts, regulations, and instruments accessible by modem from a home computer or from a public library.[4]

The Environmental Bill of Rights was criticized (prior to enactment) for raising citizens' expectations while enabling Cabinet to retain tight executive control over the operation of the legislation (e.g., by rejecting requests for review or investigation, by under-resourcing the Ministry of Environment and Energy or by ignoring the recommendations of the Environmental Commissioner (*Official Report of Debates* (*Hansard*) 1993: 3,083–4). Despite these concerns, the EBR is certainly a step towards stronger environmental democracy and, if strengthened and extended in its operation to include the above procedural safeguards, it could significantly enhance ecological citizenship and what Christoff (1996) has called 'ecologically guided democracy'.

In Australia, the jurisdiction with the most extensive rights of public involvement and enforcement in relation to environmental laws is in the state of New South Wales. The reforms introduced by the Wran Labor government (namely, public litigation rights in relation to a number of environmental statutes,[5] government financial support for the Environmental Defender's Office (EDO), which was established in Sydney in 1984, and the extension of legal aid to environmental cases) have enabled citizens and environmental organizations to bring public interest actions without having to show any personal or financial interest. Contrary to the allegations of many critics, these initiatives have not given rise to the much feared 'floodgate of litigation' in the Land and Environment Court (Comino 1994a and 1994b). The New South Wales experience has also highlighted the importance of lowering the barriers created by the high costs of litigation by providing legal aid to environmental cases. In the absence of lawyers' contingency fees and damages entitlement on the part of plaintiffs, lowering the financial barriers of litigation are unlikely to reactivate the floodgates argument.

The constitutional question

Having outlined a case for an interrelated set of substantive and procedural environmental rights, one important question now remains: to what extent, if any, should such rights be constitutionally entrenched? The answer to this question depends, first, on what we believe the purpose and function of a written constitution to be and, second, what kind of environmental rights we are talking about (substantive or procedural?).

Classical constitutional design was about limiting the exercise of political power and upholding the rule of law – protecting citizens from officials and other citizens, rather than directing or channelling power in a particular direction. Indeed, on the classical liberal view, constitutions should be ideologically and procedurally neutral and concerned only to avoid tyranny. According to this view, any effort to reflect social choices in the constitution will result in the imposition of some people's choices upon others.

Contemporary constitutional design has become much more *purposive* (although the classical concern for limiting arbitrary power has also been carried forward). This is a development that is largely in keeping with the growth of the second and third generation of human rights in the post-Second World War period. Purposive constitutions are not simply about restraining government; they are about *actively maintaining the conditions for democracy*, which should now include maintaining the social and environmental welfare of the citizenry. Modern constitutions, then, may take on any or all of the following forms: a strict charter of government powers and duties; a guardian of fundamental rights; and/or a covenant, symbol and statement of social aspiration (Murphy 1993: 8–9).

There are numerous examples of environmental provisions in constitutions, reflecting a range of different approaches to constitutional design.[6] However, most of these constitutional provisions are merely expressions of general obligations which do not create enforceable rights on the part of citizens to bring actions against the government for dereliction of duty. Even in those cases where the explicit language of rights is used, the provisions are generally intended to be symbolic rather than actionable. For example, Spain and Portugal both have environmental rights in their Constitutions (Spain,

Article 45, Portugal Article 66) yet both of these countries are taken to have poor environmental records in the European Community. However, Germany has no such law, and has very restrictive standing rules, yet it has a much better environmental record than the southern European states.

Nonetheless, the symbolic importance of broad statements of aspiration (whether in the preamble or in the main body of constitutions) should not be underestimated; not only do they provide a political foothold for substantial environmental reform, they can also assist in the interpretation of particular constitutional provisions as well as ordinary legislation.

However, taken in isolation, broad constitutional formulations of environmental rights and obligations are no panacea. Indeed, the broader the substantive formulation, the less influential and actionable such provisions are likely to be. This suggests that there is even more environmental mileage to be gained from *precise* procedural provisions in the body of the Constitution which create specific and enforceable rights, duties and decision rules. As Klipsch (1974: 229) explains in defending a constitutional right to 'environmental due process', such rights would 'have as their primary goal the broadening of democratic processes and the minimising of substantive court intervention in environmental matters'. Here, one might consider 'foundational' environmental procedural provisions such as a right to information on the state of the environment (and a corresponding duty on the part of governments to provide regular state of the environment information); a right to be informed of decisions that are likely to have a significant effect on the environment, and a right to participate in public environmental decision making.

These provisions (and related procedural rights) might be shaped and tested in the first instance by ordinary legislation and subsequently refined and distilled into workable constitutional proposals. Such a 'step-by-step' approach might serve to lower the substantial political and psychological resistance to constitutional change, particularly in Canada and Australia (where the possibilities of reform should never be underestimated). However, the general case for an interlinked set of substantive and procedural environmental rights advanced in this chapter does not stand or fall on the issue of constitutional entrenchment (although the added weight and security afforded by constitutional expression would be desirable). Rather, such rights may be enacted by any tier of government (local, state/provincial and/or national), as ordinary legislation.

Conclusion

The foregoing discussion has already answered many of the criticisms made by rights sceptics. We have seen how the rights discourse has undergone considerable expansion through the process of 'immanent critique' of the traditional rights repertoire. That is, it was precisely because the traditional liberal rights were largely abstract and formal that a widening of the discourse to include welfare rights has become necessary. The ecological critique provides an important historical sequel to the social critique, the combined effect of which is a recontextualization of the liberal ideal of individual autonomy in ways that acknowledge social interdependence, biophysical embodiment and ecological interdependence.

Moreover, we have seen that the argument that environmental rights are inappropriate because they can only be tied to individual interests has been progressively eroded by historical practice. That is, rights are increasingly invoked and recognized as providing a means of expressing collective interests, needs and identities, including those of linguistic communities, indigenous peoples and particular ecological catchments (such as the Maquiladora 'pollution haven' near the Mexico–US border). Such community rights are expressed as belonging to both the communities and the individual members of such communities; they may be pursued by individuals or by way of a class action on behalf of all individuals who bear a special connection to each other or are otherwise united by a common cause (e.g., women, ratepayers, injured workers). Far from engendering a 'muscular individualism' (Waldron 1987: 1) environmental rights provide a means of defending collective needs and building community solidarity, including community ties to the land in the case of indigenous people.

Nor should the allegation of 'middle-class bias' be taken as a reason for abandoning the push for environmental rights. Indeed, there are many circumstances in which environmental rights might serve as an important means of improving the health and quality of life of ordinary working people, in the factory, in the suburbs and in the home. Moreover, the class biases of the legal system can be addressed through such mechanisms as environmental legal aid and the establishment of a well-resourced and independent Environmental Defender's Office empowered to act on behalf of, or otherwise assist, citizens pursuing environmental claims.

In response to the feminist and post-modern objections, it is possible to make universal claims at the international level while also arguing that bodily requirements (including notions of 'environmental health') and ecological conditions and limits cannot be defined independently of specific patterns of human social, economic and technological interactions with the rest of nature (Benton 1993: 175). Accordingly, the precise scope and content of environmental rights cannot be defined independently of the particular human culture and biophysical community in which that culture is embedded (ibid.: 178). This does not, as Benton argues, imply a complete cultural relativism that blunts the edge of the critical potential of universal environmental rights, for they require 'some common core of organic functioning and absence of developmental anomaly, disability or chronic disease which can be defended as cross-culturally valid "negative" conceptions of health' (ibid.). Indeed, many of the feminist critiques of rights have acknowledged the dangers of totally abandoning rights claims (e.g., Young 1990).

Finally, it is important to emphasize that environmental rights are not offered as a panacea for the environment or for democracy. Environmental rights do not meet all of the ecological challenges presented to democratic theory and practice. Nor should environmental rights claim completeness. Indeed, there are dangers in overworking and devaluing the international rights discourse or offering vague formulations at the national level that are unlikely to be justiciable or enforceable. However, equipping the citizenry with set of interlinked substantive and procedural environmental rights would facilitate a much more systematic consideration of ecological concerns than we currently have under existing environmental laws. Such rights have the potential to broaden the scope of political representation, increase the flow of information, and strengthen the lines of responsibility and accountability between decision makers and affected communities. In this respect, environmental rights may be seen as one modest form of resistance to the endemic challenge of ecological 'problem-displacement' – whether across space, time, classes, and species or across different government agencies, departments and sub-units of government. They also strengthen the means by which 'ecological citizens' may defend the irreducible community values.

Notes

1 This paper builds on earlier work on environmental rights and democracy represented in Eckersley 1994 and 1995. I am grateful to David Bell and Peter Christoff for helpful feedback on earlier drafts of this chapter.
2 The one exception is the New South Wales Environment and Planning Act 1979, which confers third-party enforcement rights (see section 123).
3 The Draft Declaration was settled at a three-day meeting of international experts on human rights and the environment at the United Nations in Geneva in May 1994. The meeting was organized and convened by the Sierra Club Legal Defense Fund (owing to budgetary constraints facing the UN Centre for Human Rights), working with Ms Fatma Zohra Ksentini, Special Rapporteur on Human Rights and the Environment for the UN Sub-Commission on Prevention of Discrimination and Protection of Minorities. In her August 1994 final report to the Sub-Commission, Ms Ksentini included the draft declaration as an appendix and recommended that it serve as the basis for eventual adoption of a UN General Assembly resolution on human rights and the environment (correspondence, Sierra Club Legal Defense Fund Inc, 28 November 1994).
4 Other key measures include:

(A) the creation of public rights to comment on, or call for a review of, or appeal against, environmental policies, acts, regulations and instruments posted on the registry; it remains the responsibility of the minister to decide whether or not to review the request.
(B) the creation of an independent office of Environmental Commissioner, appointed by the Legislative Assembly to serve as a general watchdog; to supervise, review and comment on the operation of EBR and on compliance by ministries and to report to the Provincial Parliament, and to handle requests for review of policies, acts, regulations and instruments by the public (by passing them on the minister).

(C) a requirement that fourteen specified Ministries provide a 'Statement of Environmental Values' showing how the ministry will take the environment into account in its decision making, to be placed on the electronic registry for comment. (In November 1995 the Ministry of Finance was exempted from this requirement bringing to thirteen the number of designated Ministries.)

(D) the creation of public rights to call for an investigation into any failure to comply with the law.

(E) wider rules of standing and rights to sue anyone suspected of breaking any existing law and causing significant harm to a public resource (however, contrary to the practice in the United States, no award of damages is available to those who sue).

5 These include the Environmental Planning and Assessment Act, the Heritage Act, the National Parks and Wildlife Act as well as legislation dealing with hazardous chemicals, uranium mining and wilderness (Bonyhady 1993: 71).

6 Many states in the US and many European countries have environmental provisions in their constitutions. For example, the Florida Constitution, Article II, s. 7 states that 'It shall be the policy of the state to conserve and protect its natural resources and scenic beauty. Adequate provision shall be made by law for the abatement of air and water pollution and of excessive and unnecessary noise' (Klipsch 1974: 235, note 168). Another example is the Michigan Constitution, Article 4, s. 52 of which provides that 'the conservation and development of the natural resources of the state are hereby declared to be of paramount public concern in the interest of the health, safety and general welfare of the people. The legislature shall provide for the protection of the air, water and other natural resources of the state from pollution, impairment and destruction' (Klipsch 1974: 235–6, note 172). Article 21 of the Dutch Constitution states that 'the government is charged with the care of the habitability of the country as well as the protection and improvement of the environment'.

References

Aiken, W. (1992) 'Human rights in an ecological era', *Environmental Values* 1, 3: 191–204.

Bailey, P. (1993) *Bringing Human Rights to Life*, Annandale, NSW: The Federation Press.

Beck, U. (1992) *The Risk Society: Towards a New Modernity*, New York: Sage Publications.

Benton, T. (1993) *Natural Relations: Ecology, Animal Rights and Social Justice*, London: Verso.

Bonyhady, T. (1993) *Places Worth Keeping: Conservation, Politics and the Law*, Sydney: Allen and Unwin.

Christoff, P. (1996) 'Ecological citizens, ecologically guided democracy and the state', in F. Mathews (ed.) *Ecology and Democracy*, Portland, OR: Frank Cass.

Comino, M. (1994a) 'The Sydney EDO: past experiences and future challenges', Paper presented at *Defending the Environment: A Public Interest Environmental Law Conference*, 7–8 May, Australian Centre for Environmental Law, Law School, University of Adelaide, Adelaide.

—— (1994b) *EDO Submission to the Federal Government*, Sydney: Environmental Defenders' Office.

Courchene, T.J. and Walsh, C. (1994) 'Globalization and the new technoeconomic paradigm: implications for constitutional federalism', paper presented to the Conference on 'Redesigning the State: The Politics of Mega-Constitutional Change', Australian National University, 27–9 July 1994 (pre-conference version).

Dryzek, John S. (1987) *Rational Ecology: Environment and Political Economy*, New York: B. Blackwell.

Dworkin, R. (1984) 'Rights as trumps', in J. Waldron (ed.) *Theories of Rights*, edited by Oxford: Oxford University Press.

—— (1990) *A Bill of Rights for Britain*. London: Chatto and Windus.

Eckersley, R. (1994) 'Connecting ecology to democracy: the rights discourse revisited', paper presented to the European Consortium for Political Research Conference, Madrid, Spain, 17–22 April 1994. A revised version of this paper appears in B. Doherty and M. de Geus (eds) (1996) *Democracy and Green Political Thought: Sustainability, Rights and Citizenship*, London: Routledge.

—— (1996) 'Liberal democracy and the environment: the rights Discourse and the struggle for recognition', in F. Mathews (ed.) *Ecology and Democracy*, Portland, OR: Frank Cass.

Klipsch, R. (1974) 'Aspects of a constitutional right to a habitable environment: towards an environmental due process', *Indiana Law Journal* 49, 2: 203–37.

Livingston, J. (1981) *The Fallacy of Wildlife Conservation*, Toronto: McCelland and Stuart.

Lowi, T. (1979) *The End of Liberalism: The Second Republic of the United States*, New York: W.W. Norton.

Mackay, M.B. (1994) 'Environmental rights and the US system of protection: why the US Environmental Protection Agency is not a rights-based administrative agency', *Environment and Planning* A 26: 1761–85.

Marks, S. (1980–81) 'Emerging human rights: a new generation for the 1980s?', *Rutgers Law Review* 33: 435.

Mathews, F. (ed.) (1996) *Ecology and Democracy*, Portland, OR: Frank Cass.

Murphy, W. (1993) 'Constitutions, constitutionalism and democracy', in D. Greenberg *et al.* (eds) *Constitutionalism and Democracy: Transitions in the Contemporary World*, New York: Oxford University Press.

Official Report of Debates (Hansard), (1993) No. 60, Third Session, 35th Parliament, Legislative Assembly of Ontario, Tuesday 28 September, 1993: 3,083–4.

Pain, N. (1992) 'The right to a healthy and safe environment: can international law provide the answer?', in R. Harding (ed.) *Ecopolitics V Proceedings*, Kensington, NSW: Centre for Liberal and General Studies.

Rehling, D. (1991) 'Legal standing for environmental groups within the administrative system–the Danish experience and the need for an international charter on environmental rights', in N. Fuhr and G. Roller (eds) *Participation and Litigation Rights of Environmental Associations in Europe*, Frankfurt am Main: Peter Lang.

Sierra Club Legal Defense Fund, Inc. (1994) Written correspondence, 28 November .

Stone, C. (1974) *Should Trees Have Standing?: Toward Legal Rights for Natural Objects*, Los Altos, CA: William Kaufmann.

Stone, C. (1987) *Earth and Other Ethics*, New York: Harper and Row.

Tarlock, A.D. (1988) 'Earth and Other Ethics: The Institutional Issues', *Tennessee Law Review* 56: 43–76.

Waldron, J. (ed.) (1987) *Nonsense Upon Stilts: Bentham, Burke and Marx on the Rights of Man*, London: Methuen.

World Commission on Environment and Development (WCED) (1990) *Our Common Future* (Australian edn), Melbourne: Oxford University Press.

Yeager, P. (1991) *The Limits of the Law: The Public Regulation of Private Pollution*, Cambridge: Cambridge University Press.

Young, I.M. (1990) *Justice and the Politics of Difference*. Princeton, NJ: Princeton University Press.

INDEX